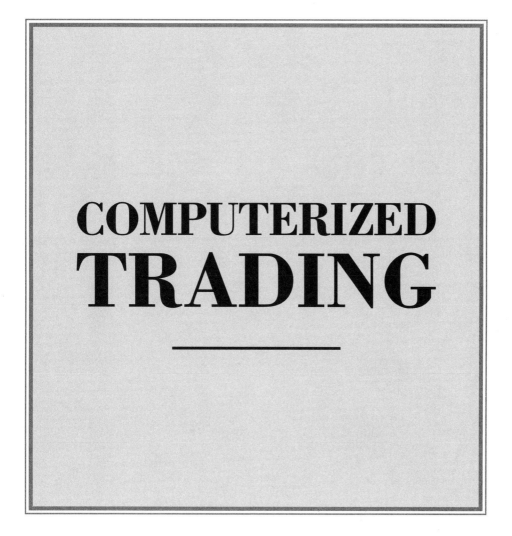

COMPUTERIZED
TRADING

COMPUTERIZED
TRADING

Maximizing Day Trading
and Overnight Profits

Mark Jurik

Editor

NYIF

NEW YORK INSTITUTE OF FINANCE

NEW YORK • TORONTO • SYDNEY • TOKYO • SINGAPORE

Library of Congress Cataloging in Publication Data
Computerized trading : maximizing day trading and overnight profits /
    Mark Jurik, editor.
        p.   cm.
    Includes index.
    ISBN 0–7352–0077–7
        1. Investments—Computer network resources.   2. Investments—Data
    processing.   I. Jurik, Mark.
    HG4515.95.C66   1999
    332.64'0285—dc21   98-41212
                                                                             CIP

This publication is designed to provide accurate and authoritative information in regard to the subject matter
covered. It is sold with the understanding that the publisher is not engaged in rendering legal, accounting, or other
professional service. If legal advice or other expert assistance is required, the services of a competent professional
person should be sought.

> *. . . From the Declaration of Principles jointly adopted by a Committee of*
> *the American Bar Association and a Committee of Publishers*
> *and Associations.*

Printed in the United States of America

10 9 8 7 6 5 4 3 2 1

ISBN 0-7352-0077-7

TradeStation® is a registered trademark of Omega Research, Inc.

ATTENTION: CORPORATIONS AND SCHOOLS

Prentice Hall books are available at quantity discounts with bulk purchase for educational, business, or sales
promotional use. For information, please write to: Prentice Hall Special Sales, 240 Frisch Court, Paramus,
New Jersey 07652. Please supply: title of book, ISBN, quantity, how the book will be used, date needed.

NEW YORK INSTITUTE OF FINANCE
An Imprint of Prentice Hall Press
Paramus, NJ 07652
A Simon & Schuster Company

Prentice Hall International (UK) Limited, *London*
Prentice Hall of Australia Pty. Limited, *Sydney*
Prentice Hall Canada Inc., *Toronto*
Prentice Hall Hispanoamericana, S.A., *Mexico*
Prentice Hall of India Private Limited, *New Delhi*
Prentice Hall of Japan, Inc., *Tokyo*
Simon & Schuster Asia Pte. Ltd., *Singapore*
Editora Prentice Hall do Brasil, Ltda., *Rio de Janeiro*

To today's children, who now leave kindergarten already knowing how to boot an operating system. To the young college graduates, often facing the dilemma of choosing between their lovers and their laptops. And to their poor parents, like my mother, who still think software utilities are manufactured by Rubbermaid®.

Contents

PART IV

Advanced Indicators and Forecasting

Appendices

Preface

One of the advantages of the Internet is that you can easily gauge the pulse of the masses. For example, questions repeatedly asked on forums related to financial trading indicate a constant need for certain information not commonly available. Questions like the following appear over and over:

- Will this endeavor cost me lots of money just to get started?
- What's the best time frame (hourly, daily, etc.) to trade in?
- What are the basic ways to enter and exit a market?
- How should I evaluate my trading system?
- What is the best way to receive live data?
- How should I build a neural net based trading system?

To satisfy the novice trader's need for information, I agreed to be the editor of *Computerized Trading*. This book discusses a broad range of topics related to using computers for investing and trading the financial markets. Twenty authors have contributed chapters discussing their favorite topics. Topics are presented in a progressively more advanced sequence, beginning with basic trading methods, through system testing and evaluation, all the way to advanced indicators and forecasting. *Computerized Trading* also includes a comprehensive list of data vendors and, for the first time ever, a description of how real-time data is collected and processed, and the various methods of data distribution. This is essential reading when your data feed is acting up and you do not have a clue what has gone wrong.

As editor of *Computerized Trading*, I have made sure that each chapter is informative, contributes to the big picture, and is organized with the other chapters in logical sequence. I have included an introduction and summary for each of the book's four parts, to make the book even more user friendly.

Part I discusses the basic trading skills and methods needed by the novice. We begin by comparing trading styles to prepare you for the psychological pressures awaiting you. Chapters 2, 3, and 4 review technical indicators and their general use. Chapters 5 and 6 show ways you can enter and exit a trade, and Chapter 7 covers basic money management techniques, an essential part of any trading strategy.

Part II discusses the important issue of testing and evaluating your trading system. Chapter 8 comments on backtesting methodology and Chapter 9 reviews numerous ways to assess system performance. It is foolish to trade for real without a complete understanding of both your own and your system's strengths and weaknesses.

Part III discusses intermediate-level issues. Chapter 10 delves into the psychological issues required to master trading. Chapter 11 shows how to quantify a market's upside and downside potential by creating trading zones. Chapter 12 reveals a technique for switching among time frames. Chapter 13 supports the practice of using diversification to improve system reliability.

Part IV discusses the advanced issues of constructing market models as powerful indicators. Chapter 14 illustrates by examples the power of including intermarket analysis. Chapter 15 notes the importance of using the correct paradigm for modeling the market and how, by failing to do so, current models fall short of exploiting some market inefficiencies. In particular, the author shows how an improper paradigm is skewing modern option pricing models—information that can be exploited by the savvy trader. Chapter 16 reveals how properly preprocessing financial data prior to modeling can greatly enhance system accuracy. Chapter 17 offers an example of how to model the market using the Statistical Data Mining technique. Chapter 18 is a complete case study on building an advanced trading system.

The appendices cover the practical issues of gathering knowledge and data. Appendix A provides a brief overview of the issues when selecting a financial data provider as well a list of data vendors and their services. Appendix B discusses, in fine detail, how financial data is generated and transmitted through vendors to your computer, and all the things that can go wrong along the way. Appendix C includes Web hyperlinks to three of my collections: (1) financial book reviews written by real traders, (2) quality trading system programmers for Omega Research products, and (3) worthwhile software companies whose products are useful in market forecasting. Appendix D is a short true story about lessons learned, as relevant today as it was decades ago. Appendix E introduces all the contributing authors to this book

Editing a book this size was a task whose sheer enormity overwhelmed me. So, in addition to the authors of each chapter, I relied heavily on the contributions of many experienced traders, especially through these four moderated forums on the Internet:

- ati@sciapp.com
- scilink@sciapp.com
- omega-list@eskimo.com
- realtraders@listserver.com

To make it easier to find up-to-date information about a product or service mentioned in this book, I have included identifying hyperlinks to relevant Web sites. However, to ensure these hyperlinks will not age, I have included only those links that point to original domains and not to accounts within an Internet service provider (ISP).

I hope you will carefully consider *all* the issues discussed in this book *before* deciding what to purchase. Your adventure in computerized trading will cost you a small fortune. Oh, yes it will.

May you acquire an even greater fortune.

Mark Jurik

Introduction

Playing the markets is very much a competitive sport, and to be in the small circle of winners you must commit time, effort, and money. More than you might guess. You will need to make many decisions regarding these three issues, especially when you intend to use a personal computer as part of your trading system.

Can you imagine any institutional investor playing with billions of dollars and not having an entire computer facility dedicated to analyzing the markets? Facing this opposition, do you stand even a remote chance of making a profit? Yes, but salvation will not come from a basket of nifty indicators that thousands of others already use. To chisel out profit from the market's inefficiencies, you are going to need market insight, trading skill, and all the edge you can get, including computerized trading.

By "market inefficiencies" I am referring to any market behavior that can be predictably exploited. The tulip mania of seventeenth-century Holland was the result of people anticipating the demand of others, who in turn were anticipating the demand of others, and so on. Consequently, tulip prices rose astronomically, followed by the inevitable crash. A few speculators made fortunes in a short period of time. This is a classic case of an inefficient market.

Has modern technology, with all its rapid information transmission and processing, virtually eliminated market inefficiencies? Could the masses be so wrong in modern times? Well, yes. There is mounting evidence that the market is still filled with opportunities, and that as new financial instruments appear, they create both inefficiencies and predictabilities that await exploitation. This is due to the diverse makeup of traders—people have different investment horizons (short- or long-term), attitudes toward risk (those with deep pockets versus those without), sensitivity to news and public opinion (mob psychology), and trading technology (which affects response times).

Inefficiencies also occur because the "markets" are people, making the same greedy, panicked decisions day in and day out—dumping a position at the bottom, jumping into already overbought markets. (Remember the craze for junk bonds?) As a consequence, not all value is immediately discounted. Predictable behavior still remains. For example, market action alternates between clusters of high and low volatility, and certain price behaviors, such as trendiness, are more predictable within these clusters.

What has changed since the seventeenth century is the level of sophistication needed to both find and profit from market patterns. Computers and advanced pattern matching are at home here, as are the hordes of physicists and mathematicians who have been crawling around Wall Street ever since the cold war ended.

Because of this high-tech onslaught, good old reliable cycles have little staying power. They are exploited and discounted as soon as they are discovered. In the past 5 years, there has been a tangible drop in the profitability of simple, standard systems based on canned indicators such as moving averages, the Relative Strength Index (RSI), or stochastics. One trader lamented, "I doubt that even the Turtles could make the same money today using the same methods as a decade ago."

So what is left for the individual investor? Will all the good opportunities be taken by large institutions that can afford to hire Ph.D. analysts? Well, no. Considering that 90 percent of all traders are losing money in the markets, there is lots of treasure to be had. But you will need more than pencil and paper to get your share. Profitability requires sophisticated analysis that can dig out short-term persistance in price/volume behavior, a brief incident of cyclic action, correlation between two or more markets with predictive value, and so on. To gather, analyze, and detect profitable market inefficiencies, you will need at least one computer. It will not guarantee profits, but it can provide the sophisticated evaluation of market activity that simply was not necessary a decade ago.

To succeed, you need to find those investment techniques that work for you. This includes having faith in your system, as well as having effective money management and entry-exit timing. Faith depends not only on how well your system is performing, but also how well you understand what it is doing. It is all too easy to get cold feet and try to outsmart your system, only to end up worse off than if you stuck to your guns.

Acknowledgments

I take this opportunity to express my thanks to many people who have, in various ways, helped me attain my goal of preparing a book that I wish I could have purchased years ago.

Of course, my thanks to all the authors for their contributed chapters. Also, thanks to the innumerable contributors to Internet user-group forums. Their collective interaction produces a wisdom greater than its parts. Special acknowledgment goes to Bob Brickey, Larry Erhart, Gerrit Jacobson, Dick Crotinger, and Robert Pisani for taking the time to contribute either material or comments to my chapter on datafeeds.

I also want to express gratitude to Bob Klein, who initially offered me this role as editor, and who took care of all "behind the scenes" activities, including finding the right publisher. Finally, I am grateful to my wife, who patiently let her "space cadet" take this adventure, and to Ellen Schneid Coleman, the executive editor at Prentice Hall. I cannot count how many times she agreed to wait "just a few more weeks" for the manuscript.

PART I

Basic Trading Skills and Methods

Part I discusses the basic trading skills you will need to begin designing and testing your own trading strategies. Chapter 1 offers a comparison of trading styles to prepare you for the psychological pressures that accompany different trading methods. Chapters 2, 3, and 4 provide several viewpoints that together paint a broad picture of technical indicators and their applications. Chapter 5 and 6 show ways to enter and exit a trade and Chapter 7 covers basic money management techniques, an essential part of any trading strategy.

After you have read Part I, I recommend that you acquire low-cost trading simulation software to design and test basic trading strategies on historical data. Low-cost software products to consider include Omega Research SuperCharts *(www.omegaresearch.com)*, Equis MetaStock *(www.equis.com)*, Nirvana Systems OmniTrader *(www.nirv.com)*, Titan Trading Analytics PowerPlay *(www.titantrading.com)*, Trendsetter Software Professional Analyst *(www.trendsoft.com)*, Flexsoft Technical Analysis Scanner *(www.flexsoft.com)*, Street Logic Software Wall Street Quest *(www.pacific-coast.com/StreetLogic)*, and Windows on Wall Street "WOW."

CHAPTER 1

Trading Methods

JOE DINAPOLI

This chapter discusses judgmental versus nonjudgmental trading systems and position trading versus intraday trading. Judgmental approaches call on the trader to make decisions within a given criterion or context, whereas nonjudgmental systems are strictly mechanical.

The trading methodology I use involves judgment. It is the way I like to trade. Judgmental techniques have inherent advantages over nonjudgmental techniques. Flexibility, as inspired by the human mind, and the speed with which the trader can make necessary adjustments in response to changing market conditions are two of the strongest reasons to trade using judgment. From teaching, however, I know that many of you may have preconceived notions about approaches to trading that are inconsistent with reality. Since achievement in any field begins with fundamental understanding, I am going to explain basic realities of trading approaches. First we will go through a reality check, then some history, so you can see why and how I have reached certain conclusions. We will consider judgmental versus nonjudgmental trading methods; then position versus intraday trading approaches.

REALITY CHECK

The Beach Boys had a memorable song that began, "Wouldn't it be nice . . ."

In actuality, there is usually a difference between expectation and reality. With enough effort, we can strike a balance between them. Likewise, such is the promise of both judgmental methods and nonjudgmental trading systems. We will examine nonjudgmental trading systems first.

This chapter has been excerpted and substantially edited from the book *Trading with DiNapoli Levels: The Practical Application of Fibonacci Analysis to Investment Markets,* by Joe DiNapoli, Coast Investment Software, 1998. Used by permission of the author.

NONJUDGMENTAL APPROACHES

Wouldn't It Be Nice . . .

- Once you have the development in place, your research and your work are over. Your trading system is fixed, stationary, and immutable. Stress is nonexistent since the decision-making process is out of your hands and in the purview of a machine. Thorough and precise (hypothetical) testing techniques have left little to chance. Everything has been taken into consideration, so your confidence is strong.
- You can arrange for signals to be implemented by a hired trader or broker and thereby avoid the tedium of monitoring the markets yourself.
- "It" (the "system," the "program," the "solution") can generate an adequate income flow, which will enable you to go to Fiji and stick your toes in the sand.

The Reality . . .

- The work never ends. When system historical extremes are exceeded, you are back to tweaking, testing, and massaging the parameters.

  In fact, you better have two independent systems, or maybe three, or four, to even out the equity swings. Oh yes, there will not only be some tweaking and massaging, it is more likely that outright replacement of a system or two will occur, as one or the other goes sour altogether.

  What about stress? You don't know stress until you experience pervasive impotence. You feel utterly helpless to affect results as you watch your system(s) dictate one absurd order after another. You just know that profit is going to evaporate and go to a loss. When that happens, you cannot do *anything* but watch and obey the signals it generates. Hey Mack, pass the Maalox®, *now!*

  You learn that the $100 for slippage and commission you thought would be extravagant, was in fact sorely inadequate. You forgot about limit moves, 40 tick runs without looking back, worst possible fill situations and. . . . The data you did the testing with was supposed to be okay, but really was not all that good. Your confidence in your testing techniques is hitting a new low along with your account size.

- The broker who is executing your trades seems to be missing entries on some of the biggest moves and . . . *why couldn't he get that stop right!* Or, the trader you hired cannot resist putting his vast experience (one year) to work "improving" what you have struggled so long to perfect.

- The only way to get enough capital to properly fund four systems over the 15 futures contracts you have found necessary to trade for adequate system diversification is to take in, and manage money. Now you have disclosure statements, CFTC (Commodities Futures Trading Commission) oversight, a staff, and more NFA (National Futures Association) compliance issues than you ever dreamed existed.

WHAT ABOUT JUDGMENTAL APPROACHES?

Wouldn't It Be Nice . . .

- You study under the best of the high-powered pros. You achieve a 90 percent win ratio through unexcelled market understanding.
- You live where you want, trade when you want, and rid yourself of the employee hassles that have been bugging you for years.
- You turn a modest amount of money, through skill and diligence, into a veritable mountain of pure financial muscle. You leave an ever-growing portion of it in a high-yielding money market account whose proceeds will allow you to zip off to Fiji whenever you choose.

The Reality . . .

- You learn from one high-powered pro, then from another high-powered pro, and although you find some real benefit here and there, you never quite achieve what you expected. In fact, after years of efforts; $30,000 in seminars, books, software, and trading courses; your profit is only barely able to cover your overhead. You haven't been able to touch that $50,000 you're out from past trading losses!
- If you cannot find a way to get *really* profitable and hit a big home run, your savings will be gone in not so many months. You start wondering if you will become someone else's employee.
- The stress and time demands of constantly focusing on that screen, being there for the open, and tangling with the overnight Globex session have you wondering if you will ever get to the local beach. As for Fiji, is there a contract on them? What's the tick size and . . . where do Fijis trade?

Okay, things are neither quite as rosy nor quite as bad as outlined here, but they easily can be. In fact, they can be worse! What follows are some unqualified observations from my direct involvement: the odyssey *I have experienced.* These are not hypothetical events; real-time living is being described here, so you can see how I arrived at certain conclusions. Then, perhaps you can better decide for yourself where you might best fit in.

SOME HISTORY

Around 1980, I decided to investigate the futures markets. The plan was to switch from the vehicles I had been trading to what I knew was the most demanding and potentially rewarding game in town. The timing of the switch had to do with my view of my station in life. By that time, I was "well heeled" enough to take what I expected would be a rough transition. I also thought my knowledge level and trading expertise had reached a level that would allow me to meet this new challenge. I quickly realized two things. It was a good thing I had waited until I was well heeled, and the challenge was a bit more than I had anticipated. Here are the highlights of the odyssey, how I got started in, and eventually became successful at trading futures.

After about a year of trading poorly, I managed a much sought-after meeting through a social contact with an extremely successful and reclusive commodity trading advisor (CTA). This man was reputed to have made a bazillion dollars over the past five years in agricultural futures. I wish I could describe this bizarre person to you, but perhaps someone would recognize him, and one prerequisite for his tutelage was that I never reveal his identity. Of course, I never have.

After a few pleasantries, this cerebral type began our discussion of futures: "What if you were a Martian and you came to earth to trade commodities." Hmm. . . . "You look at this action, that action, another action, and so on. Not being able to speak English, you simply watch actions. Prices fluctuate." He went on, "You talk with your Martian friends about these actions and you wonder about appropriate reactions." I looked at him as if he were Moses holding the Commandments behind his back and musing about the fit of his sandals. After an hour of this much cloaked "benefit," I was so befuddled and confused I was willing to settle for which way soybeans might be going. I could only hope that information would allow me to get back the cost of my travel to see him!

This man was the first of three mentors I was fortunate enough to have. Their kindness and willingness to share with me weighed heavily in my decision to begin teaching in 1986.

So what was all this about Martians? It took me a while to figure it out, but he held the key to the gold box and he wasn't about to share it with a stranger whose intentions, interest, and sincerity were unknown. This meeting was the first of many that stretched over a period of about three years. I learned a lot from this man who traded strictly and competently from the basis of a nonjudgmental system. But, strangely enough, none of what I learned was what I was after in that first meeting. He taught me that:

- There are no absolute heroes, only heroes for a while.
- All nonjudgmental systems eventually fail (stop making money). Your hope is to be using one while it is working.
- Excellent information can be gleaned from a true expert once trust, eligibility, and prerequisites in your knowledge base are established.
- Nonjudgmental systems are lucky to achieve 50 percent winning trades; 30 percent is acceptable.
- Trading a nonjudgmental system is difficult and stressful. It requires tremendous concentration, diligence, and self-discipline.
- There is an awesome level of challenge, fulfillment, and discovery in the entire trading process.

ELABORATION OF KEY POINTS

Heroes

It turns out my friend was a hero of epic proportions during the market moves of the 1970s. His nonjudgmental, fundamentally based, mathematical system was very cleverly put together. It fell apart, however, after the inflation peak of the late 1970s and after subsequent avenues of supplies (grains) opened up overseas.

System Failure

With substantial personal resources, cash, and experience, he diligently proceeded with a staff and mainframes to replace what he had lost. One of the more interesting dead ends he explored was a detection of randomness, or lack thereof, to determine if a tradable trend existed. It was sort of like a Directional Movement Index gone mad. That one worked great for two years, then it stopped making money. When later it bombed out, it bombed out big. Through consultations with other traders, joint ventures, and the like, he was funneled down the corridor of many of my other system-developing friends (i.e., some form of volatility breakout system seems to best handle the test of time). Most would agree, however, that these systems have a poor win/loss ratio and employ significant funds to satisfy their diversification requirements. All this number crunching revealed a hopeful aspect: some systems can last up to 5 or perhaps even 10 years before falling apart—if you happen to get on to one of those early on, you can do awfully well, at least for a time.

Apprenticeship

My naive idea that this individual would share his earned knowledge with me on our first encounter was absurd. That he would recognize my sincerity and my obvious worthiness was also absurd. It took years of doing for him, before he shared with me. He knew I needed to be ready to hear what he had to tell me. He also knew that when he told me what he knew, *I would realize how little he knew.*

That is exactly what happened. When we reached that point, I went on. In the many encounters with bright and successful traders of fixed systems in the ensuing 16 years, I have not had reason to materially change what I had learned from my first mentor.

During the time I was working with this man, I ran into my first really good trading tip, given to me by my second mentor. He was an extremely successful *judgmental* trader, who (I think out of pity) told me to study displaced moving averages. Of course, after telling me to study DMAs, he had to explain what they were. By doing so, he was finally able to get me out of his presence and go back to his mainframe.

In those days, the only truly successful traders I found all had mainframes, and they were incredibly eccentric and reclusive. I had spent less than 15 minutes with this person, but now I had a direction. Three years later when I compared the results of my research with his, the similarities were astonishing. It took another 15 minutes to compare our research. This was the second and final meeting I ever had with this man. Now I, too, had a profitable and reasonably consistent judgmental method to trade.

The method was far from perfect, however, about 50 percent winners, and it gave back a lot. Although I had a reasonable methodology, I was totally unsatisfied. Necessity being the mother of invention led to my first important independent discovery, the "Oscillator Predictor™," a true leading indicator. With it, I was able to capture profit and avoid risky entries.

Not until my third mentor told me about an Italian mathematician named Fibonacci did my techniques really begin to click. Number three was also eccentric. He did not own a mainframe and was anything but reclusive. This man was certainly the most dazzling trader I had ever met. Definitely judgmentally based, he nailed down highs, lows, intermediate rally highs, intermediate retracement lows. You name it! His trading style went beyond any rational expectation I had ever entertained, and he did this live time while I watched him! It was not until he taught me what he was doing in one short afternoon that I discovered these techniques were not nearly enough for consistent, profitable trading. As experience (time) stole yet another hero from me, I saw him go from riches to rags, to insolvency, to debt. The Holy Grail sure seemed to have a lot of holes that needed mending. After many years of my own experience, I have made repairs based on the following hard-won conclusions.

JUDGMENTAL TRADING

The most important trading tool you have is not your computer, your data service, or your methodology. *It is you!* If you are not right—*you do not trade.*

- Trading breaks are essential, particularly for intraday players. Three- to seven-day breaks every three to six weeks is what I have determined is best for me.
- Take significant time off; about three to six months every year, if you trade intraday, at least one to three months, if you trade daily-based or above.
- For four or five days a week spend at least one hour doing something you like that does not involve the markets or your computer. I like working with my hands, restoring cars or otherwise fixing or building things.
- The definition of a professional is one who makes the least number of mistakes, not the one who makes no mistakes. If you make one serious mistake, take yourself off trading for three days. If you make three mistakes in a short time period (over two consecutive days), take yourself off trading for three days.
- If you have not been trading for 10 days or more, do not trade size (large positions) for at least one week.
- Separate yourself into two halves, the trader and the manager. The trader cannot trade without the express permission of the manager. The manager watches for crucial signs of fitness (e.g., mistakes, irritability, stress in the trader's personal

life, telltale black shading under the eyes). Get the idea? It is the manager's job to get the trader away from the phone before the disaster occurs. Just look at the Barings fiasco if you doubt the need for competent management.

In the late 1980s, a local I had trained who had achieved consistent and considerable profitability, began just as consistently, losing money. His personality seemed to be undergoing a change and it was obvious his personal life was under some stress. I first suspected drugs, but on further reflection I narrowed it down. One night when we were talking market and he was complaining bitterly about "unexplained" losses, I asked him how long it was before his new child was to be born. "Three months," he said, "and how the hell did you know?"

Being "fit" to trade is of crucial importance. Systems or methods allowing for discretion depend on the quality of that discretion both in execution and size. If the discretion goes, you can wipe out in a week what it has taken you months to accumulate.

There are knowledgeable, honest, and sincere traders available who like to teach and have the qualifications to make themselves understood. Seek them out, get their material if you can afford it, and befriend them. Much of what they can offer to you in casual conversation will be invaluable to your success. Someone helped them. Approach them correctly and if they can, they will help you.

Judgmental trading can lead to incredibly favorable win/loss ratios. Don't let them go to your head. If you attain dramatic profits very quickly, your ego can blow way out of proportion. Always remember *you are only one trade away from humility.*

During the trading decision-making time, you can afford no interruptions. None! Zero! If your office is in your home and you trade intraday, get a lock to separate yourself from anyone sharing the premises *and use it.* I warned one of my clients, a chiropractor who traded out of his home in northern California, about this repeatedly. This trader suffered a $40,000 loss when his wife casually walked over and dropped their infant in his arms just before a crop report. Experience can be a tough teacher, but to many it is the only teacher.

The speed with which you can adapt to changing market conditions is considerably faster with a judgmental rather than a nonjudgmental trading approach. This can prevent those huge drawdowns that may accompany blind (fixed) system failures. For those engineers who are reading this, consider a mechanical feedback system that dampens and focuses responses as a function of the speed of the transducers. If the feedback system is quick enough, it keeps up with the changes. But if it gets behind, it can go 180 degrees out of phase and tear itself up! It works the same with trading.

Trading a judgmental system is difficult, and requires tremendous concentration, diligence, and self-discipline.

There is tremendous challenge, fulfillment, and discovery in the entire trading process. The bottom line is that there are certain inherent advantages and disadvantages to either market trading approach. I have chosen the judgmental approach. It is largely a question of matching your talents, your psyche, your financial resources, and your objectives with the challenges and advantages already cited. There is no way I have ever seen of avoiding a lot of work and a lot of stress. Prepare yourself for it, or if it is too hot, get out of the kitchen now!

POSITION TRADING VERSUS INTRADAY TRADING

Not only must you decide whether to trade judgmentally or nonjudgmentally, you also must consider the time frame that best suits you. You need to be sure the time period you have chosen is best for the *approach* you are using.

With respect to applying the methodology this book *(Trading with DiNapoli Levels)* teaches, it is easy. Essentially you apply the same general criteria to a five-minute chart that you would apply to a monthly. Where *you* best belong is the tougher question.

My experience indicates that it is suicidal for a new trader, operating off the floor, to trade intraday. What is "new"? "New" refers to anyone trading *actively* for less than one year. If you are a part-time or casual trader, you had better give it three to five years before going to intraday trading. A better question, however, would be: What is "intraday"? My definition is that it describes the activities of a trader who is actively observing price action during the day and making decisions based on what appears to be unfolding at that time.

A daily-based (or above) trader may choose an entry or exit point to be *acted on during* the *next* day without being construed as being an intraday player.

What is a position player? The true answer is, it depends on perspective. To a floor trader, the five-minute trader is a position player. To a daily-based trader, a weekly-based trader is a position trader, and so on. For our purposes, however, we will consider a position trader as daily-based or above. As you drop the time frame, the decision-making time is compressed and the stress is increased. As you drop the time frame, the number of decisions increases radically. You have seven times the number of decisions going from daily- to hourly based, 12 times the number of decisions, going from hourly to five-minute. The opportunity is certainly accelerated, but I would not expect a savvy boxing promoter to put a promising newcomer into the ring with Mike Tyson, just to see if he could learn to handle the big time more quickly. After all, he might lose more than an ear in the process!

Five Disadvantages of Intraday Trading

1. You need experience—lots of it—with particular emphasis on order entry techniques and a thorough understanding of floor operations.
2. You need excellent brokerage and clearing services.
3. You have high overhead costs in software, quote delivery fees, equipment, and transaction costs.
4. So much of your time is taken up by the trading activity, you cannot make money doing anything else.
5. Stress levels increase dramatically.

Three Advantages of Intraday Trading

1. You can trade many more contracts with a given amount of capital.
2. You have many more trading opportunities than are available to a position trader.
3. If your trading capital is severely limited and you are otherwise qualified, you have trading opportunities that allow for much closer stops. Obviously, the typical range on a five-minute bar is smaller than the typical range of a daily bar. (This point is really a variation of item 1.)

AN ALTERNATIVE

Given today's technology, there is a way to gain substantial benefits from a mix of the traditional paths. Here is how it works.

Get delayed intraday quotes from a quality vendor and have the capacity to display the bars graphically on an intraday basis. You can use, let's say 30- and 60-minute time frames, to help make daily-based decisions that can be acted on *during the next day*. The idea is to come home after work and make your decisions in the relative calm of the evening with the added accuracy and flexibility of intraday charting capability. You can set stops, entries, and such to be acted on during the *next* day. It may even be possible to set up some contingency orders, depending on your work environment and/or brokerage relationships. The advantages are substantial. You avoid the need for excellent brokerage services and a thorough understanding of floor operations. You avoid expensive software, on-line feeds, and equipment. You can make money doing something else. You can trade somewhat more contracts and have far greater opportunity than a traditional position player, and have closer stops. The analysis of your trading opportunities will be thorough. What is most important, however, is that you will operate with less stress than an intraday player, giving you an opportunity to grow into the trading experience rather than to be intimidated by its nature and seeming unpredictability.

CONCLUSION

Aspects of Judgmental Trading Techniques

1. You can benefit from an extremely flexible market approach.
2. You will have a highly flexible personal schedule.
3. You have the potential for dramatic gains (or losses) quickly.
4. You will have potentials for extremely favorable win/loss ratios.
5. There is an absolute necessity for strict personal management.
6. There is an absolute necessity for a separate and adequate trading environment.

7. Relatively small amounts of capital can be adequate to achieve your goals.
8. A focus on relatively few markets is not only acceptable, but also preferable.

Aspects of Nonjudgmental Trading Techniques

1. Poor win/loss ratios are the rule, not the exception.
2. Historical hypothetical testing techniques are typically badly flawed for a wide variety of reasons.
3. Most nonjudgmental systems ultimately fail; the aim is to attempt to use one while it is working.
4. Volatility breakout systems seem to best stand the test of time.
5. Multiple systems, traded over a wide variety of markets are necessary to smooth out the equity curve.
6. Relatively large amounts of capital are necessary for system and market diversification, as well as for the inevitable drawdowns.
7. If system and market diversification is achieved, large amounts of capital are employable.
8. Constant implementation of trading signals is essential (no breaks).
9. Locating adequate help to implement the system signals is a challenge in itself.

Aspects of Nonjudgmental and Judgmental Trading

1. An excellent lifestyle is attainable if trading goals are met.
2. Fulfillment, challenge, and discovery are possible outcomes of the trading experience.
3. Stress levels, if not properly managed, can lead to utter destruction of your psyche and physical self.
4. Financial ruin will accompany a frivolous or ill-advised approach.
5. The workload is awesome and unending; it must be properly managed.
6. You will have the potential to meet, and have as friends and colleagues, some of the best and brightest people on the planet.

CHAPTER 2

Popular Trading Indicators

ROBERT M. MELANCON, RIA

Technical analysis is based on the premise that human nature remains more or less constant and that people will respond to changing economic, monetary, and psychological factors in the future in much the same way as they have responded in the past. The challenge for the technical analyst, then, is to identify the prevailing psychological trend in the market, recognize when changes in that trend are at hand, and attempt to profit from the new trend for as long as it remains in effect. Technical indicators are tools that have been developed over time to assist the technician in identifying these changes in the prevailing trend.

With the advent of the personal computer, technical indicators are now limited only by the bounds of one's imagination. There are price-based indicators, volume-based indicators, breadth-based indicators, sentiment-based indicators, and the like. There are also seasonally based indicators, celestial-based indicators, Super Bowl-based indicators and even indicators based on the length of women's skirt hems. The purpose of this chapter, however, is not to examine every indicator imaginable, but rather to acquaint the reader with the development, application, and limitations of a few of the more popular and reliable ones in use.

TREND IDENTIFICATION

Before setting about the task of identifying trends and trend reversals, it is first necessary to understand what a *price trend* is. Around the turn of the century, Charles Dow, considered the father of technical analysis, observed that during a market advance prices tended to move upward in a series of steps or waves, with each new high and low progressively higher than the one preceding it (see Figure 2.1). As long as this pattern of progressively higher peaks and valleys remained uninterrupted, the primary trend of the market was considered to be positive. Conversely, during market declines prices tended to move lower in a series of progressively lower highs followed by progressively lower lows.

Dow further observed that once a trend was established (either upward or downward), it tended to stay in effect until it was broken. Once violated, though, it

FIGURE 2.1 UPTRENDS AND DOWNTRENDS.

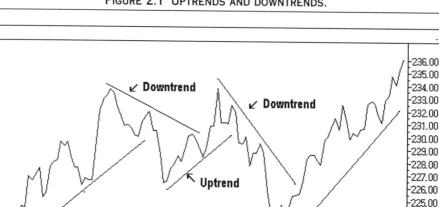

usually meant an end to the prevailing trend and the likelihood of a reversal in direction. As simplistic as it may seem, this elementary concept of *peak-and-valley progression* paved the way for the earliest forms of technical analysis: pattern recognition.

CHART PATTERN RECOGNITION

When a primary trend comes to an end, prices usually enter a sideways consolidation period before either resuming the preceding trend or reversing direction. The price patterns resulting from this consolidation phase frequently give the analyst highly profitable clues as to future price direction. Some patterns, such as wedges, pennants, and flags, are considered continuation patterns and can be useful in preventing a premature exit from a position. Others, such as the double or triple top (bottom) and "head and shoulders" formations are considered highly reliable reversal patterns and can be invaluable in giving advance warning of an impending trend reversal. Still other patterns, such as right-angled and symmetrical triangles (sometimes called *coils*), can be either continuation or reversal formations and thus serve as a valuable caution flag for the investor. Besides their usefulness as a barometer of future trend direction, chart patterns also serve a highly useful role in projecting the extent of an ensuing price move. While beyond the scope of this chapter, a thorough understanding of chart pattern recognition cannot be overemphasized as a basic requirement for the serious technical analyst.

MOVING AVERAGES

Another of the early price based indicators is the *moving average.* The purpose of moving averages is to smooth out the fluctuations of incremental price movement, and provide the technician with a sort of moving trend. Although there are a number of different kinds of moving averages, the most common are the *simple, weighted,* and *exponential* moving averages. A simple moving average is nothing more than a summation of a number of periods of data, divided by the number of periods. Each time a new increment of data is added, the first or initial increment of data is dropped. Thus the moving average "moves" or changes along with the price data it is averaging.

Weighted moving averages are similar in concept to simple moving averages except that additional weight is given to the more recent data. Exponential moving averages are similar in construction and give similar results to weighted moving averages, but are far more simple (and faster) to calculate. Thus they are frequently the moving average of choice in technical analysis. With the advent of the personal computer, however, virtually any form of moving average, including advanced and centered moving averages, can be calculated in a flash with the touch of a button. But because they are used extensively in most technical indicators, a thorough understanding of the various types of moving averages is essential before proceeding further.

TECHNICAL INDICATORS

Due in large part to the power and broad accessibility of the personal computer, technical analysis has taken a quantum leap from the early study of chart patterns and moving averages to a formidable array of technical indicators and trading systems. For the most part, these indicators fall into four major categories: *sentiment* indicators, *monetary* indicators, *market structure* indicators, and *other* indicators.

Sentiment Indicators

Based primarily on crowd psychology, sentiment indicators measure the buy and sell expectations of the various market participants. Unlike most other indicators, though, their interpretation is contrary in nature. For example, according to the well known *Advisory Sentiment Index,* the more investment advisors that are bullish, the more likely it is that they are already fully invested, and therefore there is less new money available to drive the market higher. Without liquidity to drive prices higher, the most likely course for stocks is *down* as those already fully invested begin taking profits. Therefore, the more bullish investment advisors are as a group, the more bearish the outlook for stocks.

As the popularity of sentiment indicators has taken hold, it has become more and more difficult to know whether the emotions being measured are the *actual* opinions of those surveyed or the *opposite* of their true feelings, based on contrary opinion.

For example, if you polled a room full of informed investors as to their opinion on the direction of the market, they might all feel that it would advance. But if the investors all knew that the others also thought it would advance, they might then reverse their stance based on contrary opinion. Because of the "double negative" potential of sentiment indicators, some feel they have lost much of their usefulness. Following are several of the more popular sentiment indicators in use today:

Advisor's Sentiment Index   Member's Short Ratio
Confidence Index   Odd Lot Balance Index
Gross Trinity Index   Odd Lot Short Ratio
Insider's Buy / Sell Ratio   Public Short Ratio
Installment Debt Indicator   Put / Call Ratio
Large Block Ratio   Put / Call Open Interest
Margin Debt   Short Interest Ratio
Margin Requirements   Specialist / Public Ratio

Monetary Indicators

Monetary, or flow-of-funds, indicators seek to measure the *capacity* of various market participants to buy or sell stocks. The greater the availability of capital to fuel a market advance, the more likely prices are to rise. On the other hand, the lower the amount of cash available (e.g., by institutional investors), the less likely stocks are to advance. In fact, since mutual fund managers may ultimately have to sell stocks in their portfolios to raise cash for redemptions, low cash reserves can actually represent potential for *lower* prices.

Like sentiment indicators, flow-of-funds indicators also suffer from a major disadvantage. Although they are effective in measuring the capacity of market participants, they fail to measure the *intention* of the participants to put those reserves to work. For example, if mutual fund cash levels are low, it may represent a potential *negative* for the market for the reason previously cited. However, it may also represent a potential *positive* for the market since a higher proportion of their reserves have been put to work buying stocks. Conversely, a high institutional cash position may be a *positive* since it represents a pool of liquidity to fuel a market advance, or it could mean that the managers are *negative* on the market overall, and are therefore selling stocks. In addition, the reporting of monetary data is usually somewhat delayed making it of little use in the timing of investment decisions. Both sentiment and monetary indicators can serve a useful purpose, though, both as a backdrop to the overall market psychology and as confirming indicators. Examples of monetary indicators include:

Fed—Discount Ratio Spread Index   Mutual Fund Net Purchases Index
Money Supply (M1, M2, M3)   Net Free Reserves
Mutual Fund Cash / Assets Ratio   Ninety-Day T-Bill versus Discount Rate

Fed—Prime Rate Spread Index

Short Interest Ratio

Yield Curve

Zweig Fed Indicator

Three Steps and a Stumble

Two Tumbles and a Jump

Market Structure

The most valuable technical indicators are those that deal with the actual structure or characteristics of the market itself. Whereas early technical indicators (such as chart pattern analysis and moving averages) dealt primarily with price action, modern market structure indicators can be divided into four major camps:

1. *Price.* The level of enthusiasm.
2. *Time.* The duration of the move.
3. *Volume.* The degree of interest or conviction.
4. *Breadth.* The extent of participation.

When used in combination, these indicators represent the most powerful of all tools in the analyst's arsenal. However, without a thorough understanding of their construction and application, these tools not only can prove meaningless, but also can be counterproductive. The balance of the chapter, therefore, will focus on the construction and application of several of the more popular of these indicators. Although the list is almost limitless, following are a few of the better known price, time, volume, and breadth indicators in use today:

Market Structure Indicators

Price, Volume, and Time

Accumulation/Distribution Index

Accumulation Swing Index

Average True Range

Bollinger Bands

Bollinger %B

Bolton-Tremblay Indicator

Bull and Bear Power

Chaiken Money Flow

Chaiken Oscillator

Commodity Channel Index

Cumulative Volume Index

Daily Volume

Demand Index

Directional Movement

Double Momentum Oscillator

Dow Theory

Ease of Movement

Force Index

Haurlan Index

Herrick Payoff Index

High Low Logic Index

Intraday Intensity Index

Linear Regression Analysis

Linear Trend Indicator

Mixed Momentum Index

Money Flow Index

Morris Volume RSI

Moving Averages
Moving Average Convergence-Divergence
Negative Volume Index
On-Balance Volume
Parabolic SAR
Percentage Bands
Positive Volume Index
Price Momentum
Price Phase Indicator
Price Volume Trend
Split Volume Moving Average
Standard Deviation
Stochastics (%K, %D)
Swing Index
Relative Strength Index
TRIX
Up / Down Volume Oscillator
Ultimate Oscillator
Volatility Index (Chaiken)

Volatility Index (Wilder)
Volume Accumulation Percentage
Volume Oscillator
William %R
Zig Zag

Breadth

Absolute Breadth
Advance-Decline Line
Advance Decline Oscillator
Breadth Thrust Indicator
High-Low Differential
Market Facilitation Index
McClellan Oscillator
McClellan Summation Index
Moving Balance Indicator
Open TRIN
STIX
Traders Index (TRIN)

Other Indicators

Over the years, many other indicators have come along that have less to do with sentiment, monetary policy or market structure, and more to do with cycles, fads, or chance. Some of them, such as the seasonal indicators, appear to be grounded in logic and can at least be tied somewhat to the economic and/or business cycle. Others seem to be purely fad and seem designed more to profit their promoter than the technicians who use them. Still, those who follow these indicators swear by them, and profess to profit by their signals. The bottom line, though, is that if you do not fully understand the indicator and can explain why it produces the results it does, better leave it alone. Tuition in the school of technical analysis can be expensive! Following are some of these indicators:

Days of the Month
Days of the Week
First Five Days in January
January Barometer
Pre-Holiday Periods

Presidential Election Cycle
Celestial/Astrological
Super Bowl
Women's Skirt Hems

INDICATOR CONSTRUCTION

Most technical indicators fall into a group called momentum indicators in that they attempt to measure the velocity of directional movement in whatever is being evaluated. One reason momentum indicators are so popular is that, unlike price-based indicators, which typically generate buy and sell signals *after-the-fact,* momentum indicators actually give an indication of a change in trend direction *before* the actual change in price itself. To better understand this concept, consider a simple momentum oscillator of today's price minus the price 10 days ago, or the *10-day rate-of-change.*

As Figure 2.2 illustrates, we begin on day 10 when the closing price is 48.50. The price 9 days prior (on day 1) was 50.75. So when we subtract today's price (48.50) from the price 9 days ago (50.75) it results in a value of −2.25, which is plotted below the zero line. By following this simple procedure each following day, we develop a momentum curve that we then plot directly above or below the price curve for the same time period. As the price moves down by the same increment each day, the curve becomes a straight horizontal line between days 10 and 14. Then on day 15 the price turns up by 25 points while the momentum plot turns up by 50 points. Thus price momentum is accelerating twice as fast as is the price. The momentum curve continues this rate of change until day 23 when the change becomes constant once again, even though price continues to advance at the same rate.

On day 28 price begins to level out at 50.75, yet the momentum curve begins to drop. Should price continue to move horizontally, the momentum curve will continue to fall until the 38th day (10 days later) at which time both the momentum curve and

FIGURE 2.2 PRICE VERSUS MOMENTUM. BOTTOM HALF SHOWS EXAMPLE PRICE
ACTION AND TOP HALF SHOWS THE 10-DAY RATE OF CHANGE.

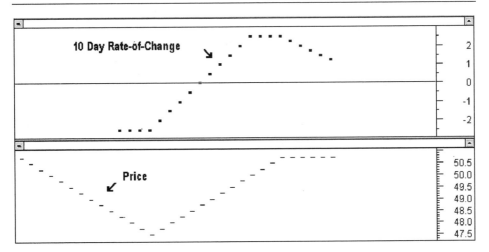

price will be moving horizontally. When plotted in this manner, momentum always changes direction in advance of price. That is because the momentum curve is reflecting the rate of change, or velocity, of price movement.

Momentum indicators can be constructed to be either oscillator based or threshold based. The momentum curve in an oscillator-based indicator revolves (or oscillates) above and below a zero line. Buy signals are generated when the oscillator curve reaches an extremely low (oversold) level and turns up. Sell signals are generated when the oscillator curve reaches an extremely high (overbought) level and turns down.

How high is high and how low is low depends upon what is being measured as well as the number of periods in the calculation. As with all technical analysis, interpretation is an *art form* and requires a substantial amount of experience in order to get a "feel" for each indicator's individual behavior.

Threshold-based momentum indicators are constructed so that the momentum curve travels between an absolute scale of 0 and 100. When the momentum curve travels to the high end of the range, the issue is considered overbought. Conversely, when the curve travels toward the low end of the range, the issue is considered oversold. Buy and sell signals are generated when the issue reaches an extreme, changes direction, and penetrates a predetermined threshold. Here again, sensitivity of the indicator is determined by what is being measured as well by the time parameter selected.

WEIGHT OF THE EVIDENCE

As mentioned, to build an effective timing system, it is not enough just to know about the existence of technical indicators, one should thoroughly understand how they are constructed and what they measure. One of the biggest traps most aspiring technicians fall into is following several indicators with different names, but that all measure the same thing (e.g., volatility, cyclicality). That is like posing the same question to several people of different languages. Although their responses may sound different, they are still basically answering the same (single) question. And whether you receive 5 or 50 responses to the question, it still only addresses one part of the equation.

A better approach would be to follow a handful of indicators that are very well understood, reliable, and selected to measure different aspects of market behavior. This way the technician can evaluate the "weight of the evidence" from a number of perspectives before making an investment decision. The following are several popular indicators that, when combined, can provide a meaningful assessment of an issue's underlying strength.

Bollinger Bands (BB)

One aspect of a stock's behavior that the technician will want to know is the issue's current volatility compared with its volatility over the past x number of days. To measure such volatility-based price action John Bollinger of Bollinger Capital Management developed a technical indicator called *Bollinger Bands* (see Figure 2.3).

FIGURE 2.3 PRICE CHART WITH BOLLINGER BANDS ABOVE AND BELOW PRICE.

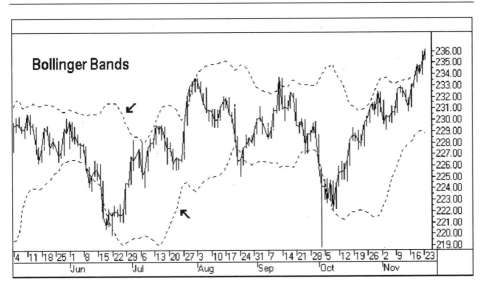

Bollinger Bands are trading bands based on the volatility of prices. However, they differ from ordinary trading bands in that they are based on a standard deviation above and below a simple moving average as opposed to a fixed percentage. As a result, the spacing of the bands is determined by the volatility over the past *x* number of periods (usually days). Thus, the greater the volatility the broader the Bands, and the lower the volatility the narrower the Bands. Normally, Bollinger Bands are constructed using 2.0 standard deviations above and below a 20-day simple moving average.

Bollinger set forth the following rules for interpreting Bollinger Bands:

- Sharp moves in the market tend to occur after the Bands tighten, and the closer to the average the better. Since reduced volatility denotes a period of consolidation, the first increase in volatility after a consolidation tends to mark the start of the next move.
- When prices move outside the Bands (either upward or downward), it signals a continuation of the move until prices move back inside the Bands.
- Moves starting at one Band tend to move to the opposite Band before reversing.
- Rallies and reactions that temporarily take prices outside the Bands usually represent exhaustion and are associated with trend reversals.

The parameters for Bollinger Bands are the number of periods used in the simple moving average and the standard deviations that define the upper and lower Bands. The greater the number of periods in the moving average, the less reactive the Bands. Conversely, the fewer the number of periods in the moving average, the more reactive the

Bands. Note in Figure 2.3 how price tends to reverse direction after reaching either the upper or lower Band.

Volume Accumulation/Distribution (V-A/D)

It is generally accepted in technical analysis that volume leads price. When a stock breaks out of a consolidation pattern on increasing volume, for example, it is considered a valid breakout and the expectation is that price will move higher. However, if a breakout is followed by lethargic volume, it is considered suspect. Therefore, an issue's current volume relative to its recent volume can be highly useful not only in assessing the viability of an issue's current trend, but also the likelihood of a change in price direction.

One indicator that can prove helpful in depicting the price-volume relationship is called Volume Accumulation/Distribution. Developed by Marc Chaikin and based on earlier work by Larry Williams, the indicator is calculated by adding (or subtracting) a percentage of the period's volume to a cumulative total. The percentage is determined by the relationship among the day's high, low, and close. When the close is nearer the high, a larger percentage of volume is *added,* and when the close is nearer the low, a larger percentage of the volume is *subtracted.* A close exactly at the midpoint of the day's range would cause the indicator to be unchanged (see Figure 2.4).

Because it is a summation indicator, the actual values will depend on the number of periods under consideration. However, the actual value is of little importance; it is the direction of the indicator line that matters. If the line is pointing up, the stock is considered to be under accumulation, and the steeper the line the greater the buying

FIGURE 2.4 VOLUME BARS AND THE VOLUME ACCUMULATION LINE.

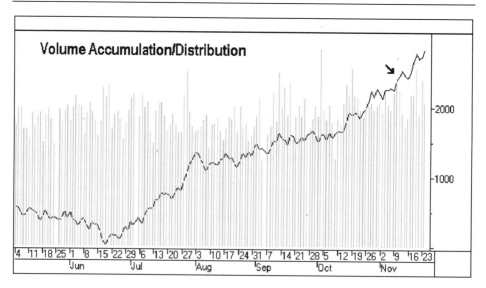

pressure. If it is pointing down, it is considered to be under distribution, and the steeper the slope the greater the selling pressure. A buy signal is generated when the indicator line turns from down to up, and a sell signal is just the opposite. Also, divergences from price direction and/or nonconfirmations of new highs or lows can be a significant early warning of an impending change in price trend. The only variable parameter in the calculation of Volume Accumulation/Distribution is the number of periods under consideration.

Commodity Channel Index (CCI)

Many technicians believe that markets (e.g., stocks, funds, commodities) move in waves or recognizable patterns over time. And whether attributable to naturally occurring events (the normal business cycle, presidential election campaigns, the planting/harvesting sequence of certain commodity crops, etc.) or a more cosmic phenomenon (the alignment of the earth and stars or gravitational forces), markets do appear to have some cyclical appearance. Notice, for example, Figure 2.5 shows the recurring cycle peaks in the following weekly chart of the S&P 500 Index from 1970 to 1995.

The technician's task, then, is to determine the extent to which an issue is exhibiting cyclical behavior, and to take advantage of those cycles that are the most reliable or tradable. One indicator that was designed to do just that is the Commodity Channel Index, published by Don Lambert in 1980. The CCI evaluates how the current typical price deviates from the mean typical price to determine when issues are

FIGURE 2.5 PRICE CYCLICALITY. THE S&P 500 HAS VISIBLE PRICE
CYCLES WHOSE PEAKS ARE MARKED BY ARROWS.

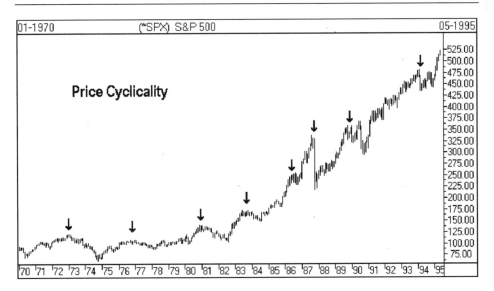

near the tops or bottoms of their cycles. It differs from other cyclical indicators, though, in that its calculation is based on a *mean deviation* rather than a *standard deviation*. Although originally developed for use with commodities (thus its name), the Commodity Channel Index may be used equally well with stocks, funds, indexes, and so on (see Figure 2.6).

The CCI is designed to oscillate in a range of between +100 and −100, which captures 70 percent to 80 percent of random price fluctuations, and within which the issue is considered to be exhibiting normal price cyclically. When it moves outside this range, it signals that price may have begun trending. Trading rules as originally advanced by Lambert were:

- Buy long when the indicator breaks above +100, and sell long when it breaks back below +100.
- Sell short when the indicator falls below −100 and cover short when it breaks back above −100.

This approach however, is very short term and tends to leave the trader on the sidelines most of the time. A better approach may be to buy long (cover shorts) when the CCI breaks above −100 moving up, and selling long (enter shorts) when the CCI breaks below +100 moving down. The CCI has one variable parameter, which is the number of periods over which the calculation is made.

FIGURE 2.6 COMMODITY CHANNEL INDEX. AN EXAMPLE OF THE CCI LINE.

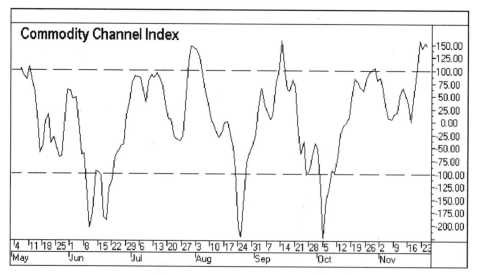

Relative Strength Index (RSI)

Developed in 1978 by J. Welles Wilder, the Relative Strength Index is one of the most popular and reliable indicators in the technician's arsenal. Often confused with "relative strength" (which is merely a ratio of the price of an issue divided by an index of the overall market), the RSI is an oscillator that measures the relative *internal* strength of an issue's average upward price movement against its average downward price movement over a selected time frame (see Figure 2.7). It is computed on a scale of 0 to 100, with a value over 70 representing an overbought situation and a value under 30 representing an oversold situation. (Based on my experience, however, 70 and 30 should not be taken as absolutes, but rather as areas or zones near which an overbought/oversold condition might occur.)

Wilder also recommends looking for divergences between the oscillator and price action, as well as failure swings at or near the 70/30 overbought/oversold levels, and chart formations in the indicator itself, as additional signs of a potential price reversal. Although the RSI can be calculated over virtually any time span, Wilder recommends a 14-day period. The shorter the time span, the more sensitive (and volatile) the oscillator. The longer the time span, the slower and more stable the oscillator.

Moving Average Convergence-Divergence (MACD)

Another helpful piece of information for the technical analyst is the degree of an issue's price/trend deviation. Price/trend deviation is determined by dividing the price itself by a moving average of the price. Since the moving average represents the trend

FIGURE 2.7 RELATIVE STRENGTH INDEX. AN EXAMPLE OF THE RSI LINE.

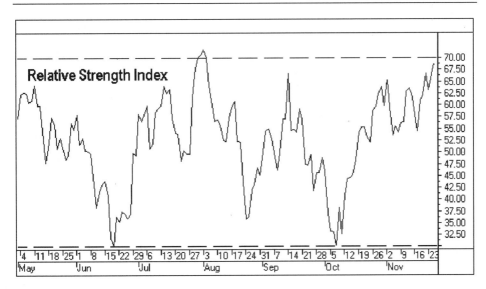

of the issue, the resulting calculation reflects just how slow or fast price is rising or falling in relation to its trend.

A popular and useful indicator of trend deviation is called the Moving Average Convergence-Divergence Index. Developed by Gerald Appel in 1979, MACD is nothing more than an oscillator constructed from the difference between two exponential moving averages, one of shorter-term duration and the other of longer-term duration. While any time period may be used, Appel recommends a 12-period exponential moving average for the shorter term and a 26-period exponential moving average for the longer term. The indicator gets its name from the fact that the shorter-term moving average is constantly converging toward, or diverging from, the longer-term moving average.

The difference between the two moving averages, called the MACD or differential line, is plotted as an oscillator curve. A 9-period exponential moving average of the differential line, called the signal line, is then plotted beside the differential line. Buy signals are generated when the differential line is negative and then crosses from below to above the signal line. Conversely, sell signals are generated when the differential line is positive and then crosses from above to below the signal line (see Figure 2.8).

Because the indicator is constructed of moving averages, it serves to smooth out the data in highly volatile issues. (*Note.* At first glance, it may appear to novice technicians that the two lines on the MACD plot represent the short-term and longer-term exponential averages. Actually, the difference between the two moving averages

FIGURE 2.8 MOVING AVERAGE CONVERGENCE-DIVERGENCE.
AN EXAMPLE OF THE MACD LINE.

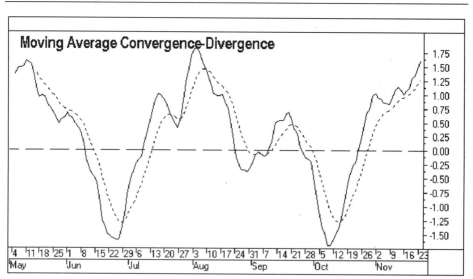

is a single curve [usually plotted as a solid line], and the other curve [usually plotted as a dashed line] is a 9-period exponential moving average of the first.)

Stochastics (STOC)

To complete the technical assessment of an issue, it is useful to know where the issue is currently trading relative to its price range over the past x number of periods. This is important because of the tendency for prices to close near the upper end of their trading range during an advance, and near the lower end of their trading range during a decline. Once the advance nears its end, prices begin closing farther and farther away from the high end of its trading range. During declines, the opposite is true. Prices tend to bottom out and then begin trading farther away from the low end of their trading range as the trend reverses direction. The stochastics oscillator, developed by George Lane, is a momentum oscillator designed to give the analyst a quantitative measurement of "position in range."

Although the term *stochastic* as used by Lane actually has no relation to the true definition of the word—"a naturally occurring random process"—its usage as applied in technical analysis refers to the term "stochastic equation." The indicator attempts to define the points in a rising or falling trend at which prices tend to cluster around the highs or lows for the period under consideration since this is the point at which trend reversals are signaled. The indicator consists of a family of oscillator curves, known as %K, Slow %D, and Fast %D, which are plotted and interpreted in a manner similar to the RSI.

The first curve, %K, represents the position of the close relative to the issue's range over the preceding x number of periods and is therefore the most important. Fast %D is merely a smoothing, usually a 3-period simple moving average, of %K. Slow %D is typically a 3-period moving average of Fast %D, but all the curves can be changed to suit the issue and time frame under consideration.

According to Lane, oversold conditions exist below 20 and overbought conditions exist above 80. Buy signals are generated when both %K and Slow %D are below 20 and turn up, with %K breaking above %D. Sell signals are generated when both %K and Slow %D are above 80 and turn down, with %K breaking below Slow %D. Signals may also be generated by price divergence. The only variable parameters with stochastics are the number of periods in the trading range, and the number of periods used in the smoothing of Slow %D and Fast %D (see Figure 2.9).

STRENGTH IN NUMBERS

As mentioned before, indicator interpretation is an *art form* requiring a great deal of skill and experience on the part of the technician. While each of the preceding indicators is considered a "standard" in its own right, no one indicator should ever be depended on exclusively, for there is no Holy Grail in technical analysis. Rather, each

FIGURE 2.9 STOCHASTICS. AN EXAMPLE OF A STOCHASTICS LINE.

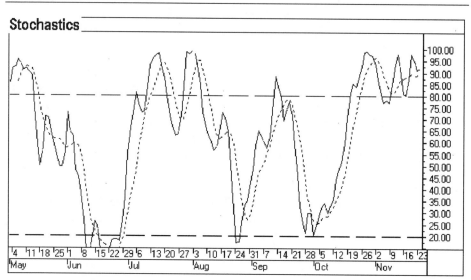

FIGURE 2.10 INDICATOR CONFIRMATIONS. A COMPOSITE OF VARIOUS
INDICATORS ON THE SAME PRICE TIME SERIES.

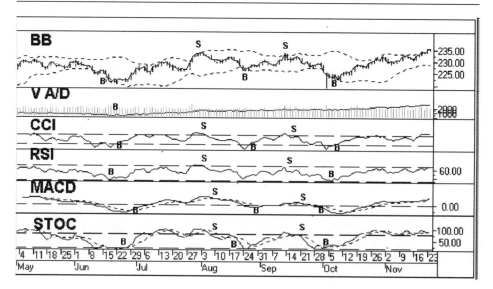

should be seen as solving only one piece of the puzzle. Their true value can be realized only when used in concert with other (dissimilar) indicators to provide an overall composite picture of an issue's underlying trend strength and direction.

The more evidence there is to support the indicators' confirmation of one another, the more valid the conclusion—and the higher the probability of profit. For example, Figure 2.10 shows how powerful the ensuing price move was when the buy (B) and sell (S) signals of each indicator (volatility, accumulation/distribution, cyclicality, internal strength, trend deviation and position in range) confirmed each other.

A WORD OF CAUTION

When momentum oscillators move rapidly from oversold to overbought levels and vice versa, or when the oscillator curve reaches an extreme high/low reading, it may seem that it is exceptionally strong evidence of an impending change in price direction. In actuality, moves of extraordinary proportions in momentum oscillators, either in duration or magnitude, are usually an indication of exceptional price strength and strong evidence in favor of a continuation in trend direction. In these instances, it is wise to ignore the signals generated by these oscillators and rely instead on trend-based indicators.

Some indicators, like momentum oscillators, are only effective in trading markets, and can be counter productive (and quite expensive) in trending markets. Other indicators, like those based on moving averages, are primarily effective in trending markets and can be counterproductive in trading markets. The secret to success with technical analysis, then, lies in the art of knowing the kind of market you are in and, therefore, upon which indicators to rely.

CHAPTER 3

Combining Trend Analysis with Indicator Readings

DAVID VOMUND

Which technical indicator is the most effective? This frequently asked question is difficult to answer because most indicators work well only in a particular market environment. Most indicators can be classified into two categories defined by the market environment (trending or trading) in which the indicators are effective.

In strong trending markets, some indicators work very well while others fail to give good results. In consolidating or trading markets, those indicators that failed during trending market environments often work best. Before analyzing a security with a set of indicators, it is essential to determine the trend of the security and then apply the appropriate indicators in the analysis.

DETERMINING THE TREND

There are several methods to help determine whether a security is in a trending or nontrending (trading) environment. The ADX indicator, developed by Welles Wilder, is designed to flag trending securities. Those securities with an increasing ADX indicator, especially when the indicator is above 30, are in a trending environment while those with a decreasing ADX are in a trading environment. This indicator is generally only helpful to short-term traders.

My preferred method of determining whether a security is in a trending or a trading environment is to simply look at a chart of the security along with its 28-day moving average. When price rarely crosses the moving average, the security is in a trending environment. However, if price constantly crosses the moving average, the security is in a trading environment.

Nike (NKE) is an example of a strong trending stock. The top half of Figure 3.1 shows Nike along with its 28-day moving average. Notice that Nike never fell below its 28-day moving average from March until June. The moving average acted as support as the stock moved higher.

FIGURE 3.1 TRENDING AND TRADING STOCK. NIKE IS IN AN UPTREND AS
IT SELDOM CROSSES BELOW ITS MOVING AVERAGE. LOUISIANA PACIFIC IS
IN A TRADING ENVIRONMENT AS ITS MOVING AVERAGE IS OFTEN CROSSED.

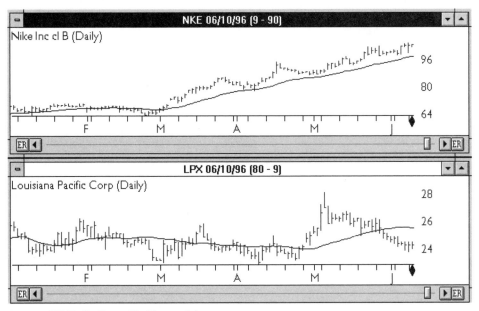

Source: AIQ's TradingExpert. Used by permission.

The lower half of Figure 3.1 displays a nontrending security, Louisiana Pacific
(LPX). This security would be a poor choice for a buy-and-hold type of investment
since its price is almost at the same level in June as it was in January. As it moved sideways, the 28-day moving average was crossed on several occasions. During this period, the 28-day moving average failed to act as support or resistance for LPX.

CLASSIFYING INDICATORS

With the trend of a security determined, we can now classify indicators into two categories: those that work best in trending markets and those that work best in trading markets. Table 3.1 shows some well-known indicators classified into these two
categories.

Generally, indicators that work well in nontrending market environments are
those that give overbought/oversold readings. The theory is that when a security rises
too far too fast it becomes "overbought" and therefore retreats. The opposite is true for
oversold conditions. These indicators work well in nontrending environments because
an overbought reading is registered whenever the security rallies to the upper end of its

TABLE 3.1 INDICATOR CLASSIFICATION

Trending	Non-Trending
McClellan oscillator	RSI
Directional movement index	Stochastic
MACD	
Moving average crossover	
Positive volume index	
SK-SD	

trading range. Conversely, the security becomes oversold when it nears the lower end of its trading range.

Indicators that work well in trending environments are generally those that tend to remain positive as long as the security continues to rise or those that remain negative as long as the security decreases. Moving averages are a common element in many of these indicators.

Note: Some indicators, such as On Balance Volume and Money Flow, are not listed since they do not give strict buy and sell signals.

NONTRENDING INDICATORS

To demonstrate the effectiveness of a nontrending indicator, we will again examine Louisiana Pacific (LPX). Figure 3.2 shows LPX charted with its 21-day stochastic, an indicator that works well for nontrending securities. A stochastic buy signal is registered when the indicator moves out of oversold territory by rising above the lower horizontal line (corresponding to a value of 20). A sell is registered when the indicator falls below the upper horizontal line (corresponding to a value of 80). We have drawn arrows on the LPX price chart that correspond to the buy and sell signals generated by the Stochastic indicator.

Notice that the stock tends to fluctuate between $23 and $27. When the stock falls to the lower end of this range, a stochastic buy signal is often registered. A corresponding sell is registered when the security rises to the upper end of its range. A listing of the actual signals registered in Figure 3.2 is found in Table 3.2. Each trade based on these signals is profitable. For a nontrending security, the stochastic can be very effective.

However, the stochastic indicator loses its effectiveness when a security is in a strong trend. An example of this is shown in Figure 3.3, which displays Nike (NKE) along with its stochastic indicator. The indicator gave a good buy signal in late February but proceeded to give a series of sell signals even as the security moved higher. The stochastic will almost always have you exit from strong performing securities too early.

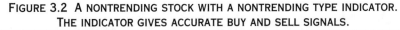

FIGURE 3.2 A NONTRENDING STOCK WITH A NONTRENDING TYPE INDICATOR.
THE INDICATOR GIVES ACCURATE BUY AND SELL SIGNALS.

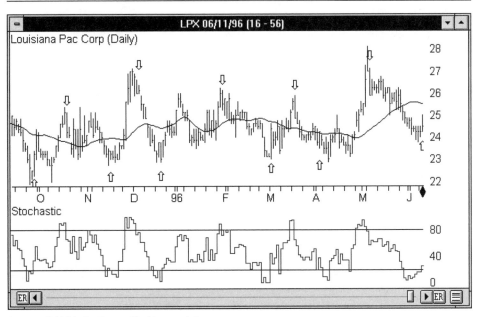

Source: AIQ's TradingExpert. Used by permission.

TRENDING INDICATORS

Now we will examine the effectiveness of an indicator that works well in trending
market environments. In Figure 3.4, Nike is charted along with its Directional Movement Index (DMI). Using the DMI, a buy is registered when the indicator moves
above zero and a sell is registered when it falls below zero. On the Nike price chart, arrows correspond to the DMI buy and sell signals. In almost every month shown on
this chart, the DMI remained positive. Other than two short-lived sell signals, the

TABLE 3.2 STOCHASTIC SIGNALS FOR LOUISIANA PACIFIC

Buy Date	Buy Price	Sell Date	Sell Price	Percent Change
9/28/95	23.250	10/19/95	24.250	4.30
11/15/95	23.375	12/5/95	26.000	11.23
12/19/95	23.750	1/31/96	25.500	7.37
3/4/96	24.375	3/19/96	24.875	2.05
4/3/96	24.250	5/7/96	25.875	6.70

FIGURE 3.3 A TRENDING STOCK WITH A NONTRENDING INDICATOR. THE INDICATOR
GIVES SEVERAL BAD SIGNALS AGAINST THE DIRECTION OF THE TREND.

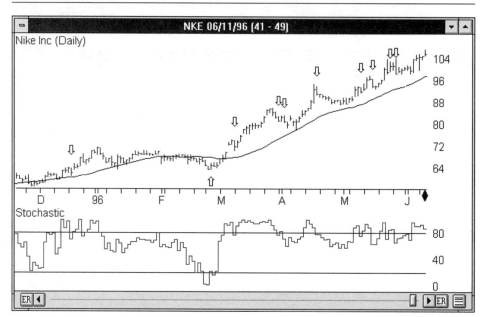

Source: AIQ's TradingExpert. Used by permission.

FIGURE 3.4 A TRENDING STOCK WITH A TRENDING INDICATOR. THE INDICATOR
IS BULLISH FOR THE MAJORITY OF THE ADVANCE.

Source: AIQ's TradingExpert. Used by permission.

TABLE 3.3 DMI SIGNALS FOR NIKE INC.

Buy Date	Buy Price	Sell Date	Sell Price	Percent Change
12/1/95	58.500	2/14/96	67.000	14.53
3/5/96	69.500	4/9/96	81.000	16.547
4/10/96	82.375	6/19/96	100.375	21.851

indicator kept us in the security as the security moved higher. The actual signals registered are listed in Table 3.3.

The DMI worked well for this trending security, but loses its effectiveness for nontrending securities. Figure 3.5 is a chart of Louisiana Pacific (LPX) along with its DMI. Looking at the arrows, we see many signals were registered but the majority of them turned out to be whipsaws. The actual signals registered in this example are listed in Table 3.4. The majority of the signals were unprofitable.

FIGURE 3.5 A TRADING STOCK WITH A TRENDING INDICATOR. THE INDICATOR
FREQUENTLY GIVES WHIPSAW SIGNALS.

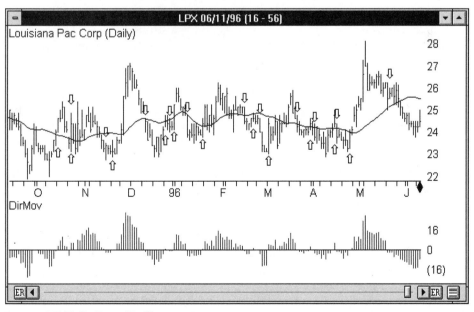

Source: AIQ's TradingExpert. Used by permission.

TABLE 3.4 DMI SIGNALS FOR LOUISIANA PACIFIC

Buy Date	Buy Price	Sell Date	Sell Price	Percent Change
10/16/95	24.625	10/23/95	23.500	−4.569
10/24/95	24.375	11/15/95	23.375	−4.103
11/20/95	23.125	12/12/95	24.500	5.946
12/26/95	24.500	12/28/95	24.250	−1.020
1/2/96	25.250	1/10/96	23.875	−5.446
1/19/96	24.375	2/15/96	24.500	0.513
2/22/96	24.625	2/27/96	24.000	−2.538
3/4/96	24.375	3/21/96	24.250	−0.513
3/29/96	24.375	4/2/96	23.750	−2.564
4/16/96	24.375	4/17/96	23.750	−2.564
4/25/96	24.000	5/20/96	25.500	6.250

TRENDING SECURITY, NONTRENDING INDICATOR

When an indicator that works well in a nontrending market is applied to a trending security, it tends to give bad signals against the trend. Does this mean the indicator should be ignored? Not so fast. By making adjustments to an indicator's interpretation, we can effectively apply a nontrending indicator to a trending security.

The first adjustment is to simply ignore all signals against the trend of the security. These indicators give frequent sell signals during a strong advance. These signals should be ignored. This does not mean you should not have an exit system in place. It means that the exit system should not involve the use of nontrending indicators.

The second adjustment is to change the requirements for buy or sell signals so that the indicator gives signals in the direction of the overall trend. Using defaulted values (values recommended by the developer), a stochastic or Relative Strength Index (RSI) rarely gives a buy signal for a strongly advancing security. As a result, the oversold levels should be adjusted upward so the indicator will give buy signals. Instead of the normal default value of 20 for the stochastic, the oversold level should be raised to 50 for a strongly advancing security. Then a stochastic buy is registered anytime the indicator falls below and then rises above a value of 50.

An example is found in Figure 3.6, which displays the Dow Jones Industrial Average for 1995's strongly advancing market. We know the market is in a strong uptrend because its 28-day moving average is not broken. Using the default buy and sell values for the stochastic, the indicator failed to give a single buy signal in 1995 but gave sell signals almost every week of the year. Not very effective.

By making our adjustments, we identify the strong trend and therefore ignore the sell signals from all nontrending indicators. By raising the oversold level of the stochastic, buy signals are registered when the indicator falls below and rises above 50,

FIGURE 3.6 A TRENDING MARKET WITH A NONTRENDING INDICATOR.
BY USING 50 AS A BUY LEVEL, THE STOCHASTIC GIVES ACCURATE
SIGNALS IN THE DIRECTION OF THE TREND.

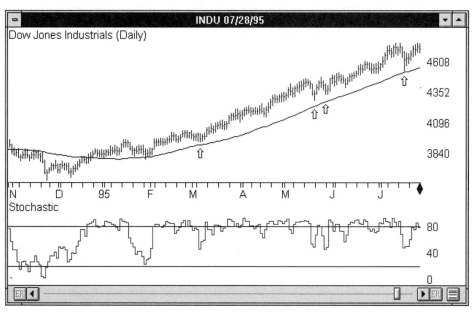

Source: AIQ's TradingExpert. Used by permission.

which happened in early March, twice in May, and again in July (see arrows on the price chart in Figure 3.6).

NONTRENDING SECURITY—IMPROVING THE ODDS

Almost every security is in a trend, but sometimes it is necessary to look at more data to find what the trend is. Plotting only the last few months may show that no trend is in place while a two-year chart may reveal that the security is in a definite uptrend. A good example of this is Mirage Resorts at the end of 1995. Figure 3.7 shows a chart of Mirage Resorts (MIR) using daily data. We see a nontrending security as the stock crosses its 28-day moving average often.

By plotting the same stock using weekly data, we get a different picture (Figure 3.8). The stock began a strong rally in early 1995 as it rarely crossed below its 28-week moving average. Whereas the daily chart shows a stock in a trading range, its weekly chart reveals an uptrending stock that is currently undergoing temporary consolidation.

Once the long-term trend is determined, we can improve our odds by trading only in the direction of the long-term trend. On the daily chart, the stock is consolidating so

FIGURE 3.7 A NONTRENDING STOCK AS IT FREQUENTLY CROSSES ITS 28 DAY MOVING AVERAGE OFTEN.

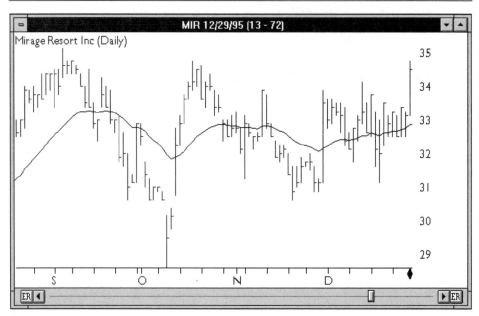

Source: AIQ's TradingExpert. Used by permission.

FIGURE 3.8 DETERMINING THE TREND. USING WEEKLY DATA, WE SEE MIRAGE RESORT IS IN AN OVERALL UPTREND.

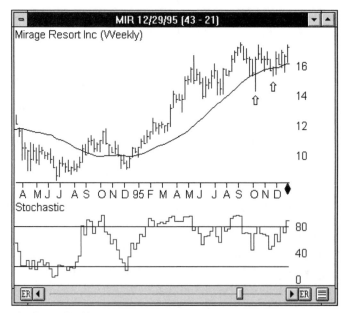

Source: AIQ's TradingExpert. Used by permission.

the stochastic or an RSI indicator is appropriate. Since the overall trend is up, we can improve the accuracy of the signals by acting only on the buy signals.

Performing the same type of analysis on MIR's weekly chart also shows that we should be concentrating on the long side. Using weekly data (Figure 3.8), we see the stock is trending higher over the long term. For an uptrending stock, we know to ignore sell signals from indicators that work best in trading markets. However, by making adjustments to the oversold levels of these indicators, we see that MIR's stochastic gave two oversold buy signals in the fourth quarter of 1995 as its value fell below and then rose above the 50 level.

CONCLUSION

Indicators can be classified into two categories: those that work in trending markets and those that work in nontrending markets. Unless adjustments are made to an indicator's interpretation, you can get into trouble when you apply the wrong type of indicator in a given market environment.

An indicator that works well in a trading market will constantly give signals opposite the trend for a strong trending security. When a security is in a nice uptrend, ignore overbought sell signals. Conversely, if you apply an indicator that works well in trending situations to a nontrending security, you will trade often but will end up selling at about the same level as the purchase price.

It is best to apply nontrending type indicators to securities that are in a trading range and to apply trending type indicators to securities that are in a trend. When using nontrending type indicators, it is always best to follow the signals that are in the direction of the security's long-term trend.

Forecasting with Mobility Oscillators

MEL WIDNER

The Mobility Oscillator, a technical indicator that measures how easily prices can move, is useful for assessing developing market conditions and anticipating price moves, even when conditions are relatively quiet.

CONGESTION AND MOBILITY

Does a market remember what it did previously? Each individual trader or investor in that market certainly remembers. Does the ensemble of traders and investors that make up a market have a collective memory? Can this be measured? Does this memory influence the future? Consider the following scenario and analysis, and judge for yourself.

If a trader enters or exits the market at a particular level, then that level becomes important to that trader, who will base future decisions on the entry or exit point. If the trader has entered the market and the market moves in either direction by some amount, the position may be closed for profit taking or as a stop loss. If the trader had exited the market previously, then he or she may reenter for similar reasons. The amount of the move and the time frame depend on the style and risk tolerance of the trader.

While a single action is not so important, the accumulation of actions for all traders in the market has significance. The composition of the market is varied. Some investors or fund managers may use fundamental analysis to determine entry and exit points based on assessed value. The fundamental levels are important as they can persist and, once evident, can reoccur and be reused in the future. There is also a cadre of traders and analysts who are watching the tape, trying to spot a trend, pattern, or an extreme or overdone condition. Trends and reversals are usually important for this group and they will jump on or off for a variety of reasons. These and other transactions cannot be hidden and are reflected in the price or index value.

If the price remains in a narrow range for a period of time, for whatever reason, then this price range becomes a region of congestion. There has been a balance of buyers and sellers, and over time, their numbers accumulate. If the market moves far enough, then they may react creating a breakout. The losers will stop out and the winners will ride the trend. Other trend followers will jump on, and the process will continue until a new support or resistance level is tested.

From another viewpoint, the number of available buyers and sellers influences price changes. If initially there are about the same number of buyers and sellers and the price goes up, some additional new sellers, stimulated by the higher price, enter the market and the price is pushed back and equilibrates. Similarly if the price goes down, some additional buyers enter pushing the price back. For these supply-and-demand conditions, the reaction to a price move is stabilizing.

In some cases, the numbers of previously available buyers and sellers can be greater than the number of new buyers and sellers that can be stimulated by a move. As a result, the reaction to a price move is not always stabilizing. In fact, the opposite can occur. For example, if a move begins in a price range of high congestion and moves to a region of lesser congestion, then there can be fewer potential traders to counteract the move and the move can continue. This is destabilizing. If the move begins in a region of low congestion toward a region of higher congestion, there can be more traders to counteract and absorb the action. In this case, the reaction is overstabilizing.

Congestion may be viewed as a memory of the market that can influence future price movement. If price is moving about within a region of low congestion, there are few traders to counteract the moves and the price movement is considered mobile. Further, when prices move *toward* lower congestion, the move is likely to continue and the price is considered mobile. Conversely, when prices move either within high congestion or toward a region of higher congestion, then price is considered immobile. The ability or ease of a price to move is referred to as Mobility. That is not to say that price of high mobility will move, but that it is *easier* to do so.

External factors can change this scenario. Essentially anything that can cause significant numbers of new traders, who are not active, to enter the market will change the story. Changes in market conditions and departures from the previous history or expectations will do so. Earnings and growth potential, or lack thereof, are long-term drivers. News and unexpected events can lead to randomness or unpredictability. Other markets can influence a particular market indirectly. Sometimes these are factored in price, sometimes not. Divergence sometimes occurs and can lead to correction or equilibration.

Momentum is also an important factor. If a price move has sufficient inertia, then stopping it may take more than a region of congestion, or a support or resistance level. Not only are there traders sitting on the price level, there are those riding the trend. Therefore, momentum should be captured in the analysis process. This is possible by developing a historical record of congestion and price movement.

The premise to be explored is that price history contains a memory of previous events and that this will influence future events. So what is memory and how do you measure it? The most straightforward approach is to consider memory as simply a tally of that which has happened for some previous period. Pick a previous period and analyze the price action. One means of doing so is to calculate how prices are distributed over the price range of that period. This distribution is called a Price Distribution Function (PDF). The PDF shows the amount of time that the price has spent within subdivisions of its price range for some previous period. If the amount of time spent is large, then there is congestion; and if the time spent is small, then there is a lack of congestion. An example of a PDF is shown in Figure 4.1 as a bar graph. High bars represent high congestion and low bars represent low congestion. The inverse relationship between congestion and mobility, as viewed by PDF analysis, is illustrated in Figure 4.1.

Distribution functions related to price are not by any means new. For example, the Black-Scholes model, a common tool for estimating the value of options and derivatives, utilizes a distribution of price changes to determine volatility. The data is assumed to fit a lognormal distribution, a standard distribution function form. Its volatility is derived, assuming this particular form, for subsequent evaluation. The analysis here is different. The PDF is a distribution over price, not price changes. It is simply a numerical distribution function computed by sorting data into bins. The shape is determined by the data history and can be virtually anything. There is no

FIGURE 4.1 CONGESTION AND MOBILITY. CONGESTION, AS MEASURED BY A PRICE DISTRIBUTION FUNCTION (PDF), DEFINES MOBILITY. THE PDF IS SIMPLY A TALLY OF PRICE ACTION FOR A RECENT PERIOD. WHEN CURRENT PRICE IS IN A REGION OF LARGE CONGESTION (THE CENTER OF THE BULGE), THEN MOBILITY IS SMALL AND MOVEMENT IS DIFFICULT. WHEN CURRENT PRICE IS IN A REGION OF LOW CONGESTION (THE EXTREME LEFT OR RIGHT OF THE BULGE), THEN MOBILITY IS LARGE AND MOVEMENT EASIER. PRICE MOVEMENT FROM HIGH CONGESTION TO LOW CONGESTION IS ALSO EASIER.

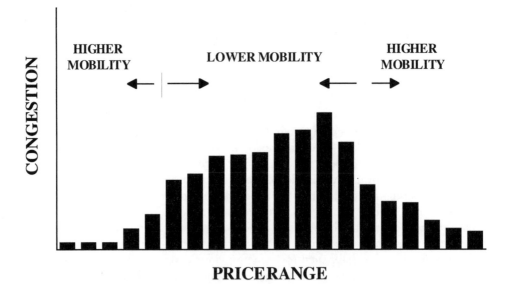

attempt to fit a particular form. A bar graph representation of the PDF not only is useful for interpretation, but also accurately reflects the method that was used to determine the distribution. Each bar is defined for one interval or bin and the bar height is a measure of congestion within that bin.

Up to this point, we have considered a single time period and a single PDF for that period. When a long history of data is analyzed, then each bar will have a lookback period and PDF for each bar. This series of PDFs can be plotted bar by bar to view the time dependence. This plot is a complicated 3-D surface. While rich with information, is it not easy to interpret. There are too many trees and not enough forest. To have a more practical tool, it is necessary to distill the PDF to a simpler, oscillator form that represents the level of congestion as well as one that captures the momentum, direction, and extreme conditions. And it must have a single numerical value for each bar so that it can be used to make trading decisions. This oscillator has been constructed and is called the Mobility Oscillator (MO). This oscillator and its smoothed companion, the Slow Mobility Oscillator (MOS), provide insight into price behavior and have utility as a forecasting tool.

In the discussion to follow, mobility analysis is described in detail, step by step. The six steps are:

1. Measuring congestion—Price Distribution Functions (PDF).
2. PDF examples and interpretation.
3. Reference points (support, resistance, and moving averages).
4. Mobility Oscillators.
5. Applications and interpretation of the Mobility Oscillators.
6. Steps for assessing price mobility.

One final point. Besides providing a useful trading tool, this chapter also provides an example of how an oscillator is constructed. To develop an oscillator from a hypothesis, determine parameters that characterize the hypothesis, determine reference points for these parameters, and combine the parameters to produce the oscillator. Once accomplished, then test the method by back-testing and by adjusting variables that make up the parameters. Sometimes refinement of the method is needed. Keep the analysis as simple as possible and avoid curve fitting. This was the process followed for developing the Mobility Oscillators.

MEASURING CONGESTION—PRICE DISTRIBUTION FUNCTIONS (PDF)

The PDF is a distribution of price action for a fixed period of time. The computing procedure is straightforward. Select a particular time. Tabulate the high, low, and close data from that time over a look-back period of N bars. The range of the PDF is just the range of prices from the minimum low $L_{min} = Min(L_j)$ to the maximum high

H_{max} = Max(H_j) over the look-back period from $j = 1$ to N bars. This is the same range as is used for stochastics and may implicitly capture some of the same features.

Next divide the range into M equal intervals or bins separated by boundaries. The range is bounded by the lowermost boundary L_{min} and the uppermost boundary H_{max}. The boundary values B_i are

$$B_i = L_{min} + \frac{i-1}{M} \times (H_{max} - L_{min})$$

for $i = 1$ to $M + 1$, where M = number of intervals.

The number of intervals M should be chosen no larger than necessary, but large enough to delineate any important structure. The interval size should be smaller than the smallest bar height by some factor, say two or so.

Figure 4.2 shows an example of a short S&P100 history ($N = 14$ bars) with the price range divided into 10 intervals ($M = 10$). The interval boundaries are extended through the data history.

FIGURE 4.2 PRICE DISTRIBUTION FUNCTION (PDF) CONSTRUCTED FROM 14 DAYS OF DATA. THE PRICE RANGE FOR THE 14-DAY PERIOD IS DIVIDED INTO 10 INTERVALS AND THE PRICE DURATION WITHIN EACH INTERVAL IS PROJECTED TO THE RIGHT. THE PDF IS A BAR GRAPH TILTED ON ITS SIDE. THE BAR LENGTH IS PROPORTIONAL TO THE AMOUNT OF CONGESTION.

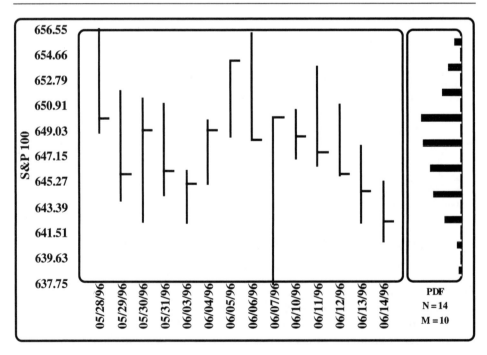

Weightings and spreads for each bar are chosen as follows. Each bar, within the look-back period, is equally weighted. It is also assumed that it is equally likely that prices will occur anywhere between the low and high for that bar. In other words, the price is uniformly distributed between the high and low of each bar. These choices allow the contribution of each bar to be easily divided within each interval and tallied. This is simple and minimizes the number of adjustable parameters. Some variations on the assumptions have been tried by the author, but found to add little to the discussion presented here.

The next step is to calculate the fraction of time or frequency of occurrence of the price within each of the intervals (the PDF values). One method for doing this would be to go bar by bar, compute the fraction of the total bar that falls within each interval, and then tally these fractions for each interval over all bars to get the PDF. Although this is perfectly valid, it is not the most numerically efficient.

A more efficient method is to first compute a Cumulative Price Distribution Function (CPDF) for the same intervals. The PDF is then the difference between adjacent values of the CPDF. The CPDF values represent the fraction of all the price action that is below the interval boundary values. Since we assumed that the price for any bar j is uniformly distributed between the high and low values H_j and L_j, then the term T_{ij} represents the fraction of the bar j that is below boundary B_i:

$$T_{ij} = 1 \qquad\qquad \text{for } B_i \geq H_j$$
$$T_{ij} = (B_i - L_j)/(H_j - L_j) \quad \text{for } H_j > B_i > L_j$$
$$T_{ij} = 0 \qquad\qquad \text{for } L_j > B_i$$

The $CPDF_i$ collects all the individual fractions T_{ij} below boundary B_i and normalizes by the number of bars N. This gives the fraction of the price action during the look-back period that is below boundary B_i:

$$CPDF_i = \text{Sum}(T_{ij})/N \quad \text{for } j = 1 \text{ to } N$$

Note that $CPDF_1 = 0$ as there is no price action below B_1 and that $CPDF_{M+1} = 1$ as all the price action is below B_{M+1}.

Normally the terms T_{ij} and the CPDF are only a means to an end (i.e., parametric variables) and are not viewed or printed, unless to familiarize the reader with the process. By using Visual Basic macros to perform the calculations, all the intermediate steps can be done within the macro. It is not necessary to store these variables in a worksheet. Should the reader choose to use standard spreadsheet methods for the preceding calculations, however, it would be necessary to insert these terms in a spreadsheet. This latter choice is possible, but very cumbersome, and I do not recommend it based on my experience.

The PDF is given as

$$PDF_i = CPDF_{i+1} - CPDF_i \quad \text{for } i = 1 \text{ to } M$$

The value of PDF_i represents the fraction of the price action between the boundaries B_{i+1} and B_i. The PDF_i value is assigned at the interval center at BC_i, the central price, where

$$BC_i = (B_i + B_{i+1}) / 2 \quad \text{for } i = 1 \text{ to } M$$

The values of the PDF, as defined, represent the fraction of the look-back period that the price has spent in each respective interval. For this definition, the magnitudes of the PDF values depend on the number of intervals M. To remove this dependence, simply normalize PDF_i by dividing each value by the interval size $\Delta B = (H_{max} - L_{min})/M$. This normalization is not necessary for the following discussion, may be confusing, and thus is omitted here. However, if the reader wants to make absolute comparisons between PDFs, then it would be important to include this normalization.

Figure 4.2 includes a plot of the PDF distribution to the right of the High-Low-Close plot. Note that the bar chart has been turned 90 degrees, on its side. This is a convenient way of viewing the distribution function as it combines the time history with the PDF with a shared ordinate axis and range on the same scale. For the example in Figure 4.2, the high $H_{max} = 656.55$ was on 5/28/96 and the low $L_{min} = 637.75$ on 6/7/96. This defines the price range. For $M = 10$, the interval $\Delta B = (656.55 - 637.75) / 10 = 1.88$.

The value of M should be large enough to resolve all the structure present. That is, $M > (H_{max} - L_{min}) / \Delta$, where Δ is the smallest interval that is to be resolved. Typically Δ values range from the minimum of the bar height (high–low) to the average of the bar height for the look-back period. These recommended M values, named MRX and MRA, are shown in Table 4.1 for comparison, assuming two bins per Δ. The reader may also want to adjust M and observe changes to the PDF as a basis for selection.

PDF EXAMPLES AND INTERPRETATION

Tabulation of the input data for the example given in Figure 4.2 as well as boundary values and the CPDF and the PDF are shown in Table 4.1. These are loaded onto a worksheet for viewing. Next, the T matrix is computed following methods and formulas previously outlined, and the columns are summed and normalized to give the CPDF and PDF.

Table 4.2 gives the same output as the sheet given in Table 4.1, except that the parametric variables are not shown. Only output data is shown. This is the format that is used in my practice for routine analysis and is calculated using Visual Basic macro functions in EXCEL. Accompanying the sheet in Table 4.2 is a bar chart of the PDF as shown in Figure 4.3.

For the example shown in Figure 4.4, the current close was below the peak. The subsequent price moved further lower on the several following days. The mobility

TABLE 4.1 SPREADSHEET SHOWING CALCULATION OF PRICE DISTRIBUTION FUNCTION (ILLUSTRATION VERSION)

DATA INPUT	LAST	N (<=100)	M (<=40)		COMPUTED OUTPUT					HMAX	LMIN	MRA	MRX			
RUN	06/14/96	14	10							656.55	637.75	6	11			
	OEX	OEX	OEX					****** T(I,J) MATRIX VALUES ******								
J	DATE	HIGH	LOW	CLOSE	JI	1	2	3	4	5	6	7	8	9	10	11
1	05/28/96	656.55	648.92	649.93	1	0.00	0.00	0.00	0.00	0.00	0.00	0.01	0.26	0.51	0.75	1.00
2	05/29/96	651.97	643.84	645.83	2	0.00	0.00	0.00	0.00	0.18	0.41	0.64	0.87	1.00	1.00	1.00
3	05/30/96	651.43	642.33	649.09	3	0.00	0.00	0.00	0.12	0.32	0.53	0.74	0.94	1.00	1.00	1.00
4	05/31/96	651.06	644.25	646.02	4	0.00	0.00	0.00	0.00	0.15	0.43	0.70	0.98	1.00	1.00	1.00
5	06/03/96	646.06	642.19	645.11	5	0.00	0.00	0.00	0.31	0.80	1.00	1.00	1.00	1.00	1.00	1.00
6	06/04/96	649.82	645.11	649.06	6	0.00	0.00	0.00	0.00	0.03	0.43	0.83	1.00	1.00	1.00	1.00
7	06/05/96	654.21	648.60	654.21	7	0.00	0.00	0.00	0.00	0.00	0.00	0.08	0.41	0.75	1.00	1.00
8	06/06/96	656.24	648.37	648.40	8	0.00	0.00	0.00	0.00	0.00	0.00	0.08	0.32	0.56	0.80	1.00
9	06/07/96	650.01	637.75	650.01	9	0.00	0.00	0.15	0.31	0.46	0.61	0.77	0.92	1.00	1.00	1.00
10	06/10/96	650.55	647.00	648.61	10	0.00	0.00	0.00	0.00	0.00	0.04	0.57	1.00	1.00	1.00	1.00
11	06/11/96	653.77	646.42	647.44	11	0.00	0.00	0.00	0.00	0.00	0.10	0.36	0.61	0.87	1.00	1.00
12	06/12/96	650.98	645.73	645.80	12	0.00	0.00	0.00	0.00	0.00	0.27	0.63	0.99	1.00	1.00	1.00
13	06/13/96	647.90	642.24	644.57	13	0.00	0.00	0.00	0.20	0.54	0.87	1.00	1.00	1.00	1.00	1.00
14	06/14/96	645.24	640.80	642.32	14	0.00	0.00	0.16	0.58	1.00	1.00	1.00	1.00	1.00	1.00	1.00
				B		637.75	639.63	641.51	643.39	645.27	647.15	649.03	650.91	652.79	654.67	656.55
				CPDF		0.00	0.01	0.03	0.12	0.26	0.42	0.61	0.81	0.91	0.97	1.00
				BC		638.69	640.57	642.45	644.33	646.21	648.09	649.97	651.85	653.73	655.61	
				PDF		0.01	0.02	0.09	0.14	0.16	0.19	0.20	0.09	0.06	0.03	

HMAX and LMIN are computed as are MRA and MRX, the estimates of the required M values based on average and minimum daily price range. The T matrix is shown here for illustration and is a parametric variable that is normally not used for working calculations of the PDF.

TABLE 4.2 SPREADSHEET SHOWING CALCULATION OF PRICE DISTRIBUTION FUNCTION (WORKING VERSION)

INPUT DATA	LAST DAY	N (<=100)	M (<=80)	COMPUTED DATA			MRA	MRX
RUN	06/14/96	14	10				6	11
	OEX	OEX	OEX					
J	DATE	HIGH	LOW	CLOSE	I	B	CPDF	BC	PDF
1	05/28/96	656.55	648.92	649.93	1	637.75	0.0000	638.69	0.0110
2	05/29/96	651.97	643.84	645.83	2	639.63	0.0110	640.57	0.0224
3	05/30/96	651.43	642.33	649.09	3	641.51	0.0333	642.45	0.0862
4	05/31/96	651.06	644.25	646.02	4	643.39	0.1195	644.33	0.1396
5	06/03/96	646.06	642.19	645.11	5	645.27	0.2591	646.21	0.1582
6	06/04/96	649.82	645.11	649.06	6	647.15	0.4173	648.09	0.1941
7	06/05/96	654.21	648.60	654.21	7	649.03	0.6114	649.97	0.2017
8	06/06/96	656.24	648.37	648.40	8	650.91	0.8131	651.85	0.0928
9	06/07/96	650.01	637.75	650.01	9	652.79	0.9059	653.73	0.0623
10	06/10/96	650.55	647.00	648.61	10	654.67	0.9682	655.61	0.0318
11	06/11/96	653.77	646.42	647.44	11	656.55	1.0000		
12	06/12/96	650.98	645.73	645.80					
13	06/13/96	647.90	642.24	644.57					
14	06/14/96	645.24	640.80	642.32					

A more useful format for PDF calculations with the same input data format but a more streamlined output format than in Table 4.1. The distribution functions are listed along columns instead of rows, as in Table 4.1.

FIGURE 4.3 PRICE DISTRIBUTION FUNCTION (PDF) CONSTRUCTED FROM 14 DAYS OF
OEX DATA. THE PDF VERSUS BC IS OBTAINED FROM TABLE 4.2. THE BIN
CONTAINING THE LAST CLOSE IS HIGHLIGHTED.

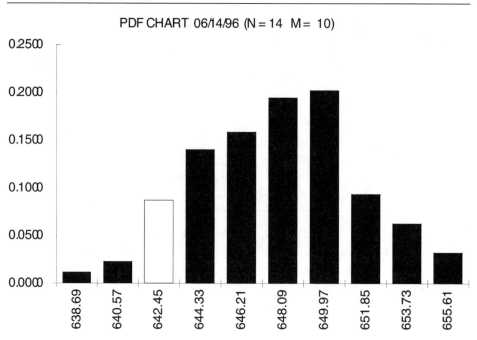

analysis would suggest that it is easier to move lower than higher for these conditions
and the subsequent price movement was consistent with this. To properly assess the
situation, however, requires additional information and an assessment of the momentum to be discussed shortly.

Distribution function shapes can vary. They can be symmetric about the center
of the range, peaked to one side or the other, skewed, and even have multiple peaks.
Quite often, prices will form bottoms or tops and sometimes steps. This is quite natural before or after a large move, for example. These flat regions correspond to regions
of congestion and will produce corresponding peaks in the PDF. The PDF analysis
gives a precise means of observing this behavior. Figure 4.5 is an example of a distribution function with multiple peaks. This is not too common for short periods of 14
days, but happens occasionally. For this example, during the look-back period, the
OEX moved from a level (flat region) of about 610 to another level of about 640. The
move was quick, and little time was spent between these levels. Although this is apparent from simple examination of the time series history, the PDF provides a means
of quantifying these conditions for precise comparisons and analysis.

Multiple peaks are more common for longer look-back periods than for shorter
ones since it is more likely the price movement will experience cycles or steps within a

FIGURE 4.4 PRICE DISTRIBUTION FUNCTION (PDF) CONSTRUCTED FROM 14 DAYS
OF OEX DATA WITH M = 20. THIS CHART IS PRODUCED WITH THE SAME CONDITIONS
AS IN TABLE 4.2 EXCEPT M = 20. THERE IS AN IMPROVEMENT IN RESOLUTION OVER
FIGURE 4.3. THE MAGNITUDES OF THE BARS IS ABOUT 2 TIMES LESS THAN THAT
OF FIGURE 4.3 SINCE THE INTERVALS ARE 2 TIMES SMALLER AND THE PDF IS NOT
NORMALIZED BY THE INTERVAL SIZE. THE IMPORTANT THING IS THAT THE SHAPE IS
ESSENTIALLY THE SAME AS THAT IN FIGURE 4.3.

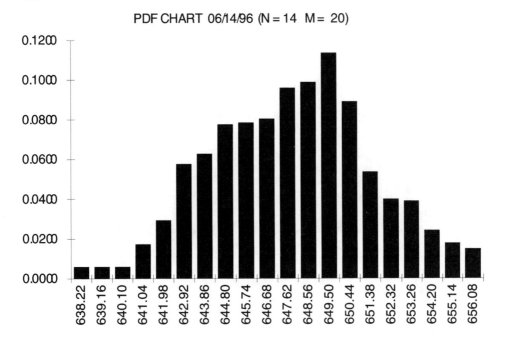

longer period. An example of this is shown in Figure 4.6. Here a history of 39 bars
was used for the look-back period. To properly resolve the structure of the PDF more
intervals were also used ($M = 30$). The longer time periods are useful for long-term
reference; however, it is difficult to construct a responsive, meaningful oscillator when
multiple peaks are present. Nonetheless, these plots have value for establishing longer-
term congestion and for comparison with support and resistance levels.

REFERENCE POINTS

To evaluate market conditions analytically, it is necessary to have points of comparison or reference points. For example, the current price may be compared with the
maximum and minimum price values over some look-back period as is done in stochastics. In stochastics, the current price is gauged between these references and the

FIGURE 4.5 PRICE DISTRIBUTION FUNCTION (PDF) CONSTRUCTED FROM 14 DAYS
OF OEX DATA WITH M = 40. THIS CHART IS AN EXAMPLE OF MULTIPLE PEAKS.
THE LOWER PEAK IS A SHORT-TERM BOTTOM, FOLLOWED BY A SHARP RISE TO
THE UPPER PEAK. AT THE UPPER PEAK THE OEX IS PAUSING AND FORMING A TOP.

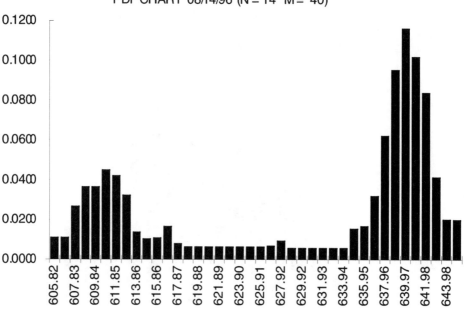

PDF CHART 08/14/96 (N = 14 M = 40)

proportion between these two positions defines the Stochastics Oscillator. Similarly, trendlines can be used to project the highs and the lows as a reference. When we let the maximum projected high and the minimum projected low over a look-back period define the stochastic range, we have a form of "Projection" oscillator. In general, reference points can be a particular price value on a previous date, an extreme price value within a recent interval, or an average or other statistical measure. The following will relate several common references to the PDF analysis.

Support and resistance levels are common reference points used to describe market behavior. They are local maxima or minima over a period. If a particular high is greater than the prior N bars highs and greater than the following N bars highs, then that high qualifies as a resistance level. Correspondingly, if a particular day's low is less than the prior N bars and less than the following N bars, then that low qualifies as a support level. Of course, today's support may become tomorrow's resistance and conversely. Generally the greater the period or value of N, the more significant the level. Too short a period gives a large number of levels, some of which may be insignificant, while too long a period may omit important levels. Traders must determine their own time horizon for their particular market and back-test to pick a good

FIGURE 4.6 THE PDF FOR A LONGER TIME PERIOD. IF A LARGER TIME INTERVAL IS SELECTED THERE IS MORE STRUCTURE IN THE PDF. IN THIS CASE, THERE ARE TWO PRINCIPAL PEAKS CORRESPONDING TO TWO STEPS IN THE PRICE HISTORY. THE PRICE SPENDS LITTLE TIME IN THE CENTRAL REGION AND AT THE END POINTS OF THE RANGE WHERE THE DISTRIBUTION VALUES ARE LOW.

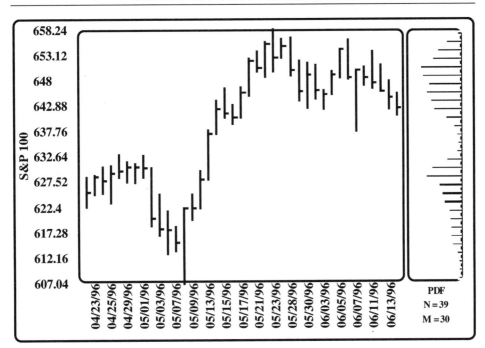

value. For example, for a 5-day time horizon for OEX daily data, I find $N = 4$ days (−4 days to +4 days) to be a good choice.

The PDF, if plotted for long look-back periods, implicitly includes the congestion levels as well as support and resistance. This can be seen in Figure 4.7, where the support and resistance levels clearly match with low spots in the PDF. The support and resistance levels determined with $n = 4$ are traced to the right on the chart. All the 59 data points that are plotted are used to construct the PDF on the right of the chart. The PDF and the support resistance levels define bands of high and low mobility. Combining this information is useful for forecasting.

Why particular values of support and resistance have significance is not clear, but they do. It could be a reoccurrence of an overvalued or undervalued condition or an exhaustion of one side or the other. My own favorite explanation is that it is an obvious reference point with strong public belief that it is important, therefore it is important. It is a self-fulfilling prophecy, a belief whose consequences are quite real and the consequences reinforce the belief.

FIGURE 4.7 A PLOT OF THE NASDAQ COMPOSITE INDEX SHOWING SUPPORT
AND RESISTANCE LEVELS. SUPPORT AND RESISTANCE LEVELS FALL OUTSIDE
CONGESTION REGIONS AND ARE PRESENT WHERE THE PDF IS SMALL. THIS REFLECTS
THE OBSERVATION THAT THE PRICE OR INDEX SPENDS LITTLE TIME NEAR THESE LEVELS.
EXPECT A BOUNCE OR A BREAK THROUGH NEAR THESE LEVELS, BUT NOT STAGNATION.

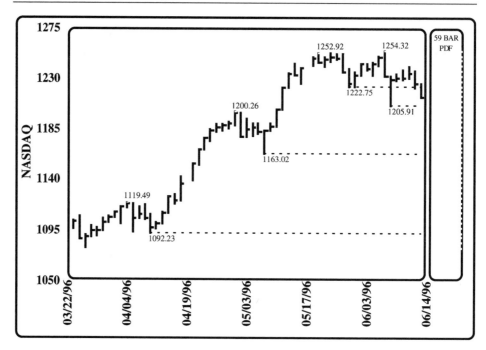

Another common reference is the simple moving average. This is simply an average of some number of data points, say M data points, that is plotted at the last time
value. Mathematically, the average best corresponds to the time at the center of the interval of M points, and by plotting it at the last time value, a delay is introduced of
half the interval size. While smoothing that is accomplished by the average is good,
the delay is often viewed as undesirable. Nonetheless, the simple moving average is
widely used and quite often seems to provide support or resistance to prices.

Why is this? One possible explanation might be that market congestion plays a
role in price behavior. It turns out that for short periods, simple PDF structures usually result. The simple moving average is an approximate means of defining the location of congestion for this situation. The delay that is introduced is appropriate and
even desirable for comparing the congestion to current price. For longer time periods
and complex PDF structures, the average may be less meaningful. For example, consider a PDF with two congestion peaks. These peaks then define congestion levels,
whereas the average might fall between the peaks at the wrong level. For short periods,

the PDF, in most cases, has only one peak and the simple moving average is a often a reasonable approximation to the location of this peak.

One method that I have found convenient for observing congestion I refer to as "Price Layers." A layer plot is simply a trace forward of a price. Extend (draw horizontally) each closing price forward for a fixed time interval. The extension should be long enough to represent a cycle period, as identified by inspection of the prior history or by Fourier analysis or some other frequency analysis. If the drawn lines are closely spaced, then there is clustering that reflects the presence of congestion. If the lines are widely spaced, then there is evidence of a lack of congestion. The line plots also give some representation of the range of prices over a brief period by observing the extreme top and extreme bottom lines at any given time.

Several patterns are frequently evident in layer plots, flat tops, flat bottoms, and flat steps. An example of steps is seen in Figure 4.8. A clustering of layers often

FIGURE 4.8 A TIME HISTORY FOR THE NASDAQ PRESENTED AS A LAYER PLOT AND CORRESPONDING PDF FOR THE 59-DAY PERIOD. THE LAYERS, WHICH ARE SIMPLY HORIZONTAL EXTENSIONS OF THE DAILY CLOSES, PROVIDE A GRAPHICAL PICTURE OF CONGESTION. GROUPINGS OR CLUSTERING OF THESE LAYERS CORRESPOND TO CONGESTION, AND WIDE SPACES, THE LACK OF CONGESTION. THIS PLOT SHOWS A STRONG UPTREND WITH THREE MAJOR STEPS AND CONGESTION PEAKS. THE LAST STEP IS A TOP FORMATION WITH SUCCESSIVELY LOWER HIGHS WITH THE PRICE MOVING BELOW THE UPPER CONGESTION PEAK.

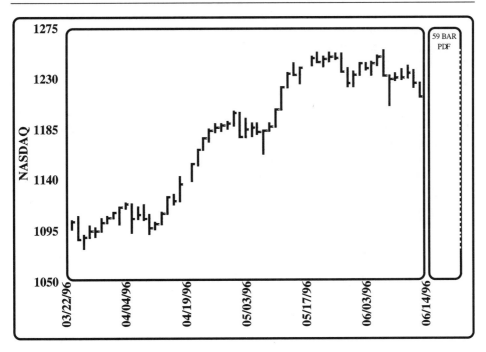

represents a value close to the mode of the PDF and spaced layers correspond to valleys in the PDF. Breaking through the layers gives an advance warning of an upcoming test of support or resistance. Other variations are also possible as extensions of combinations of the high, low, and close. This approach is a means of assessing congestion in a very qualitative way. It can be plotted by either programming graphics in Visual Basic or by repeatedly plotting price values with varying incremental delays.

In summary, PDFs provide additional references for analysis such as the peak or peaks and the minimum values of the distribution. There are alternative ways of viewing congestion such as price layering. PDFs also complement other analysis references such as support and resistance and averages. A PDF can identify regions between support and resistance levels as being either high congestion or low congestion, an important piece of information.

MOBILITY OSCILLATORS

As mentioned, direct viewing of PDF functions for mobility analysis of a time history is possible, but can be difficult since the structure can be complex. What is needed is to boil down the PDF into an oscillator that gives a precise measure of congestion and mobility and reflects previous market movement. Since the PDF implicitly includes this and other reference information on price, it is a matter of sorting out the information and framing it in a useful form.

The first step in construction of an oscillator is to find suitable reference points. In this case, there are several possibilities. There are price references for the look-back period: the high, the low, the average, and the mode. For example, a comparison between the current price with the high, low, and average or mode for the period could be made. In fact, I tried this with some success, resulting in an oscillator similar to the Stochastic Oscillator with the mode as an internal reference point to give direction. While this price reference method was somewhat useful, it did not give a precise comparison of congestion levels. Consequently, the analysis was reformatted using congestion as the basis for comparison and for the references.

This resulted in what is referred to as the Mobility Oscillator. That is, the maximum congestion level of a look-back period is the peak value of the PDF that occurs at the price mode value and is the upper reference point. The lower reference is the minimum possible congestion level and is zero. The current congestion level, the PDF value at the current price value, is compared with these references. A simple, linear proportionality of the current congestion level to the upper and lower reference congestion levels gives the gauge. Next, a direction can be assigned by comparing the current price with the mode. This is described mathematically as follows.

The value of the price at the peak of the distribution function is the mode. The mode is the most likely value for the price during the look-back period, the value where the price spent the most time. It represents the price where there was maximum congestion for the look-back period and lowest mobility. For the analysis here, the mode is easy to observe and to calculate directly from the distribution function. It is determined as

$$PDF_{im} = PDF_{max} = Max(PDF_i) \quad \text{for } i = 1 \text{ to } M$$

where *im* is the interval number containing the maximum PDF value. The Price Mode *(PM)* is the price value at the center of the interval containing PDF_{max}. Since the PDF is defined over intervals and not at points, the interval center is chosen as the best value for the interval:

$$PM = BC_{im}$$

The Mobility Oscillator (MO) is now constructed from the PDF. The intent here is to gauge mobility by determining the amount of congestion at the current price and then comparing it with the extremes in congestion for the look-back period. In addition, the MO is constructed to provide a sense of direction, large and positive when there is an upward bias and large and negative when there is a downward bias.

To accomplish this, first form the ratio of the value of the PDF in the interval containing the current price with the maximum PDF value. When this ratio is one, then the current price is sitting in the interval with the mode and there is maximum congestion. When the ratio is equal to zero, there is minimum congestion. To convert from congestion to mobility, this ratio is subtracted from one since maximum congestion represents minimum mobility and conversely. This gives a direct relationship rather than an inverse relationship. The MO is assigned a positive sign when the current close is above the mode and a negative sign when below the mode. If the current price is below the mode, then there is downward mobility, and if it is above the mode, there is upward mobility. Convert the entire expression to a percentage by multiplying by 100.

$$MO = 100 \, (1 - PDF_C/PDF_{max}) \quad \text{for } C_n > PM$$
$$MO = 0 \quad \text{for } C_n = PM$$
$$MO = -100 \, (1 - PDF_C/ PDF_{max}) \quad \text{for } Cn < PM$$

where C_n is the current price and PDF_C is the PDF value for the interval containing the current price. Normally C_n is the current close; however, other options are possible such as the current high, current low, average of current high and low, or the average of the current high, low, and close. One of these alternatives can sometimes provide confirmation or reduction in noise.

The MO ranges from −100 to +100. If the price is above the mode, it is supported and is "upwardly mobile" and if below the mode it is resisted and "downwardly mobile." It is not to say that the price will move up or down, but rather it may be easier to do so based on what it did previously. Price momentum should also be considered as well as the potential for surprises, such as the release of economic data.

MO values near zero correspond to large congestion and are important for forecasting. When the MO is moving toward zero, from either above or below, price action is contracting and the market is pausing, waiting, and building something. Congestion building often occurs before a large move, and the MO is a useful indicator under these circumstances. This behavior appears to be analogous to the narrowing of the Bollinger Bands that is frequently observed prior to a large move. When the MO moves away from zero, the price action is expanding and there is mobility. Sometimes the MO will have momentum and move rapidly through zero. This confirms the move as a strong move that will likely continue. Congestion building also frequently occurs after a large move and is a good indicator of when the move is over.

It is also useful to define the Slow Mobility Oscillator (MOS) as

$$MOS = EMA(MO)$$

where EMA represents the Exponential Moving Average. Typical smoothing periods for the moving average are a portion of the look-back period; for example, for $N = 14$ bars use about 7 bars for smoothing. This slows and smooths the MO and can be used to identify direction as well as crossing signals that indicate change.

APPLICATION AND INTERPRETATION OF MOBILITY OSCILLATORS

Consider several examples of mobility analysis applied to recent data. The first example, Figure 4.9, is a recent OEX history. Here a top with a large cycle below the top characterizes the price history. The MO (dark lower line) and the MOS (lighter lower line) are plotted on the same time scale as the OEX high-low-close data. Crossings of the MO and MOS have significance, although in some cases the noise level is high and whipsawing is possible.

The MO moving toward zero precedes principal moves. This represents congestion building. The MO builds congestion prior to major moves and gives some warning of what is to come. However, price action can be erratic just prior to the move so be careful of direction. Also note that congestion building following a move often signals the end of the move.

Figure 4.10 shows mobility analysis for a long and steady uptrend of the OEX in early 1995. Even this relatively steady trend consists of many small steps where the market flattens out and pauses for a few days before continuing higher. The MO reflects this behavior by approaching zero during these steps signaling congestion building. This does signal a move, only here it is up to the next rung on the ladder. Note that the MO remains positive, with the price above the mode of the PDF reflecting the upward bias for the price trend.

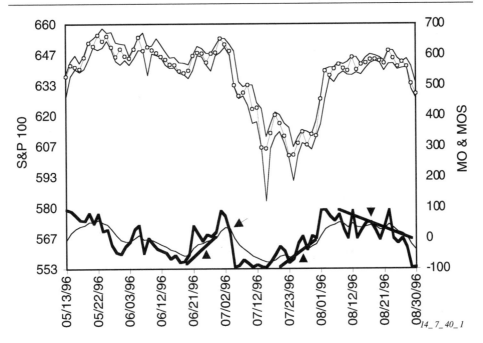

FIGURE 4.9 MOBILITY ANALYSIS FOR RECENT OEX DATA. HERE A TOP WITH
A LARGE CYCLE CHARACTERIZES THE PRICE HISTORY. THE MO (DARK LOWER LINE)
AND THE MOS (LIGHTER LOWER LINE) ARE PLOTTED ON THE SAME TIME SCALE
AS THE OEX HIGH-LOW-CLOSE DATA.

Figure 4.11 shows a significant move to the upside in early 1996. There is evidence of congestion building prior to moves, although the action can again be erratic just prior to a large move. This is seen with the very brief, but significant, dip prior to the up move. The MO picks up the dip with an abrupt move to negative territory and crossing of the MOS in time for damage control. The next congestion building phase signals the up move and there is follow-through with the MO remaining positive for a long period. Once again, the congestion slowly builds signaling the move is over. Slowly building congestion is a more reliable signal with less likelihood of an abrupt reversal prior to the major move.

Other examples of mobility analysis are shown in Figures 4.12 and 4.13. These examples show several features including the fast and slow Mobility Oscillators. The Mobility Oscillators use a look-back period of 14 bars, a smoothing period of 10 bars, and 40 intervals for the PDF. The PDF for the entire plot period, 59 bars, is shown at the right, tilted on its side, for reference. These plots were produced using Visual Basic macros in EXCEL.

Figure 4.12 shows the rise, sell-off, and bounce of the NASDAQ Composite in the summer and fall of 1995. The rising periods generally correspond to positive

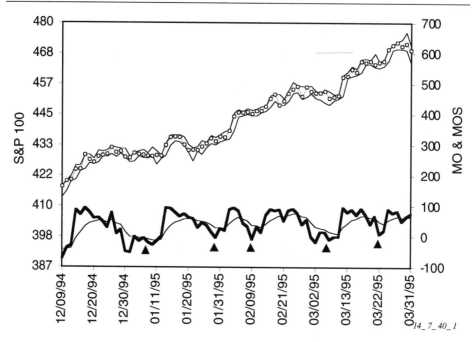

FIGURE 4.10 MOBILITY ANALYSIS FOR A LONG AND STEADY UPTREND OF THE
OEX IN EARLY 1995. EVEN THIS RELATIVELY STEADY TREND CONSISTS OF
MANY SMALL STEPS WHERE THE MARKET FLATTENS OUT AND PAUSES FOR A
FEW DAYS BEFORE CONTINUING HIGHER.

values for the MO. The sell-off is preceded by a MO move to negative territory and crossing of the MOS. The MO remains in negative territory throughout the sell-off.

In Figure 4.13, analysis of NASDAQ Composite data shows a slide during the early summer and a partial recovery in late summer. The MO is in negative territory for essentially the entire slide until the double bottom occurs. The MO shows congestion building around the end of July followed by an upward move. This upward movement has stagnated and congestion is once again building. The NASDAQ appears to be preparing for a move.

STEPS FOR ASSESSING PRICE MOBILITY

The eight steps for assessing price mobility and trading are described in this section. The numerical methods are derived from the formulas given in the text. While it is possible to perform the analysis directly on a spreadsheet, it is recommended that macro programs be used to efficiently manage the calculation of the Price Distribution Functions. Visual Basic macro programs with EXCEL were used for the analysis presented here and are described further in the included references.

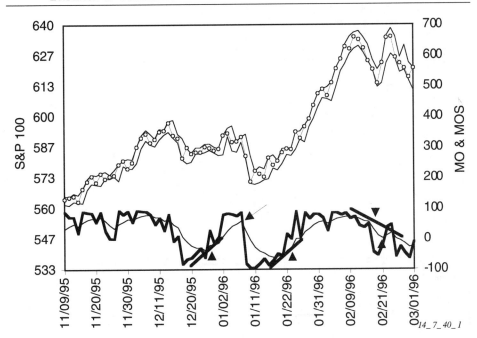

FIGURE 4.11 A SIGNIFICANT MOVE TO THE UPSIDE IN EARLY 1996. THERE IS
EVIDENCE OF CONGESTION BUILDING PRIOR TO THE LARGE UPWARD MOVE.

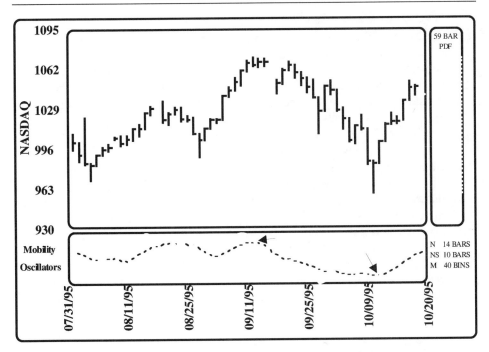

FIGURE 4.12 THE RISE, SELL-OFF, AND BOUNCE OF THE NASDAQ
COMPOSITE IN SUMMER AND FALL 1995.

FIGURE 4.13 ANALYSIS OF NASDAQ COMPOSITE DATA. THERE IS A SLIDE
DURING THE EARLY SUMMER AND A PARTIAL RECOVERY IN LATE SUMMER.

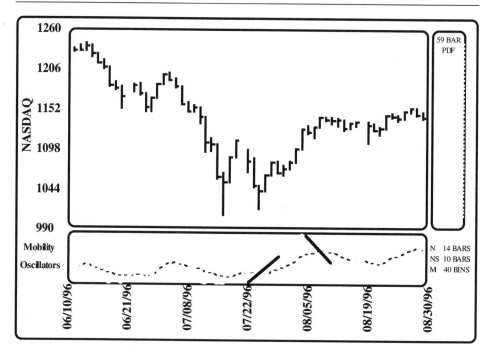

1. Select an issue and a data history of high, low, and closing data.

2. Apply numerical methods that represent the formulas given earlier to compute
   the mobility oscillator and slow mobility oscillator. Select a look-back period to
   coincide with your trading horizon. The look-back period should be as long as
   possible, but short enough to avoid multiple peaks in the PDF. The period
   should be short enough to be responsive to significant moves (e.g., the value of
   14 days for OEX daily data seems to work well). The smoothing period should
   be shorter than the look-back period, typically one-half to one-third (a value
   from 5 to 7 days works well for the cited example).

3. Compare high, low, and closing data with MO and MOS on the same time scale.
   This can be accomplished using EXCEL charts with MO and MOS plotted on
   the secondary axis. Generally the MO is reasonably smooth; however, sometimes
   there is an abrupt change. In this case, it is helpful to display the PDF also for
   more detail as a separate bar chart. Sometimes the abrupt change is meaningful,
   and sometimes it is the result of multiple peaks in the distribution and abrupt
   changes in the mode. If there is complex structure, new emerging peaks, or old
   declining peaks, then be careful. The mode reference point may be switching dis-
   continuously and an apparent change in momentum may be a false signal.

Crossings of the MO with the MOS is quite often a sign of changing direction, but not always, depending on the high-frequency noise level in the oscillators.

4. Identify congestion building patterns by noting when the MO approaches zero from larger values. The move can approach zero from above or from below. This is a warning of a potential upcoming move. As the oscillator crosses through zero, the direction of the price move usually follows in the same direction as the oscillator move, but not always. Sometimes there is a little reverse blip before the stronger move in the other direction. Be careful.

5. Consider other indicators for confirmation of an upcoming move and its probable direction. For example, the 30-year T-Bond is useful for the OEX as are other related markets such as the NASDAQ Composite that may show confirmation, divergence, or a leading indication.

6. Select a position that manages risk, for example, credit spreads. Establish entry points for a position. These could be at peak congestion, after a crossing, or off a bounce. There are advantages to buying positions when congestion is building or low as things are quiet and premiums reflect low, short-term volatility. There are advantages to selling positions when mobility is high and premiums are high, reflecting high, short-term volatility.

7. Establish exit conditions. If there is nothing better, then use stop-loss and trail stops. A better choice might be placement near support and resistance levels. Another strategy might be the conditions of another market.

8. Back-test the preceding before executing to match the analysis to the issue, the trading time horizon, and trading style.

CONCLUSION

Do markets remember what they did previously? I think so, at least to some degree. Building on this premise, an analysis method was constructed to quantitatively describe and measure prior market price action. Price Distribution Functions (PDF) give a precise picture of where the market price previously spent time. PDFs can be further concentrated into a practical forecasting tool, the Mobility Oscillator (MO). Examples are provided that support the validity of this analysis and show a relationship with mobility and future price behavior. There are always exceptions as the market depends on things other than past history, so exercise caution. Changing conditions such as interest rates, economic data, and world events influence the situation, especially if the news is unexpected and extreme. Sometimes these things are "in the market," sometimes not. In any case, the Mobility Oscillator forecasting approach offers signals during times when other oscillators that identify extreme conditions are often in-between signals. It also identifies developing conditions well in advance that may lead to movement. Given enough data and the ability to pick and choose, of course, just about any claim can be supported. I invite you to try the method, back-test, become familiar with common patterns and interpretation, and judge for yourself.

REFERENCES

Achelis, Steven B., *Technical Analysis from A to Z,* Chicago: Probus Publishing, 1995.

Bollinger, John, "Using Bollinger Bands," *Technical Analysis of Stocks and Commodities,* June, 1992.

Lane, George, "Lane's Stochastics," *Technical Analysis of Stocks and Commodities,* February, 1984.

McMillan, Lawrence G., *Options as a Strategic Investment,* Paramus, NJ: New York Institute of Finance, 1986.

Murphy, John J., *Technical Analysis of the Futures Markets,* Paramus, NJ: New York Institute of Finance, 1986.

Visual Basic User's Guide, Microsoft Corporation, 1993–1994.

Widner, Mel, "Gauging Mobility with Price Distributions," *Technical Analysis of Stocks and Commodities,* February, 1996.

Widner, Mel, "Signaling Change with Projection Bands," *Technical Analysis of Stocks and Commodities,* July, 1995.

Widner, Mel, "Rainbow Charts," *Technical Analysis of Stocks and Commodities,* July, 1997.

Widner, Mel, "Automated Support and Resistance," *Technical Analysis of Stocks and Commodities,* May, 1998

CHAPTER 5

Entering a Market

LEE ANG

Trading is a game of odds. Having a strong disciplined mind-set, statistical proven strategies, and strict money management are crucial in stacking the odds in your favor.

A trade consists of an entry and an exit. The entry and exit of a trade are what constitute the implementation of a sound strategy. Most people feel that having a good entry is 50 percent of the game. I think it is at least 75 percent of the game. A good entry allows you to limit losses to a minimum in a losing trade, a higher chance of a profitable exit, and more money being made on a profitable trade.

Before showing you how I trade successfully with my entry strategies and methods, I will first explain the basic types of entries.

BASIC TYPES OF ENTRIES

A market order is used to buy or sell stock or futures at the market. This means the floor broker or the specialist on the exchange must execute the order promptly at the most favorable price possible. Market orders are normally filled at the ask (offer) price. For example, if Microsoft is quoted as 123 bid and 123¼ offer, a market order will likely fill you at 123¼.

A limit order is used when the trader has imposed a limit price that precludes the floor broker from paying more on a buy order or selling for less on a sell order. This limit assures the trader at least the price he or she wants if the order is executed. For example, if you place a limit to buy Apple Computers at 27¼, your fill must at most be 27¼. However, you would run the risk of not getting an execution if the price stays beyond your limit or there is not enough liquidity to fill your order when the price is at your limit.

A buy stop order is an order that gets executed only if the price rises to a specified price. Once the price hits the stop, it will be executed as a market order. A sell stop order gets executed only if the price falls to a specified level, which will then be executed as a market order.

Stop orders are not to be confused with limit orders. The buy limit order is usually placed below the current market and must be executed at the limit or better. The buy stop order is placed above the current market and may be executed at the price specified on the stop, *above or below it,* because it is executed at the market after the stop price is touched.

Unlike a sell limit order, a sell stop order is placed below the current market level and, when triggered, may be executed at the price specified on the stop, *above or below it,* because it is executed at the market after the stop price is touched.

A more complex type of order is the stop limit order. A buy stop limit order becomes a limit order once the current price rises to a specific stop. A sell stop limit order becomes a sell limit order once the current price drops to a specific stop.

USES OF LIMIT AND STOP ORDERS

A buy limit order may be used to establish a new long position or to liquidate an old short position. A sell limit order may be used to establish a new position or to liquidate an old one. A stop order is used to limit a loss, protect a profit, or establish a new position.

Limit orders are very useful when trading slow, choppy, liquid markets. Scalpers of fractions of a point place limit orders all the time. In most liquid markets, trading is so slow and choppy that there is always a second or third chance of getting filled at your favored limit price since the market moves toward and away from that limit in a choppy fashion.

Stop and limit orders are useful tools for portfolio managers who trade hundreds of stocks with big buy and sell orders. They allow the manager time to focus on other work instead of constantly monitoring the quotes to execute a trade.

Never use limit orders in fast, illiquid markets. The chance of getting filled at your limit is slim when a market is moving rapidly. In fast, illiquid markets, always get in and out using market orders.

THE EXPECTED RETURN EQUATION IN ENTERING THE MARKET

The expected return equation is one of the most overlooked mathematical formulas used to enter a market. I have spoken to many traders and was amazed how few traders really understand the formula. Traders who do not know how to use the equation are relying on pure hunches to trade the market and, therefore, will not last long.

Here's the formula:

$$\text{Net Expected Return } \textit{for a specific trade} = (\text{Avg gain} \times \text{Win odds}) - (\text{Avg loss} \times \text{Loss odds}) - \text{Slippage} - \text{Commission}$$

where . . .
   Avg gain = Average profit made on a winning trade
   Avg loss = Average loss on a losing trade
 Win odds = Chance (%) of a winning this trade. For example, a 50% chance of winning.
 Loss odds = Chance (%) of a losing this trade.

If the net expected return is a positive number, then you have a good trade or sound entry. If it is a negative number, then you should avoid that trade.

For example, based on one or two technical indicators or chart, you feel that Microsoft has a 4 points upside (Avg gain), a 2 point downside (Avg loss or your stop) with a winning chance of 60 percent to a losing chance of 40 percent, then your net expected return on that trade is

$$\text{Net Expected Return per trade} = (60\% \times 4 \text{ pts}) - (40\% \times 2 \text{ pts}) - 0.125 \text{ slippage} \\ - 0.125 \text{ of commission} = 1.35 \text{ pts}$$

Since the trade generates a 1.35 points expected net return, it is a great trade and entry should be taken immediately.

You may say this mathematical equation looks fairly easy to apply so why isn't everybody getting rich off it? The real skill in applying this equation successfully and, therefore, trading successfully is being able to evaluate your win odds, loss odds, avg gain, avg loss as accurately as possible. A slight misjudgment in any one of the factors would turn a profitable net return trade to a net loss. That is the art of trading: being able to subjectively assign odds in different scenarios and market situations and quantify them through the Net Expected Return Equation.

This is why trading will always remain an art as well as a science.

USING TECHNICAL INDICATORS AND TOOLS TO TIME AN ENTRY

The most important part of entering the market involves selecting the best technical tools to time your entry.

There are many different technical tools and indicators traders can use to time an entry. A combination of indicators can provide high risk/reward entry points. Technical indicators appear to work best in stocks or markets not widely followed.

The following are simple technical indicators that are widely used.

Support and Resistance of a Price Chart

Support and resistance are extremely popular nowadays and are effective entry tools because of their simplicity. Once price hits a strong support on a chart or a crucial resistance, an entry could be triggered.

FIGURE 5.1 STOCK CHART SHOWING SUPPORT AND RESISTANCE LINES.

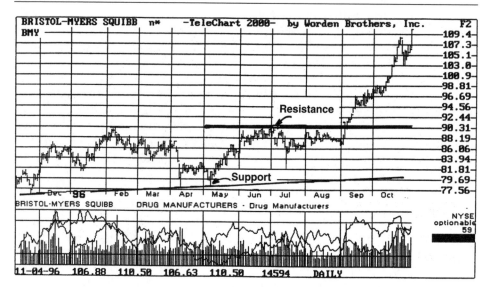

For an example, look at Figure 5.1. Bristol-Myers is a good trading stock to apply support and resistance. When the stock hits a crucial support, it bounces off immediately and initiates an uptrend. And when it hits a crucial resistance it retraces before testing the resistance again. Support and resistance have more significance if they are new yearly low or highs due to psychological buying and selling.

The key idea is to buy support and sell resistance. Support on the chart should be wide and tested numerous times to verify the significance of the support. The more significant the support, especially if price is at a yearly or historic low, the higher the odds the support will hold. This is also true for resistance. It should also be wide in time and tested on several occasions.

Playing Breakouts and Breakdowns—A Popular Strategy

Understanding how support and resistance work helps in playing breakouts and breakdowns. When price breaks above a crucial resistance, it is called a breakout. A breakout will trigger a buy signal. A breakout of a crucial resistance point with good volume is a good entry if the price closes above the resistance. When price breaks below a significant support, it is called a breakdown and will initiate a sell short signal.

Breakouts and breakdowns are popular strategies, but depending on which market you trade, they can be difficult to apply because of many false signals. However, from my own experience, the cup and handle breakout pattern strategy suggested by William O'Neil of *Investors Daily* works very well in a bullish market.

Referring to Figure 5.2, United Technologies goes through the cup and handle pattern before breaking out to the upside strongly with above average volume. To prevent getting false signals or breakouts, the cup should be as wide and round as possible and not a V shape. And the handle should be small and not drag below 50 percent of the height of the cup.

The longer the time it takes to establish the cup formation, the more powerful the rally. And lastly, the breakout should always accompany big volume, which indicates huge buying interest.

In Figure 5.3, Spyglass breaks below a crucial support level, which happens to be its new yearly low, and prices break down.

The Reversal Roles of Support and Resistance

Once price breaks below a support, that support line becomes its resistance. Referring back to Figure 5.3, Spyglass experienced difficulty rising back above the break down point. That support line has become a resistance line. Hence, one should sell short or avoid buying Spyglass once it rises to that line.

Conversely, once price breaks above a crucial resistance line, the resistance becomes the support line. Referring back to Figure 5.2, UTX found support at the breakout point after it has gone through the cup and handle pattern.

FIGURE 5.2 STOCK CHART SHOWING A CUP AND HANDLE
PATTERN WITH A BREAKOUT TO THE UPSIDE.

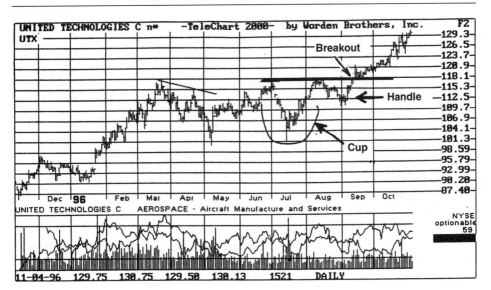

FIGURE 5.3 STOCK CHART SHOWING A DOWNWARD TRENDLINE AND SUPPORT LINE.

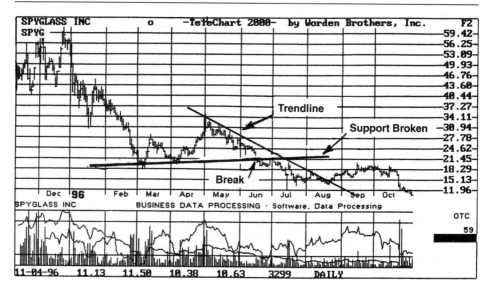

Once again, one should not apply support and resistance strategies blindly to any markets or stocks. Picking the right stocks that work consistently and combining that with other technical tools is the key.

Trendlines—A Popular Tool

Another popular tool is the trendline method. In Figure 5.4, Eli Lilly bounces off support and resistance at points A, B, and C before breaking though D with a strong uptrend. One can draw an upward sloping line from left to right below price during this uptrend to find good entry levels. The best way to play an uptrend stock is when the stock occasionally pulls back to or close to its trendline. That will be your buy entry since the trendline is the support line in an uptrend and therefore offers minimal downside risk. The odds are very good if the uptrend is backed by improving or strong fundamentals.

A sell short entry is initiated when price rises to an established strong downtrend line. In Figure 5.3, Spyglass is going through an obvious downtrend. The downtrend line is drawn form left to right above the prices. See how difficult it is for the stock to break above the trendline? The downtrend line is a strong resistance line for this stock and one would sell short the stock once price hits the line or comes close to that line. If the downtrend is accompanied by deteriorating fundamentals in the stock, the odds are even better for a good entry.

FIGURE 5.4 STOCK CHART SHOWING SUPPORT AND
RESISTANCE LINES AT BREAKOUT TO THE UPSIDE.

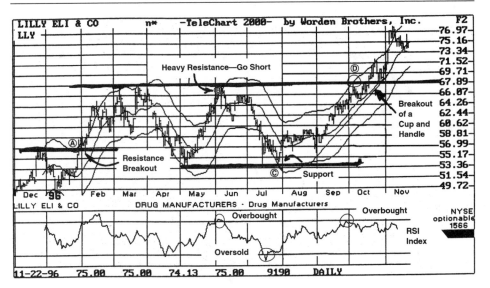

MECHANICAL ENTRY METHODS USING MORE ADVANCED TECHNICAL INDICATORS

The Moving Average and the Moving Average Crossover Method

A moving average curve can be defined as the mathematical average price for the past *N* days. Nine-day and 14-day moving averages are quite popular and widely used. A popular entry method is the moving average crossover method (see Figure 5.5). Moving averages of two different time periods are used. When the shorter time period moving average (solid line) crosses over the longer time period moving average (dotted line), a buy signal is triggered. And when the shorter time period moving average crosses below the longer time period moving average, a sell short signal is activated.

I do not encourage the use of moving averages or moving average crossovers. The simple reason is different people use different time periods for their averages. Some prefer a 15-day average to a 9-day average. Some prefer a 15,10-day crossover to a 14,7-day crossover. It is highly subjective, and the lack of consensus weakens the self-fulfilling prophecy needed as a catalyst to make a technical indicator effective and profitable.

This is true of any technical indicator. An unknown, unfollowed indicator will not be effective and an overly used indicator used in a widely followed market or stock would not be profitable either. *You want an indicator with a good degree of consensus in a stock or market not too widely followed.*

FIGURE 5.5 MOVING AVERAGE CROSSOVER STRATEGY. TOP HALF OF THE CHART
SHOWS PRICE LINE AND TIMES WHEN TO BUY AND SELL, AS DETERMINED BY
THE CROSSING OF TWO MOVING AVERAGES SHOWN IN THE LOWER HALF OF THE CHART.

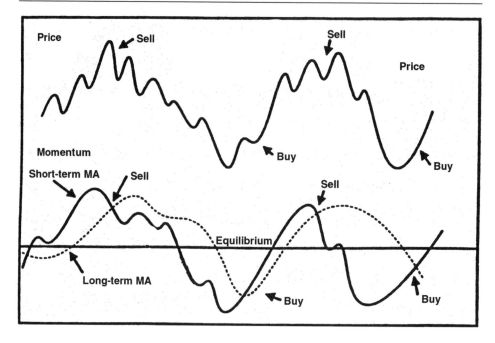

Overbought/Oversold Indicators: The Relative Strength Index (RSI) and Stochastics

The overbought/oversold indicators are extremely useful indicators to structure good risk/reward trades. However, I do not prefer using them alone as trading strategies. They should be used, like any other indicators, as tools to be combined with other indicators.

Relative Strength Index

The RSI is defined as the Relative Strength Index introduced by Welles Wilder in 1978. It is a cyclical indicator that tells us when prices are overbought or oversold. It is an effective tool to apply in a sideways market or choppy, slow, nontrending market. Avoid using it in long, violent trending markets as these markets stay overbought or oversold for long periods of time.

$$RSI = 100 - (100 / (1 + RS))$$

where RS equals the average of the closing values of the up days divided by the averages by the closing values of the down days.

A 14-day RSI works well with many stocks I trade. For example, in Figure 5.6, I used a 14-day RSI to trade Morgan Stanley. My strategy is simply to buy when RSI dips at or below the 25 level and short it when it rises above the 75 level. The two buy entries and two sell entries, as in Figure 5.5, are near perfect entries. However, my *exits* are based on support and resistance and not based on RSI. RSI is only my entry tool.

Morgan Stanley is a good stock to apply RSI because of its sideways volatile nature with big price ranges. That nature is due to its underlying fundamentals. So you have to do some fundamental research and historical chart analysis to pick the proper stock or market to use the RSI. Never apply any technical indicator to a market or stock blindly. Homework is the key.

Traders have used the RSI in many unaccountable ways. But the basic idea is to buy a market when it is oversold and sell the market when it is overbought. Some traders like to buy when the RSI starts dipping below the 25 RSI line, and some only buy when it moved below that line and just recently crossed back above the 25 line. On the sell side, some traders like to sell when the RSI starts crossing above the 75 RSI line, and some only sell when it has moved above that line and just recently crossed back below the 75 line.

There are many other ways to play the RSI but the basic idea is never to buy an overbought market and never sell into an oversold market. Always buy an oversold situation and sell into an overbought market.

FIGURE 5.6 PRICE CHART SHOWING BUY AND SELL
POINTS AS DETERMINED BY THE RSI INDEX.

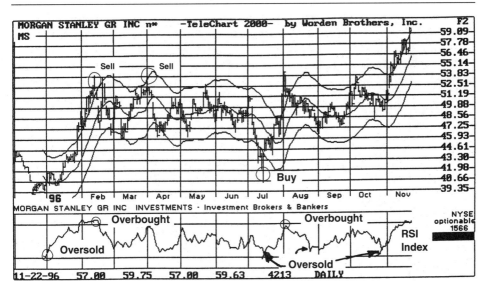

Stochastics

The stochastics indicator was invented by George Lane. Like the RSI indicator, it is a cyclical overbought/oversold indicator and is used similarly. Unlike the RSI, it involves two components instead of one. The formula for the first oscillator, %K, is as follows:

$$\%K = 100 \, ((C - L) \, / \, (H - L))$$

where C is today's close, H is the highest high for the last n days, and L is the lowest low for the last n days. The formula for the second oscillator, %D, is as follows:

$$\%D = 100 \, (H3 \, / \, L3)$$

where H3 is the three-period sum of C − L in the %K equation and L3 is the three-period sum of H − L.

The more sensitive of Lane's two oscillators (with more spikes) is %K, but it is %D that carries more weight and gives the major signals; %D is approximately the three-period average smoothing of %K and, therefore, less sensitive.

There are numerous ways traders in the 1990s have used the stochastics depending on the market being traded. Figure 5.7 shows the daily chart for Japanese yen spot and stochastics. As with the RSI, I like to buy when both %K and %D are below the 25 line and go long immediately when the more sensitive %K crosses over the %D line. And I would go short when both were above the 75 line and when %K dips below the %D. One can use the stochastics as an exit tool as well, but I prefer to exit my trades based on chart patterns like support and resistance.

The approaches and market for applying the stochastics should be the same as the RSI since they are both overbought/oversold indicators. Many other momentum indicators resemble the RSI and stochastics, but the main idea is the same, which is selling overbought levels and buying oversold levels in choppy nontrending markets with price big ranges. Once again, I do not agree the use of mechanical entry on any one of these indicators alone. These indicators, however, could be combined with the traditional chart indicators such as trendlines and support/resistance to improve the odds of the entry.

PUTTING EVERYTHING IN ACTION

An example will illustrate how to put these popular indicators and technical tools together for successful trading.

Referring back to the Eli Lilly chart (Figure 5.4), we have a breakout at circle "A" of a small round cup resistance pattern with good volume. The breakout point will be a good buy entry point. You should give yourself a tight stop (e.g., a 1.5 point stop) when playing breakouts since a lot of breakouts are false. I personally avoid

FIGURE 5.7 JAPANESE YEN WITH DAILY AND WEEKLY STOCHASTICS,
REFLECTING SHORT-, INTERMEDIATE-, AND LONG-TERM TRENDS.

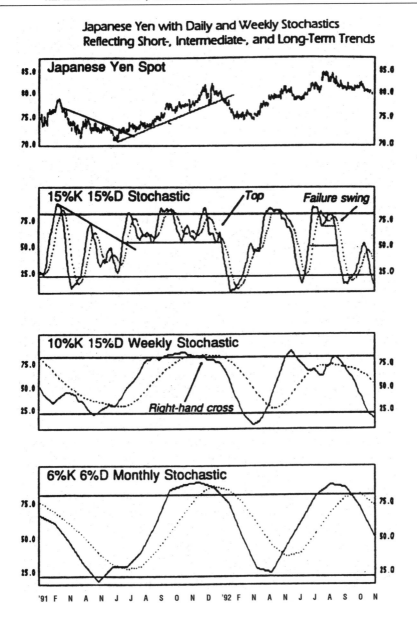

playing breakouts unless the stock has strong improving fundamentals. In the case of Eli Lilly, the whole drug and health care sector has been experiencing strong fundamentals and was considered pretty bullish at that time. And since Eli Lilly is one of the most active drug issuers in the sector, buying the breakout provides strong reward/risk.

At circle B, the stock hits a major resistance. It is normally not a good idea to short a stock with strong fundamentals on the verge of breaking out. However, aggressive traders can take on that opportunity as the 15-day RSI is extremely overbought and is turning down. Give yourself a half-point stop above the breakout point, just in case you are wrong. The potential gain in this trade is huge as the trading range goes from 53.25 to 66.875, a 13.625 range! But never assume you are going to gain the whole downside move on the full 13.625 points. I always try to take profits at half the trading range since that is where the reward/risk turns neutral (upside range equals the downside range) or turns negative, since there will be fewer smart traders selling.

So how profitable is this trade? Using the expected return equation:

$$\text{Net Expected Return per trade} = (\text{Avg gain} \times \text{Win odds}) - (\text{Avg loss} \times \text{Loss odds})$$
$$- \text{Slippage} - \text{Commission}$$

Assuming win odds and loss odds at 50 percent each and avg gain equals half the 13.625 pt range = 6.81 pts, avg loss at 1 pt stop. The Net Expected Return per trade = $(50\% \times 6.81\text{pts}) - (50\% \times 1 \text{ pt}) - 0.125$ slippage $- 0.125$ of commission = 2.65 pts, and is a pretty good risk/reward trade. That is how I quantify my trades using charts and the expected return equation. Traders should develop the habit of using the expected return equation since charts that look good to the human eyes might not necessarily produce positive return trades. Assigning the odds on the win/loss ratio takes skill and subjectivity.

As it turned out, Eli Lilly did retrace all the way to circle C, a strong support line. That is a very good buying point since the support is strong, RSI is oversold, and Eli Lilly and the drug sector have good fundamentals. But what's more important is that the expected return equation is positive on that trade. Give yourself a 1-point stop and take profits at half the trading range at $60.

Once again the trade turns out to be an excellent one as the stock rallied all the way back to the high of the year testing its resistance again at circle D. At D, aggressive traders could once again repeat what we did at circle B by selling short. However, this time we are stopped out of this trade with a 1-point loss as Eli Lilly broke out of the resistance with a powerful cup and handle pattern.

Smart traders should immediately reverse their trades and buy the breakout giving it a half-point to 1-point stop. As it turned out, Eli Lilly stayed above the breakout point and went higher. Note that when playing breakouts, the RSI is always pretty overbought. Therefore, unless the underlying stock has strong improving fundamentals, traders should be less reluctant in playing it.

Always look at the whole range of variables before initiating an entry. The variables include chart patterns such as support/resistance, momentum indicators such as the RSI, the underlying fundamentals of the instrument, and most important of all, the expected return equation. Being able to structure strong risk/reward trades with the preceding tools makes the trader a wizard above all competitors.

CONCLUSION

- Never apply any technical indicator to a market or stock blindly. Homework is the key.
- Always look at the whole range of variables before initiating an entry.
- Buy an oversold situation and sell into an overbought market.
- Assigning the odds on the win and loss ratios of a trade takes skill and subjectivity.

CHAPTER 6

Exiting a Market

JOSEPH LUISI

Every trader and investor knows the frustration of missing a trade or the anxiety they feel when in a trade. It is very difficult to pull the trigger after a series of losing trades. What can be more difficult is not knowing what to do once you are in the trade. How long should you hold onto the position? Where do you place stops? Do you even need stops? When should you exit the position? In this chapter, we are going to look at the importance of having a good exit strategy and knowing how and when to exit a market. This is of vital importance because it is only when you exit a position that you determine your profit or loss.

Although this seems basic, indeed it is not. We will look at various technical and nontechnical ways to exit a market. Keep in mind it is very easy to enter the market; you simply pick up the phone and buy or sell. Exiting is the hard part because trade management comes into play. You also are dealing with the emotional ups and downs of your position either making or losing money. There are many different types of exit orders and ways to place your stops; each one has its own special purpose.

THE VALUE OF STOPS

Once you are in a trade and, more important, *before* entering a trade, you should place a stop in the market. Some people use mental stops; however, you need to have great discipline to adhere to your mental stops once they are hit. It becomes too easy to wait and hope that the market moves back in your direction. I would strongly recommend placing your stop with your broker. Placing stops will minimize your losses, help to ensure profits, and reduce risk. Stops should be placed in an area that, if hit, will prove your analysis wrong. Remember you got into a position for a reason. There needs to be a point where your reason is no longer valid—this is where the stop comes in. If you feel that the market is going lower, to what point must the market move for your analysis to be considered wrong. For example, I feel the market will move lower, but if price is rising and a certain price is hit then the market wants to go higher and I am wrong (see Figure 6.1).

FIGURE 6.1 PLACE A STOP BELOW THE MARKET TO PROTECT A LONG POSITION.

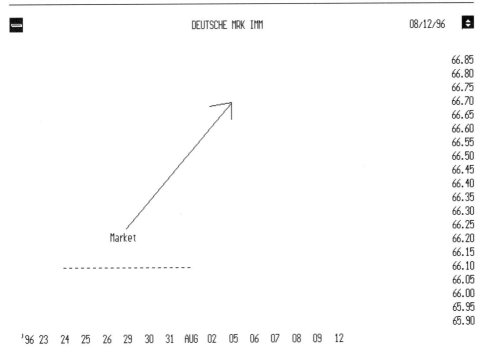

THE DOLLAR STOP

This is the most basic and simple approach to stop placement. You simply figure out the maximum dollar amount that you are willing to lose (risk) on that particular trade. You may have a $20,000 account ready to trade the S&P 500. You can decide that $500 is the most that you are willing to lose per trade. This will represent 1 point in the S&P. Therefore every time you enter the market you add or subtract one point and place your stops accordingly. You want to make sure that the dollar loss gives enough room for the trade to work. If this stop is too tight, many potential winning trades will be stopped out before they have a chance to work out. With the S&P 500, a $100 stop is too tight and you will be stopped out too often for your trades to work out.

On the other hand, you want to make sure that the amount you are willing to risk is not so large that your capital base is depleted if you encounter a series of losing trades. In our example, a $1,000 stop would be too wide. Five losses in a row will reduce your capital by 25 percent and that is too high. There is no right answer; you just need to use common sense, look at the market you are trading, and choose an appropriate level.

More volatile times call for a wider stop and quiet (less volatile) times a tighter stop. You will also want to determine from what value the stop will be calculated. Will

FIGURE 6.2 PLACING A STOP TO LIMIT RISK TO EXACTLY $500.

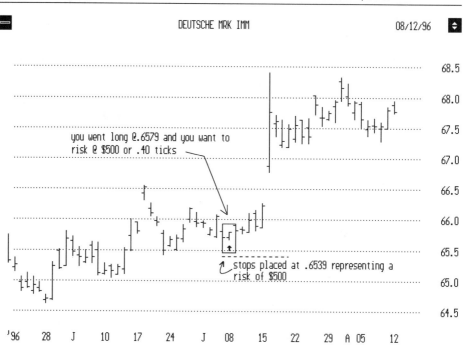

DEUTSCHE MRK IMM   08/12/96

you went long @.6579 and you want to
risk @ $500 or .40 ticks

stops placed at .6539 representing a
risk of $500

it be from the entry price? Or from the previous day's high or low? In Figure 6.2, determine your maximum dollar loss for the trade *before* establishing your position. With the Deutsche mark, we will use 0.40 tick, which represents $500. Once the stop is placed, we wait for the trade to work out. The benefit of using a dollar stop is you can determine how many times you can be wrong before pulling the plug. A $10,000 account using a $500 stop can have 10 losing trades in a row and still have 50 percent of the capital remaining.

BREAKEVEN STOPS

This technique is more for trade management than for initial placement. This is by far one of the most important stops. The importance of this stop is preservation! When a trade moves in your anticipated direction by a certain amount, you should immediately bring your initial stop to breakeven. The breakeven level is your entry price. Remember the initial stop is the one you placed when you first entered the trade. With the breakeven stop in place, you will be able to relax and let the trade work its course knowing the worst possible outcome is that you will lose only commissions.

Some judgment is involved with this method, so study it carefully. The market should move in your direction by a certain amount before you place this stop. You want to make sure that by placing this stop you will not be taken out prematurely. Sometimes this may occur, but the benefits far outweigh any potential trades that are stopped out prematurely. If you went long the Swiss franc at .7640 and the market moves to .7650, placing a breakeven would hurt your chances of success because in the course of the markets fluctuation .10 ticks can easily be hit. Therefore, use an amount that gives you some room. If the Swiss franc trades to .7700, now would be an ideal time to place the breakeven. If the market has moved .60 ticks in your direction, chances are it will continue; however, if it reverses your risk is zero and you can wait for the next trade.

Remember that you can always get back into a trade if you are stopped out at breakeven and you still feel the market will move in your direction.

In Figure 6.3, we bought on the close of July 8, 1996, at .6579. Our initial stop had us risking $500 or .40 ticks; this is placed at .6539. On July 15, the market closed above .6620, thus allowing us to raise our stops to breakeven. No matter what happens from here on out, we will only lose commissions.

FIGURE 6.3 RAISING THE STOP TO BREAKEVEN LEVEL.

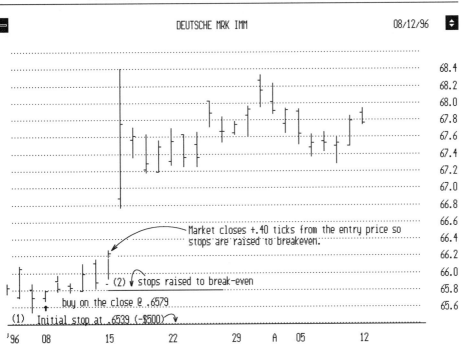

TRENDLINES

When you first enter a position, you place your initial stop. As the market moves in your direction, you place your breakeven stop. Now you can look at the various ways to adjust your stops. The trendline technique is one of those ways.

Trendlines are lines drawn connecting a series of lows or highs in a market. An uptrend line connects higher lows. A downtrend line connects lower highs. Generally to form a trendline, you need to connect three or more points. The more points you connect, the stronger (more reliable) that trendline is. A trendline that connects two points is not as reliable as one that connects four or five.

Draw a trendline and place your stops just below the value of the trendline; every day as the value changes, adjust your stop accordingly. Remember that the trendline does not change; only the value of the line changes as each day goes by. As the market moves in your direction, this trendline stop will increase in value until eventually you are stopped out. This will ensure that as the market moves, you will partake in the movement as well.

Trendlines are more of an art than a science so make sure that you are comfortable with trendlines and know how to draw them correctly. If at the time of entry, no

FIGURE 6.4A A DOWNTREND LINE PLACED ON LOWER HIGHS. STOPS ARE CONSTANTLY ADJUSTED AT THE VALUE OF THE DOWNTREND LINE, UNTIL THE LINE IS BROKEN.

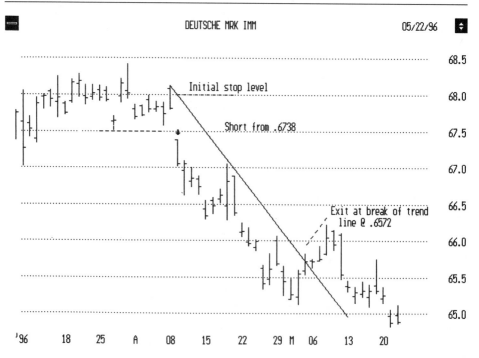

clear trendline is evident, then wait until the market moves so you can draw the trendline and place stops accordingly. Then, as the market trends in your direction, you are following the market as well.

Once we place our initial stop, we may need to keep this stop in place until a clear trendline emerges if one has not been established. In Figure 6.4a, the market rallies (possible stop running) on August 18, then continues to sell off. We will use this high to connect our downtrend line. From this point forward, we will adjust our stops to the level of the trend line. If the market continues to move in your direction with a greater velocity, it might be necessary to draw a second trendline at a steeper angle to keep up with the market and to avoid excessive giveback. This will enable you to lock in a greater profit. Take a look at Figure 6.4b.

FIGURE 6.4B A FASTER TRENDLINE WAS CREATED TO KEEP UP WITH FASTER PRICE ACTION. BY DRAWING A SECONDARY TRENDLINE THE POSITION WAS EXITED AT 11.50 INSTEAD OF 113 WHERE THE ORIGINAL TRENDLINE FELL.

TRAILING STOPS

Trailing stops have the advantage of keeping you in a trade as the market moves in your direction. As the market moves, you trail your stops until eventually you get stopped out. There are several methods that you can use.

Parabolic SAR

The first method is the Parabolic SAR. This indicator was introduced by Welles Wilder in his book *New Concepts of Technical Trading Systems.* This method is a trend-following method that is always in the market either long or short. This system is not too bad as long as the market is trending. When the market gets choppy, this method works very poorly. As a stop technique, it works great. It is not the scope of this chapter to explain each indicator and how it is calculated, but here is a brief description of how the Parabolic SAR works.

FIGURE 6.5 THE DAILY VALUES OF THE PARABOLIC. THE VALUES ARE SHOWN AS DOTS. THE DOWN ARROWS ABOVE THE DOTS SHOW HOW WELL IT WORKS DURING A TREND. USING THE PARABOLIC AS A STOP NOTICE HOW THE STOP POINTS FOLLOW THE MARKET LOWER. THE PARAMETERS ARE .20 STEP VALUE AND 2 MAXIMUM.

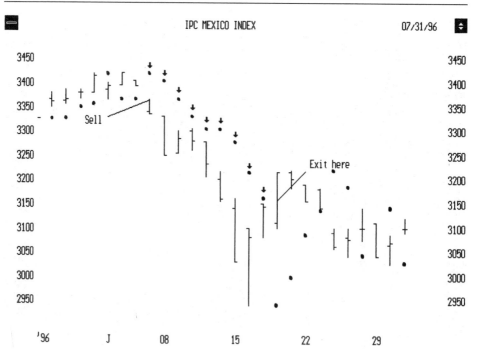

This indicator has two components: the step, which is the size that the Parabolic will rise/fall as the market makes new highs/lows and the maximum value that the SAR can obtain. As a rule of thumb, most technicians use .20 as the step value and 2 as the maximum value. The Parabolic will continue to rise/fall with time until eventually prices break the Parabolic level and the Parabolic reverses direction (see Figure 6.5). Its shape resembles a parabola as it follows the market up and down.

Once you are in a trade, you can set your stops to the level of the Parabolic and every day thereafter change your stop accordingly. Figure 6.5 shows that as the IPC Mexico Index sells off, the Parabolic follows it down as well. When the market hits the Parabolic point, the signal reverses.

Moving Average

In a similar fashion, a moving average is a great tool for determining stop placement. A moving average takes a series of data points for the past number of days that you determine and averages them. For example, if you choose 10 days of closing prices, you add the closing prices for 10 days and divide that number by 10. As you add the next day's closing price, you drop the oldest price, producing a running total of the most recent 10 days.

When you buy and sell, you can place your exit stops at the same level as the moving average, as in Figure 6.6. As the market moves, your stop level automatically follows and you can periodically call your broker to change your stop. There may be times when you enter long and the moving average is above the market, or enter short when the moving average is below. When this occurs, place your initial stop and wait until the moving average moves to the appropriate side before using it to adjust your stops. You can decrease waiting time by using a shorter length for the moving average.

Use a time period for the moving average that is far enough away to prevent a false move stopping you out prematurely, but do not make the moving average value so distant (slow) that you give up a substantial portion of your profits to avoid getting stopped out. If you are trading short-term, a 5- or 10-period moving average works well. For the longer term, a 15- to 25-day period is good. This balancing act has no perfect answer.

There are many different types of moving averages (simple, weighted, exponential, adaptive), so experiment and visually look at the market and time frames and choose the average that works best for you. First try a simple moving average. If you are swing trading and short-term oriented, a more advanced moving average designed to have less lag might work better.* Figure 6.7 shows the difference between a simple and an advanced moving average. Notice that for the same number of days, they look very different. Compare moving average types and lengths to find the one that works best for you.

---

*Some simple low-lag moving averages are (DEMA) Difference Exponential Moving Average and (KAMA) Kaufman Adaptive Moving Average. More sophisticated versions include the Kalman Filter and (JAMA) Jurik Adaptive Moving Average.

FIGURE 6.6 USING A 10 PERIOD MOVING AVERAGE. IF YOU USE THIS
AVERAGE AS YOUR EXIT STOP, YOUR TRADE IS EXITED WHEN PRICE
BREAKS THROUGH THE MOVING AVERAGE LINE.

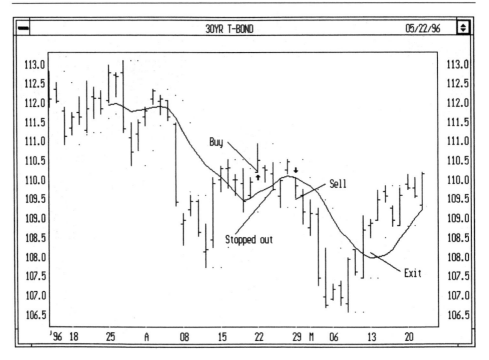

Incremental Approach

The third type of trailing stop you can use is the incremental approach. This is where you adjust your stops incrementally and on occasion, not on every bar. When a position is initiated and you have your initial stop in place, wait for the market to either move or close by a certain amount beyond your stop and then raise your stop by a predetermined increment. For example, every time the S&P 500 closes by one point or more beyond your stop, you might raise your stop by 0.25 ticks until eventually you are stopped out.

The second approach takes into account intraday moves. For example, whenever the S&P 500 moves one point or more beyond your entry, you place a stop at ½ point from your entry. As the market continues to move by one point, you continually raise your stops. If the market does not move, you keep your stop until you get stopped out or you exit for another reason. This is a great technique because it lets the market move in your direction before you take any action with your stops.

FIGURE 6.7 COMPARING THE PERFORMANCE OF A SIMPLE AND
TIME-SERIES MOVING AVERAGE. WHEN LOOKING FOR A MOVING
AVERAGE FOR A STOP, NOTICE HOW THE TIME-SERIES AVERAGE ADAPTS
TO CHANGES IN THE MARKET QUICKER THAN A SIMPLE MOVING AVERAGE.

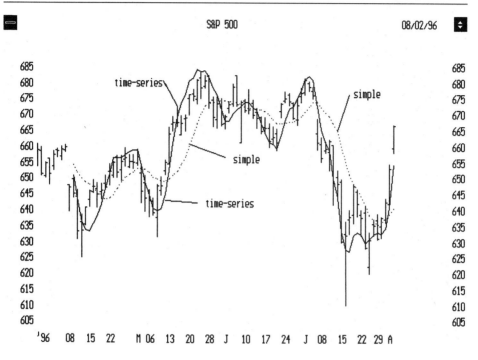

In Figure 6.8, we shorted on July 7. Once the initial stop is set, we do nothing until the market closes 10 or more points from our entry. As the market moves, we lower at levels 2 (breakeven), 3, and 4. At level 5, we get stopped out.

Trailing Highs and Lows

The technique of trailing highs and lows ensures that if the market rallies in your direction you will be able to partake in some if not all of the move. The basic premise is that if your initial analysis is correct, then the market should not take out the previous lows/highs or previous several days of lows or highs.

Once you are in a position, you place your stop at the high/low for the previous day or days and move your stop each day to the next day's high/low until eventually you are stopped out. A short-term trader who entered long might use the previous day's low as a stop. Each day, the trader would change the stop to reflect the level of the previous day's low. For example, in Figure 6.9, stops were at the previous day's high

FIGURE 6.8 AN INCREMENTAL APPROACH. STOPS ARE INCREMENTALLY LOWERED TO
LEVELS 2, 3, 4, AND 5. WE DECIDE TO SELL ON THE CLOSE WHEN THE UPTREND LINE
IS BROKEN. INITIAL STOPS ARE PLACED AT THE PREVIOUS DAYS HIGH. EVERY TIME THE
MARKET CLOSES 10 POINTS FROM OUR ENTRY PRICE, WE LOWER STOPS 5 POINTS UNTIL
WE ARE STOPPED OUT. POSITION WAS EXITED AS PRICE CROSSED BACK OVER LEVEL 5.

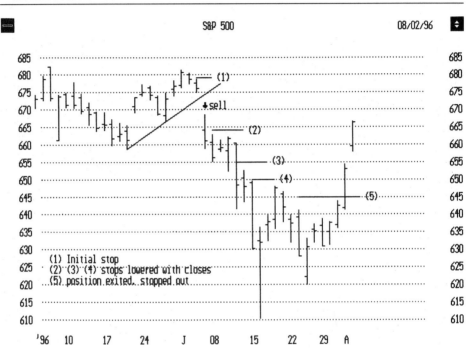

when short and the previous day's lows when long. Hold until you get stopped out.
Make sure initially that the previous day's high/low is not to far away. We do not want
to incur any more risk than is necessary.

Another variation is to add/subtract an increment to the high/low that you use
to reduce the chance that a false move would stop you out of your position. Perhaps
in a long position you can use the previous day's low minus 0.1 ticks. Look at the market you are trading and determine what levels work best. Perhaps a two-day low works
better than the previous day's low. You may decide that the low of the last three bars is
better. Experimentation is recommended. Longer-term traders can use weekly or
monthly highs/lows for their stops.

In Figure 6.10, experiment to find the best number of ticks to add to the
high/low. On June 10, we go long. On June 11, the market takes out the previous two
days of lows by several ticks and then continues to rally. We could have avoided getting stopped out by adjusting it downward by a predetermined amount.

FIGURE 6.9 PLACING STOPS AT THE TRAILING DAY'S HIGHS AND LOWS.
EXIT LONG AND SELL WHEN PRICE CROSSES BELOW THE STOP. EXIT
SHORT AND BUY WHEN PRICE CROSSES OVER STOP.

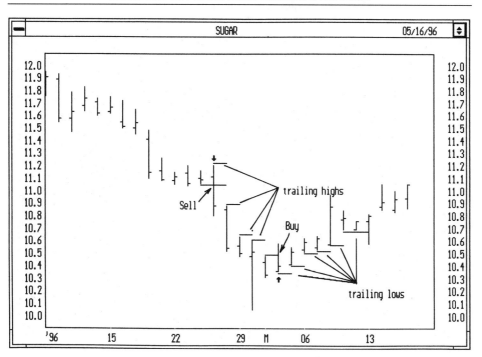

INDICATORS

Indicators are used mainly for analyzing the markets, but you can also use them for a stop approach as well as an exit strategy. We will look at several of the more popular indicators and how you can include them in with your current approach for stop techniques.

Stochastic

Stochastic is a popular overbought/oversold indicator developed by George Lane. In general, whenever the indicator goes above 70–80, the market is considered to be overbought (look for a sell-off). When the indicator drops below 30–20, the market is considered to be oversold (look for a rally). As a stop technique, we can look at the value of the indicator rather than the levels used for its original analysis.

Once you enter a position, look at the value of a stochastic. Place your initial stop and look to exit a long position when the indicator falls for one day or for two

FIGURE 6.10 STOPS INCREMENTALLY LOWERED TO LEVELS 2, 3, 4, AND 5.
POSITION WAS EXITED AS PRICE CROSSED BACK OVER LEVEL 5. BY TRAILING
THE LOWS WITH .10 TICKS, YOU COULD HAVE AVOIDED BEING
STOPPED OUT PREMATURELY.

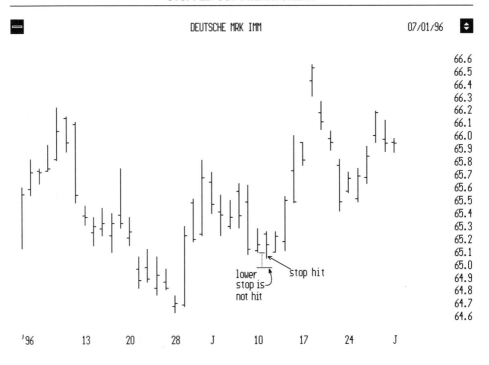

consecutive days. This will enable you to avoid getting stopped out by random moves in the market. Such moves usually do little to change the value of a technical indicator.

The Relative Strength Index (RSI) is another popular indicator that you can use.

Figure 6.11 shows a 10-period stochastic indicator and an exit when the stochastic was high and turned down.

Momentum

Momentum and least squares momentum are two of my favorite indicators. A five-bar momentum of the closing price is simply the difference between today's closing price and that of five bars ago. Least squares momentum (LSM) is a method used to smooth out the momentum indicator and alleviate some of the "noise" that indicators can have. This technique is a bit more involved than the other techniques discussed so far. To make a five-bar LSM of the closing price, first fit a straight (regression) line through the most recent five closing price points. The LSM is the slope of this regression line. Make sure that you are comfortable with an indicator's

FIGURE 6.11 A 10-PERIOD STOCHASTIC INDICATOR AND AN EXIT
WHEN THE STOCHASTIC WAS HIGH AND TURNED DOWN.

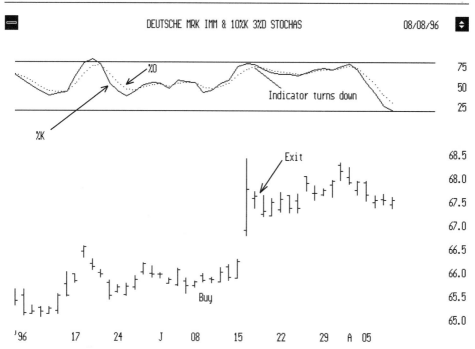

behavior and how to properly use it. For example, when using these indicators for exits, be sure that their time frame is similar to the time frame of your trading.

Try to find trends where the market and indicator coincide or the indicator leads the market slightly. Make sure the indicator moves with the market. When you are in a position, try to lighten up or get out whenever the indicator turns the other way. What we want to do is look for an early warning sign of weakness, the indicator turning.

Figure 6.12 uses a 10-period least squares momentum indicator and an exit when the indicator begins to turn up. Again, we are looking for signs of a market turn to exit our positions.

TIME STOPS

Time stops are very simple and easy to use. They place a time limit on your trade. Experience shows us that whenever you enter a trade, within a few days the market should confirm your analysis by moving in your anticipated direction. If the market fails to move, perhaps your original analysis is wrong. A time stop of three days gives the trade three days to work out. If after three days, you have not been stopped out or

FIGURE 6.12 A 10-PERIOD LEAST SQUARES MOMENTUM INDICATOR
AND AN EXIT WHEN THE INDICATOR BEGINS TO TURN UP.

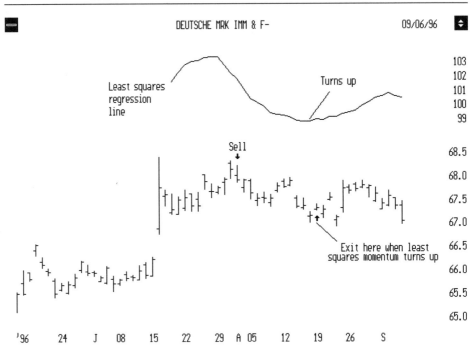

a profit is not made, exit the position. Usually you will be taking a small loss when this occurs.

The time window's length depends on the time frame you are trading in. For a short-term trader, 3 to 5 days may be sufficient. For a longer-term trader, perhaps 10 to 20 days is better. For a day-trader, 15 minutes may be a long enough time frame. What you will find is that if the market hasn't moved within your time frame eventually you will be stopped out anyway and at least you can get out with less of a loss or even a small profit.

This technique forces you to analyze a market to determine the appropriate time needed to work out. This can be very frustrating if you give a trade 3 days and on day 4 the market takes off in your anticipated direction. Keep two things in mind: One is that you can always get back into a trade at a later time if you still feel that your initial analysis is correct. Two, preservation of capital is key. If the trade is not working after the time stop you have chosen, your capital may be better used in another trade or market. You should not tie up all your capital on a trade waiting while other better opportunities may be out there.

Be careful during quiet markets and markets that are trapped in a tight range. These markets go nowhere for days and even weeks until eventually the market explodes. If you are in this type of market, you may want to give the trade a little bit longer than normal to work out. Keep the type of market you are trading in mind when you formulate your time stop. For example, you enter a market and realize that for the past 3 weeks the market has been very quiet trapped within a defined range trading back and forth. If you originally only intended to give the trade 3 days to work out, perhaps 5 or 7 might be better. Conversely if a market has been very volatile, you may want to shorten the time stop. Figure 6.13 uses three days for the trade to work out. Why three days? Only experimentation and testing can give you a fair number of days to use. Keep in mind that this approach takes discipline because it is very difficult to exit a position when you still might have a possibility of the trade working out.

PROFIT OBJECTIVE STOPS

Profit objective stops are predetermined levels of profit at which you will exit a position. For example, 0.4 ticks may be what you determine to be a reasonable profit per trade with the market you are trading. You will set a market order to get out of a position once 0.4 ticks is reached in your anticipated direction.

FIGURE 6.13 A TIME STOP. THE POSITION TAKEN ON AUGUST 13 TIMED OUT AFTER THREE DAYS OF NO ACTIVITY.

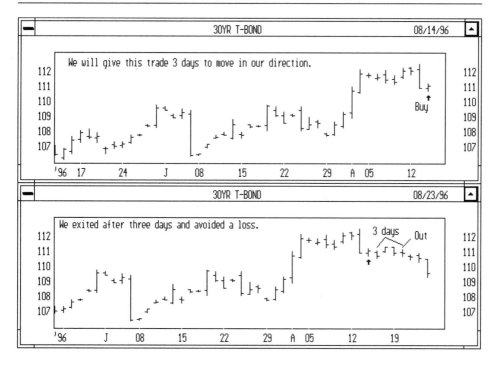

The advantage of this technique is that during choppy, sideways markets, a *trailing* stop can produce losses or fail to produce any significant gains. In contrast, if your *profit target* is not set too far away during trending and choppy markets, the trading range is usually large enough to stop you out with profit. Because of this, profit targets will increase the percentage of winning trades during choppy markets, and this increase must occur to be profitable. Remember that you are only taking small bites out of a trade that could be potentially a big winner. Therefore, you want to increase the number of winning trades to make up for missing some big moves.

The main disadvantage is that when the market does move greatly in one direction, you will not be holding a position. Depending on which market you trade, you should use a profit objective that is great enough to produce a decent profit after commissions and slippage (the difference between your exit price and your actual fill). However, it should be small enough that the percentage of winning trades is at a level that will offset your losses.

If you are going to use a profit objective stop, keep in mind that you must be able to watch the market rally well beyond your objective from time to time. The benefit is that you will be confident in knowing you have a system producing more winners than losers. In Figure 6.14, we decided to go long at the break of the high (65.3) of May 29. We went long and placed our initial stops. With this trade, we had a profit objective of

FIGURE 6.14 PROFIT OBJECTIVE STOP. THE LONG POSITION
WAS STOPPED OUT BY A PROFIT OBJECTIVE SET AT $625.

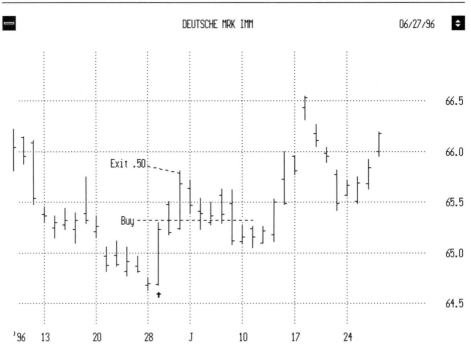

½ point ($625). The very next day, we exited the position with our profit objective at 65.8. With the market closing very strong from our initial entry, we might have brought stops to break even. Two days later, you would have been stopped out at breakeven. Even though you would have lost no money, without using a profit objective stop you would have missed an opportunity to make a profit.

Figure 6.15 shows a period in the sugar market where sideways choppy trading occurs. Arrows were placed at swing high and lows to show you what would have happened if you bought and sold at these points. If you used a trailing stop (moving average), most of these positions would show little profit or breakeven trades. However, if you had used a profit objective stop of 0.2 ticks, every trade would have made you money. It is very important for traders to know what type of market they are in and use the appropriate stop strategy.

DOUBLE AND REVERSE

This next strategy is very risky and somewhat advanced. Before trying this technique, study it carefully. This is an effective strategy for you to turn your losses into potential

FIGURE 6.15 THIS CHART SHOWS HOW A SIDEWAYS CHOPPY MARKET USING A PROFIT OBJECTIVE STOP WOULD SHOW A PROFIT ON EVERY TRADE.

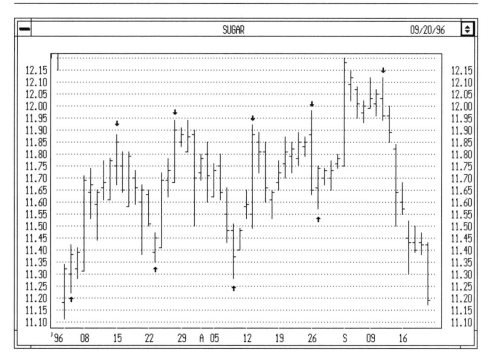

profits or breakeven trades. This strategy should be used only in markets that are liquid and volatile. You want to make sure that the market partakes in wide swings
throughout the day, as in the currency market or the S&P 500.

The basic premise of double and reverse is that when you are stopped out, you
will double up on the opposite position to recoup your losses. With twice as many
contracts, it will take half the initial move to get even. When even, you can reevaluate
the current situation to make adjustments. Again this is a risky strategy, but if used
correctly it can deliver great results. If you are wrong, however, this strategy could potentially double your losses. If you use it correctly, you can eliminate many potential
losing trades or reduce the initial loss.

When your stop is hit, you are counting on the market continuing in that direction long enough to recoup the amount of your original loss, since you only need
half the original move. Markets prone to false breakouts help this strategy, as well as
those times when many stops are hit causing a swing in the opposite direction. You
then use this swing to recoup your loss.

In Figure 6.16, all through May the Canadian dollar moved lower in a downtrend. If we sold on May 22 at the low of 72.87, then for the next couple of days it appeared that the trade was working out. However, the market reversed quickly. If your

FIGURE 6.16 DOUBLE AND REVERSE. IN THIS SCENARIO, LOSSES
FROM THE SHORT POSITION WOULD HAVE BEEN QUICKLY COMPENSATED
BY GAINS FROM A DOUBLE AND REVERSE STRATEGY.

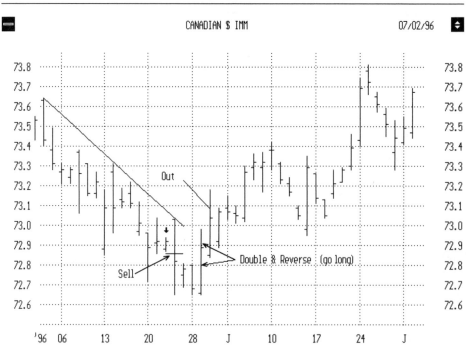

exit method used the trendline, you would have stopped out with a loss on May 29. You could have then saved this loss by using the double and reverse stop. By moving your stops to breakeven, fewer losses would have occurred if you were trailing the position with the highs of the previous day.

MULTIPLE POSITION EXITS

This next section is more advanced but the ideas and techniques are useful if you trade multiple positions. I strongly recommend not trading multiple positions until you feel comfortable trading with the markets and techniques you already use. Also, make sure that you have adequate capital to incur inevitable losses.

If you trade multiple positions, I strongly recommend trading in multiples of two (2,4,6). If you do not, it will be more difficult to determine where to exit each position. You can, however, take any of the techniques we have discussed and use them with as many positions as you choose to hold.

The first technique will combine the profit objective stop with the trailing stop. Choose the trailing stop that works best for you. By using this technique, you will exit half of your positions at the profit objective and use the trailing stop for the second half. This is a great technique because you can hit the profit objective fairly easily and this will ensure making some profit on the trade even if the other position is stopped out. When initially entering the position, remember to place an initial stop to protect your capital. Next set your profit objective stop and your trailing stop. If your profit stop is hit, just keep adjusting the trailing stop until you exit the second position. This will enable you to take advantage if the market starts to explode into a trend. You will be there in your position to take advantage of the move. If the market trades choppy, at least you can somewhat limit your losses due to a partial profit from the first position.

Another method is to stagger your stops by placing one tighter than the other. If your analysis is correct, then the trade should work out from the onset. However, there are times when the markets drop a little before rallying and vice versa. If your stop is too tight, then you will be taken out before the trade has a chance to work out. To counter this, you can place a loose stop on half your trade and a tight one for the other half—perhaps one at $300 and one at $500 for a maximum loss of $800 rather than both stops at $500.

Another method you can use if you trade multiple positions is to stagger your profit objectives. For example, say your system automatically exits your position at a ½ point profit (0.5 tick). You can exit the first position at 0.3 tick and the second at the original 0.5 tick stop. The 0.3 tick profit objective should be easier for the market to hit, thereby increasing your percentage. If the 0.3 tick objective is hit, the market turns, and you get stopped out, at least you have some profit to help offset the loss of the second position.

There are numerous ways you can combine different stops when you are trading multiple positions. Experiment and make sure that the combination enhances your returns rather than increases the losses or the chances of losses occurring. In

FIGURE 6.17 COMBINING STOPS. TWO SHORT POSITIONS WERE ENTERED
WHEN THE STOCHASTIC TURNED DOWN. THE FIRST WAS EXITED BY A PROFIT STOP OF
0.5 TICKS AND THE SECOND WAS EXITED WHEN THE PREVIOUS DAY'S HIGH WAS BROKEN.

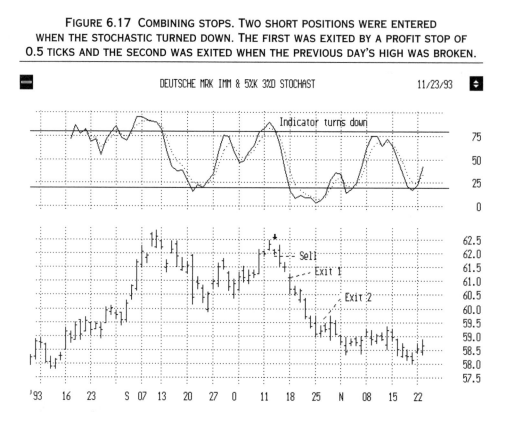

Figure 6.17, we decided to sell soon after the 5-day stochastic turned down. It turned on October 13. We then sold on the break of the low of the signal. Our initial stops were placed and we chose to exit our first position at 0.5 ticks in our favor and exit the second position whenever the previous day's high was broken. This method enables you to use the best that each stop technique has to offer.

VOLATILITY

Volatility is the trading range of a market. Traders view it to determine whether a market has good profit potential. A volatile market can provide good trading opportunities because of its large wide swings as well as its ability to trend. Less volatile markets tend not to move as quickly and it is harder to take advantage of small swings. Volatility is a double-edged sword. High volatility markets can be very dangerous because tight stops get taken out more frequently as big moves occur often in both directions.

Volatility is very important for stop analysis because you need to be aware of the type of market environment you are in (volatile, nonvolatile). When markets exhibit a high degree of volatility, your stops should be a little wider to compensate for the wide swings. Perhaps you may decide to trade fewer contracts to control risk better. You may also decide to raise profit objectives because you have a greater chance for the market to move farther. The opposite is true when markets exhibit less volatility: you can use tighter stops and you may consider smaller profit objectives as well. Perhaps you can consider trading more contracts since the risk is less and the stops are tighter.

Volatility is an important consideration when you look at the *type* of stops to use as well as the placement. Most software packages contain volatility studies that you can use. Look at historical volatility for the past several weeks and months to get a feel for where the volatility of the market has been and is now. Figures 6.18 and 6.19 show two methods of determining when a market's volatility is low. The volatility indicator in Figure 6.18 shows a period of one month wherein volatility has fallen from 5 to 1. Notice how the market is trading between 65.5 and 66.0. Figure 6.19 shows the daily range (high minus low) again during the same time frame. Notice how the market's range is under 0.4 ticks. If you are trading during this time frame, you will want to adjust your strategies (stops, targets, time) to reflect the market's inactivity.

Remember that volatility is a double-edged sword and that there will be times when a market becomes too volatile to trade. The risk in a very volatile market becomes one not worth taking. Sometimes it is better to wait for volatility to fall back before trading again.

FIGURE 6.18 DETERMINING LOW VOLATILITY. AS PRICE FORMED A CLASSICAL PENNANT FLAG PATTERN, INDICATING A POTENTIAL BREAKOUT, VOLATILITY SHRANK FROM 5 TO 1.

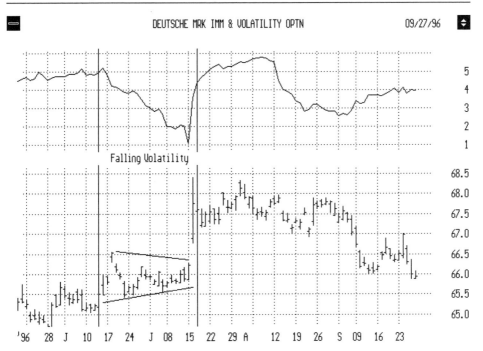

FIGURE 6.19 AN INACTIVE MARKET. DURING THE SAME TIME WINDOW AS IN
THE PREVIOUS FIGURE, THE DAILY TRADING RANGE INDICATOR HOVERS BELOW 0.5.

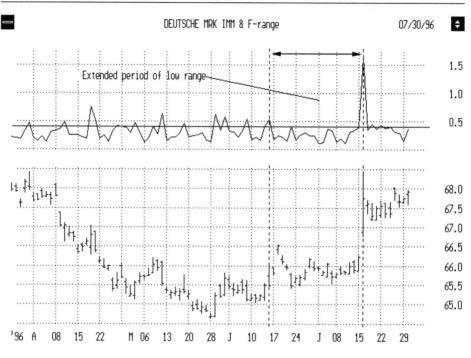

OPTIONS

Commodity options can also be used as a stop technique. While it is not within the
scope of this chapter to explain how the options market works and how the pricing of
options is determined, there are many good books on the topic. Options can be complex, and experienced traders should use this technique.

Options represent the right to sell/buy a futures contract at a predetermined
price in the future. The two sets of options are puts and calls. Puts represent the right
to *sell* a futures contract at some predetermined price at the expiration date of the option. For example, an October .6700 Swiss franc put gives the buyer the right to sell a
Swiss franc futures position at the strike price of .6700 at expiration in October if the
futures market is trading below the strike price. Calls represent the right to *buy* a futures contract at some predetermined price at the option's expiration date.

Whenever a position is initiated, you can look to buy cheap options to protect
your position. For example, suppose you decide to buy the Swiss franc at .6700. You
can buy a .6600 or .6650 put to protect your position. If the market moves against
your contract position, the option will increase in value, thereby offsetting most of
the loss incurred by the contract. However, if the market moves in your anticipated

direction, the option will decrease in value and expire worthless. Your loss on the option will be the premium you paid to acquire it. You need to take that into account when formulating your stop strategy. You do not want to pay too much for the option and you want to use the closest expiration date if you are trading short term. If you are a long-term trader, perhaps you will need to go out several months to protect yourself. If your initial analysis is wrong and the market sells off, you can recoup some or all of the loss that occurred.

Another good technique for use with options is to lock in a profit. Suppose you are long from a price of 500 and the market is now at 600. You can place a sell stop at 550 and sell a 550 call naked (all by itself), receiving the premium as payment. If the market falls below 550 you exit your futures position, the option becomes worthless, and you made a profit (550 − 500 plus the premium). If the market continues to rally and stay above 550 past expiration date, you lose your futures position to the option holder for the strike price of 550, but you still made a profit (550 − 500 plus the premium).

These are just two simple strategies you can use with options. There are numerous strategies, both simple and complex, that can be used with options.

CONCLUSION

Exiting a position is an important aspect to trading. If you cannot properly exit a position, you will never achieve success in trading. Exiting is more complicated than simply picking up the phone and calling your broker. A proper exit strategy is crucial in preserving your capital and ensuring profitable trades. Once you enter into a position:

- You have to set your initial stop. You will need to determine your risk parameters and examine the type of market and trade you are in. Will this trade last three days or three weeks?
- Once the initial stop is placed, you will then need to monitor the position. When is the appropriate time to bring your stops to breakeven?
- Determine if you will take a predetermined amount out of the market or if you will trail the market until you get stopped out. If you decide to use a trailing stop, you will have several to choose from.

Once you are stopped out of the position, hopefully with a profit, the whole process starts over again with the next trade. This chapter has highlighted the importance of stops and a proper exit strategy. There are numerous techniques, and you will need to experiment and use the ones that you find most comfortable. The techniques you use should make sense to you and your style of trading.

CHAPTER 7

Basic Money Management

JOSEPH LUISI

The key to any successful trading venture is money management. It is probably the single most important aspect in trading. Money management can be loosely defined as how a person manages his or her money in the financial markets, the person's bankroll so to speak. This can consist of factors such as the number of contracts to trade, the number of markets to trade in, exiting a position, and loss control. Money management can be as simple or as complex as a trader wants it to be. In this chapter, we will start with the basics of money management and move on to more complex topics. Each idea or topic will show how you can apply money management to your trading to help ensure your success.

Money management has been one of the least understood aspects of trading. For this reason, it is also the most essential to master—without it, failure is imminent. In its most basic form, money management in trading means that traders should spend 70 percent of their time on developing and using money management and 30 percent of their time looking for low-risk, high-profit trading opportunities. In contrast, many traders feel that a successful system can make them rich without regard to money management. Many systems can be 80 percent accurate and still lose money due to over-trading and bad risk-to-reward ratios. By risk-to-reward ratio, I mean a system that has 9 profitable days in a row making $100 a day can be wiped out on day 10 with a $900 loss. The system is 90 percent accurate, yet no money is made. To be successful, a trader only needs to be accurate 51 percent of the time and sometimes not even that. Most successful money managers use systems that are only 40 percent to 50 percent accurate, but they have very strict money management standards and their risk-to-reward ratio is very high. Having a money management plan is critical. All the top traders interviewed in *Market Wizards,* Harper Business, 1993, by Jack Schwager had a reason for stating that money management is the most important element in trading. It is!

THE BASIC TERMS

The following terms are used in this chapter:

- *Average loss* The total of all your losses divided by the total number of losing trades.

- *Average profit*   The total of all your profits divided by the total number of winning trades.
- *Capital*   The amount of money in your trading account at any given time. This can also be referred to as equity.
- *Drawdown*   This represents a cumulation of losses from your last winning trade. Drawdown can be measured on an intraday, daily, and end-of-trade basis. A series of losing trades can accumulate into one large drawdown.
- *Equity*   Represents the profit or loss on a given trade, added to the previous equity value. Generally, the trader starts with an initial equity amount of $10,000 and as trades are taken or followed, the outcome profit or loss is added or subtracted to the initial equity and a running total is kept. For example, if trade results were +100, +200, −100, and +300 for a starting capital of 10,000, the equity after each trade would be 10,000, 10,100, 10,300, 10,200, and 10,500.
- *Fast market*   A market in which the action (prices) are moving wildly, usually after some surprise news or economic report is released. During this time, the brokers on the floor are not held to your orders at the price you give. Now you can see why slippage becomes an important factor.
- *Gross profit/loss*   The total profit or loss from a trade not including commissions and slippage.
- *Largest losing trade*   The biggest dollar-losing trade compared with all losing trades in a given series or number of trades.
- *Largest winning trade*   The biggest dollar winning trade compared with all winning trades in a given series or number of trades.
- *Limit Move*   The maximum that a market can move up or down in a single trading day.
- *Losing trade*   A trade that produced a loss once a trade is over.
- *Margin*   The amount of money a trader needs to put up to trade one contract of a particular market. This amount is set by the exchanges and can be changed.
- *Net profit/loss*   The total profit or loss from a trade including commissions, slippage, and any other factors included in your exit price.
- *Percent losing trades*   A running total of the number of losing trades divided by the total number of all trades.
- *Percent winning trades*   A running total of the number of winning trades divided by the total number of all trades.
- *Slippage*   A term used to define the difference between the price you get on a trade versus the actual fill from your broker. This usually represents a few ticks. In fast markets, it can become many ticks. This can be important when comparing results on paper versus actual market results. The two can be very different.
- *Starting capital*   The amount of money used to start your trading account.

- *Volatility* This is related to market action. The wider the swings, the more volatile a market is.
- *Winning trade* A trade that produced a profit once the trade is over.

USING BASIC MONEY MANAGEMENT IN TRADING

Probably the single most important money management concept in trading is determining the number of contracts to trade. While no one approach is the best, some guidelines to follow include looking at margin requirements. Each futures contract has a posted margin that you must have in your account to trade one position for that market. These margins are posted by the exchanges that the market trades in. The exchanges constantly monitor the markets and margins can be raised or lowered. Margins generally rise when a market becomes more volatile. An example in the Deutsche mark futures is a margin of $1,250. This is the minimum to trade one contract.

Maintenance margin is calculated to determine how much you will truly need once a position is established. Most beginners trade using the margin posting in the following way. They will reason that a $10,000 account can trade eight ($10,000 / $1,250) Deutsche mark futures. This approach is entirely wrong because of the market's volatility and the leverage involved. An account can get wiped out very quickly using this formula. Therefore, most people use a factor of the margin such as two or three times margin per position. If the margin is $1,000 and you use a three times factor, you would trade one position for every $3,000 you have available.

Another method is to allocate a *percentage* of your account per trade. For example, if you allocate 2 percent per trade and you have a $100,000 account, that would be $2,000. On a contract that has a $1,000 initial margin, you could trade two contracts. The problem with this technique is that when you have a small account, say $10,000, a 2 percent allocation is $200. There are no markets that have a margin that low. For smaller traders, a suggestion would be to set a plan according to the amount of money you have to trade. If you have a $10,000 account, you may decide to trade two markets and only one contract per market. Every time the account grows by $5,000, you may add another contract or keep the contracts the same and add another market to trade. There really are no hard-and-fast rules. Just be very conservative when starting, and remember that if you are trading well, one contract can make you a lot of money. Perhaps wait until your account size has doubled before adding more contracts. When you experience a series of losing trades, you will be glad that you are trading conservatively.

Determining what markets to trade is a more subjective task. Here are some suggestions:

- What areas interest you? Does the stock market get you excited? Interest rates or foreign currencies?

- What is your trading method or trading system? Is it short term? Long term? Trend following or countertrend? Some markets historically trend better than others.

- Always look for liquid markets because they give you the ability to get out if you so choose. Remember many markets have limit moves and these limit moves occur fairly frequently. Once a limit is hit, no further price movement can occur in the same direction, thereby killing liquidity.

- Are your system results based on a basket of markets or are you focused on one market?

- The last and most important thing to consider is the amount of capital you have to trade. You may love the stock market and want to trade the S&P 500, but if you only have $8,000 to trade, you cannot trade that market. The margin for the S&P 500 is $10,000 per contract. Based on the money you have available for trading, look to the markets that suit your trading and fall within your money parameters.

ADVANCED MONEY MANAGEMENT

What most traders do not realize is that the same time and precision they put into their trading and system development, they can also put into money management strategies and techniques. The same techniques that you use to analyze the markets can be applied to equity and money management.

Equity Charts

Next to the actual market charts, equity charts are the most important charts that a trader can keep. Equity represents the profit or loss on a given trade added to the previous equity value. If you ever notice the nice advertisements for systems for sale and a chart that looks like a rocket taking off, this represents the equity chart of that particular system's trading results. An uptrending equity line represents a series of profitable trades; for example, +$200, +$300, +$500. A downtrending equity line represents a series of losing trades; for example, −$100, −$500, −$300.

Generally, the trader or system being tested starts with an initial equity amount, say $10,000. As trades are closed out, the outcome (profit or loss) is added to the initial equity and a running total is kept. Figure 7.1 shows an uptrending and downtrending equity chart. As trades accumulate, an equity line forms that looks similar to a line chart of a particular market.

You should analyze your equity very carefully to get an idea of how your trading is faring. If you are trading well, the equity line should be uptrending. If the trading is poor the line will be falling or downtrending. If your results are mixed, the line will be moving sideways. Each of these scenarios can be very insightful to traders who can step back and look objectively at the results. Uptrending equity charts are what we all strive for because this represents winning trades over time. Profits are outweighing losses. The steeper the slope the better because that means your money is growing rapidly.

FIGURE 7.1 TWO SAMPLE EQUITY CURVES.

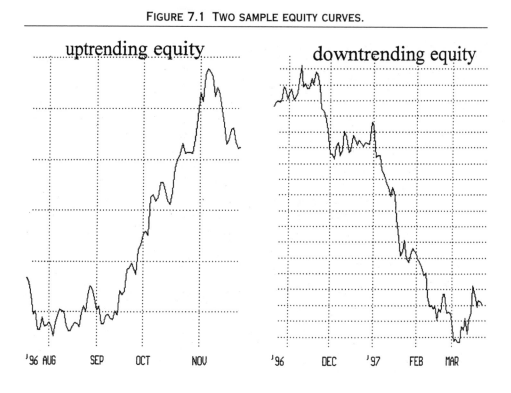

Take a look to see how smooth this line is. How about the zigzags in the line? Are there any that represent a fairly sizable loss or series of losing trades? If the opposite is occurring and the equity line is pointing downward, you should be very concerned. This situation represents more losses over time than winners or big losses that cannot be overcome by the winning trades. This situation is what every trader tries to avoid. If this situation is happening, you need to analyze your trading or system to determine what is causing the losses. Are you following your plan? Has the market changed? If you are trading a trend-following system and now the markets are trendless and choppy, this could cause losses as you get whipsawed. A sideways equity chart represents profits and losses that generally are equal over time. The losses and profits cancel out. In this situation, equity is trapped between two levels, for example, $10,000 and $12,000. If this is the scenario, you need to analyze why losses occur after your winning trades. Perhaps the risk-to-reward ratios should be higher.

Equity Line Techniques

Trendlines

The same analytical techniques applied to markets can also be applied to equity charts. Trendlines connect important highs and lows to project the anticipated

FIGURE 7.2 EQUITY CURVE CROSSES UNDER A TRENDLINE, INDICATING IT IS TIME TO REDUCE TRADES.

direction. By connecting a series of significant lows, we have an uptrend line. By connecting a series of significant highs, we have a downtrend line. If you can draw an uptrend line, your equity is rising and your trading is going well. A break of the uptrend line can signal a start of losing trades. Figure 7.2 has an uptrending equity where an uptrend line can be drawn. Eventually, a series of losing trades causes the equity to drop below the trendline. This would be a good time to suspend trading to preserve capital. When your equity breaks below an uptrend line this could represent an area to reduce your trading. You can even just paper-trade your signals until the equity rises to form another uptrend line. A break below a trendline can signal the start of a losing streak. Drawing trendlines is more of an art that an exact science.

If you are unable to draw a trendline, perhaps the results of the trading are choppy, you should analyze the reasons why. If the system you have been following shows a terrible downtrending equity, you might be tempted to throw out the system. You might consider still following the system and drawing a downtrend line. If the equity breaks the trendline going upward, this could signify a good area to start taking signals. Maybe there was a good reason that the system and systems equity had fallen such as low volatility, or a choppy market. When the equity rises and breaks a downtrend line, the reasons for the system performing poorly could have changed.

Moving Average

A simple moving average taken of the equity line can provide some valuable insight. A trader can suspend trading or lighten up on position size when equity is below the moving average. I recommend withdrawing to the sidelines completely when the equity line is below its moving average and simply continue tracking or paper-trading the system's trades. When the equity goes above the moving average, trading should resume. This technique ensures capital preservation, in case the system never returns to profitability (i.e., an equity line that goes to zero).

Furthermore, use a moving average that is slow enough so the equity line is not constantly crossing the moving average. Make sure it is not too slow, or a series of big losses will need to occur for the equity to fall below the moving average. A moving average length of 10 to 25 days is usually sufficient (see Figure 7.3). In addition, experiment with different moving averages to find the one that works best for you. Keep in mind that there are about a half dozen different moving averages. Each one is a little different than the next. Some have less lag, some weight present data heavier than older data, and others adapt to the market environment. Some include a volatility component. Experiment to find one that works well. My studies show that a simple moving average seems to work the best.

Stop and Start Trading with Equity

The logic behind Start and Stop Trading is simple. If a system is performing poorly and experiencing losses, equity will start to fall. As equity falls, it will eventually cross below its own moving average. When this happens, why not just simply stop

FIGURE 7.3 COMPARING AN UPTREND LINE TO AN APPROPRIATELY
SMOOTH MOVING AVERAGE OF THE EQUITY CURVE.

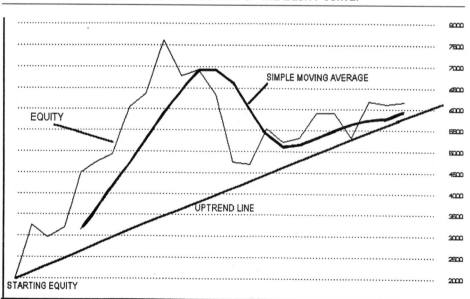

trading? Continue paper-trading and following the signals until the equity rises above the moving average and then start trading again (see Figure 7.4). The drawback is that you will miss the profitable trade that brought the equity above the moving average. Another drawback occurs if the results are choppy—a good profitable trade that brought the equity above the moving average could be followed by a losing trade. In this scenario, if you take the second trade (since the equity would then be above the moving average), that trade is a loss.

In the following example, I used a volatility trading system provided through Investograph Plus software. The market being used is the Standard & Poors 100 (OEX) from 12/31/91 to 5/20/92. The system uses an eight-day time frame and a 20 percent volatility factor for the breakout. Commissions used were $61 and every one-point move in the index will represent $266. The initial starting capital is $10,000. Initial results are shown in the Table 7.1.

Figure 7.5 shows the equity together with a 10-day simple moving average of the equity line. The following results occur if we stop trading when the equity is below the moving average. Figure 7.6 has the periods marked where the equity is below the average. Results are in the "Modified System" column of Table 7.1. Figure 7.7 shows the new equity curve with the new results. A much smoother equity curve resulted.

FIGURE 7.4 SHORT AND STOP TRADING. TRADING IS SUSPENDED WHEN EQUITY FALLS BELOW THE TRENDLINE AND RESUMES WHEN EQUITY CROSSES ABOVE THE TRENDLINE.

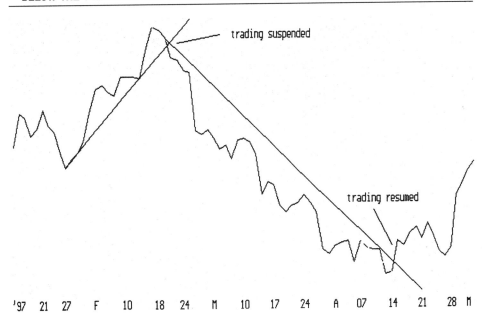

TABLE 7.1 COMPARING TRADING PERFORMANCE OF TWO SYSTEMS

	Initial System	*Modified System*
Total profits	$20,616	$23,217
Total number of trades	68	37
Winning %	52%	56%
Profit per trade	$303	$627
Highest account value	$20,616	$23,217
Lowest account value	$9,853	$9,853

FIGURE 7.5 THE EQUITY LINE OF THE INITIAL SYSTEM WITH
ITS 10-DAY SIMPLE MOVING AVERAGE.

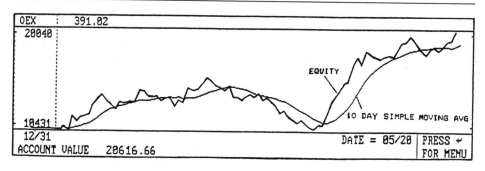

FIGURE 7.6 THE PERIODS WHERE EQUITY IS BELOW THE AVERAGE.

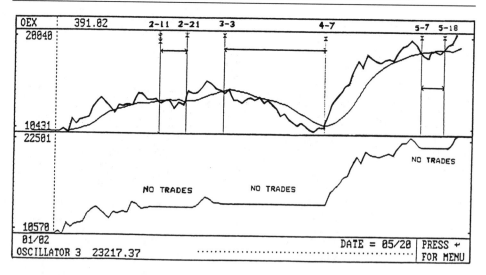

FIGURE 7.7 THE EQUITY CURVE OF THE MODIFIED SYSTEM.

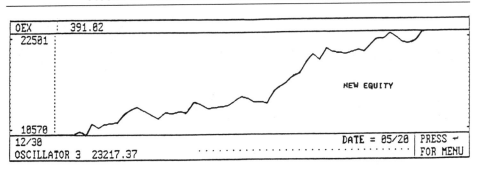

Reversing with Equity

The basic concept behind this approach is to reverse the signals given from a system when the equity is below the moving average. This approach seems counterintuitive, but take a closer look. As stated earlier, equity is composed of profit and losses from trades. These trades are based on a system that you are following. Each system design is based on a certain type of market (trending, choppy, volatile, range bound, etc.). As the market changes from one type to another, a system can start to incur losing trades. These losing trades are bunched up during the period that the market is in the type of action that your system dislikes. As the losses occur, your equity will fall and eventually go below the moving average.

While the equity is below the moving average, for the most part the system is still producing losses (more losing trades than winning trades). Therefore, the signals are wrong. What would happen if you did the opposite of the system during this time frame? Common sense would say that you would have winning trades. Now granted, you will have some winning trades when your equity is below the moving average; and eventually as the market changes, the system will start picking up winning trades and the equity will rise above its moving average. Also, keep in mind that once your equity falls below the moving average, this situation can last for a long time. Weeks and months can come and go, as you watch your system take losing trade after losing trade. An example will give you a basic idea of how this technique can work using the volatility breakout system.

As one of the more popular trading systems, the volatility breakout system has developed a following because over time it has performed quite well. In addition, many people feel that markets trade in ranges, only to break out of these ranges to form a new range or trend depending on the fundamental and economic news. This system does not predict the future direction of prices but simply reacts to the current volatility and captures the major price moves. The volatility breakout system performs poorly when the markets are in a tightly congested range. It performs well in volatile markets that are trending in nature.

The volatility breakout system is always in the market either long or short. It moves from one signal to the next. It works by calculating the true range for the number of days specified by the trader. Calculating this range requires subtracting the low from the high for that particular day. True range takes into account gaps up and down in price activity. This is a more accurate measure of a market's range. True range uses yesterday's closing price instead of today's low, if today's low is greater than yesterday's close. Also, true range uses yesterday's close instead of today's high, if today's high is less than yesterday's close. You would select the number of days to calculate the average true range. A trader who chooses five days would calculate the average true range over the previous five days.

The second parameter for the system is the breakout percentage. If the market breakout is more than a specified percentage of the average true range either above or below the previous day's close, than a buy or sell signal is generated. As a recommendation, look at 4 to 12 days to calculate the true range and 25 percent to 130 percent for the breakout. Experimentation and testing will enable you to come up with a good set of parameters. Many software packages have this system so you can just plug the numbers in and go.

We will look at one example with the Swiss Franc. This market is fairly volatile and like many of the other currencies tends to trend better and more often. Figure 7.8

FIGURE 7.8 200 DAYS OF THE SWISS FRANC.

is 200 days of the Swiss Franc ending on March 13, 1995. The market has a few up and down trends and ends with an explosive move to the upside. By looking at 200 days starting with the period ending March 13, 1995, we will use 7 days for the average true range and 65 percent for the breakout percentage. We will also take into account $32 per trade for commissions and no slippage.

Testing during this period produced results shown in the "Initial System" column in Table 7.2.

With the equity curve, we place a 25-day time series moving average. The equity curve just falters back and forth with the moving average. Where the equity is below the moving average, it generally coincides with the times that the Swiss franc is trading sideways and choppy. Can the results be improved without destroying the system's integrity? The modified system places opposite signals when equity is below the moving average. Performance results of this modified version are in the "Modified System" column of Table 7.2.

A comparison of the results shows that this simple technique can turn a mediocre system into a winner. Keep in mind that certain types of systems will not perform better by reversing the signals. This will be due to the type of system and market you are testing. Always keep your stops in place and have good exit rules. Lastly, you will need to keep separate charts to follow the original system's trades and equity while you deviate with your own alternative strategies.

Percentage Charts

As discussed earlier, it is important to know your system's percentage of winning and losing trades. These percentages can be used in chart form to provide valuable insight. The percentage charts are running totals based on the sum of all trades. You will find that your system's percent of winning trades (percentage profitable) will fall within a range of values, for example, 50 percent to 70 percent.

One way to apply this graph is to set your system's limits to, say, 50 percent profitable. If the percent profitable line of your system falls below 50 percent, all trading should cease or position size should be reduced. Conversely, when this line is rising or is above some value, say 70 percent, you could increase position size. You should be trading your heaviest when the odds of a win are in your favor.

TABLE 7.2 COMPARING TRADING PERFORMANCE OF TWO SYSTEMS

	Initial System	*Modified System*
Total profits	$6,015	$22,446
Total number of trades	49	59
Winning %	32%	69%
Profit per trade	$122	$380
Largest drawdown	$79,916	$2,710

Depending on the type of system you are trading, you will have to set the range of values. A trend following system may have good results between the 40 percent to 60 percent range, whereas a short-term oscillator system may range higher: 60 percent to 75 percent. The higher the risk-to-return ratio, the less you have to be correct to make a profit. Traders should always make sure that their trading has a good percent profitable for the system that they are trading and should be very cautious when this number decreases too rapidly. This may signal a change in the market, trending to sideways, or a system that is no longer working due to some variable.

The same chart can apply to percent losing trades as well. Figure 7.9 shows a percentage profitable chart. Notice how the percentage has stayed mostly within a range of 50–70. In this case it may be advisable to raise position size above 70 and cut size below 50.

Some systems will trade heavier when the percentage is above a certain number. I have a system that made 94 trades. Its ending equity was $51,292. As a modification, I keep a running total of the percentage profitable and double the position size from one to two contracts when the winning percentage is 57 percent or greater and keep only one contract when it's below 57 percent. This modified system's final equity is $60,112. What about drawdown since we are trading two positions? Surprisingly, the results are favorable as well. The original system's drawdown was $2,433, while the new system had a drawdown of $3,138. So for an increase in risk of $705 we added $8,820 to our bottom line, not bad! Figure 7.10 shows the two resulting equity lines.

FIGURE 7.9 A PERCENT WINNING TRADES CURVE AND TWO
THRESHOLD LINES: 50 PERCENT AND 70 PERCENT.

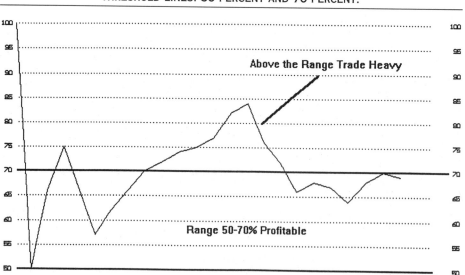

FIGURE 7.10 RUNNING EQUITY OF THE ORIGINAL AND MODIFIED SYSTEMS.

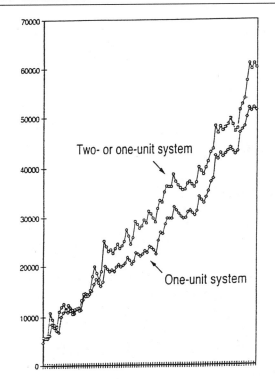

Average Profit and Loss

On a single chart, plot the profit made on each winning trade and on the same chart plot its moving average. Average profit is calculated by taking the total of the most recent N profitable trades and dividing it by N. For example, if the last trade had a profit of $800 and the most recent 10 profitable trades totaled $7,000, plot $800 and the running average $700 ($7,000/10). The profit line should, for the most part, stay on or above the average profit line. One should look to maximize profits on every trade. As you get better, profits should be greater than the average. When profits start falling below the average profit line, one should remain very cautious and reduce position size or halt trading. This again can provide an early warning sign that the markets are changing or that a losing streak is occurring (see Figure 7.11).

This chart can also be calculated for average losses as well. As you get better, the size of your losses should shrink. If your losses are increasing too rapidly, reduce position size or halt trading. You can also apply a moving average on your losses chart. This time, your goal is to have a loss that is less than its average.

FIGURE 7.11 PROFIT PER WINNING TRADE AND ITS RUNNING AVERAGE.

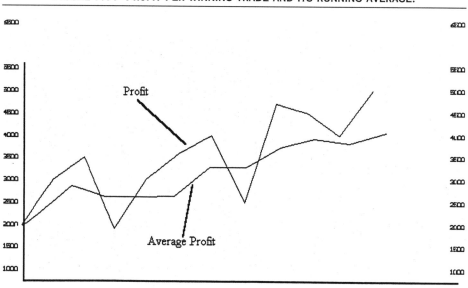

RISK VERSUS REWARD

Reward versus risk and risk versus reward. These terms have been thrown around much in various articles and books but what do they really mean? Reality says that risk versus reward is the cornerstone and foundation on which all else is based.

Risk is the amount of money that is on the line whenever you place a trade. If you do not use stops, then risk is unlimited. Theoretically, the market could fall to a point that would ruin you (e.g., being long the day before the October 1987 crash). If you have a stop in the market your risk is limited to the price of the stop. (This is sometimes not true due to other factors that we will touch upon later.) Risk can also represent the amount of money that you lost when the position is exited (closed).

Reward is the profit that is made from the trade you are in. This only occurs when the position is exited. Paper profits do not count. You could be long from 100 and the market is now at 105, giving you a 5-point profit (reward). But, what happens when the market opens 7 points lower and you exit the position? Your reward has now become your risk. Remember that only real profits and losses matter when you evaluate anything.

When you evaluate a system or trading result, you always have to consider reward relative to risk. This is also called the reward-to-risk ratio. If your system's reward-to-risk ratio is 2:1, it will make $2 for every 1$ risked. Eventually, you will come out ahead on the long run. Depending on the profitability of the system, your ratio can vary. If your ratio is 3 or 4:1, you can afford to have many more losers than winners because the size of the winnings are much greater. Ratios of 2:1, 1.5:1, 1:1 will only work with a high degree of accuracy (65%-75% or better).

Before you enter any trade, always look at how the situation may affect your risk. Is the market volatile or quiet? Has the open been gapping much? Where is my stop and if it is hit how will this affect my profit and loss? Reward will need to be calculated as well. Based on my analysis, is this going to be a big or small move? Is this trade going to take days or weeks? If the market explodes in my anticipated direction on the first day of my trade, will I take the money and run or do I have an effective strategy to deal with that?

Figure 7.12 depicts the reward-to-risk ratio in action. A nice uptrend line has formed and you decide to go short when it is broken. The market falls below the uptrend line and we are now short from .6660. We decide to have a 3:1 reward-to-risk ratio. Stops are placed at .6710, a risk of 0.5 ticks. We will place our orders to get out at .6510, a profit of 1.5 ticks, thus the 3:1 ratio. When this trade is entered, we do not know the outcome ahead of time. The only thing we know is that at the end of the trade we will have either a 0.5 tick loss or a 1.5 tick profit. One profit like this equals being wrong three times.

FIGURE 7.12 SETTING EXIT STOPS TO PRODUCE A 3:1 REWARD/RISK RATIO.

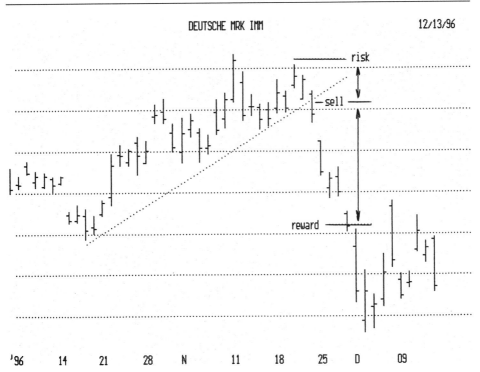

Close to Open

Unless you are a day trader, there is always the close-to-open risk. This was not much of a problem 5 or 10 years ago because when a market closed there was no more trading till the next day's session. With the increase in international trading and the need to access the markets at all times, many new after-hours trading systems were established to meet the needs of foreign investors and global traders. Globex, Project A, and Access (to name a few) are after-hours electronic systems used to match up buyers and sellers while the markets are closed.

Because of their popularity and need, markets are now experiencing big close-to-open gaps. A gap is the difference between the previous day's high and low and the new day's open. Depending on the market and events that happen overnight, the gaps could be very little or none to several hundred points. Depending on the market, you may be able to protect yourself by placing a 24-hour stop that will get you out of the market when your price is hit regardless of the time. The drawback to this is that after-hours markets are often very illiquid and prices can be hit or run up/down only to fall back in line before the market opens the next day. As with anything, there are always trade-offs.

Figure 7.13 depicts how often a market can gap. If you decided to buy the market and use the low of the previous three days as support, and a break of this support as a signal to get out, then you would have experienced a nice loss as the market gapped lower on the open by almost half a point.

You may decide the market you trade really doesn't experience big gaps so keeping stops only during the day is sufficient. If you trade the currencies, since they are much more of a global market subject to news events from other countries, a round-the-clock stop may be wise.

In evaluating your results, look to see if losses occurred due to gap openings. Maybe you need to fine-tune this area of your system. Sometimes you can use disaster stops, as I call them, in the night session to prevent a market from taking all your money and then some. These stops can be wide enough to protect you from ruin without stopping you out of a profitable position because of a slight move.

Slippage

Slippage risk is that uncontrollable part of trading that we all hate and try to avoid. Nevertheless, it occurs—sometimes more than it should. Every broker will claim to have the best execution, but in reality the normal day-to-day markets will always get you your price plus or minus a few ticks. The real dilemma occurs when you have a stop in the market and the Fed raises rates creating a "fast market" where brokers are not held to the prices. Your actual fill could be much higher or lower than your stop price. Yelling and screaming to your broker probably will not make a difference, but slippage must be taken into consideration when trading.

Are you in a position the day before an important G7 or Federal Reserve meeting? The dates of all-important economic reports are known in advance. Many times,

FIGURE 7.13 MARKET GAPS. AFTER TRADER PLACES A BUY, PRICE
GAPS PAST THE EXIT STOP AND OPENS MUCH LOWER.

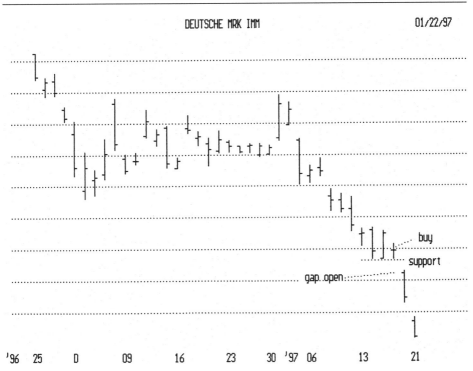

slippage is unavoidable so definitely keep this in mind and take it into account. If your slippage seems to happen more often than you would like, check to see if the market was in a fast condition. If it was not, make your broker aware that this is a concern for you, and if it keeps up, you will need to look elsewhere.

Avoiding Limit Price Moves

Severe losses can occur when stops are not available overnight when you keep a position open, or if you do not use stops, or more important, trade in markets that have limit price moves. Limit moves do not occur all too often but in some markets they can occur once every few weeks. This is unacceptable. You always want to be involved in a market that will let you get in or out at any price.

Just imagine if you are short lumber and a surprise housing number comes out, the market moves up to the daily limit (it "limits up"), and due to the fast market your order never got filled. Seven days later, the market is still limit up, and now a $500 loss is $5,000! Trust me when I say this can happen a lot all the time.

FIGURE 7.14 A FAST MARKET. IN JUST ONE MINUTE,
PRICE HAS MOVED DOWN THE EQUIVALENT OF $350.

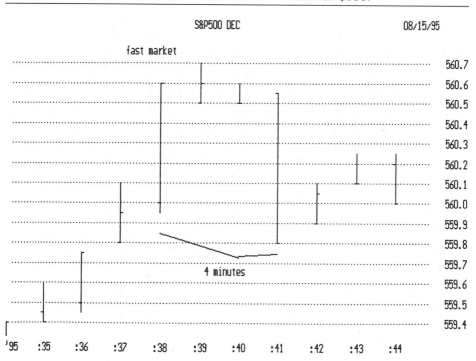

The only way to avoid this is to try to stay away from the markets that are more prone to limit moves. Also, stay away from markets that are illiquid no matter how good your results are with a system in that market. Because limit moves can be a part of trading, make sure that you are adequately capitalized so if the market does move limit for several days you can withstand the losses.

Figure 7.14 is an intraday chart of the S&P 500 on August 15, 1995. The bars represent 1-minute intervals. There is a period of 4 minutes when the market was in a fast condition. If a trader tried to go short on the fourth bar, he conceivably could have received a fill anywhere from 560.55 down to 559.80, almost .75 ticks wide during a period of just 1 minute! This is a potential slippage range of $350.

CONCLUSION

The term money management can cover a vast array of topics and techniques from something as simple as knowing how many contracts to trade to the complexity of equity analysis. Traders should never embark on a trading venture until they understand the concepts of money management. Lack of this skill is what retires so many people from the game of trading. Statistics say that the chances of small traders reaching long-term success in the markets are around 3 percent to 5 percent. Sorry to disappoint you, but that number is probably accurate.

How can you overcome such overwhelming odds? Following these five steps will help:

1. Develop a trading system designed to fit your personality, needs, equity, and temperament.
2. Develop a sound trading plan.
3. Develop and study money management principles and apply them to your overall system and analysis routine.
4. Have the discipline to follow your rules to the letter and have the knowledge to change the system if your money management signals you to do so.
5. You will need a little luck.

Start with the basics of what money management is and progress to the complex analysis. Everyone should plot his or her results and equity. That is the only way to graphically see how you are doing. Pity the trader who starts trading with $10,000 and 6 months later is down to $2,000. When asked, "What happened? Didn't you see it coming?" The trader looks off into space and says, "No."

Analyze your trading with the same vigor and scrutiny that you would use in developing a system and analyzing a market. There are always plenty of good low-risk opportunities in the market. Find them and then apply your money management.

Psychology

- Trading is a game of odds. Having a strong disciplined mind-set, statistically proven strategies, and strict money management are crucial in stacking the odds in your favor. Trading is also serious business as you can lose serious money. Expect to reorganize your life to integrate successfully all aspects of these required skills.

- Mechanized system trading (MST) is well designed to help you overcome fear. For novice investors, MST avoids the pitfalls of discretionary trading with its anticipatory forecasts that are often misleading due to optimism and overconfidence.

- Trading with a system requires tremendous concentration, diligence, and self-discipline because its trading style may not be within your comfort zone. Stress levels can lead to utter destruction of your psyche and physical self, if not properly managed. Make sure the system you design is compatible with the way you want to and are able to trade.

Markets and Time Frames

- Always look for liquid markets because they give you the ability to get out if you so choose.

- End-of-day (EOD) trading is easier than intraday (ID) trading. With EOD, you can perform calculations and plan trading strategy at your leisure anytime before market begins the next day. This permits you to hold a day job earning income. Your trading expenses are relatively low. Your clearinghouse and broker do not need to operate with split-second timing so transaction costs are small. Also, daily data is inexpensively available from many sources. You don't need a thorough understanding of entry and exit techniques and trading floor operations. Finally, stress is relatively low. (Unless you are the type that worries all day long about your trades. If that is the case, put this book down and take up another hobby. You will live longer.)

- Intraday trading is more difficult, more exciting, and potentially more rewarding. It requires you to pay attention to the markets almost continually, making calls to your broker as the need arises. It can be and should be considered a full-time job. You will have many more trading opportunities, and you can trade more contracts with a given amount of capital than by EOD. This increases your profit-loss (risk) potential. Trading on an ID basis can cost from 5 to 15 times more than EOD in monthly operating expenses. You must have the temperament for this high-stress game, or you are doomed.

Price Charts

- Novice traders erroneously tend to look for the Holy Grail indicator. There is none. Before relying on any indicator, try making mechanical systems that trade directly off price action. It will help you develop a feel and intuition for price dynamics. Learn to use your intuition and anticipate price movement. Mob psychology is to react to the market, a strategy that generally loses.
- The most important market price patterns to identify are uptrends and downtrends. An uptrend is the successive occurrence of higher highs and higher lows. A downtrend is the successive occurrence of lower highs and lower lows. Trends run along support and resistance lines that tend to continue until broken with a direction now in the opposite direction.
- Become familiar with support and resistance lines. Breakouts and breakdowns from these lines are popular strategies but they are not easy to apply due to many false breakouts or breakdowns depending on which market you trade. However, the cup and handle breakout pattern strategy works very well in a bullish market.
- Volume leads price. When a stock breaks out of a consolidation pattern on increasing volume, for example, it is considered a valid breakout and the expectation is that price will move higher. However, if a breakout is followed by lethargic volume, it is considered suspect.
- Price congestion may be viewed as a memory of the market that can influence future price movement. If price is moving about within a region of low congestion, there are few traders to counteract the moves and the price movement is considered mobile. Further, when prices move *toward* lower congestion, the move is likely to continue and the price is again considered mobile. Conversely, when prices move either within high congestion or toward a region of higher congestion, then price is considered immobile.

Indicators

- There are two categories of indicators: those that work in trending markets and those that work in nontrending (trading) markets. An indicator that works well in a trading market will constantly give signals opposite the trend for a strong trending security. When a security is in a nice uptrend, ignore overbought sell signals. Conversely, if you apply an indicator that works well in trending situations to a nontrending security, you will trade often but will end up selling at about the same level as the purchase price.
- Moving averages reduce the noise (jaggedness) in price time series, but their inherent delay or lag sometimes hinders their effectiveness, because late trade

signals can cost you profit. More advanced, low-lag moving averages are available either publicly or commercially.*

- Sentiment indicators have limited value because the public is aware of the value of taking a contrarian position, which in turn affects the sentiment indicators themselves. As for flow-of-funds indicators, although they are effective in measuring the capacity of market participants, they fail to measure the *intention* of the participants to put those reserves to work.

- Traders should never depend on one indicator exclusively. Each indicator solves only one piece of the puzzle. Traders can realize an indicator's true value by using it in concert with other (dissimilar) indicators to provide an overall composite picture of an issue's underlying trend strength and direction. The more evidence there is to support the indicators' confirmation of one another, the more valid the conclusion—and the higher the probability of profit.

- One of the biggest traps most aspiring technicians fall into is following several indicators with different names, all of which measure the same thing. To better evaluate varied perspectives on the market, follow a handful of indicators that measure different aspects of market behavior.

- Never apply any technical indicator to a market or stock blindly. Always look at the whole range of an indicator's value before assessing its meaning.

Placing Trades

- Although this may sound backward, learn to exit the market first. To do so, enter the market at arbitrary times and develop profitable stops and exit strategies. Try to stay in the good trades and exit the bad trades with a small loss. It can be done, and you will learn a tremendous amount in a very short time.

- If the net expected return for an intended trade is a positive number, then you have a good trade or sound entry. If it is a negative number, then you should avoid that trade.

- Once you are in a trade and, better still, before entering a trade, you should place a stop in the market. Placing stops will minimize your losses, help to ensure profits, and reduce risk. Place stops in an area that, if hit, will prove your analysis wrong. You will need to determine your risk parameters and examine the type of market and trade you are in. Will this trade last three days or three weeks?

- Once you have placed the initial stop, you then need to monitor the position. When is the appropriate time to bring your stops to breakeven? Determine

---

*Popular advanced moving averages include DEMA (Difference Exponential Moving Average), developed by Patrick Mulloy (see *Technical Analysis of Stocks and Commodities,* January 1994), the Kalman filter, developed by Rudolf Kalman (see *Kalman Filtering,* by Grewal and Andrews, Prentice Hall, 1993), and JMA (Jurik Moving Average), developed by Mark Jurik (see http://www.jurikres.com/catalog/ms_ama.htm).

whether you will take a predetermined amount out of the market or will trail the market until you get stopped out. If you decide to use a trailing stop, you will have several to choose from.

Money Management

- A key to any successful trading venture is money management, which can consist of factors like the number of contracts to trade, the number of markets to trade in, exiting a position and loss control. A trader should spend 70 percent of his time on developing and using money management and 30 percent of their time looking for low-risk, high-profit trading opportunities.
- Accept that you have a lot to learn and your initial performance will likely be poor. Avoid going broke by trading small lots in relatively stable markets. For example, try trading the bond market before the S&P.
- Know how much your account size needs to be, and what portion you may not use for placing trades. Assume you will need about three times margin to trade one futures contract with relative safety from drawdowns. As a rule of thumb, you can increase your survival against losing streaks by putting at risk only 5 percent of your capital per trade.
- Some risk may be controlled with good exit strategies, so predetermine your exit points before you trade.
- Measure your progress with equity charts. If you suffered a losing streak, take a breather to regain composure. Do not ever say, "I'll make it up on the next trade."

PART II

Testing and Evaluation

Will your trading strategy be profitable? Will you survive the way it trades?

The fun part of system building was just that: system *building.* Now comes the less interesting part: system testing. Here you analyze performance from many angles, looking for reasons to shoot your system down. After all, better now than when the market shoots you down.

The next two chapters underscore this common theme: you must view system performance in light of three parameters: profitability, survivability, and psychological compatibility:

1. Can you reasonably expect your system to make an overall profit?
2. Are the risks under control, or will drawdowns wipe out your account before profits roll in?
3. Can you really trade this way, or will the stress get the best of you?

A successful backtesting procedure will greatly reduce the probability that you will begin trading with either an unprofitable strategy or one that does not meet your standards. It also builds up justifiable confidence in a truly good system, and after a big loss, you will need all the confidence you can muster.

Chapter 8 discusses the importance of separating historical data into two or more test groups and shows an important, yet little-known formula for obtaining a more accurate estimation of a system's expected daily profitability.

Chapter 9 gives extensive coverage of numerous ways to assess system performance. The author breaks down the methods into the following categories: Profit Ratios, Return Figures, Sliding and Rolling Summaries, Equity Curve Analysis, Total Trades, Outlier Trades, Drawdown/Run-up, Consecutive Trades, and Time Analysis.

Books can be written on how to analyze trading systems, but these two chapters should get you started on the right track.

CHAPTER 8

Backtesting

MICHAEL DE LA MAZA

"Will my trading strategy be profitable?" After having gone through the arduous process of crafting a trading strategy, that is the question you must ask yourself. The ability to answer that question is the great promise that backtesting holds out to all traders. A successful backtesting procedure will greatly reduce the probability that you will begin trading with either an unprofitable strategy or one that does not meet your standards.[1]

By adopting a sound and rigorous backtesting approach, you will:

- Pinpoint which approaches to the market are likely to be successful and which ones are not.
- Generate good estimates of future performance for each trading strategy you test.
- Create a record of your trading strategy's historical trading performance.
- Produce data necessary for other components of your trading approach such as your asset allocation strategy.

The ability to backtest is one of the great advantages that computerized traders have over discretionary or intuitive traders. Because computerized trading strategies are clearly and objectively defined, they can be tested on historical data in a way that is all but impossible for a discretionary trading strategy. Computerized traders who do not backtest are surrendering one of the greatest advantages that they have.

In this chapter you will learn the rudiments of backtesting methodology. You will know how to execute simple backtesting protocols on your own data and you will know the benefits and shortcomings of several backtesting strategies. Most important, you will know how to employ the Markowitz/Xu data mining correction formula, which is described for the everyday trader for the first time in this chapter.[2]

THE BASICS: WALK-FORWARD TESTING

While there are many different types of backtesting procedures, most of them share a core component: walk-forward testing. The idea behind walk-forward testing is simple: A trading strategy should be tested by going back in time and running the trading strategy as if your historical data were real-time data.

An example helps to illustrate this technique. Suppose that you have developed an intermediate term trading strategy for the S&P 500 futures market and you would like to backtest this system. You have access to data going back to 1983, and your strategy uses the last 10 closing prices to determine whether or not to trade. To perform a walk-forward test of this strategy, you would begin by giving it access to the first 10 closing prices of 1983, and you would run the trading strategy on these 10 data points. You would then record the trade, if any, made by the trading strategy on day 11, along with profit and loss figures and other data you might choose to collect. Then you would replace the first closing price in the 10-day series with day 11's closing price and repeat the process. You would sweep a 10-day "window" of closing prices across your historical data and give your strategy access only to the closing prices in this window. This process is identical to the one that you would follow in real-time trading. This 10-day "window" is shown in Figure 8.1.

There are many commercial programs that automate this walk-forward testing procedure. Although these packages may be useful for some purposes, in general they are too limited to accommodate sophisticated trading strategies or backtesting protocols. Typically, custom programming is required to implement a walk-forward testing module.

FIGURE 8.1 WALK-FORWARD TESTING. AT EACH STEP, A 10-DAY "WINDOW" OF CLOSING PRICES IS AVAILABLE FOR A TRADING STRATEGY.

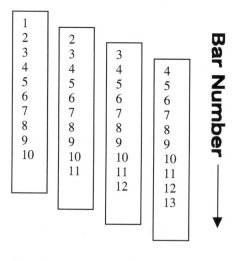

Step 1   Step 2   Step 3   Step 4 . . .

IN-SAMPLE AND OUT-OF-SAMPLE DATA

With the exception of backtesting protocols that employ the Markowitz/Xu correction (to be discussed) or something similar, all backtesting procedures make a critical distinction between "in-sample" and "out-of-sample" data. In-sample data is the data used to design the trading strategy. Out-of-sample data is the data used to test the trading strategy. A cardinal rule of backtesting is:
In-sample data should be completely separate from the out-of-sample data.

The out-of-sample data should remain "clean" and "pure" throughout the process of creating the strategy. As soon as the out-of-sample data is tainted, it can no longer serve the purpose of providing an accurate estimate of future performance which is one of the most important outcomes of the backtesting process.

One wrinkle on the standard in-sample/out-of-sample data set paradigm is the introduction of a third data set called the "tuning" set. The sole purpose of the tuning set is to provide you with the opportunity to "cheat" without ruining the out-of-sample data set. After creating your trading strategy using the in-sample data set, you then run it on the tuning set. If the results meet your criteria, then you can run the strategy on the out-of-sample data set. If, on the other hand, the results do not meet your criteria, then you can go back to the in-sample set and tune your strategy. The flowchart in Figure 8.2 illustrates this iterative process.

FIGURE 8.2 THE ITERATIVE PROCESS OF CREATING AND TESTING A TRADING STRATEGY.

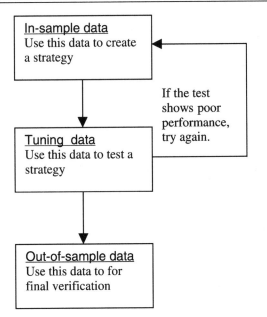

FIGURE 8.3 DIVIDING THE DATA SET INTO THREE GROUPS:
IN-SAMPLE, TUNING, AND OUT-OF-SAMPLE.

In-Sample data set	Tuning Data Set	Out-of-Sample data set
1982 1983 1984 1985 1986	1987 1988 1989 1990 1991	1992 1993 1994 1995 1996 1997

You can think of the tuning set as a psychological crutch. If, after having spent considerable intellectual, emotional, and psychological energy developing a trading strategy, you discover that it has a simple flaw when you run it on the out-of-sample data, then your options are limited. If you choose to retool the trading strategy, then your estimates of future performance will be inaccurate because the out-of-sample data set has been tainted. You will have to live with the uncertainty that you may have over-fitted, overoptimized, and "shrink-wrapped" your trading strategy around the out-of-sample data. The benefit of using a tuning set is that it gives you a second chance.

If you decide to use a tuning set in your backtesting, then the standard method is to select a period of time between the in-sample data set and the out-of-sample data set as the tuning set. For example, if you are developing a strategy for the S&P 500 futures, then your in-sample data set might range from 1982 to 1986, your tuning set might range from 1987 to 1991, and your out-of-sample data set might range from 1992 to 1997, as shown in Figure 8.3.

LEAVE-ONE-OUT TESTING

For the data partitioning strategy previously discussed, the three data sets are chosen in advance and are held fixed through the creation and testing of the trading strategy. In contrast, leave-one-out testing forces the out-of-sample data set to shift throughout the *entire* data set. With this method, the historical data set is first divided into many groups. One of these groups is temporarily assigned to be the out-of-sample set and the remaining groups become the in-sample set. Next, a trading strategy is partially developed for this particular assignment of the data groups. The cycle repeats as

TABLE 8.1 DATA GROUP ALLOCATION IN LEAVE-ONE-OUT SYSTEM TESTING

Data Groups Assigned to Be In-Sample	Data Groups Assigned to Be Out-of-Sample
1 2 3 4	5
1 2 3 5	4
1 2 4 5	3
1 3 4 5	2
2 3 4 5	1

another group is chosen to be the out-of-sample data set, the rest assigned as in-sample, and partial system development continues some more. The process repeats until all the data groups have been used as the out-of-sample data set.

An example serves to illustrate the point. Suppose you divide the historical data into five groups. Then the in-sample and out-of-sample sets are shown in Table 8.1.

THE MARKOWITZ/XU DATA MINING CORRECTION FORMULA

The Markowitz/Xu data mining correction formula is a little known but extremely powerful formula that corrects for overoptimization. You should use the Markowitz/Xu data mining correction formula whenever the out-of-sample data set has been tainted by running more than one trading strategy through it. The Markowitz/Xu formula gives an estimate of the actual return of the top-performing strategy. The intuitive idea behind the formula is that the return of the top-performing strategy should be adjusted in the direction of the average return of all the trading strategies that were run through the data set. The form of this adjustment is given by the following formula:

$$H' = R + B\,(H - R)$$

where . . .

H' is the new estimate of the return of the best strategy,
R is the average return of all of the strategies,
H is the return of the best performing strategy,
B is a number between 0 and 1.

Notice that H' will always be between the average return of all of the trading strategies and the return of the top-performing strategy. When $B = 0$ then $H' = R + 0$ $(H - R) = R$. When $B = 1$ then $H' = R + 1\ (H - R) = R + H - R = H$. The critical question is: What is the formula for B? Intuitively, B should grow smaller as the number of trading strategies grows larger. The smaller B is, the closer H' will move to R, the average return of all of the trading strategies. In addition, B should grow smaller as the variance of the returns increases. The formula for B is:

$$B = N/D$$

where

$$N = C\,(1 + 1/(n - 1) + 1/(T - 1)) - A/(T - 1)$$
$$D = C\,(1 + 1/(n - 1))$$

where

    A is the average squared difference of the daily returns of each strategy and the average daily return of all strategies,

    C is the averaged squared difference of the average daily return of each strategy and the average daily return of all of strategies,

    n is the number of trading strategies,

    T is the number of days for which you have computed daily returns

SPREADSHEET EXAMPLE

Figure 8.4 shows a spreadsheet that contains an example of the Markowitz/Xu data mining correction formula in action. The first 18 columns of the spreadsheet are organized as follows:

- Column A. Date.
- Column B. The daily returns of Strategy 1. For example, on 10/7/97, the daily return of Strategy 1 is $-.005$ or $-.5\%$.

FIGURE 8.4 AN EXAMPLE SPREADSHEET FOR CALCULATING THE MARKOWITZ/XU CORRECTION.

	A	B	C	D	E	F	G	H	I	J	K	L	M
1		Strategy 1	Strategy 2	Strategy 3	log str 1	log str 2	log str 3	str1 - avg	str2 - avg	str3 - avg	(str1-avg)^2	(str2-avg)^2	(str3-avg)^2
2	10/7	-0.0050	-0.0040	0.0037	-0.0050	-0.0040	0.0037	-0.0050	-0.0040	0.0036	2.5E-05	1.6E-05	1.3E-05
3	10/8	0.0004	0.0049	0.0010	0.0004	0.0048	0.0010	0.0004	0.0048	0.0010	1.6E-07	2.3E-05	9.9E-07
4	10/9	-0.0011	0.0002	0.0017	-0.0011	0.0002	0.0017	-0.0012	0.0001	0.0016	1.4E-06	1.6E-08	2.6E-06
5	10/10	-0.0047	-0.0026	0.0041	-0.0047	-0.0026	0.0041	-0.0048	-0.0026	0.0040	2.3E-05	6.8E-06	1.6E-05
6	10/11	-0.0037	0.0027	0.0041	-0.0037	0.0027	0.0041	-0.0037	0.0027	0.0041	1.4E-05	7.2E-06	1.6E-05
7	10/15	-0.0021	-0.0038	-0.0028	-0.0021	-0.0038	-0.0028	-0.0021	-0.0039	-0.0029	4.6E-06	1.5E-05	8.3E-06
8	10/16	0.0009	0.0050	0.0030	0.0009	0.0050	0.0030	0.0009	0.0049	0.0029	8.0E-07	2.4E-05	8.6E-06
9	10/17	0.0007	-0.0050	-0.0016	0.0007	-0.0050	-0.0016	0.0006	-0.0051	-0.0017	3.9E-07	2.6E-05	2.8E-06
10	10/18	-0.0021	0.0006	0.0016	-0.0021	0.0006	0.0016	-0.0022	0.0005	0.0015	4.8E-06	2.8E-07	2.3E-06
11	10/21	-0.0044	-0.0036	0.0030	-0.0044	-0.0036	0.0030	-0.0045	-0.0037	0.0030	2.0E-05	1.3E-05	8.9E-06
12	10/22	0.0010	0.0009	-0.0041	0.0010	0.0009	-0.0041	0.0010	0.0008	-0.0042	9.8E-07	6.8E-07	1.7E-05
13	10/23	0.0020	0.0022	0.0044	0.0020	0.0022	0.0044	0.0020	0.0022	0.0043	3.9E-06	4.8E-06	1.9E-05
14	10/24	0.0030	-0.0010	-0.0009	0.0030	-0.0010	-0.0009	0.0029	-0.0011	-0.0009	8.7E-06	1.2E-06	8.3E-07
15	10/25	-0.0030	0.0022	0.0040	-0.0030	0.0022	0.0040	-0.0031	0.0022	0.0040	9.5E-06	4.7E-06	1.6E-05
16	10/28	-0.0049	-0.0029	0.0025	-0.0049	-0.0029	0.0025	-0.0050	-0.0029	0.0024	2.5E-05	8.5E-06	5.8E-06
17	10/29	-0.0013	0.0046	-0.0010	-0.0013	0.0046	-0.0010	-0.0013	0.0045	-0.0011	1.7E-06	2.0E-05	1.2E-06
18	10/30	0.0012	0.0000	0.0028	0.0012	0.0000	0.0028	0.0011	0.0000	0.0027	1.3E-06	9.0E-10	7.3E-06
19													
20	average daily return of individual strategies				-0.0014	0.00002	0.0015						
21	individual average - global average				-0.0014	-0.00003	0.0014						
22	(individual average - global average)^2				1.984E-06	8.629E-10	2.067E-06						
23													
24													
25	n	3		number of strategies									
26	T	17		number of days									
27		5.13E-05		average daily return of all strategies (global average)									
28													
29	A	9.11E-06											
30	B	1.35E-06											
31													
32	D	2.03E-06											
33	N	1.54E-06											
34													
35	Beta	0.7607											
36													
37	Adjusted return (daily)		0.00115		1.00115								
38	Adjusted return (annual)		1.33144										

- Column C. The daily returns of Strategy 2.
- Column D. The daily returns of Strategy 3.
- Column E. The natural log of one plus the daily return of Strategy 1. The formula for cell E2 is =LN(1+B2).
- Column F. The natural log of one plus the daily return of Strategy 2. The formula for cell F2 is =LN(1+C2).
- Column G. The natural log of one plus the daily return of Strategy 3. The formula for cell G2 is =LN(1+D2).
- Column H. The difference between the daily log return of Strategy 1 and the average daily log return of all strategies. The formula for cell H2 is =E2–B27. Cell B27 contains the average daily natural log return of all the strategies.
- Column I. The difference between the daily return of Strategy 2 and the average daily natural log return of all strategies. The formula for cell I2 is =F2–B27.
- Column J. The difference between the daily return of Strategy 3 and the average daily natural log return of all strategies. The formula for cell J2 is =G2–B27.
- Column K. The square of Column H. The formula for cell K2 is =H2×H2.
- Column L. The square of Column I. The formula for cell L2 is =I2×I2.
- Column M. The square of Column J. The formula M2 is =J2×J2.

Rows 19–37 of the spreadsheet are organized as follows:

- Row 19. Blank.
- Row 20. The arithmetic average of cells E2 through E18, F2 through F18, and G2 through G18. The formula for cell E2 is =AVERAGE(E2:18).
- Row 21. Row 20 minus the average daily return of all the strategies. The formula for cell E21 is =E20–B27.
- Row 22. The square of Row 21. The formula for cell E22 is =E21×E21.
- Rows 23, 24. Blank.
- Row 25. Cell B25 is the number of trading strategies.
- Row 26. Cell B26 is the number of days for which you have computed daily returns.
- Row 27. Cell B27 is the average daily return of all of the strategies. This cell's formula is =AVERAGE(E20:G20).
- Row 28. Blank.
- Row 29. Cell B29 is the variable *A* discussed earlier. This cell's formula is =SUM(K2:M18) / (B25×B26).
- Row 30. Cell B30 is the variable *C* discussed earlier. This cell's formula is =SUM(E22:G22) / B25.
- Row 31. Blank.

- Row 32. Cell B32 is the variable D discussed earlier. This cell's formula is =B30×(1+1/(B25−1)).
- Row 33. Cell B33 is the variable N discussed earlier. This cell's formula is =B30×(1+1/(B25−1)+1/(B26−1))−B29/(B26−1).
- Row 34. Blank.
- Row 35. Cell B35 is the variable B discussed earlier. This cell's formula is =B33/B32.
- Row 36. Blank.
- Row 37. Cell D37 is the adjusted return of the third strategy (column D) which is the top performing strategy in this example. This cell's formula is =B27+B35×(G20−B27).
- To get the annual adjusted rate of return, Cell F37 is the natural exponent of D37 and cell D38 is cell F37 to the 250th power (assuming 250 trading days in one year).

Figure 8.4 shows a spreadsheet with all the numbers calculated from daily returns of three hypothetical trading system strategies. Figures 8.5 and 8.6 show, in full detail, the formulas in the spreadsheet in Figure 8.4. Note that in Figure 8.4 the return figures for the strategies (columns B through D) are expressed in a form that does not display all the significant digits that were actually used. For example, although cell B2 shows a value of −0.0050, the actual value used in the calculations was −0.00496175. So if you type in the same return figures as shown in Columns B, C, D, your results should differ slightly.

FIGURE 8.5 FORMULAS FOR THE FIRST 18 ROWS OF THE SPREADSHEET IN FIGURE 8.4.

	A	B	C	D	E	F	G	H	I	J	K	L	M
1		s1	s2	s3	log(S1)	log(S2)	log(S3)	str1 - avg	str2 - avg	str3 - avg	(str1-avg)^2	(str2-avg)^2	(str3-avg)^2
2		#	#	#	=LN(1+B2)	=LN(1+C2)	=LN(1+D2)	=E2-B27	=F2-B27	=G2-B27	=H2*H2	=I2*I2	=J2*J2
3		#	#	#	=LN(1+B3)	=LN(1+C3)	=LN(1+D3)	=E3-B27	=F3-B27	=G3-B27	=H3*H3	=I3*I3	=J3*J3
4		#	#	#	=LN(1+B4)	=LN(1+C4)	=LN(1+D4)	=E4-B27	=F4-B27	=G4-B27	=H4*H4	=I4*I4	=J4*J4
5		#	#	#	=LN(1+B5)	=LN(1+C5)	=LN(1+D5)	=E5-B27	=F5-B27	=G5-B27	=H5*H5	=I5*I5	=J5*J5
6		#	#	#	=LN(1+B6)	=LN(1+C6)	=LN(1+D6)	=E6-B27	=F6-B27	=G6-B27	=H6*H6	=I6*I6	=J6*J6
7		#	#	#	=LN(1+B7)	=LN(1+C7)	=LN(1+D7)	=E7-B27	=F7-B27	=G7-B27	=H7*H7	=I7*I7	=J7*J7
8		#	#	#	=LN(1+B8)	=LN(1+C8)	=LN(1+D8)	=E8-B27	=F8-B27	=G8-B27	=H8*H8	=I8*I8	=J8*J8
9		#	#	#	=LN(1+B9)	=LN(1+C9)	=LN(1+D9)	=E9-B27	=F9-B27	=G9-B27	=H9*H9	=I9*I9	=J9*J9
10		#	#	#	=LN(1+B10)	=LN(1+C10)	=LN(1+D10)	=E10-B27	=F10-B27	=G10-B27	=H10*H10	=I10*I10	=J10*J10
11		#	#	#	=LN(1+B11)	=LN(1+C11)	=LN(1+D11)	=E11-B27	=F11-B27	=G11-B27	=H11*H11	=I11*I11	=J11*J11
12		#	#	#	=LN(1+B12)	=LN(1+C12)	=LN(1+D12)	=E12-B27	=F12-B27	=G12-B27	=H12*H12	=I12*I12	=J12*J12
13		#	#	#	=LN(1+B13)	=LN(1+C13)	=LN(1+D13)	=E13-B27	=F13-B27	=G13-B27	=H13*H13	=I13*I13	=J13*J13
14		#	#	#	=LN(1+B14)	=LN(1+C14)	=LN(1+D14)	=E14-B27	=F14-B27	=G14-B27	=H14*H14	=I14*I14	=J14*J14
15		#	#	#	=LN(1+B15)	=LN(1+C15)	=LN(1+D15)	=E15-B27	=F15-B27	=G15-B27	=H15*H15	=I15*I15	=J15*J15
16		#	#	#	=LN(1+B16)	=LN(1+C16)	=LN(1+D16)	=E16-B27	=F16-B27	=G16-B27	=H16*H16	=I16*I16	=J16*J16
17		#	#	#	=LN(1+B17)	=LN(1+C17)	=LN(1+D17)	=E17-B27	=F17-B27	=G17-B27	=H17*H17	=I17*I17	=J17*J17
18		#	#	#	=LN(1+B18)	=LN(1+C18)	=LN(1+D18)	=E18-B27	=F18-B27	=G18-B27	=H18*H18	=I18*I18	=J18*J18
19													
20													
21													
22													
23													
24													

FIGURE 8.6 FORMULAS FOR ROWS 19–38 OF THE SPREADSHEET IN FIGURE 8.4.

	A	B	C	D	E	F	G
19							
20	average daily r				=AVERAGE(E2:E18)	=AVERAGE(F2:F18)	=AVERAGE(G2:G18)
21	individual aver				=E20-B27	=F20-B27	=G20-B27
22	(individual ave				=E21*E21	=F21*F21	=G21*G21
23							
24							
25	n	3		number of strategies			
26	T	17		number of days			
27		=AVERAGE(E20:G20)		average daily return of all strat			
28							
29	A	=SUM(K2:M18)/(B25*B26)					
30	B	=SUM(E22:G22)/B25					
31							
32	D	=B30*(1+1/(B25-1))					
33	N	=B30*(1+1/(B25-1)+1/(B26-1))-B29/(B26-1)					
34							
35	Beta	=B33/B32					
36							
37	Adjusted returr			=B27+B35*(G20-B27)		=EXP(D37)	
38	Adjusted returr			=F37^250			

Modifying this spreadsheet to calculate the Markowitz/Xu correction for your data is a simple three-step process:

1. Input the daily return of your strategies in columns B, C, and D. If you have more than three strategies, then replicate the formulas in Columns E–G, H–J, and K–M. If you have results for more than 17 days, insert additional rows just below Row 18 and copy down the formulas.
2. Input the number of trading strategies in cell B25 and the number of days in your historical test into cell B26.
3. In cell B37, change G20 to be the average daily return of the trading strategy to which you are applying the Markowitz/Xu correction. Typically, this will be the strategy with the highest average daily return. The average daily return of each strategy is computed in Row 20.

The most interesting number on the spreadsheet is B, which appears in cell B35. Remember that if $B = 0$, then return of the highest performing strategy is just equal to the average return of all the strategies. If $B = 1$, then the return of the top-performing strategy is equal to the return on the historical data set. So, the closer B is to 1, the smaller the size of the adjustment. In the case of the example shown in the spreadsheet in Figure 8.4, the natural log of the return of the top-performing strategy is reduced from .0015 (cell G20) to .00115 (cell B37).

Several modifications and improvements can be made in this correction formula. First, if you are trading a market, such as the S&P 500 futures, which has a long-term uptrend, then the return of the trading strategies should not be the absolute return, but rather the return above the uptrend. For example, if the average daily return of the S&P 500 futures is 0.04 percent and the average daily return of your top-performing strategy is .05 percent then $H = .05\% - .04\% = .01\%$. Second,

Markowitz and Xu discuss several other correction formulas for cases that have weaker restrictions. The procedure for estimating H' is considerably more complicated.

CONCLUSION

This chapter has described three approaches to backtesting trading systems:

1. The standard in-sample/out-of-sample data set approach.
2. The leave-one-out technique.
3. The Markowitz/Xu correction formula.

The purpose of a rigorous and intellectually honest backtesting procedure is to produce *good estimates of future performance*. Because intuitions about performance are likely to be poorly grounded and therefore incorrect, only a disinterested, objective approach will yield good estimates. Disciplined use of tools such as leave-one-out testing and the Markowitz/Xu data mining correction will, in the end, prevent false optimism and lead to higher profits.

REFERENCES

Kaufmann, Perry and Schwager, Jack D., *Smarter Trading: Improving Performance in Changing Markets*, McGraw-Hill, 1995.

Murphy, John J., *Technical Analysis of the Futures Markets: A Comprehensive Guide to Trading Methods and Applications*, Prentice Hall Trade, 1987.

Rotella, Robert P., *The Elements of Successful Trading: Developing Your Comprehensive Strategy Through Psychology, Money Management, and Trading Methods*, Prentice Hall Trade, 1992.

Schwager, Jack D., *Technical Analysis*, John Wiley & Sons, 1995.

ENDNOTES

1. Two books published by the New York Institute of Finance, one by Robert P. Rotella titled *The Elements of Successful Trading* and the other by John Murphy titled *Technical Analysis of Futures Markets*, provide rudimentary information about backtesting. Many of the heuristics in these two books are formalized in this chapter.

   Perry Kaufman's *Smarter Trading: Improving Performance in Changing Markets* discusses the intuitions behind backtesting for the nonacademic reader.

   Jack Schwager's well-known *Technical Analysis* discusses some of the pitfalls that are associated with poor backtesting methodology.

2. The discussion of the Markowitz/Xu data mining correction in this chapter summarizes an original article by Harry M. Markowitz and Gan Lin Xu which was published in the Fall 1994 issue of the *Journal of Portfolio Management*. This article contains the derivation for the data mining correction formula. In addition, it has an interesting discussion on holdout periods (a synonym for out-of-sample data sets).

CHAPTER 9

Evaluating Trading Performance

DAVID STENDAHL

Performance evaluation is critical to the design, development, and monitoring of a trading system. Traders and investors alike need to assess their system's true worth to build trading confidence. The tools presented in this chapter allow traders to implement a process that systematically and objectively evaluates trading performance.

The rationale for a detailed evaluation is simple—every trader has his or her own idea as to what makes a great trading system. A system that fits one person may not be appropriate for another. It is not uncommon to hear two traders talk about the same trading system that one loves and the other hates. This difference in opinions is most likely attributed to their individual trading style. One trader may be aggressive, while the other is conservative. Just because a system is historically profitable, does not guarantee that every trader will follow the system.

There are plenty of trading systems to choose from; the object is to find the one that best matches the personality of the trader. Only the individual trader can make the final decision as to the worth of a trading system. Does the trader have the reward/risk profile to trade the system? No matter how profitable a system appears, if a trader does not have the intestinal fortitude to follow it, he or she should look for another system to trade.

Throughout this chapter, we will refer to various trading systems to help in the evaluation process. A trading system is defined as a methodology that buys or sells a commodity/security for a specific reason. It can be 100 percent mechanical or totally intuitive; as long as it generates buy and sell signals, there is enough information to evaluate. A sample trade-by-trade report as outlined in Table 9.1 contains the key data necessary to perform a detailed evaluation. In general, the data consists of the entry and exit date/price information. The majority of popular technical analysis software packages as well as brokerage statements contain this information. With this basic data in hand, we are ready to evaluate the trading performance of a system.

THE EVALUATION PROCESS

The evaluation process has several parts. Each part examines trading performance from a different perspective by using specific evaluation tools that are explained throughout

TABLE 9.1 TRADE-BY-TRADE REPORT

Trade #	Date	Price	Contracts Profit	% Profit	Run-up Drawdown	Entry Eff. Exit Eff.
87	06/20/96	$670.390	1		$6,004.710	69.39%
	07/03/96	$677.640	$3,505.750	0.68%	($2,649.280)	71.41%
88	07/09/96	$660.970	1		$6,194.640	20.78%
	08/21/96	$670.670	$4,698.900	0.92%	($23,614.630)	95.07%
89	07/18/96	$641.430	1		$15,710.620	62.87%
	08/21/96	$670.670	$14,214.880	2.77%	($9,277.350)	94.11%
90	10/30/96	$711.550	1		$29,146.950	91.88%
	11/27/96	$762.160	$24,622.070	4.80%	($2,576.230)	85.82%
91	12/10/96	$759.720	1		$21,296.510	54.83%
	01/23/97	$783.950	$11,775.010	2.30%	($17,546.610)	75.55%
92	04/02/97	$764.570	1		$42,812.170	78.46%
	05/16/97	$838.270	$35,866.900	6.99%	($11,751.310)	87.32%
93	04/15/97	$757.070	1		$46,464.670	95.42%
	05/16/97	$838.270	$39,519.400	7.71%	($2,230.460)	85.79%
94	04/15/97	$757.070	1		$46,464.670	95.42%
	05/16/97	$838.270	$39,519.400	7.71%	($2,230.460)	85.79%
95	07/02/97	$904.300	1		$14,955.770	93.03%
	07/09/97	$920.980	$8,098.160	1.58%	($1,120.100)	57.50%

the chapter. Certain tools are easily calculated while others are more complex. The combination of all of these tools will provide for a complete and thorough system evaluation. To assist in the evaluation process, we will use evaluation software packages co-developed by RINA Systems, Inc. and Omega Research Portfolio Maximizer™.

An evaluation process begins with a general overview of your system's performance. Once complete we progressively work toward more specific evaluation tools to determine the system's true trading characteristics. The entire evaluation process comprises of the following separate procedures:

- System analysis.
- Profit ratios.
- Return figures.
- Sliding and rolling summaries.
- Equity curve analysis.
- Total trades.
- Outlier trades.
- Drawdown/run-up.
- Consecutive trades.
- Time analysis.

System Analysis

We begin our evaluation with the bottom line. How profitable was the system during the trading period? Some traders believe that the bigger the profit, the better the system. Although important, net profit is only one measure of a system's worth. How a system makes its profit can, in certain instances, be far more important than its actual bottom line.

As an example, look at the results of the two trading systems in Table 9.2. System A made $350K while System B made $375K during the trading period. Although System A made $25K less profit, most traders would agree that it is still the better system. This is based on System A's consistent trading compared with System B's volatile trading. The pain and suffering associated with System B is simply not apparent from its final net profit.

Valuing a system's performance based solely on its net profit can be a mistake. With today's high-speed computers and advanced trading software, almost anyone can create a winning trading system. After a few optimization runs, almost any system will produce a positive net profit based on historical data. The hard part is designing a system that actually trades well in real time and that is not curve fit to maximize net profit.

The remainder of this chapter centers on evaluation tools that look beyond the bottom line. We will focus our attention on how a system generates its net profit based on multiple reward/risk measures. At the end of a systematic evaluation, a trader should be able to answer the following questions:

- Do you over- or underestimate your system's true performance?
- How stable are your winning and losing trades?
- What is your system's pessimistic reward/risk ratio?
- How many of your trades are statistical outliers?
- How does your system compare with a buy-and-hold strategy?
- What is the average run-up and drawdown for the system?

TABLE 9.2 ANNUAL NET PROFIT AND LOSS OF TWO SYSTEMS

	System A	System B
1990	50K	−50K
1991	50K	−100K
1992	50K	−100K
1993	50K	350K
1994	50K	−50K
1995	50K	275K
1996	50K	50K
Net profit	350K	375K

And most important . . .

- Do you really know your trading system well enough to trade it with complete confidence?

The next few sections will help traders answer these tough questions to fully quantify a system's true strength and weakness.

Profit Ratios

The following ratios use net profit as a building block for more detailed oriented evaluation tools. To fully appreciate the evaluation tools listed in Box 1, let's take a look at two trading systems. The systems in Table 9.3 made the same dollar amount but their ratios tell a slightly different story. System A had a higher Profit Factor, Adjusted Profit Factor, and Average Win/Average Loss than System B. With all things equal, System A is the more efficient trading system.

This analysis is based on reward/risk ratios. In this case, reward is measured by gross profit while risk is measured by gross loss. Each of the ratios listed in Box 1 uses these reward/risk measures as a basis for calculations. Theoretically, the higher the ratio, the more efficient the system.

Every trader wants to maximize profit; successful traders maximize profit in relation to risk. Profit ratios set a higher standard of evaluation by weeding out the inferior trading systems.

Return Measures

The next step in the evaluation process is reviewing trading performance based on return. Do the system's profits justify trading the system? These results allow for

---

Box 1

PROFIT RATIOS

Profit factor: Gross profit divided by gross loss. This calculation represents how much money was made for every dollar lost. Look for a system with a profit factor of 3 or more.

Adjusted profit factor: This tool artificially deflates winning trades and inflates losing trades. The net result is a more pessimistic profit factor. Look for a system with an adjusted profit factor of 2 or more.

Ratio avg. win/avg. loss: Average winning trade divided by average losing trade. Look for a system with a ratio of 2 or more.

TABLE 9.3 PROFIT RATIOS

	System A	System B
Net profit	$100,000	$100,000
Gross profit	$140,000	$180,000
Gross loss	$ 40,000	$ 80,000
Profit factor	3.50	2.25
Adjusted profit factor	2.75	1.25
Average win/average loss	2.33	1.50

easy side-by-side comparisons between systems. System returns can be measured in several ways (see Box 2 for more information).

Return on initial capital, also referred to as return on account (ROA), is the primary measure that best evaluates trading performance. It is calculated by dividing net profit by the system's initial starting capital. A system that makes $1,000 based on initial capital of $10,000 nets a 10 percent return. However, under the same conditions, if initial capital was $100,000, the same profit would only net a 1 percent return. To accurately compare the trading performance of systems running on the same historical price data, the same initial capital must be used. Surprisingly, traders often use different starting values in their comparison not realizing the inaccuracy of their evaluation.

A system's annual return also serves an important purpose in the evaluation process. It adjusts the return on initial capital figure and presents it as an annual figure. Judging performance on an annual basis creates an even playing field to compare trading systems.

Other return calculations relate the system to its own buy/hold return. If a system fails to outperform its own buy/hold return, then questions should be raised. For example, if a system trades 100 percent of the time and nets 15 percent in a year, is it good or bad? The answer actually depends on how the underlying security behaves in a simple buy-and-hold strategy. If the security buy/hold return nets 20 percent during

---

BOX 2

RETURN MEASURES

Return on initial capital: Net profit divided by the system's initial capital.

Annual return: Return on initial capital divided by the test period in years.

System return: Net profit divided by the initial purchase price expressed in percent.

Buy/Hold return: The most recent price divided by the initial purchase price.

the same time, then the system in question may not be as good as first thought. Under the same circumstances, if the system trades less than 100 percent of the time, then its performance is subject to interpretation. Less exposure to trading translates into less risk associated with trading the system. The importance of time evaluation is discussed later in the chapter.

Performance should not be valued based on a single return measure. All these return measures play a role in the evaluation process. The importance of each measure depends on the system and its style of trade.

Sliding and Rolling Summaries

This section expands on the general overview of a system's trading performance. In the previous sections, the evaluation tools measured performance of the test period from start to end. The next step is to examine the system over various *time periods* to assure consistent performance during the trading process. After all, what good is a net profitable trading system if a trader goes broke after an early major loss? Remember that consistency breeds confidence.

Trading summaries can be based on any time frame. However, this report will examine monthly and annual periods. This detailed evaluation flushes out hidden strengths and weaknesses not readily apparent in a general overview.

A trading summary can consist of the following evaluation methods:

- Sliding Analysis. Searches for pockets of strength or weakness by examining short periods of time, one after the other.
- Rolling Analysis. Searches for sensitivity to starting dates by examining trading periods with the same end date but with different starting dates.
- Equity Curves. A graphical illustration of the system's profit/loss performance over time.

The example of two trading systems will help illustrate the advantages of examining a system over various time frames. These examples will focus on annual data; if greater detail is required, we suggest a monthly breakdown. Intraday traders should use daily and hourly breakdown periods to assure a thorough evaluation.

Both systems in Table 9.4 generated the same net profit over the same time period; however, their paths were distinctly different. Based on annual sliding analysis, System A's profit taking was consistent and System B was volatile. Based on rolling analysis, if System B was tested only on data from 1993 through 1996, then its overall net profit of $600,000 would be three times as great as that of System A. Nonetheless, we know better than to put our money on B. After all, the largest rolling period shows both systems ultimately delivered the same net profit in a 7-year span. It is best to avoid systems that generate volatile trading results. At a minimum, traders should be acutely aware of past volatility and, therefore, better prepared to trade the system into the future.

TABLE 9.4 TRADING SUMMARY COMPARISON

| | *Annual Sliding Analysis* | | | *Annual Rolling Analysis* | | |
	System A	System B			System A	System B
1990	50K	−50K		90'–96'	350K	350K
1991	50K	−100K		91'–96'	300K	400K
1992	50K	−100K		92'–96'	250K	500K
1993	50K	350K		93'–96'	200K	600K
1994	50K	−50K		94'–96'	150K	250K
1995	50K	275K		95'–96'	100K	300K
1996	50K	25K		96'	50K	25K
Net profit	350K	350K		Net profit	350K	350K

Both sliding and rolling analysis could process other evaluation measurements, such as percent gain, profit factor, and percent profitable.

Equity Curve Analysis

Viewing a system's equity curve can provide additional insight into its performance (see Box 3). Equity curve charts tally a system's net equity on a trade-by-trade basis. Until a trader sees a system's equity curve, he or she will not have a big picture of system performance. A quick review of an equity curve chart can provide the necessary mental security to trade a system.

Equity charts come in a variety of formats. Each chart centers on the same basic information but presents the data in a different manner. Since traders often

---

Box 3
EQUITY CURVES

Equity curve line: Plots the closed realized net profit per trade without regard to time.

Detailed equity: Plots the mark-to-market net profit result per bar including flat or nontrading periods.

Monthly rolling equity: Plots the mark-to-market net profit result per month.

Average monthly equity: Plots the average net profit by month.

Underwater equity: Plots a monthly equity curve with an emphasis on the magnitude and duration of percentage drawdowns between equity peaks.

have different trading expectations, it is best to evaluate trading performance with multiple equity charts. Each of these five equity charts illustrates a different aspect of trading. Reviewing all these charts paints an evaluation picture not readily seen in other formats. Figures 9.1–9.5 show five of the more important equity curve charts.

Equity Curve Line

The equity curve line chart in Figure 9.1 presents trading performance on a trade-by-trade basis. This chart does not use time on its X-axis, but rather the trade number (1st trade, 2nd trade, etc.). This all-purpose equity chart is best used as a general snapshot of trading performance.

Detailed Equity Curve

The detailed equity curve in Figure 9.2 offers greater insight into trading performance than a general equity curve chart. This chart displays net profit on a bar-by-bar basis revealing full equity drawdowns and run-ups. Flat or nontrading periods are also shown to present a detailed overview of equity performance.

Rolling Period Equity Curve

The rolling period equity curve calculates realized or unrealized profits or losses at specific periodic times. For example, an end-of-month analysis is shown in Figure 9.3.

FIGURE 9.1 GENERAL EQUITY CURVE.

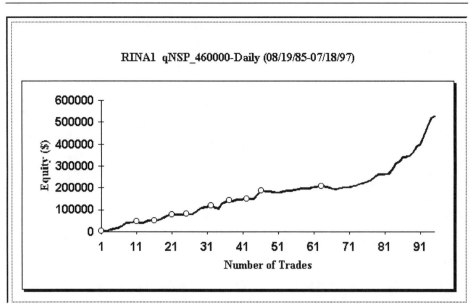

FIGURE 9.2 DETAILED EQUITY CURVE.

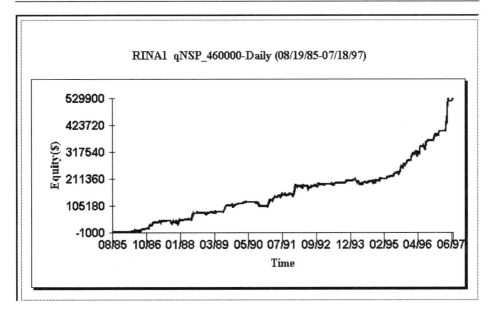

FIGURE 9.3 ROLLING EQUITY CURVE.

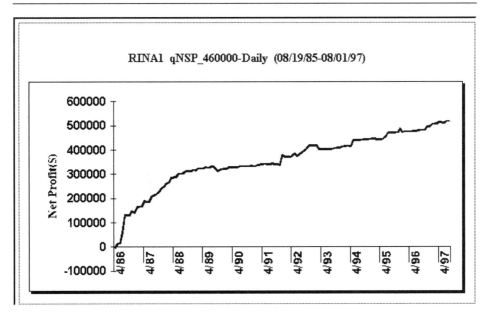

Underwater Equity Curve

The underwater equity curve serves as a pessimistic review of equity performance over time. Each bar above the zero line represents a new equity high based on monthly data. The negative curve between equity peaks represents the percent retracement from the previous high. In realistic terms, it details the pain and suffering experienced by the system over time. The duration and magnitude of monthly drawdowns are graphically illustrated in a single equity chart. Figure 9.4 is an example.[1]

Average Monthly Equity Curve

The average monthly equity chart is based on the system's individual monthly returns. The average return per month serves as a general seasonal overview of trading performance. Figure 9.5 is an example.

Total Trade Analysis

Unlike the general overview, this section fine-tunes the evaluation process and centers on the system's individual trades. The goal is to evaluate the overall performance of the system by critiquing each trade (see Box 4). This section centers on total trades; however, smaller subsets of trades should also be evaluated. These include winning and losing trades. Focusing on these trades separately helps to quantify the system's performance in even greater detail.

FIGURE 9.4 UNDERWATER EQUITY CURVE.

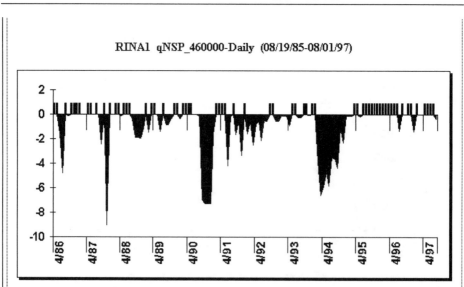

FIGURE 9.5 PROFITS PER TRADE.

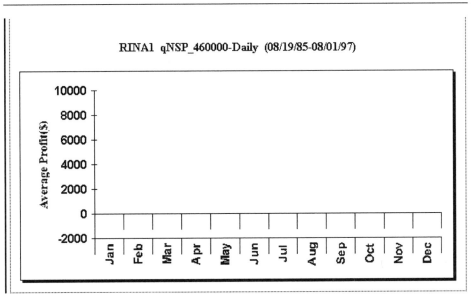

RINA1 qNSP_460000-Daily (08/19/85-08/01/97)

Special Note: The more rules used by a system, the greater its degrees of freedom (DoF). DoF represents the amount of flexibility a mathematical formula has in attempting to model data. To keep your trading system from modeling rare, mostly unrepeatable events, keep its DoF as small as possible and the data set as large as possible. Design your system to be as simple as you can reasonably make it and use as much historical data to test your system as you can.[2] The goal of having a large data set is to get your system to produce as many trades as possible in order to be statistically meaningful. Too few trades and the system could just be profitable on a fluke of the market that may never reoccur.

Box 4

TOTAL TRADES

Average trade: The average profit/loss for all the trades.

Standard deviation (STDEV): Measures the absolute variability of the returns of all of the trades. The smaller the number, the less deviation there is between trades.

Coefficient of variation: Expresses the standard deviation as a percentage of the mean. This percentage figure relates to the stability of the trades.

We begin our evaluation of total trade analysis by comparing the results of two systems. Superficially, both systems in Table 9.5 appear to be the same, with identical figures for net profit, total number of trades, and average profit per trade. Beneath the surface, however, lies a different story.

The numbers in Table 9.5 measure the volatility of the average trade. The greater the volatility the less stable the average. Both systems have the same average $2,000 profit per trade. The trades associated with System A fluctuate in a tight range around its average. Range is measured here by the standard deviation of the trades' profits. Based on its standard deviation of $714, the profit range for System A is from $1,286 ($2,000 − $714) to $2,714 ($2,000 + $714). System B on the other hand has a standard deviation of $5,335, which translates into an average trade that ranges between $7,335 and ($3,335). These are dramatically different numbers for systems that appear to be the same. The net result: System A is the more stable system.

The systems can also be evaluated based on their coefficient of variations. This statistical measure is similar to standard deviation; the smaller the figure, the more stable the trades. Coefficient of variation (CV) is calculated in a percentage format allowing for easy interpretation between systems. CV is the standard deviation of a variable (e.g., profit per trade) divided by the average value of the variable:

$$CV = 100\% \times Standard\_Deviation/Simple\_Average$$

Look for systems with coefficient of variations of 200 percent or less. Numbers larger than this indicate instability and should raise your concern.

It is easy to get lost in these numbers. Sometimes it is best to review these statistical results in a graphic format. Figure 9.6 plots individual profits per trade from a new hypothetical system. Notice the clustering of data points as trades deviate little from the average. The only exceptions were trades 92, 93, and 94. These trades are considered to be outliers, to be discussed in greater detail in the next section. Despite these outlier trades, the standard deviation and coefficient of variation for this trading system were $8,761.50 and 162.30 percent respectively (see Table 9.6). These low values reflect a system that is extremely stable in relation to its average. This high degree of stability breeds trading confidence.

TABLE 9.5 TOTAL TRADE COMPARISON

	System A	System B
Net profit	$100,000	$100,000
Total trades	50	50
Average trade	$ 2,000	$ 2,000
Standard deviation	$ 714	$ 5,335
Coefficient of variation	35.71%	266.78%

FIGURE 9.6 PROFITS PER TRADE.

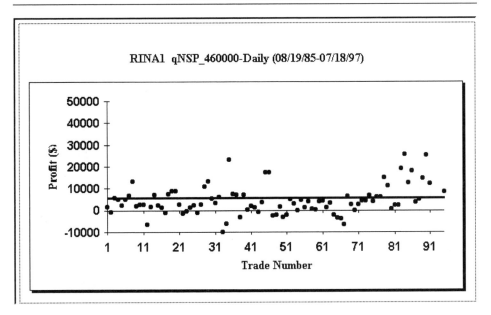

TABLE 9.6 TOTAL TRADE ANALYSIS

Total Trade Analysis

Number of total trades	95	Total stopped trades	0
Average trade	$5,398.49	Avg. trade ± 1 STDEV	$14,159.99 / ($3,3
1 Std. Deviation (STDEV)	$8,761.50	Coefficient of variation	162.30%
Run-up			
Maximum Run-up	$46,464.67	Max. Run-up Date	5/15/97
Average Run-up	$9,079.35	Avg. trade ± 1 STDEV	$18,115.44 / $43.2
1 Std. Deviation (STDEV)	$9,036.08	Coefficient of variation	99.52%
Drawdown			
Maximum Drawdown	($23,614.63)	Max. Drawdown Date	7/16/96
Average Drawdown	($4,544.12)	Avg. trade ± 1 STDEV	($16.19) / ($9,0
1 Std. Deviation (STDEV)	$4,527.92	Coefficient of variation	99.64%
Reward/Risk Ratios			
Largest Loss Ratio	52.73	Max. Drawdown Ratio	21.72
Adj. Largest Loss Ratio	44.67	Adj. Max. Drawdown Ratio	18.40

◄ ► System ╱ Annual ╱ Monthly ╱ Win | Loss ╱ Time ╱ Notes ╱   ◄ ►

Table 9.6 also lists the standard deviation and coefficient of variation values for the systems run-up and drawdown calculation, to be explained in greater detail in the next few sections.

Outlier Trades

This section centers on outlier trades. Outliers have some unusual property, such as excessive profit or loss (see Box 5). The amount of excess is measured by the number of standard deviations away from the typical (average) value. For example, if a system's average profit is $200 per trade and the standard deviation is $50, then a trade that produces $400 profit would be $((400 - 200) / 50)$ or 4 standard deviations from average.

Outliers are usually considered to be 3 or more standard deviations from average. Essentially, they are aberrations that cause system results to be unfairly positively or negatively biased. By removing outlier trades from the evaluation process, a new net profit figure can be calculated. This new select net profit figure, devoid of all aberrations, *may* offer a cleaner, more realistic trading perspective. Obviously, trend-following systems designed to accept numerous small losses to capture the infrequent big move rely on outliers to be profitable. Therefore, whether or not it is better to remove outliers requires some thought.

In general, systems that are heavily dependent on outlier trades have artificially inflated or deflated net profit results. Since outlier trades generally do not reoccur on a regular basis, they should be removed to present a more realistic trading perspective. The goal is to find a system with a select (nonoutlier) net profit figure worthy of trading.

A trading system with a few outlier trades is shown in Table 9.7. In this example, the system had a few positive outlier trades that boosted system profits. Although the system's select net profit figure is still presentable, it does make a trader think twice about the system. Is the system worth trading if it only generates $408,635 in profit without outlier trades as compared with its original $526,610? Only the individual trader can answer that question.

Box 5
OUTLIER TRADES

Select net profit: Net profit minus outlier trades.

Positive outliers: Trade values that exceed the average trade by plus three (3) standard deviations.

Negative outliers: Trade values that are less than the average trade by three (3) standard deviations.

TABLE 9.7 OUTLIER ANALYSIS

Net profit	$526,610
Positive outlier trades	117,975
Negative outlier trades	0
Select net profit	$408,635

Drawdown/Run-up

Trading in real time is far different from watching at the sidelines. Unless a trader actually lives through an adverse trading experience, it is difficult to say how he may react. It is therefore wise to evaluate profits and losses separately to get a clearer view of how much "pain" we may need to endure. To help us along, risk/reward tools evaluate a system's profitability in relation to risk. In the simplest terms, drawdown represents various measures of loss (risk), while run-up represents measures of reward (profit).

Drawdown

We will begin our discussion with drawdown. The measure of drawdown can be calculated in several ways: largest loss, maximum adverse excursion, average drawdown, largest consecutive losing series, or maximum equity loss. No matter what definition is chosen, drawdown must be calculated to gauge trading risk. If a trader is unwilling to accept the historical risks associated with a system, then the system should not be traded. Traders have a tendency to believe that major drawdowns will never occur while they are trading. A more realistic approach would be to believe that not only will it happen again, but also drawdowns may be even more severe in the future. Evaluating systems from this pessimistic point of view will help prepare traders for worst-case scenarios.

Depending on the definition of drawdown, a variety of risk numbers can be calculated (see Box 6). Each form of drawdown caters to a different personality type or trading style. There is no one correct calculation; they are all correct.

We will begin our discussion of drawdown with largest loss. This simple drawdown calculation represents the largest realized loss experienced by the system. Traders should be willing to accept this type of loss as a part of normal trading.

A better measure of drawdown is maximum adverse excursion (MAE).[3] MAE can be calculated in a number of ways. In this discussion, we will cover two formats. The first represents the single largest unrealized loss experienced by a system. The second MAE calculation averages each individual trade's largest unrealized loss. Essentially, this average adverse excursion figure (i.e., average drawdown) measures the typical risk experienced by the system.

BOX 6

DRAWDOWN

Largest loss: The largest losing trade for the test period.

Maximum adverse excursion: The largest unrealized loss based on the ultimate low for long positions or high for short positions during the trade.

Average drawdown: The addition of drawdowns for all individual trades divided by the total number of trades.

Largest consecutive losing series: The largest consecutive losing series for the test period.

Maximum equity drawdown: The largest equity dip during the test period, as measured from the highest running equity value to the lowest.

Figure 9.7 plots the individual MAE for each trade. The high of each bar represents the trade's realized profit or loss at the close of the trade. The low of each bar represents the largest unrealized loss during the trade (i.e., the largest drawdown for the trade). Realized profit or loss is the difference between the exit and entry price, less commission costs. It is the real amount of money you will either gain or lose. Unrealized profit or loss is calculated from the price roller coaster ride that occurs during a trade. This movement does not affect you unless you are required to pay up on a margin call.

Using Figure 9.7 as a reference, the system's largest realized loss of $9,726 occurred on trade number 33. However, the trade with the largest MAE occurred on trade number 88 with an unrealized loss of $23,614. Curiously, this same trade actually reversed its unrealized loss to net a profit of $4,498 at the close of the trade. The average drawdown figure for this system is $4,544. This is basically the pain that a trader should expect to experience every time a trade is initiated. This is not to say that every trade will experience this unrealized loss, but preparing for it will put a trader in the correct frame of mind to literally feel comfortable trading this particular system. If a trader is reluctant to follow a system based on any of these drawdown tools, then he should look for another system.

The first set of drawdown tools center on individual trades. To complete the evaluation, we offer two additional drawdown figures that focus on a series of trades. A system's largest consecutive losing series and maximum equity drawdown are great measures of drawdown over time. They are easy to calculate and focus the trader's attention on the bigger picture—the ability to continue to trade over time. A string of small losses may cause just as much pain as a single large loss. The largest consecutive losing series for the system reviewed in Figure 9.7 lost a total of $15,389 in four

FIGURE 9.7 PROFIT AND LOSS DRAWDOWN.

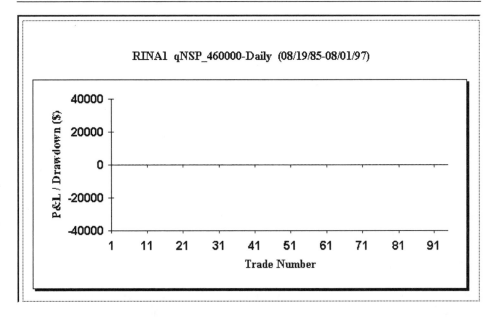

RINA1 qNSP_460000-Daily (08/19/85-08/01/97)

consecutive trades: 64–67. The largest loss for the same system amounted to $9,726. Four little losses can produce greater pain than one large loss.

A series of multiple losses can have a greater influence on trading confidence then any single loss (see Table 9.8). In the example, the maximum equity drawdown of $31,900 is more than twice the largest consecutive losing series. The more forms of drawdown calculated, the better prepared the trader will be for trading into the future. As with all drawdown measures, if the figures exceed the trader's threshold of pain, simply avoid the system.

Run-up

Traders have a tendency to overestimate their trading results by viewing their system from an optimistic point of view. The goal of this section is to temper this

TABLE 9.8 DRAWDOWN ANALYSIS

Largest loss	$ 9,726
Maximum adverse excursion	$23,614
Average drawdown	$ 4,544
Largest consecutive losing series	$15,389
Maximum equity drawdown	$31,900

optimism and quantify each trade's profit objectively. The best way to measure this performance is with a calculation called run-up. Essentially *run-up is the opposite of drawdown.* If drawdown looks for trading low points, then run-up centers on the high points.

Run-up can be calculated in several ways: largest gain, maximum favorable excursion, average run-up, largest consecutive winning series, or maximum equity gain. Each definition represents a different form of reward (see Box 7).

The largest gain is the trade that makes the most money during the trading period. Does this trade justify trading the system? That depends on whether the system was designed to rely on outliers. In general, the largest gain should not exceed 20 percent of net profit.

Another measure of run-up is maximum favorable excursion (MFE).[4] This form of run-up is the reverse of maximum adverse excursion (MAE) as mentioned in the previous section. MFE can be calculated in two formats. The first represents the single largest unrealized gain experienced by a system. The second MFE calculation averages each individual trade's largest unrealized gain. These calculations combined with the largest gain paint a general picture of reward for the system.

Figure 9.8 plots each trade's individual MFE. The high of each bar represents the trade's largest *unrealized* gain during the trade. The low of each bar represents the trade's *realized* profit or loss. The reader may want to verify that unrealized gain is never less than realized profit or loss. Using Figure 9.8 as a reference, the system's largest gain and MFE occurred, coincidentally, on trade number 93.

A system's largest consecutive winning series and maximum equity run-up round out our discussion of run-up. They are easy to calculate. The largest consecutive winning series for the system reviewed in Figure 9.7 gained a total of $43,999. The largest single gain for the same system was $39,519 (see Table 9.9).

Since a system can have many run-ups and drawdowns, it is possible to evaluate the standard deviation of each as well as the coefficient of variation (CoV). The CoV

Box 7

RUN-UP

Largest gain: The largest profitable trade for the test period.

Maximum favorable excursion (MFE): The largest gain based on the ultimate high for long positions or low for short positions during the trade.

Average run-up: The average MFE figure for each individual trade.

Largest consecutive winning series: The largest consecutive winning series for the test period.

Maximum equity run-up: The largest equity increase during the test period, as measured from the lowest running equity value to the highest.

FIGURE 9.8 PROFIT AND LOSS RUN-UP.

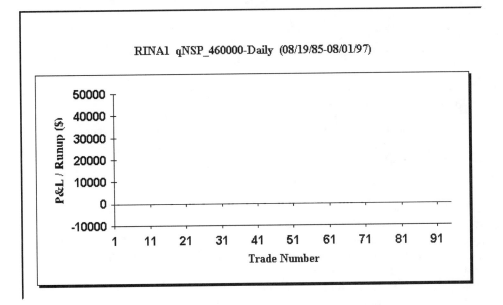

RINA1 qNSP_460000-Daily (08/19/85-08/01/97)

for run-ups and drawdowns should be 150 percent or less. Values greater then this have a tendency to generate inconsistent results when used with money management techniques.

Reward/Risk Ratios

Reward/risk ratios center on a system's profitability in relation to risk. Theoretically, the larger the ratio the better the system.

The previous section on drawdown and run-up sets the stage for a few simple yet powerful ratios. Countless ratios can be created, but in this discussion we will center on only three (see Box 8). Each formula attempts to critique performance on a risk-adjusted basis. They are simple to calculate and extremely informative. All too

TABLE 9.9 RUN-UP ANALYSIS

Largest gain	$ 39,519
Maximum favorable excursion	$ 46,464
Average run-up	$ 9,079
Largest consecutive winning series	$ 43,999
Maximum equity run-up	$528,776

BOX 8

REWARD/RISK RATIOS

Largest loss ratio: Largest loss divided by net profit. Look for a ratio of 0.1 or less.

Max drawdown ratio: Maximum adverse excursion (MAE) divided by net profit. Look for a ratio of 0.1 or less.

Average run-up/drawdown ratio: Average run-up divided by average draw-down. Look for a ratio of 1.5 or more.

---

often, individual traders center on risk or reward calculation never bothering to combine the two into a simple ratio.

Two trading systems are shown in Table 9.10. Although System A made $100,000 more than System B, the additional profit does not justify the risks associated with its trading. Based solely on these simple ratios, System B is the better of the two systems because its profitability was much more risk averse. *Reward/risk ratios point out that sometimes less profitable systems can be more desirable.*

Consecutive Trades

Short-term trading confidence, or a lack thereof, often stems from the number of consecutive winning and losing trades produced by a system. After a winning streak, you can become overly confident and believe that your system is infallible. Conversely, after a few losing trades, you may become easily discouraged, risk averse, and perhaps even reluctant to trade. In either case, *the trading principles behind your system have remained constant, while your perception of the system has changed.* By tracking the performance of consecutive trades, you can gain additional insight into the personality of your system and thereby trade with greater confidence.

This discussion of consecutive trade analysis begins with a definition. A streak is defined in this chapter as a sequence of only winning or only losing trades that occur

TABLE 9.10 REWARD/RISK ANALYSIS

	System A	*System B*
Net profit	$1,000,000	$900,000
Largest loss ratio	0.12	0.03
Max drawdown ratio	0.20	0.07
Average run-up/drawdown ratio	1.00	2.00

in consecutive order. The winning or losing streak ends when a trade results in a gain or loss in the opposite direction of the series. Calculations based on consecutive series data can produce two very powerful evaluation tools:

1. Average gain (or loss) of a winning (or losing) streak.
2. Average gain or loss for the trade that ends the streak.

The first calculation takes an average net gain of all winning streaks or an average net loss of all losing streaks. In general, the more winning (or losing) trades there are within a streak, the larger the magnitude of the streak's average performance. This measurement can determine a system's profitability during periods of extended strength or weakness.

The second calculation centers on the average return for the trade that ends the streak. This figure can determine how abruptly a system reverses its course of action after a consecutive series of wins or losses. We like to end a streak with a small loss or large gain. Therefore, a small losing reversal is preferred for ending a winning streak, while a large winning reversal is preferred for ending a losing streak.

Table 9.11 shows the consecutive winning series for a real trading system used by the author. All numbers in this table are quoted in S&P 500 Index points. This system generated a number of consecutive winning trades, and as expected, the longer the streak, the larger the average net gain. In addition, notice the inverse relationship between the average streak gain and the loss size of the trade that ends the streak. As the average streak's net gain increased, the loss size of the ending trade decreased. An explanation for this is that a system that trades exceptionally well has most likely found its preferred trading zone, and it would be unusual for a system that is trading "red hot" to immediately turn "ice cold." Consequently, the system ends its winning streak with a relatively small loss. *This is the mark of a well-designed system.* Knowing a system's historical tendency during and after a consecutive series of trades will help you build confidence in your trading system.

TABLE 9.11 CONSECUTIVE WINNING SERIES

Streak Size	Number of Streaks	Average Net Gain	Average Loss of Next Trade
1	4	9.40	−4.15
2	3	8.48	−2.44
3	1	25.64	−2.21
4	2	30.05	−1.65
5	2	31.67	−1.12
6	0		
7	0		
8	1	31.99	−0.42

To put this into a real world trading perspective, consider the following true story.

An investor, after months of comparing trading services, finally decided to subscribe to a trading service with an impressive track record. The service was in the midst of a small winning streak, making the investment decision all the easier. As time passed, the service continued to extend its winning streak. The investor, thrilled with these results, felt reassured in his decision to subscribe to the service. After a few more winning trades, the investor began to feel a little uneasy, knowing that all winning streaks must eventually end. As the winning streak persisted, the investor completely centered his attention on the next losing position. The more the service won, the more uncomfortable the investor became. Eventually the investor, consumed with fear of a major loss, decided to pull out of the service. When asked why the investor had left the service, the response was "Why wait for a major loss?"

The only thing that changed in this case was the investor's perception. Trading logic did not dictate that the next losing trade had to be a major loss. If the system had been evaluated using the consecutive series data in the first place, then the investor would have been better prepared to trade using this system. *Fear of the unknown always weighs heavier in our mind than that which is known.* Preparing for the unknown begins with a thorough system evaluation.

Time Analysis

This section centers its evaluation strictly from the standpoint of time in or out of the market. The longer a position is exposed to the market, the more risk it assumes. This form of analysis can be used on the entire system or on individual trades (see Box 9).

Box 9

TIME ANALYSIS

Total time in the market (periods): The time in which the system is actually trading.

Percentage of time in the market: The total time in the trades divided by the total time for the test period (in a percentage). If a system trades more then 80 percent of the time, make sure its reward/risk ratios are in line with other comparable systems. Time in the market is another measure of risk.

Longest flat period: This figure notes the longest period in which the system did not trade. Consider this to be a patience factor. Note that the longer the flat period the more patience a trader must possess to follow the system.

TABLE 9.12 PERCENTAGE OF TIME IN THE MARKET

	System A	*System B*
Net profit	$100,000	$100,000
Percent-in-the-market	60%	100%

Table 9.12 shows a simple side-by-side comparison of two trading systems. We can evaluate them based on percent-in-the-market.

With all things equal, and with time as the only variable, System A made its profits in 40 percent less time in the market than System B. This smaller exposure to the market translates into less risk and ultimately, a more efficient trading system. If you were to account for the interest earned on the idle cash position, then System A becomes the clear winner. By factoring time into the evaluation process, traders will improve their overall understanding of a system and its true performance.

Time can also be used in the evaluation of a system's individual trades. These calculations serve as historical reference points, especially useful for option traders where time to expiration is a critical factor in evaluating price.

Table 9.13 shows the results of a trading system that remains in an average trade for approximately 10 days and is then idle for about 48 days. This information should be used to compare open (in the market) positions to the system's historical tendencies. Trading action may be required, should the duration of the open position strongly deviate from the average. This type of review increases trading confidence in the underlying position.

These calculations can also reveal potential system design flaws. Although the intended trading strategy may be correct, your system's design may not match the time-based trading results. For example, the numbers in Table 9.13 reflect a trading strategy that trades in short-term spurts. If the system had been originally designed as a longer-term, trend-following system, then the design would definitely have a problem.

Quite often the difference between a professionally evaluated system and a quick review performed by a novice investor is the use of time. If traders are going to profit in the real world, they must factor time into their evaluation.

TABLE 9.13 TIME ANALYSIS

Time-in-the-market	561
Percent-in-the-market	17.96%
Longest flat period	163
Average time in trades	9.84
Average time between trades	47.80

CONCLUSION

The historical profitability of a system is not enough to justify its trading. Greed and fear affect every trader. This chapter laid groundwork for measuring aspects of a trading system that will likely affect greed and fear. The more that the trader can learn about a system in the evaluation stage, the more confidence the trader will have trading it real time.

No matter how profitable a system appears, if a trader does not have the intestinal fortitude to follow it, he or she should look for another system to trade.

Fear of the unknown always weighs heavier in our mind than that which is known. Preparing for the unknown begins with a thorough system evaluation. Test first—trade second.

During long run-ups and drawdowns, the trading principles behind your system remain constant; it is your perception of the system that changes.

At the end of a systematic evaluation a trader should be able to answer the following questions:

- Do you over- or underestimate your system's true performance?
- How stable are your winning and losing trades?
- What is your system's pessimistic reward/risk ratio?
- How many of your trades are statistical outliers?
- How does your system compare to a Buy-and-Hold strategy?
- What is the average run-up and drawdown for the system?
- Do you really know your trading system well enough to trade it with complete confidence?

ENDNOTES

1. Schwager, Jack, For additional information on underwater equity curve, see *Schwager on Futures: Technical Analysis,* John Wiley & Sons, 1995.
2. Jurik, Mark, For further insight into the phenomenon of degrees of freedom (DoF), see "Developing Indicators for Financial Trading," in *Virtual Trading,* Probus, 1995.
3. Sweeney, John, For a discussion of maximum adverse excursion (MAE), see *Campaign Trading,* John Wiley & Sons, 1995.
4. Ibid.

Why Test?

- System performance must be viewed in light of all three parameters: profitability, drawdowns, and stress. Before you consider opening up a trading account, are you sure your system is reliably profitable? Will drawdowns wipe you out first? Is it trading in a way you can tolerate? Can you go for long periods of no trading, or too much trading? The only way to know is by subjecting your system to extensive backtesting.

- The more thoroughly you test your system in advance, the less stressful your trading session will be. Does your system perform better than buy and hold or a random buy/sell process? How does it compare with a fixed rate, no-risk investment? Is system performance sensitive to precise values for its parameters? Will a slight change cause a significant decrease in profits? Is system performance on out-of-sample data significantly poorer than on in-sample data?

- Backtesting will help you pinpoint which approaches to the market are likely to be successful and which ones are not. It will also produce a record of your system's historical trading performance, necessary for developing a diversified asset allocation strategy.

- Testing your system requires skill because sloppy testing makes it easy to convince yourself you have a "winning system" despite its flaws. For example, to have a meaningful evaluation, your system should produce a statistically significant number of trades, at least 100. A small number of trades, no matter how perfect, is easy to produce and nearly impossible to reproduce.

General Procedure

- If there is enough data to do so, in-sample data should be completely separate from out-of-sample. Better still, create a third set that can be used in conjunction with the in-sample set to build, test, and reject preliminary systems. This way, the optimization process of building and testing runs without the out-of-sample data. Lastly, any system that passes the preliminary build-and-test phase is then subjected to out-of-sample data for final analysis.

- Whether you should include outlier trades in your test results depends on your strategy. For example, a system designed to suffer lots of small losses while waiting for big, rare, profitable breakouts depends on outlier trades. Removing outliers from that scenario will portray a losing system, which in reality may not be the case at all.

- After you backtest your system on historical data, I advise a round of forward-tests to measure its real time performance. Various brokers are willing to set up an account to let you simulate trading.* This will help you answer questions about slippage and timeliness as well as help you master the skill of placing trades.

- When designing a mechanical system, remember that all systems eventually fail, so you will need to periodically update the trading strategy.

Measurements

- System analysis measures overall net profitability. This is important, as no one will trade a system expected to lose money. However, do not let this be your only consideration. Reward/risk ratios point out that sometimes less profitable systems can be more desirable.

- Of all the profit ratio measurements available, I find profit factor (PF) to be the most useful. It tells me how many dollars I gain for each dollar I lose in trading. Don't consider a system whose PF is less than 2.

- The annual return on account (AROA) is another favorite measure of mine. It is the ratio of a year's net profits to the total cost of placing those trades in that year (i.e., margin costs + maximum drawdown), averaged across all the years the system was tested.

- Instead of averaging AROA, list the ratio for each year in a table. This sliding window method illuminates any particularly bad years, giving you the opportunity to analyze a system weakness.

- The Markowitz/Xu data mining correction formula adjusts your estimate of a system's average daily return by considering the number of systems that were run through the out-of-sample set.

- The coefficient of variation is a good way to measure, for comparison purposes, the steadiness or consistency of a system's trade-by-trade performance. Look for systems with coefficient of variations of 200 percent or less. Larger numbers indicate instability and should raise your concern.

---

*TradeComp International *(www.tradecomp.com)*, Larax Software *(www.larax.com)*, and AudiTrack *(www.auditrack.com)* permit simulated trading.

PART III

Assessing the Market and Yourself

Trading in the real world can be very stressful. One big loss may be so unnerving that you will be tempted to begin overriding your trading system's recommendations. Further losses ensue, followed by more stress and overrides. Once that spiral starts, it is downhill all the way. To avoid this emotional trap, Chapter 10 presents important tasks that you, not your system, should perform. You will discover how to enter a trading session with a clear mind, why you should create a financial objective large enough to be uncomfortable, and how to separate trading events from your emotional reactions.

After you learn how to create and apply basic indicators, the next step is to create trading zones that quantify market behavior. This may facilitate your selecting one type of trade over another. Chapter 11 presents two new methods for quantifying market behavior: zone analysis and subsequent performance analysis. The author also briefly covers basic issues regarding system testing and evaluation.

One of the more exciting ideas to come along this past few years is trading on sliding time scales. That is, you start your trade using 5-minute charts and gradually scale up to daily charts. Chapter 12 shows how you can control risk with a few basic rules and formulas for assessing the best bar length and trading interval that corresponds to a predetermined level of risk exposure.

One of the best known ways to lower risk is to diversify. Chapter 13 goes beyond discussing market diversification and carries the philosophy to time frame and system diversification as well. The advantages and shortcomings of modern portfolio theory are also reviewed. Lastly, the author presents a method for safely increasing the complexity of your trading system.

CHAPTER 10

Trading to Win:
The Psychology of Trading

ARI KIEV, M.D.

For the past 30 years, I have been involved in developing stress management and personal empowerment programs for individuals experiencing stresses or challenges in their lives. In the past 6 years, I have developed a training program for traders designed to reduce stress and maximize trading performance. This program is a proactive approach based on the application of certain fundamental principles of goal directness, self-monitoring, and a willingness to manage emotional responses. To tap the trader's potential for creativity and flexibility, the program centers around a conscious commitment to specific financial objectives, development of a flexible trading strategy, and adherence to money management and risk control rules.

At weekly seminars, I help groups of traders identify habitual trading patterns and the underlying thoughts associated with them so that they can implement practical steps necessary for trading in line with their goals. The critical distinction is in teaching traders to separate trading events from their own interpretations and emotional reactivity so that they can see the repetitiveness of their behavior, which causes them to repeat the past and remain in performance plateaus year after year. However motivated, it takes considerable time and effort for traders to get past their resistance to self-examination and personal change and to become conscious of their own decision-making processes and habitual actions. However, they must do this to recognize when they are trading compulsively and to act more consistent with their trading objectives.

The principles of my proactive approach teach traders to see how their trading is colored by their perceptions and their past experiences. They encourage traders to refine their awareness of their own perceptions so as to get closer to appreciating reality as it is. Successful traders remember past trades, good and bad, and are careful to differentiate between what happened and what they think happened. They continually seek to tell the truth about their trades, to mark their day's results to the market so that they can see what they did and differentiate that from what they felt. They do this so that in the future they are governed by the facts and their relationship to what they did. In this way, they correct their daily experiences so that their memories are clear, and they move forward with corrected perceptions about the market.

165

PROMISING THE RESULT

A critical aspect of proactive trading is to make a conscious commitment to a financial objective greater than what you are accustomed to achieving. You must do what it takes to realize this objective. This means relinquishing any inclination to trade in terms of comfort and safety, to bypass self-doubts in response to the uncertainty of the marketplace, and to allow your choice of price, volatility, and size of positions taken to be guided by parameters commensurate with your goals. The trading objective provides a lens for trading experientially rather than in terms of habits or fears. The conscious decision to follow a proactive strategy, rather than passively waiting for market or trade trends to govern decisions, allows traders to stretch beyond their habitual stopping points.

Committed traders do not allow their emotional reactivity to limit their trading, nor do they retreat at the first setback. They recognize when their old habits and fixed notions come into play, especially in a negative market, but do not allow them to influence their decisions as long as their original decision remains tenable.

It is important to recognize that an unconscious expectation of failure may hold you back from being as committed and successful as you can be. One trader I know, named Ben, routinely hesitates to buy a stock at the very moment he recognizes its potential. Invariably by the time he buys, the stock has made 50 percent of its move. This delay in acting is often followed by public self-flagellation that draws attention to his failure. If he is to grow as a trader, Ben must relinquish his "dance of failure" which lets him be "right" about being "wrong."

Another trader, Phil, was dominated by memories of "crashing and burning" and was afraid to use larger amounts of his trading capital to buy and hold volatile stocks. Slowed by his chronic fears of disaster, he had to learn that the manifestations of anxiety were identical to those of excitement. He had to learn to ride out the anxiety and take greater risks by putting in larger orders of higher priced stocks and using more of his allocated capital in line with his strategic objectives. In effect, traders must learn to notice the impact of their unconscious fears and expectations on their trading behavior and use their discomfort to empower them to make conscious choices based on their stated goals.

THE VALUE OF PROACTIVE TRADING

To succeed, traders must separate their comfort needs and defensive responses from trading reality. The proactive approach encourages traders to relinquish their preoccupation with losses that may lead to a negative spiral. If no buyers are willing to take traders out or if a rush of sellers occurs, proactive traders can begin to look for new opportunities without becoming so focused on getting their money back that they use all their effort in fruitless activities.

Proactive trading is a useful standard against which to identify conservative responses to uncertainty. Proactive trading is especially valuable in times of adversity when most people are taken out of their games by their own reactivity and self-protective responses. Rather than be governed by their own cautious responses to trading dilemmas or market downturns, proactive traders continually assess whether they are utilizing an appropriate amount of capital or need to trade larger or more volatile positions. In the process, they are more willing to embrace the inherent paradox of excitement and discomfort associated with taking risks.

CENTERING

Centering, or entering into a meditative state of consciousness, is one of the most critical skills for reducing anxiety and tension and decreasing the impact of distracting stimuli. It helps you distance yourself from the sequence of emotional responses and negative interpretations of stressful and unsuccessful trades that trigger panic, denial, rationalization, and avoidance—all of which perpetuate the circle of failure.

By recognizing the automatic nature of your negative thinking, you can turn off your self-doubt and self-criticism and adjust your behavior to respond to events in a disciplined way. Centering lets you turn off fearful, automatic thoughts that project negative images onto events. Centering reduces misinterpretation by minimizing distractions and the inclination to focus on past mistakes or worry about future events. It leads to increased control over the autonomic nervous system enabling you to stretch objectives and the tape action with a minimum of preconceived notions and fears.

One of the best illustrations of the centering process is demonstrated in archery where any tension created by trying to control anxiety will be reflected in the tension applied to the bow and the arrow at the moment of release. Thus, the skilled archer allows thoughts to pass through his mind without reacting to them so that they do not interfere with his actions. The best shots occur when the arrow is released effortlessly.

Being centered enables you to commit to a specific trading objective and then maintain sufficient discipline to follow your trading strategy rather than be disturbed by fears of losing, which may lead you to trade too cautiously. Once centered, you are able to follow the market trend, cut your losses, and let your profits run. Most important, you can follow your own rules and not keep trying to explain your results in terms of market vagaries.

Through centering, your greatest asset is your ability to control your own actions. You will learn that uncertainty is more an internal factor than a factor in the marketplace, that your internal concept of the marketplace influences your interpretations of events and trading decisions. As such, you find value in maintaining a centered state so that your fears and emotional reactions to market fluctuations do not influence your trading.

Through a conscious process of centering, which also can occur spontaneously when it is called "being in the zone," you can choose to break the endless loops of destructive trading. When you are centered, you are better able to continue to follow your trading strategy, despite carrying a continuing loss. You can be more proactive in pursuing your own concepts and are not afraid to climb aboard a trade after it has begun rather than assume it has reached its limit. You do not have to be "first" to a trade or certain of the outcome before trading. You are able to be less emotional and reactive and can focus more narrowly on your trades. You are confident about your decisions and do not dwell on past errors. If you are a day trader, you are assiduous about marking your profits and losses daily. You are able to expand as you succeed and not shut down if you lose. You are willing to cut your losses rather than ride them out to avoid admitting to them.

Stress and Trading Success

Stress is a natural response to uncertain events. The stress response, which is associated with an increased flow of adrenaline, increases alertness to stimuli and enhances performance. The stress response prepares you physically and psychologically to trade by increasing blood flow to the brain, increasing your capacity for memory retrieval and your ability to handle complex situations in which stocks are moving in unpredictable patterns. The stress response can enhance your ability to concentrate on the tape, observe your own internal trading signals, and maintain your pace and strategy in the face of conflicting signals. Emotional arousal can also keep you from getting bored if things are slow, from being distracted if things are hectic, or from being paralyzed or confused if your positions are dropping precipitously.

Beyond the optimum level of stress, however, stress responses become negative and are experienced as anxiety associated with declining performance. Fear intensifies the stress reaction, which in turn may lead to distraction and errors. Negative memories from the past may be reactivated leading to fear of failure or criticism, misinterpretation of data, and misinterpretation of your own responses. This may be followed by further anxiety, decision paralysis, and a retreat to a comfort zone of defensive trading.

To keep stress responses within reasonable limits, most traders learn to trade within a comfortable range. When the stressed trader approaches a range that is uncomfortable, rather than hold on to or increase a position in a rising stock to maximize profits, he may sell too soon to take a quick profit. While most traders tend to be better at cutting their losses than extending their profits, some may hold on to losing positions too long, hoping that their positions will reverse rather than acknowledging their loss. Others, afraid of duplicating past market disasters, may panic at any hint of failure. They may engage in elaborate self-induced ruses to avoid acknowledging their losses and may end up losing far more than they would have had they sold out when they first realized their positions were failing.

As anxiety mounts, you may become fearful and uncertain and second-guess your decision. You may become depressed and convinced you are destined to failure, especially in the face of significant profits or losses. Numerous fears come into play when trading beyond the psychological comfort zone, irrespective of your performance. These fears include fear of losing and disappointing others, fear of shame and embarrassment for not succeeding, and fear of making errors and looking bad. For some, fears of going broke or trading beyond the comfort zone are related to anxiety about attaining positive results and competing with others.

Different situations present different challenges and trigger different reactions. Some traders have trouble accepting success and experience significant anxiety as their profits rise, often sabotaging themselves as soon as their profits exceed certain amounts. Most traders also agree that they lose more often when they worry about losing. This may be related to performance anxiety.

PERFORMANCE ANXIETY

Mental errors produced by anxiety can lead to increased tension, narrowing of attention, and yet more errors. Anxiety may cause traders to neither respond effectively to incoming data nor rely on internal models to recall past successful patterns. As a trader, any increase in anxiety may distract you from the stock activity you are following and lead to excessive focusing on your own internal bodily reactions, further increasing your anxiety.

Efforts to reduce anxiety, paradoxically, may create a new set of programmed responses that can undermine trading flexibility. These can be temporary or permanent handicaps to good performance or to the capacity to keep growing and improving as a trader. These behaviors may be adaptive temporarily in the present, but once they become fixed patterns they have a rigidity of their own. As a trader, you must maintain a certain level of consciousness about what you are doing, so that you can keep adapting to new circumstances rather than continuing to repeat what you have just learned to do.

Typical symptoms of performance anxiety include palpitations, difficulty breathing, distractibility, muscle tension and cramps, noise sensitivity, severe hand trembling, and loss of appetite. These symptoms usually recede as trading begins. Indeed, performance anxiety seems to occur mostly before and after the trading day, not so much during it. The better the trader, the more he or she can tune these negative thoughts out and fine-tune excessive stress responses to focus all his or her professional skill on the task of trading.

STOPPING POINTS IN TRADING

The stopping point is the whole sequence of events, reactions, interpretations, and automatic decisions that may keep you from being fully engaged in trading opportunities. You may rationalize your position because it appears to be consistent with your goals, when in fact it may be a cover for a life principle of risk avoidance.

All trading is influenced by lifelong beliefs and habits that are operating for you when you trade. It is important to consider these distinctions. To the extent that your trading is dominated by long-standing life principles you may not be maximizing your opportunities. Instead, you may be limited or stopped by your underlying assumptions of the world.

Traders can be stopped for a day or longer by their fearful automatic thoughts of losing, which may be consistent with their self-concept. Such fear leads to the misinterpretation of events, greater distractibility, and the inclination to focus on past mistakes or to worry about future events. In this state of mind, traders cannot analyze the market and plan their trading objectives clearly.

Such traders often buy small volumes of numerous low beta-stocks or trade more stocks than they can handle. Their knowledge of stocks and their continued failure to play up to their abilities perpetuate a self-image of being "bright losers," which may be a reenactment of a central emotional theme from childhood. Some of these overly cautious traders are afraid to use all their own market assessments. Paradoxically, some won't buy a stock if others are in it because they do not want to be thought of as being a "follower" or being "late to the party."

Trading to win is to risk going beyond the familiar and to enter the zone of uncertainty. A stopping point prevents these traders from committing to their trading objectives and maintaining sufficient discipline to follow a winning trading strategy.

Trapped by their own anxiety, these stopped traders are unable to follow the market trend, cut their losses, or let their profits run. They are unable to follow their own rules and have trouble recognizing that their greatest asset is their ability to control their own actions. The stopped trader does not recognize that his fears and emotional reactions to market fluctuations significantly influence his trading.

Some traders are stopped by their egotism. They are often aggressive but inflexible and unwilling to admit error. They may be able to ride out considerable pain and uncertainty on the way down to make a profit by selling short, but are unable to switch positions and take a long position on the same stock when it reverses direction. They may be stopped by the same conviction that enables them to stay short for a long time, and they may lose all profit on the upside that they made on the downside.

Beneath this inflexibility is a false sense of self based on past successes. After bad days, one trader I know looked back to his successful choices to demonstrate he was right in his perception. He defended himself by having a self-concept as a home-run hitter who had a "few" bad days. He blamed his precipitous losses on "bad luck," tended to avoid preparation, and got in too soon and out too late. He was easily influenced by criticism and kept seeking approval, while simultaneously rebelling to gain reassurance. His stopping point is his need to receive support and approval, his inability to acknowledge support when it is given, and his inclination to blame his failure on the advice of others.

Another pattern of egotism can be seen among contrarians who refuse to use stop losses. An erroneous sense of their own ability prevents them from developing flexibility. Their sense of self repeatedly asserts, " That's the way I am and always will be." They are invariably frustrated because their self-concept (which they believe is not modifiable), not their trading strategy, governs their trading.

KNOW YOUR STOPPING POINTS

Recognizing your own stopping points is the first step to managing fear and building trading discipline. Traders may find it difficult to relinquish old habits because doing so means acting contrary to their underlying negative self-concepts. While this may be rationalized as the fear of failure, it is really the fear of change. These traders are afraid to commit to a larger objective.

The second step is to ask yourself a series of questions about whether you are functioning in terms of your potential:

- Are you willing to let go of the life principles that keep you from learning new trading techniques?
- Are you willing to define a larger trading objective and strategy and then commit to trading in those terms?
- Are you willing to record entry and exit points as well as a stop point for the trades you want to make?
- Are you willing to mark your profits and losses to the market so you know where you are at the end of the day?
- Are you willing to analyze your trades to see what strategic elements are missing from your unsuccessful trades?
- Are you willing to develop parameters of measuring your performance so you know what you need to do?

Stopping points keep traders from maximizing their results. To overcome these stopping points, you must begin to view market events as neutral and learn to handle them in terms of your conscious objectives, not in terms of old beliefs. Remember, the *stopping point is that point in time where your fears and beliefs keep you from entering fully into the next moment and keep you trading in repetitive and possibly destructive patterns.*

RECOVERY FROM THE LAST TRADE

Trading is a complex activity that requires increasing self-correction in the face of ever-changing market conditions. To reach trading mastery, you must learn how to recover from previous trades, profitable or not, to relinquish the emotional impact of your most recent success and failures, and to focus on upcoming trades. This entails learning psychological skills designed to access the mind-set of successful trading.

Relaxation or meditation is particularly useful in quieting the mind of self-doubts and focusing positively on the next moment. For example, tennis players begin their recovery process by shifting their racquets to their nonplaying hands between points. Then they walk back from the net consciously adopting a confident posture associated with a positive mental image to create a winning mind-set and reduce negative reactions to past events.

Traders can also pay special attention to their bodily preparation. Tighter muscles lead to tension, slowed reflexes, and diminished ability to visually track and assess the movement of rapidly moving stocks. Shortness of breath may reduce endurance, hamper concentration, and trigger panic attacks. With relaxation and deep breathing exercises, you can master these anxious responses and enter into a calm, meditative state so that you can access past, positive memories and prepare yourself to enter the "zone." These affirming memories recreate your sense of purpose and help build a positive set of expectations that will increase your ability to take calculated risks in following your trading strategy.

Recovery also requires that you implement steps consistent with your trading strategy, such as deciding on the number of shares you need to trade to realize specific objectives and measuring parameters to track your performance. You also can measure your efficiency in terms of your ability to generate a certain return relative to the amount of risk you are willing to take. With experience in controlling your downside risk, for example, you may be able over time to trade bigger while maintaining the same degree of risk. Using this kind of productivity/risk measure, you should be able to determine whether you are taking appropriate risks with your capital, without being so risk-adverse as to miss significant opportunities for profitable trading.

SYSTEMS TRADING

The goal-directed strategies that comprise the essence of a trading-to-win approach should, in general, be at the core of systems trading. Ideally, the systems model enables you to trade in terms of a specific objective or financial target and to boil down market action into a formula or strategy, built around your own trading principles, rules, and assumptions. It enables you to test your hypotheses against historical data before and after you start trading. Given a large enough historical database to cover all situations, this approach assumes that the market is not time bound and that whatever happens reflects some new combination of past events, so that when you actually implement your trading strategy you are not caught off balance.

Systems programs are especially designed to maximize your capacity to concentrate on the most critical variables and to keep expanding your trading volume consistent with the best strategy for realizing your objectives. Systems programs help to quantify the different risk/reward opportunities in the marketplace by giving you a spread of information to track performance and determine the extent to which you are following your model.

The development and application of such a model is less stressful for the systems trader who, in contrast to the discretionary trader, does not need to focus as much attention and energy on being centered and focused in the face of stress, or on mastering self-doubt and other emotional responses. These human responses are inherently resolved in systems trading by your capacity to handle more information exponentially, which increases your control over future choices.

While systems programs provide you with a layer of distance between your decisions and emotions, they do not relieve you of the responsibility for the consequences of your decisions. You must still endure the ups and downs of trading, especially if you are emotionally reactive. System programs also do not eliminate problems that result from their limitations of flexibility and the false expectations that people sometimes impose on them.

SYSTEMS TRADING AND STOPPING POINTS

A systems model is particularly well designed to assist in bypassing many of the stopping points that are built into the personalities of traders. To the extent that the result is built into the programming strategy, the system can bypass the stopping points that interfere with clear thinking and strategic implementation.

Systems trading ignores the emotional response to a loss that often leads traders to start thinking about failure the moment they experience a loss. In so doing, the system offers freedom from the human response whereby thoughts of failure set in motion a self-fulfilling prophecy of failure.

Systems trading also bypass emotional responses to winning trades. The system does not react emotionally to successful trades, which eliminates the chance of having losing days follow profitable days as occurs for so many discretionary traders. Systems trading allows you to overcome any personal tendency to play below your potential or hold back out of fear of success.

MAINTAINING YOUR RATE OF RETURN AS YOU EXPAND

Systems traders look at subtle below-eye-level phenomena with measurable variables and follow a rigorous discipline of testing their signals in the laboratory before ever using them. Discretionary traders learn from experience and spend little time testing hunches in a systematic way in a laboratory. They are more flexible and opportunistic and do not systematically approach the entire market the same way each time.

The best discretionary traders are pattern recognition machines who employ much historical experience, intuition, current information, and the like in a complex system designed to forecast the stock trajectory. First-rate discretionary traders are better under a greater variety of situations than computerized programs because of their greater adaptability to changing markets. Computer, quantitative programs, however, can handle more data and more trading rules. Each model has an expected rate of return and a set of rules tested on historical data that enable you to ratchet up the rate of return by defining specific expectations and decision elements and then calculating the size you must trade to meet that expectation.

Discretionary traders are more volatile and less predictable but perhaps better equipped to adapt their style to short-term market fluctuations and other events that give them a trading edge. Accustomed to rapid shifts in response to rapid changes, discretionary traders who may use systems models to enhance their own trading, are often inclined to modify their systems without modeling them, or override their systems without knowing it. As might be expected, they tend to have higher error rates than the more disciplined systems traders who are committed in principle to adhere to their models and tend to rely almost totally on their systems to trade.

Systems traders develop experience in the laboratory, testing the effects of different hypotheses on the data that they have and testing their hypotheses on historical data. In doing this work, they must learn to pay special attention to biases, transaction costs, and the need for simulations to match reality. As such, they must test hypotheses with data from many different markets. This laboratory testing period can be stressful. Traders may lose time while testing the system and may also discover when they are ready to use the strategy that because the markets have changed, it may not work.

However, an advantage of systems trading is that you have more data to inform you. If your simulations are making money and you are losing money in your trading, you can look to see whether something in your model dropped out of your trading. You can also keep testing to see what you need to add to your model. You can ask easily answered questions and control the process of trading without the stress and emotional responsivity that distract so many discretionary traders from their objective.

Systems trading is perfectly designed for proactive trading. You can establish specific trading objectives and criteria, and you can keep measuring your performance to ensure that all of the relevant data is available and scientifically examined and measured in terms of your hypotheses.

But systems trading is not without its problems. In addition to technical failures, insufficient testing of the simulation model, and lack of congruence between the simulation model and reality, systems do not entirely insulate you from your own emotional reactivity to the success and failure of your trades. By deciding in advance of trading which principles to follow and knowing assumptions of the system, it is easier to make decisions based on your system's computations.

Systems traders lack the flexibility of discretionary traders in their day-to-day execution of orders. One trader described the working realities of systems trading as if he were in a "foxhole with no time to relax." "I have to keep working to make my statistics work out," he said. "I cannot miss a trade which may make my whole day by taking time off to take a break."

Systems traders are trading in a narrow range and must pay close attention to the system's signals, or they run the risks of missing a trade. Their opportunities are limited, and they must keep trying to execute well by paying attention and trying to minimize costs by getting good prices and reducing slippage. They cannot take a day off or change the instruments they are using if they are having a bad day. They have less control over the implementation of their prescribed strategy. The ability to keep to their strategy is thus both a strength and at times a weakness of systems traders. On the other hand, discretionary traders have greater flexibility, but perhaps less ability to determine what they have been doing right and what they have been doing wrong.

The evolution of systems programs involves progressive development of designs for making more effective systems, the capacity for making quantum leaps and expanding incrementally, and then suddenly plateauing and going from plateau to plateau. Systems designers must evolve over time. Unlike discretionary traders who have less comparable competition and who cannot be so readily modeled, systems programs can be readily stolen or modeled to the extent that different designers are working on similar issues and problems. While the systems trading cannot be reverse engineered, it can be copied by putting together bits of information about what the systems trader seems to be interested in. System traders have additional stresses such as development problems, security problems, problems associated with keeping their system going, and all the problems associated with developing the software needed for running the system and keeping it updated.

Systems traders can benefit from learning how to turn off self-doubt, manage stress, and stay focused in pursuing the testing and implementation of their system. The same issues would hold for:

- Ramping up.
- Making decisions about when to extend themselves and to exploit their system fully.
- Deciding when they have developed enough data to implement a system.
- Dealing with the stress of discovering that what worked in the laboratory does not always immediately apply to the real world.

Some traders, especially beginners, may bring erroneous and magical expectations to systems trading. One false expectation is that the system will do your work and relieve you of responsibility for results. If you are a perfectionist, you may spend too much time looking for a systems model to help you to decide on which stocks to trade, when to trade, and when to get out. While such a system might definitely provide a sense of security about making the right trades, the perfectionist runs the risk of postponing actual trading so that he doesn't develop skill in trading.

In actual fact, while systems can collect and analyze large quantities of data, they cannot make your decisions. You have to call the markets, decide when to place your order, and whether to buy on the bid or on the offer. You have to take responsibility for missing a trade or the slippage in executing a trade. In fact, you are never free of the responsibility for how your trading goes. You must make an effort to understand the assumptions of your system and when it is time to go back to the laboratory to test them.

Moreover, in systems trading, it is axiomatic that you do the trade based on the system's signal rather than overriding it and following your hunches. If you are committed to the system, you may have to do things that are counterintuitive, and therefore stressful, at those times when you believe the system may be wrong.

When you develop a system program by simulating events without knowing how the system will work in the real world, you want to do enough simulations so that you can predict what your profit will be based on the size of your sample. If you do not do this, it can be extremely stressful. You cannot know if reality will confirm your simulations until you step into the unknown and test them.

More stress can occur if the system's trading rules are not compatible with your personality. You may have difficulty holding on to a position because of your need to scalp or trouble getting out of a position given a predisposition to hold dropping stocks. You may also find it stressful to hold as many positions as the system allows you to hold, because of a need to be in control of all your trading and discomfort in having to delegate some of these functions to a system. This sometimes gives rise to an urge to override the system, but the best systems traders prefer to stop trading and try to improve the program rather than override it.

THE USE OF SYSTEMS BY DISCRETIONARY TRADERS

Some traders use systems programs to measure volume as a percentage of price, sorting data by highs and lows, positives and negatives. Systems are useful for confirming the value of a trade in a stock with a good story, for confirming perspectives, and generating new ideas. They are particularly useful when a good stock is trading poorly and you cannot find an explanation. The systems program enables you to analyze more data than you can by yourself. It watches all 3,000 stocks at once and sometimes comes up with recommendations on stocks you have not followed for years. This system is less accurate in certain other situations such as a secondary, a buyback, an arbitrage, or overseas stock where the ratio may get "messed up."

Reliance on systems trading can help traders by providing a more accurate picture of the market than they might get ordinarily, especially in stressful situations where they might be inclined to misperceive the system's program trend in the market. In this sense, it can give discretionary traders a greater sense of confidence about what is happening and what they ought to do. A systems program keeps traders in the right type of market, days and weeks, where their inclination might be to get out.

Conversely, in a market at an all-time high, where the market is becoming resistant and starting to turn around and catching traders flatfooted, a systems program may help a discretionary trader to get out when he might be inclined to wait before selling.

If you are a discretionary trader with sufficient time energy and inclination, you can develop a systems model that will give you signals that will fit your style. When you build your own, you know its assumptions and can build in the parameters and corrections you want. It can be especially valuable, if you are a master trader, to build a program around some of your own trading perspectives. Your program could, therefore, alert you to more opportunities while multiplying the extent to which it is gathering and analyzing information about more stocks along the lines of your most successful criteria and choices.

In general, though, it would be difficult to model all the rules of the expert trader, and it certainly would not be able to model your intuition very well or your capacity to do the innovative, uncomfortable things when you are in the zone. As a discretionary trader, you can factor many more things into your system that others do not know about or cannot figure out and can, therefore, develop your own niche in the marketplace.

The use of system programs is often motivated by a desire to reduce anxiety levels and to take the emotion out of trading decisions. Discretionary traders often turn to such programs to increase their sense of confidence about their decisions. Nevertheless, when some traders go beyond their comfort levels, they may at times feel compelled to override their computer signals resorting to old ways of trading in the face of stress.

CONCLUSION

One of the big advantages of a systems program is the ability to maintain attention to the marketplace and a consistent degree of flexibility not subject to fluctuations in fears and emotions. It is always able to assess incoming data, with the same dispassionate perspective as has been built into it, and it does not freak out when things go contrary to plans. If you are using such a system, you only need to be able to make decisions about the information and analysis gathered and presented by it.

Such a program does not get depleted of energy and develop fatigue, depression, and errors. It does not lose capacity to focus on events by being preoccupied with its own internal, psychological state. Its data acquisition and reasoning capabilities are not vulnerable to the distortions of anxiety and can keep mental errors down to a minimum. Systems programs do not anticipate repeated failure that intensifies anxiety and throws off performance.

The great virtue of computerized programs is their steadfastness under dramatically changing and unpredictable market conditions. Again, this is one of the best reasons to supplement your trading with a systems program. Unlike the human trader, the computer can treat each trade independently and is not constricted by negative or repetitive thoughts from the past that predict and produce poor performance.

REFERENCE

Kiev, Ari, *Trading to Win: The Psychology of Mastering the Markets,* New York: John Wiley & Sons, 1998.

CHAPTER 11

Quantifying a Market's Upside and Downside Potential

TIMOTHY W. HAYES

If you are setting out to become a serious trader, you can seek to use a subjective approach that lends itself to trading decisions based on myriad opinions and gut emotions, or you can seek an objective approach that instills discipline into a trading system. The latter is the less risky option, and potentially the more rewarding.

But if handled incorrectly, the objective approach can mislead you into thinking that your system is helping you make money, when in fact it is leading you astray. When the quantification process fails to deliver, instead producing misleading messages, the subjective approach is no worse an alternative—a misguided quantification effort can be worse than none at all. The predicament is how to make your quantification efforts truly pay off in the form of more profitable trading.

A good starting point for testing and optimization is to understand the potential pitfalls in each step of the process. You must also decide the time frame you want to focus on. Are you interested in day trading or only a few trades a year? You must also identify your level of risk tolerance—how much risk are you willing to take, and for how much reward? And you must decide how you will use the indicators that result from your testing. You may decide to combine your indicators into composite models, a "weight-of-the-evidence" method that would reduce the risk of big losses if an individual indicator were to go awry. Or you could use the signals as individual inputs for fine-tuning your model-based trading decisions.

This chapter will start with the issues to keep in mind when embarking on the optimization process, and it will then take a closer look at several methods of quantifying market performance following indicator signals.

Adapted from "The Quantification Predicament," Ned Davis Research. Used with permission. In recognition of this essay, the author was the recipient of the 1996 Charles H. Dow Award. Sponsored by Dow Jones Telerate, the Market Technicians Association, and *Barron's,* the award recognizes "an outstanding original work or a significant extension of a previously known work that best expounds on the principles of technical analysis." The author's original essay detailed the need to quantify technical indicators and determine their value and role in a truly objective market outlook. He has adapted it here for the trader interested in the basics on testing and optimization.

THE CONCERNS

There are several reasons quantification must be handled with care. The initial concern is the data used in developing the indicators. If it is inaccurate, incomplete, or subject to revision, it can do more harm than good, issuing misleading messages about the market that is under analysis. The data should be clean and contain as much history as possible. When it comes to data, more is better—the greater the data history, the more numerous the like occurrences, and the greater the number of market cycles under study.

This leads to the second quantification concern—sample size. The data may be extensive and clean, and the analysis may yield an indicator that foretold the market's direction with 100 percent accuracy. But if, for example, the record was based on just three trades, the results would lack statistical significance and predictive value. In contrast, there would be few questions regarding the statistical validity of results based on more than 30 observations.

The third consideration is the benchmark, or the standard for comparison. The test of an indicator is not whether it would have produced a profit, but whether the profit would have been any better than a random approach, or no approach at all. Without a benchmark, "random walk" suspicions may haunt the results.[1]

The fourth general concern is the indicator's robustness, or fitness—the consistency of the results of indicators with similar formulas. If, for example, the analysis would lead to an indicator that used a 30-week moving average to produce signals with an excellent hypothetical track record, how different would the results be using moving averages of 28, 29, 31, or 32 weeks? If the answer was "dramatically worse," then the indicator's robustness would be thrown into question, raising the possibility that the historical result was an *exception* to the rule rather than a good *example* of the rule. An indicator can be considered "fit" if alterations of the formula would produce similar results.

Moreover, the nonrobust indicator may be a symptom of the fifth concern, and that is the optimization process. Much has been written about the dangers of excessive curve fitting and overoptimization, often the result of unharnessed computing power. As analytical programs have become increasingly complex and able to crunch through an ever-expanding multitude of iterations, it has become easy to overoptimize. The risk is that armed with numerous variables to test with minuscule increments, a program may be able to pick out an impressive result that may in fact be attributable to little more than chance. The accuracy rate and gain per annum columns of Figure 11.1 compare results that include an impressive-looking indicator that stands in isolation (top) with indicators that look less impressive but have similar formulas (bottom). One could have far more confidence using an indicator from the latter group even though none of them could match the results using the impressive-looking indicator from the top group.

What follows from these five concerns is the final general concern of whether the indicator will hold up on a real-time basis. One approach is to build the indicator

FIGURE 11.1 RESULTS FROM HYPOTHETICAL INDICATOR TESTS.
THE FIVE RESULTS IN THE TOP HALF OF THE TABLE SHOW ONE WITH
OUTSTANDING PERFORMANCE, WHILE ALL FIVE IN THE BOTTOM HALF OF
THE TABLE HAVE SIMILAR PERFORMANCE.

SUMMARY RESULTS FROM HYPOTHETICAL INDICATOR TESTS

These results contain an impressive-looking EXCEPTION to the rule ...

Number of Trades	Moving Average (Periods)	Buy Level	Sell Level	Accuracy Rate (%)	Gain/Annum (%)
40	70	100	110	50	11.2
39	71	99	111	50	11.3
37	72	98	112	65	15.1
37	73	97	113	52	10.1
36	74	96	114	50	9.8

These results would all be good EXAMPLES of the rule ...

50	20	15.6	8.6	55	11.8
49	21	15.8	8.4	56	12.0
48	22	16.0	8.2	56	12.1
47	23	16.2	8.0	57	12.1
46	24	16.4	7.8	56	12.0
Buy-Hold Gain/Annum					6.3

and then let it operate for a period of time as a real-time test. At the end of the test period, its effectiveness would be assessed. To increase the chances that it will hold up on
a real-time basis, the alternatives include out-of-sample testing and blind simulation.
An out-of-sample approach might, for example, require optimization over the first
half of the date range and then a real-time simulation over the second half. The results
from the two halves would then be compared. A blind-simulation approach might include optimization over one period followed by several tests of the indicator over different periods.

Whatever the approach, real-time results are likely to be less impressive than the
results for the optimization period. The reality of any indicator developed through
optimization is that, as history never repeats itself exactly, it is unlikely that any optimized indicator will do as well in the real-time future. The indicator's creator and user
must decide how much deterioration can be lived with, which will help determine
whether to keep the indicator or go back to the drawing board.

TRADE-SIGNAL ANALYSIS

With these general concerns in mind, the various quantification methods can be put to use. The first, and perhaps most widely used, is the approach that relies on buy and sell signals, as shown in Figure 11.2. When the indicator meets the condition that it deems to be bullish for the market in question, it flashes a buy signal, and that signal remains in effect until the indicator meets the condition that it deems to be bearish. A sell signal is then generated and remains in effect until the next buy signal. Since a buy signal is always followed by a sell signal, and since a sell signal is always followed by a buy signal, the approach lends itself to quantification as though the indicator was a trading system, with a long position assumed on a buy signal and closed out on a sell signal, at which point a short position would be held until the next buy signal.

The method's greatest benefit is that it reveals the indicator's accuracy rate, a statistic that is appealing for its simplicity: all else being equal, an indicator that had generated hypothetical profits on 30 of 40 trades would be more appealing than an indicator that had produced hypothetical profits on 15 of 40 trades. Also, the simulated trading system can be used for comparing other statistics, such as the hypothetical per

FIGURE 11.2 VALUE LINE COMPOSITE SHOWING BUY AND SELL SIGNALS.

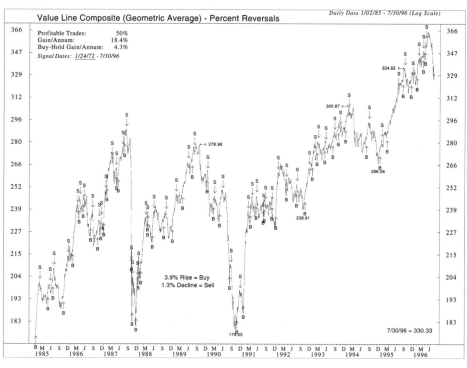

Source: Ned Davis Research. Used by permission.

annum return that would have been produced by using the indicator. The per annum return can then be compared with the gain per annum of the benchmark index.

But the method's greatest benefit may also be its biggest drawback. No single indicator should ever be used as a mechanical trading system—individual indicators should instead be used as tools for interpreting market activity. Once the most reliable indicators are identified, they should be combined into models that can offer increased reliability for dictating trading actions.

The drawback is the tendency to make little or no distinction between the hypothetical and the actual. The signal-based method does not specify actual records of real-time trading performance. If they were, the results would have to account for the transaction costs per trade, with a negative effect on trading results. Figure 11.3

FIGURE 11.3 TOP HALF OF CHART SHOWS HOW MUCH PROFIT IS MADE TRADING ON THE SIGNALS IN FIGURE 11.2 WHEN NO COMMISSION COSTS WERE CONSIDERED. THE BOTTOM HALF SHOWS HOW JUST A ¼% TRANSACTION COST CAN SIGNIFICANTLY REDUCE PROFITS.

SUMMARY RESULTS FOR INDICATOR IN FIGURE 11.2
-- NO TRANSACTION COSTS

VALUE LINE GEOMETRIC $627,079   1/24/72 - 7/30/96

LAST	PROFIT	NUMBER	DAYS	GAIN	BATTING	MODEL	BUY/HOLD	$10,000
SIGNAL	CURRENT	OF	PER	PER	AVERAGE	GAIN PER	GAIN PER	INVESTMENT
"Sell"	TRADE	TRADES	TRADE	TRADE		ANNUM	ANNUM	
5/07/96	6.1%	240	37	1.9%	50%	18.4%	4.3%	$627,079

Maximum Drawdown: -4.68%

SUMMARY RESULTS FOR INDICATOR IN FIGURE 11.2
-- INCLUDING TRANSACTION COSTS OF 1/4 PERCENT PER TRADE

VALUE LINE GEOMETRIC $189,425   1/24/72 - 7/30/96
LAST	PROFIT	NUMBER	DAYS	GAIN	BATTING	MODEL	BUY/HOLD	$10,000
SIGNAL	CURRENT	OF	PER	PER	AVERAGE	GAIN PER	GAIN PER	INVESTMENT
"Sell"	TRADE	TRADES	TRADE	TRADE		ANNUM	ANNUM	
5/07/96	5.6%	240	37	1.4%	45%	12.7%	4.3%	$189,425

Maximum Drawdown: -4.68%

summarizes the indicator's hypothetical trade results before and after the inclusion of a ¼ percent transaction cost, illustrating the impact that transaction costs can have on results. The more numerous the signals, the greater the impact.

Also, as noted in the results, another concern is the maximum drawdown, or the maximum loss between any consecutive signals. But again, as long as the single indicator is for perspective and not for dictating precise trading actions, indicators with trading signals can provide useful input when determining opportune periods for entering and exiting the market in question.

Several other testing methods can also be used to confirm a trading signal, supporting the case for market strength or weakness. A buy signal, for example, could be confirmed by a bullish-zone reading from an indicator that uses zone analysis.

ZONE ANALYSIS

In contrast to indicators based on trading signals, indicators based on zone analysis leave little room for doubt about their purpose—they do not even have buy and sell signals. Rather, zone analysis recognizes black, white, and one or more shades of gray. It quantifies the market's performance with the indicator in various zones, which can be given such labels as "bullish," "bearish," or "neutral" depending on the market's per annum performance during all the periods in each zone. Each period in a zone spans from the first time the indicator enters the zone to the next observation outside the zone. Unlike the signal-based approach, the indicator can move from a bullish zone to a neutral zone and back to a bullish zone. An intervening move into a bearish zone is not required.

Zone analysis is therefore appealing for its ability to provide useful perspective without a simulated trading system. The results simply indicate how the market has done with the indicator in each zone. But this type of analysis has land mines of its own. In determining the appropriate levels, the most statistically preferable approach would be to identify the levels that would keep the indicator in each zone for roughly an equal amount of time. In many cases, however, the greatest gains and losses will occur in extreme zones visited for a small percentage of time, which can be problematic for several reasons:

1. If the time spent in the zone is less than a year, the per annum gain can present an inflated picture of performance.
2. If the small amount of time meant that the indicator made only one sortie into the zone, or even a few, the lack of observations would lend suspicion to the indicator's future reliability.
3. The indicator's usefulness must be questioned if it is neutral for the vast majority of time.

A good compromise between optimal hypothetical returns and statistical relevance would be an indicator that spends about 30 percent of its time in the high and low zones, like the indicator in Figure 11.4. For an indicator with more than four years of data, that would ensure at least a year's worth of time in the high and low zones and would make a deficiency of observations less likely. In effect, the time-in-zone limit prevents excessive optimization by excluding zone-level possibilities that would appear the most impressive based on per annum gain alone.

Another consideration is that in some cases, a closer examination of the zone performance reveals that the bullish-zone gains and bearish-zone losses occurred with the indicator moving in particular directions. In those cases, the bullish or bearish messages suggested by the per annum results would be misleading for a good portion of the time, as the market might actually have had a consistent tendency, for example, to fall after the indicator's first move into the bullish zone and to rise after its first move into the bearish zone.

It can therefore be useful to subdivide the zones into rising-in-zone and falling-in-zone, which can have the added benefit of making the information in the neutral zone more useful. This requires definitions for "rising" and "falling." One way to define those terms is through the indicator's rate of change. In Figure 11.5,

FIGURE 11.4 DOW JONES INDUSTRIAL AVERAGE (DJIA) AND AN INDICATOR WITH APPROXIMATELY 30 PERCENT OF ITS TIME IN THE HIGH AND LOW ZONES.

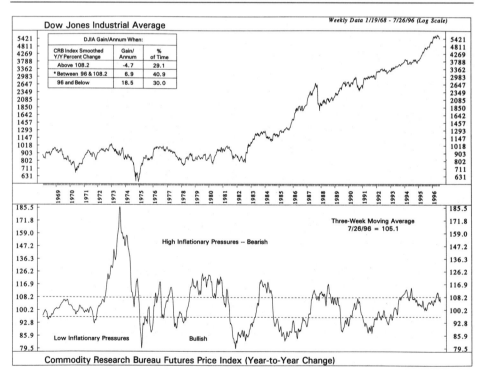

CRB Index Smoothed Y/Y Percent Change	Gain/ Annum	% of Time
Above 108.2	-4.7	29.1
* Between 96 & 108.2	6.9	40.9
96 and Below	18.5	30.0

Source: Ned Davis Research. Used by permission.

FIGURE 11.5 STANDARD & POOR'S (S&P) 500 STOCK INDEX WITH "BIG MO" STOCHASTIC INDICATOR. THE PERCENT GAIN PER ANNUM OF THE MARKET IS BETTER CLASSIFIED WHEN THE INDICATOR'S DIRECTION AS WELL AS LOCATION IS CONSIDERED.

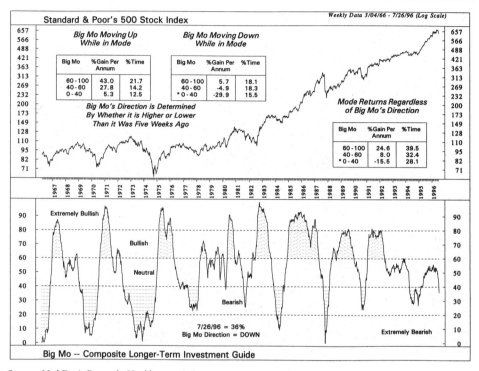

Source: Ned Davis Research. Used by permission.

which applies the approach to the primary stock market model used by Ned Davis Research, their "Big Mo" indicator is "rising" in the zone if it is higher than it was five weeks ago and "falling" if it is lower. Again, the time spent in the zones and the number of cases are foremost concerns when using this approach.

Alternatively, "rising" and "falling" can be defined using percentage reversals from extremes, in effect using zones and trading signals to confirm one another. In Figure 11.6, for example, the CRB (Commodity Research Bureau) Index indicator is "rising" and on a sell signal once the indicator has risen from a trough, whereas it is "falling" and on a buy signal after the indicator has declined from a peak. Even though the reversal requirements resulted from optimization, the indicator includes a few poorly timed signals and would be risky to use on its own. But the signals could be used to provide confirmation with the indicator in its bullish or bearish zone, in this case the same zones as those used in Figure 11.4. For example, in late 1972 and early 1973 the indicator would have been rising *and* in the upper zone, a confirmed bearish message. The indicator would then have peaked and started to lose upside

FIGURE 11.6 DJIA AND CRB INDICES. CHART SHOWS DJIA'S
ANNUAL GAIN AS A FUNCTION OF CRB'S ZONE LOCATION.

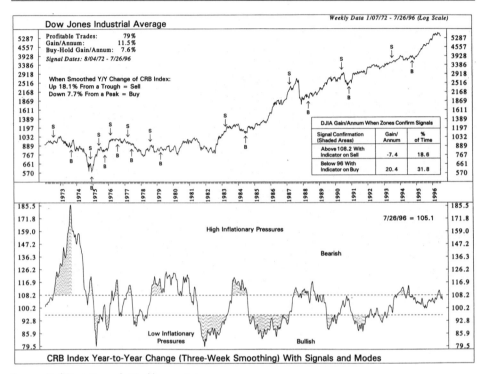

Source: Ned Davis Research. Used by permission.

momentum, generating a "falling" signal and losing the confirmation. That signal would not be confirmed until the indicator's subsequent drop into its lower zone.

The chart's box shows the negative hypothetical returns with the indicator on a sell signal while in the upper zone, and on a buy signal while in the lower zone. In contrast to the rate-of-change approach to subdividing zones, this method fails to address the market action with the indicator in the middle zone. But it does illustrate how zone analysis can be used in conjunction with trade-signal analysis to gauge the strength of an indicator's message.

SUBSEQUENT PERFORMANCE ANALYSIS

In addition to using signals and zones, results can be quantified by gauging market performance over various periods following a specified condition. In contrast to the trade-signal and zone-based quantification methods, a system based on subsequent performance calculates market performance after different specified time periods have elapsed. Once the longest of the time periods passes, the quantification process becomes inactive, remaining dormant until the indicator generates a new signal. In contrast, the other two approaches are always active, calculating market performance with every data update.

The subsequent-performance approach is thus applicable to indicators that are more useful for providing indications about one side of a market, indicating market advances or market declines. And it is especially useful for indicators with signals that are most effective for a limited amount of time, after which they lose their relevance. The results for a good buy-signal indicator are shown in Figure 11.7, which lists market performance over several periods following signals produced by a 1.91 ratio of the 10-day advance total to the 10-day decline total.

FIGURE 11.7 SIGNALS BASED ON 10-DAY TOTAL OF NYSE (NEW YORK
STOCK EXCHANGE) ADVANCES OVER 10-DAY TOTAL OF NYSE DECLINES. CONCEPT
COURTESY OF DAN SULLIVAN, MODIFIED BY NED DAVIS RESEARCH.
ALL-PERIOD RESULTS ARE BASED ON DATA FROM 6/23/47 THROUGH 6/30/96.

Signal Date	10-Day A/D	Trading Days Later					
		5	**10**	**22**	**63**	**126**	**252**
06/23/47	1.96	-0.1	2.9	5.3	0.3	0.1	3.7
03/29/48	2.05	2.2	3.2	5.8	11.2	4.0	0.6
07/13/49	2.06	1.4	1.9	3.5	7.0	15.2	28.4
11/20/50	2.01	1.5	-1.7	-1.4	10.0	9.8	18.8
01/25/54	2.00	0.5	1.1	0.3	8.3	18.2	36.4
01/24/58	2.00	-0.1	-0.4	-3.1	0.6	10.3	31.4
07/10/62	1.98	-1.4	-2.0	0.9	0.0	14.0	21.5
11/07/62	1.91	2.4	3.5	4.8	10.3	17.3	21.1
01/13/67	1.94	1.4	1.1	2.6	2.9	5.6	6.9
08/31/70	1.91	1.1	-1.8	-0.5	3.9	15.5	17.9
12/03/70	1.95	1.5	1.7	3.6	11.1	14.1	5.0
12/08/71	1.98	1.0	3.5	6.2	10.6	10.4	20.2
01/08/75	1.98	2.8	2.7	12.0	20.9	37.2	41.4
01/06/76	2.05	2.5	6.6	8.3	12.7	11.3	10.9
08/23/82	2.02	0.2	2.6	3.9	14.6	22.6	34.0
10/13/82	2.03	1.9	-0.9	2.4	6.7	13.9	24.6
01/21/85	1.93	1.3	2.3	1.4	0.4	7.6	20.1
01/14/87	2.19	2.9	6.3	7.3	10.7	22.1	-5.4
02/04/91	1.96	4.7	5.8	6.9	6.1	7.8	16.7
01/06/92	1.99	-0.5	1.7	1.8	1.5	4.3	3.4
Median		1.4	2.1	3.6	7.7	12.6	19.4
Mean		3.1	2.0	3.6	7.5	13.1	17.9
Mean - All Periods		0.2	0.3	0.7	2.0	4.1	8.3
% Cases Higher		80	75	85	100	100	100
% Cases Higher All Periods		56	57	60	63	67	70

Signals based on 10-day total of NYSE advances over 10-day total of NYSE declines. Concept courtesy of Dan Sullivan, modified by Ned Davis Research. All-period results based on data from 6/23/47 through 6/30/96.

Source: Ned Davis Research. Used by permission.

In its most basic form, the results might list performance over the next five trading days, 10 trading days, and so on, summarizing those results with the average gain for each period. However, the results can be misleading if several other questions are not addressed. First of all, how is the average determined? If the mean and the median are close, as they are in Figure 11.7, then the mean is an acceptable measure. But if the mean is skewed in one direction by one or a few extreme observations, then the median is usually preferable. In both cases, the more observations the better.

Second, what is the benchmark? While the zone approach uses relative performance to quantify results, trade-signal analysis includes a comparison of per annum gains with the buy-hold statistic. Likewise, the subsequent-performance approach can use an all-period gain statistic as a benchmark. In Figure 11.7, for instance, the average 10-day gain in the Dow Industrials has been 2 percent following a signal, nearly seven times the 0.3 percent mean gain for *all* 10-day periods. This indicates that the market has tended to perform better than normal following signals. That could not be said if the 10-day gain was 0.4 percent following signals.

A third question is how much risk has there been following a buy-signal system, or reward following a sell-signal system? Using a buy-signal system as an example, one way to address the question would be to list the percentage of cases in which the market was higher over the subsequent period, and to then compare that with the percentage of cases in which the market was higher over any period of the same length. Again using the 10-day span in Figure 11.7 as an example, the market has been higher after 75 percent of the signals, yet the market has been up in only 57 percent of all 10-day periods, supporting the significance of signals. Additional risk information could be provided by determining the average drawdown per signal (i.e., the mean maximum loss from high to low following signals). The mean for the 10-day period, for example, was a maximum loss of 0.7 percent per signal, suggesting that at some point during the 10-day span, a decline of 0.7 percent could be considered normal. The opposite approaches could be used with sell-signal indicators, with the results reflecting the chances for the market to follow sell signals by rising, and to what extent.

Along with those questions, the potential for double counting must be recognized. If, for example, a signal is generated in January and a second signal is generated in February, the four-month performance following the January signal would be the same as the three-month performance following the February signal. This raises the question of whether the three-month return reflects the impact of the first signal or the second one. Moreover, such signal clusters give heavier weight to particular periods of market performance, making the summary statistics more difficult to interpret.

Problems related to double counting can be reduced or eliminated by adding a time requirement. The signals in Figure 11.7 used the condition that in a 50-day window, if the ratio reaches 1.92, drops to 1.90, and then returns to 1.92 two days later, only the first occurrence will have a signal. This time requirement eliminates the potential for double-counting in any of the periods of less than 50 days, though the longer periods still contain some overlap in this example.

Another application of subsequent-performance analysis is shown in Figure 11.8, which is not prone to any double counting. The signals require that three

FIGURE 11.8 CONFIRMATION OCCURS, AND A CASE IDENTIFIED, WHEN THE DJIA AND THE INDEX IN QUESTION BOTH REACH 52-WEEK HIGHS, THE FIRST SUCH JOINT OCCURRENCE IN AT LEAST A YEAR. CHART IS SORTED BASED ON PERCENTAGE OF CASES IN WHICH THE INDEX WAS HIGHER OVER THE SUBSEQUENT 52-WEEK PERIODS (SHADED COLUMN). "% ALL PERIODS" IS THE DJIA'S MEAN GAIN FOR ALL 26-, 39-, 52-WEEK PERIODS STARTING WITH THE BEGINNING OF THE DATA IN QUESTION.

PERFORMANCE OF DOW INDUSTRIALS FOLLOWING INITIAL INDEX CONFIRMATION
(JOINT 52-WEEK HIGHS FOR THE FIRST TIME IN A YEAR)

Confirming Index	Cases	------ 26 Weeks Later ------			------ 39 Weeks Later ------			------ 52 Weeks Later ------			Latest Case
		% Higher	Mean % Gain	% All Periods	% Higher	Mean % Gain	% All Periods	% Higher	Mean % Gain	% All Periods	
New York Utilities	7	100	8.79	5.53	100	13.59	7.98	100	16.62	10.35	5/12/95
World Composite	6	100	8.47	5.85	80	9.74	8.88	100	12.91	11.78	9/15/95
Weekly New Highs	9	89	7.79	3.53	78	10.09	5.27	100	14.41	6.98	3/31/95
NYSE Weekly Volume	10	70	6.64	3.53	67	5.16	5.27	89	6.91	6.98	7/14/95
S&P 500 Composite	22	73	5.13	3.53	73	9.92	5.45	82	14.78	7.47	2/10/95
NYSE Composite	20	63	4.02	3.72	68	8.10	5.68	79	13.29	7.60	2/10/95
AMEX Composite	9	67	3.53	5.53	67	8.20	7.98	78	13.62	10.35	3/31/95
OTC Composite	9	56	3.77	5.53	67	7.73	7.98	78	12.38	10.35	3/17/95
Dow Transports	22	77	5.26	3.53	73	8.62	5.45	76	9.99	7.47	4/13/95
S&P High-Grade Index	12	67	5.46	3.53	75	9.73	5.27	75	10.77	6.98	2/17/95
S&P Industrials	12	58	1.66	3.53	58	4.34	5.27	75	10.15	6.98	2/10/95
NYSE Financials	11	45	0.59	3.53	55	4.86	5.24	73	10.06	6.92	4/07/95
Dow Utilities	23	70	6.00	3.27	65	7.63	5.05	73	9.18	6.95	5/05/95
Weekly A/D Line	12	58	2.44	3.53	67	5.30	5.27	73	7.31	6.98	4/13/95
S&P Low-Priced Index	11	55	1.26	3.53	40	2.88	5.27	70	7.31	6.98	7/14/95
Value Line Composite	14	50	1.35	3.53	50	3.74	5.27	69	6.26	6.98	4/13/95

Confirmation occurs, and a case identified, when the DJIA and the index in question both reach 52-week highs, the first such joint occurrence in at least a year. Table is sorted based on percentage of cases in which the index was higher over the subsequent 52-week periods (column shaded). "% All Periods" is the DJIA's mean gain for all 26, 39, and 52 week periods starting with the beginning of the data series in question. Table updated through 4/04/96.

conditions are met, all for the first time in one year—the Dow Industrials much reach its highest level in a year, another index must reach its highest level in a year, and the joint high must be the first in a year. The significance for the various indices can then be compared in conjunction with their benchmarks (i.e., the various all-period gains). Figure 11.9 uses twelve of those indices to show how subsequent performance analysis for both buy signals and sell signals can be used together in an indicator. For each time span, the chart's box lists the market's performance after buy signals, after sell signals, and for all periods.

REVERSAL-PROBABILITY ANALYSIS

Finally, the subsequent performance approach is useful for assessing the chances of a market reversal. In Figure 11.10, the "signal" is the market's year-to-year change at the end of the year, with the signals (years) categorized by the amount of change—years with any amount of change, those with gains of more than 5 percent, and so on. In this case, the subsequent-performance analysis is limited to the year after the various

FIGURE 11.9 S&P 500 INDEX, A COMPOSITE OF 12 INDICES LISTED IN
FIGURE 7.8. FIGURE 11.SHOWS HOW SUBSEQUENT PERFORMANCE ANALYSIS
FOR BOTH BUY SIGNALS AND SELL SIGNALS CAN BE USED TOGETHER IN AN INDICATOR.
FOR EACH TIME SPAN, THE CHART'S BOX LISTS THE MARKET'S PERFORMANCE
AFTER BUY SIGNALS, AFTER SELL SIGNALS, AND FOR ALL PERIODS.

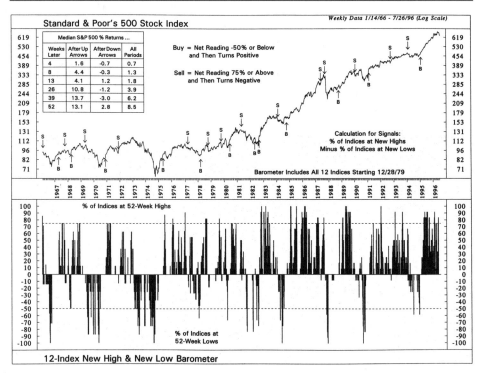

Source: Ned Davis Research. Used by permission.

one-year gains. But the analysis takes an additional step in assessing the chances for a
bull market peak within the one- and two-year periods after the years with market
gains, or a bear market bottom within the one- and two-year periods after the years
with market declines.

This analysis requires the use of tops and bottoms identified with objective criteria for bull and bear markets in the Dow Industrials.[2] The reversal dates show that
starting with 1900, there have been 30 bull market peaks and 30 bear market bottoms, with no more than a single peak and a single trough in any year. This means
that for any given year until 1995, there was a 31 percent chance for the year to contain a bull market peak and a 31 percent chance for the year to contain a bear market
bottom (30 years with reversals/95 years).

Using this percentage as a benchmark, it can then be determined whether there
has been a significant increase in the chances for a peak or trough in the year after a

FIGURE 11.10 DJIA YEARLY CLOSE AND THE DJIA YEAR-TO-YEAR CHANGE. FOR ASSESSING THE CHANCES OF A MARKET REVERSAL, THE SIGNAL IS THE MARKET'S YEAR-TO-YEAR CHANGE AT THE END OF THE YEAR, WITH THE SIGNALS (YEARS) CATEGORIZED BY THE AMOUNT OF CHANGE—YEARS WITH ANY AMOUNT OF CHANGE, THOSE WITH GAINS OF MORE THAN 5 PERCENT, AND SO ON.

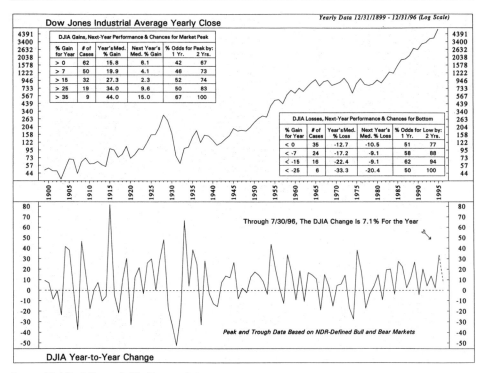

Source: Ned Davis Research. Used by permission.

one-year gain or loss of at least a certain amount. The chart's boxes show the peak chances following up years and the trough chances following down years, dividing the number of cases by the number of peaks or troughs. For example, prior to 1995, there had been 31 years with gains in excess of 15 percent starting with 1899. After those years, there was a 52 percent chance for a bull market peak in the subsequent year (16 following-years with peaks/31 years with gains of more than 15%). The chances for a peak within two years increased to 74 percent, which can be compared to the benchmark chance for at least one peak in 61 percent of the two-year periods (since several two-year periods contained more than one top, this is not the exact double of the chances for a peak in any given year). The analysis could also be applied to peaks and troughs identified using criteria for identifying shorter term peaks and troughs.

    A major difference in this analysis is that in contrast to signals and zones, which depend on the action of an indicator, this approach depends entirely on time. Each signal occurs after a fixed amount of time (one year), with the signals classified by what they show (a gain of more than 5%, etc.). Depending on the classification, the risk of a peak or trough can then be assessed.

CONCLUSION

Each one of these methods can help in assessing a market's upside and downside potential, with the method selected having a lot to do with the nature of the indicator, the time frame, and the frequency of occurrences. The different analytical methods could be used to confirm one another, the confirmation building as the green lights appeared. An alternative would be a common-denominator approach in which several of the approaches would be applied to an indicator using a common parameter (i.e., a buy signal at 100). Although the parameter would most likely be less than optimal for any of the individual methods, excessive optimization would be held in check. But whatever approaches are used, it needs to be stressed that each one of them has its own means of deceiving. By better understanding the potential pitfalls of each approach, indicator development can be enhanced, indicator attributes and drawbacks can be better assessed, and the indicator messages can be better interpreted, resulting in more profitable trading.

The process of developing a market outlook must be based entirely on research, not sales. The goal of research is to determine *if* something works. The goal of sales is to show that it *does* work. Yet in market analysis, the lines can blur if the trader decides how the market is supposed to perform, then selling himself on this view by focusing only on the evidence that supports it. What is worse is the potential to sell yourself on the value of an indicator by focusing only on those statistics that support your view, regardless of their statistical validity. As shown by the hazards associated with the methods described in this chapter, such self-deception is not difficult.

As a trader, your research goals should be objectivity, accuracy, and thoroughness. Using a sound research approach, you can determine the relative value of using any particular indicator in various ways. And you can assess the indicator's value and role relative to all the other indicators analyzed and quantified in a similar way. The indicator spectrum can then provide more useful, profit-building input toward a research-based market view.

ENDNOTES

1. This is a reference to Burton Malkiel's *A Random Walk down Wall Street* (New York: Norton, 1990), which argues that stock prices move randomly and thus cannot be forecasted through technical means.

2. A bull market requires a Dow Industrials rise of 30 percent after 50 days or 13 percent after 155 days. A bear market requires a 30 percent decline after 50 days or a 13 percent decline after 145 days. Value Line Composite reversals of 30 percent since 1965 also qualify. This applied to the 1990 high and low. Results use the equivalent high and low dates in the Dow Industrials.

CHAPTER 12

Choosing a Bar Length or Trading Interval

CYNTHIA A. KASE

In discussing the importance of time interval or duration in trading, we will examine six major areas:

1. Is it practical to trade intraday, that is, using less than daily bars?
2. What is the relationship between bar length and the length of the trading day?
3. What is the importance of risk in choosing bar length?
4. Does the quality of the market (trending vs. choppy) impact the choice of length?
5. Which is best, trading bars based on time, or based on volume?
6. Why and how should investors trade using multiple time frames?

Price charts were produced using TradeStation®. TradeStation® is a registered trademark of Omega Research, Inc.

INTRADAY OR NOT?

Trading intraday means that the bars we are using are less than one day in length (e.g., an hourly bar). Trading intraday bars is not the same as day trading; in day trading you look at tick charts to open and close a position within one day.

The term "tick" has several meanings. Formally, a tick is considered by an exchange as the minimum allowable price change. A tick can also mean a transaction or price change as broadcast by a data vendor. Some data vendors broadcast each and every transaction, such as S&P Comstock. Other data vendors broadcast prices as they change, such as DBC Signal. Thus, if we are to count the number of ticks in a given day, we would most likely get a slightly higher number from an S&P Comstock datafeed, than from DBC Signal. When evaluating tick volume, you should keep in mind the number of ticks broadcast by your data vendor in a given day. In wheat, if three transactions took place, $300.2, $300.4, and $300.4, we would get a tick volume count of three from S&P Comstock and two from Signal.

Unlike the equities market, commodity volume is not broadcast during the trading day and thus cannot be employed as a trading tool. Thus, as a proxy, we use tick volume.

A certain number of transactions are necessary to provide the liquidity necessary to trade an intraday bar. We must decide how comfortable we are with the corresponding lag time in getting filled and with the uncertainty of waiting to fill an order. Certainly, a market that trades, for example, only four times an hour will have very high bid offer spreads and may pose an unacceptable risk to the trader. Our guideline for a market that is liquid enough to trade is a minimum of one transaction every two minutes.

For this section of the chapter, we will focus on March 1997 Wheat. The contract opens at 9:30 A.M. central time and closes at 1:15 P.M. Thus, we have a 225-minute day. If we look for a trade at least every 2 minutes, we need a market that trades a little over 110 times a day. We would prefer to see, of course, a trade each minute or better or 225 trades or more per day.

Figure 12.1 is a daily chart of March 1997 Wheat. The bottom curve is a 5-day moving average of tick volume. Since the moving average is above 225, this market is liquid enough for us to trade on an intraday basis. The following formula can be used for evaluating the average tick volume indicator. The first line produces a time series

FIGURE 12.1 DAILY BARS OF WH7 AND A   FIGURE 12.2 DAILY BARS OF WZ7 AND A
    MOVING AVERAGE OF TICK VOLUME.   MOVING AVERAGE OF TICK VOLUME.

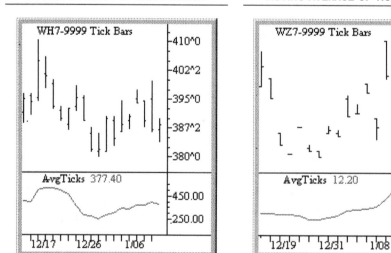

Produced using TradeStation, a registered trademark of Omega Research Inc. Used by permission.

X that adds the number of upticks and downticks for each bar. The next line takes a simple moving average of X, five samples at a time:

$$X = \text{upticks} + \text{downticks}$$

$$Y = \text{average }(X, 5)$$

$$\text{plot1 }(Y, \text{"average tick volume"})$$

Now moving forward to the December 1997 Wheat chart, (Figure 12.2) we see an average over a 5-day period of roughly 12 ticks, not enough for us to bother to trade with intraday trading. Consequently, we relied primarily on daily bars.

BAR LENGTH AND TRADING DAY

When setting up time bars longer than the nominal 15 minutes, it is important to take into consideration the number of minutes in a day. For example, in natural gas we have 310 minutes during the normal day session. This means that if we set up our charts with an hourly bar, we will end up with a 10-minute bar at the end of the day. Similarly, if we look back at the March Wheat chart and set an hourly chart for this market (which trades for 3¾ hours), we will end up with a 45-minute bar at the end of each day.

Referring to Figures 12.3 and 12.4, we see on the left a 30-minute chart and on the right a 25-minute chart. The 25-minute chart has nine evenly spaced bars, each with exactly 25 minutes. The 30-minute chart has nine bars, the last of which is a 15-minute bar. Certainly, if we treat the 15-minute bar just like a 30-minute bar, we would be effectively weighting it by a factor of 2. We may do this; however, the trader

FIGURE 12.3 THE 30-MINUTE BARS. THEY PRODUCE A 15-MINUTE INTERVAL AT THE END OF EACH TRADING DAY.	FIGURE 12.4 THE 20-MINUTE BARS. THEY DIVIDE EACH DAY EVENLY.

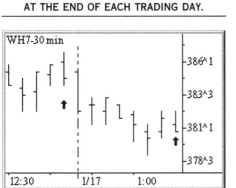
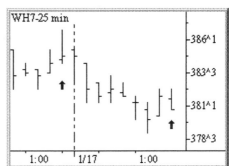

should have a particular purpose for doing so. Although not always possible, if one can trade a bar length that divides the day into even increments, meets risk criteria, and generates a Fibonacci number of bars per day (3, 5, 8 etc. bars per day), this is preferable as the Fibonacci sequence catches natural market rhythms. The first few Fibonacci numbers are 1, 2, 3, 5, 8, 13, 21, 34, 55 . . . . Each additional number in the sequence is the sum of the two numbers preceding it.

BAR LENGTH AND RISK

Many traders are taught to set stops based on what they can afford to risk. For example, if a trader can afford to risk $1,000 and wants to trade five wheat contracts, he would set his stops at 4 cents. (One cent in a wheat contract is equivalent to $50, so 4 cents is $200, and five contracts total $1,000.) This method, while serving to keep the trader from losing much more than he can afford, is a very ineffectual method for trading profitably. The reason is that market risk is not determined by what a trader can afford to lose, but by market volatility and its variability.

If this trader sets his stops narrower than dictated by volatility, that is, sets his stops within the band of erratic, random noise in the market, he will continually be stopped out by the noise. Consequently, he will not be in the market long enough to either enter or exit a trade properly. Conversely, if the trader sets his stops too wide, simply because he can afford to take a greater loss than the market dictates, he will give back more profit than necessary before exiting his trade.

For readers who may not be familiar with how to set stops based on volatility, two methods are described, both based on price range. Range is directly proportional to volatility. Risk is also directly proportional to volatility. The system I developed—Kase exit system—is based on true range. In this system, we take the average true range and its standard deviation. The true range as the chart shows is the maximum of either of the three following values:

1. The high minus low (see Figure 12.5A).
2. The high minus the previous close (see Figure 12.5B).
3. The previous close minus the low (see Figure 12.5C).

In essence, the true range is very similar to the high/low range but captures any gap between the previous day's close and the current day's activity. If the market gaps up whereby the low of the following day is above the close of a day on which we were short, we are going to lose money equivalent to that gap plus the high/low range. The same would be true if we are long going into a gap down day as well. Thus, gaps on the chart need to be considered when looking at risk.

The Kase DevStop© system is based on a method that incorporates three stops. To calculate the first stop, take the average (mean) and standard deviation of true range over a set of N bars. Next, add the standard deviation to the mean. Finally, if your position is long, subtract the resultant value from the largest profit point, or if

FIGURE 12.5 TRUE RANGE. IT IS CALCULATED FROM THE LARGEST
VALUE OF EITHER THE HIGH MINUS LOW (IN 5A), THE HIGH MINUS YESTERDAY'S
CLOSE (IN 5B), AND YESTERDAY'S CLOSE MINUS TODAY'S LOW (IN 5C).

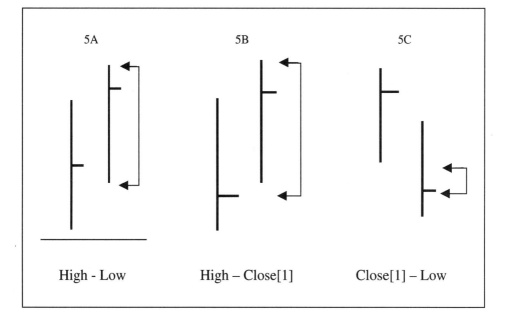

FIGURE 12.6 S&P COMSTOCK RANGE DISTRIBUTION, SHOWING RIGHT HAND SKEW.

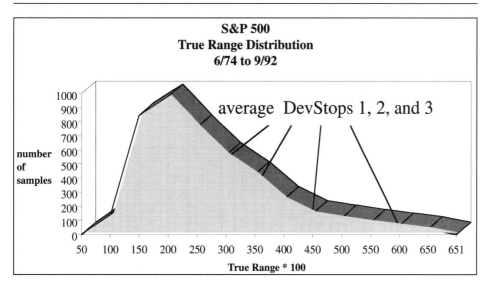

short, add. The second and third stops are set by adding approximately two and three standard deviations to the mean, respectively, but slightly increased to account for skew in our assumption that price range is log-normally (as opposed to normally) distributed. Figure 12.6 shows the distribution of S&P prices.[1]

The "Kase Average Risk" or KAR is formulated to show the amounts at risk at DevStops© 1, 2, and 3. Similarly, another method for measuring risk is called "Value at Risk," or VAR. VAR is a standard technique used by risk managers to assess risk over a given time frame. The default risk is a two standard deviation move against the current price, based on volatility. However, unlike KAR, the VAR method uses volatility based on close-to-close price changes and not true range. For traders placing only market-on-close or market-on-open orders (MOC or MOO orders) and unable to execute during the trading day, this approach may be of interest.

The following formula can be used for calculating VAR lines modified for intraday futures. In this formula, "close[BB]" represents the closing price BB bars ago, and N specifies the number of samples needed for the standard deviation and average functions. Scaling variable Z by 1, 2, and 3 produces the three VAR lines.

input: BB { default value = 4 }

input: N {default value = 30 }

$W = Log (close / close[BB])$

$X = stddev (W, N)$

$Y = X \cdot average (close, N)$

$Z = average (Y, 30)$

plot1 $(Z \times 1$, "risk at 1 stdev")

plot2 $(Z \times 2$, "risk at 2 stdev, VAR line")

plot3 $(Z \times 3$, "risk at 3 stdev, max line")

To return to the case of the trader who does not want to lose more than $200 per contract under normal conditions, assume that this trader has been using a 45-minute March 1997 Wheat chart. In Figure 12.7, the middle set of four curves (KAR group) show the average risk as well as the three amounts of risk at DevStops© 1, 2, and 3. The VAR method produced the bottom set of lines. The second line from the bottom in the KAR group is at the 6 cents per bushel level at the most recent bar. This means average risk is at $300 per contract. This is more than the trader wants to risk; however, if use used only a 4 cents stop, he would frequently be stopped out on noise. On the other hand, when the trader drops down to trading a 15-minute bar chart, analysis in Figure 12.8 shows the risk is just under 4 cents per bushel or $200 per contract. Therefore, our trader would need to trade a 15-minute chart or smaller to stay within his risk limit.

Using the VAR model, we come up with similar average risk of a little over 4 cents for the 15-minute chart but jump to 8.6 cents at the second standard deviation on the 45-minute chart. We can see also that the maximum amount of risk we have to

FIGURE 12.7 45-MINUTE WH7 (MARCH 1997 WHEAT) WITH KAR AND VAR RISK LINES.

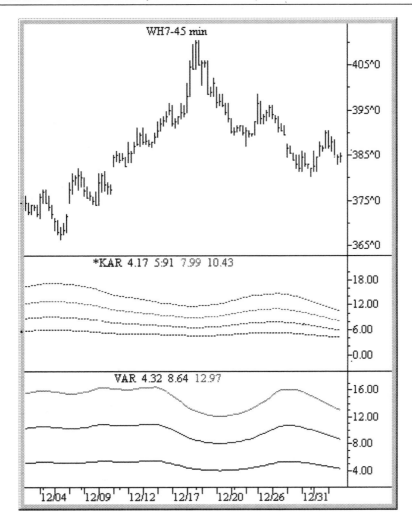

take raises considerably as well, from 6.7 cents on the 15-minute chart to just about 13 cents on the 45-minute chart. These charts illustrate the necessity of choosing a stop that is consistent with the volatility and its variability in the markets.

MARKET QUALITY

Another important element in setting time bar duration length is the quality of the market. That is, is the market trending or oscillating in the particular time frame

FIGURE 12.8 15-MINUTE WH7 (MARCH 1997 WHEAT) WITH KAR AND VAR RISK LINES.

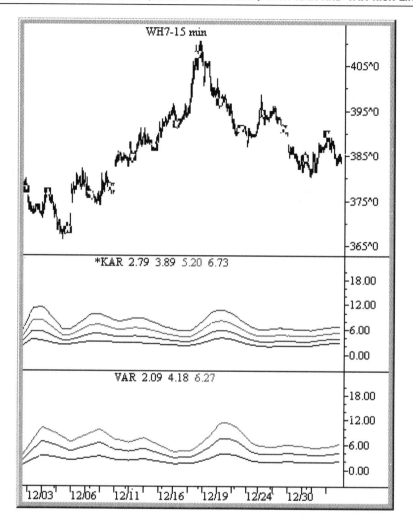

that we normally trade? If the market is trending, we may not only trade in the time frame that we normally trade, but may enlarge it provided that our risks are under control. However, in an oscillating market, even the best of systems will whipsaw once the oscillations attain a sufficiently small cycle length. Thus, in an oscillating market, we want to drop down to a lower time frame. The point here is that price action oscillating in a larger time frame may behave as small trends in a smaller time frame.

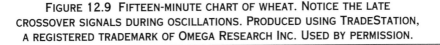

FIGURE 12.9 FIFTEEN-MINUTE CHART OF WHEAT. NOTICE THE LATE
CROSSOVER SIGNALS DURING OSCILLATIONS. PRODUCED USING TRADESTATION,
A REGISTERED TRADEMARK OF OMEGA RESEARCH INC. USED BY PERMISSION.

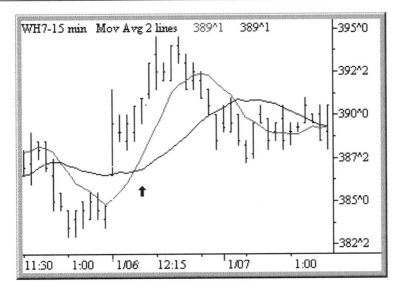

Examine the 15-minute March 1997 Wheat chart in Figure 12.9. Using a simple moving average crossover system with periods of 9 and 18, we see that we get a
crossover following a gap open late morning on the sixth. This type of late crossover,
whipsaw behavior is typical of oscillating markets. Also, given that oscillations are
generating single highs and lows, we cannot rely on traditional momentum divergence indicators to give us much help. Remember that momentum divergence requires two highs or two lows in price to be compared with their respective
momentum levels.

If we drop down to the 5-minute chart (see Figure 12.10), our moving averages
cross the Friday earlier. Thus, we are already long into the gap open and have a reasonable chance of making profitable trades provided we see the oscillations exceed
slippage and commissions. When the oscillation heights are too small to cover overhead costs, one may stand aside and not trade for awhile. If you are willing to accept
risk in an oscillating market, then you can trade with a very large time frame, daily or
higher, whereby you will ride the general trend but also suffer a combination of normal risk plus risk induced by the height of the oscillations.

FIGURE 12.10 FIVE-MINUTE CHART OF WHEAT. NOTICE THE IMPROVED CROSSOVER TIMING. PRODUCED USING TRADESTATION, A REGISTERED TRADEMARK OF OMEGA RESEARCH INC. USED BY PERMISSION.

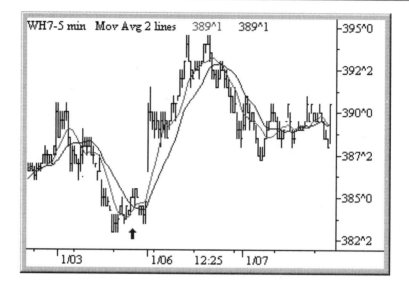

TIME VERSUS VOLUME BARS

As discussed earlier, true volume, the number of contracts traded, is not available for futures on a live broadcast basis. Nevertheless, we can use tick volume as a proxy.

A number of charting packages such as Omega Research TradeStation and Aspen Graphics provide tick volume bars. Tick volume bars simply increment each bar by the number of ticks as opposed to the number of minutes. With regard to a tick bar, the open is the price of the first transaction that occurred in that bar's set of ticks, the high is the highest priced transaction in that set, the low is the lowest priced transaction, and the close is the last transaction of the set.

Tick volume bars are superior to time bars in most cases because they form more quickly during periods of high activity and more slowly in periods of quite activity. This produces visually cleaner signals.

We can compare the 15-minute March 1997 Wheat chart (Figure 12.11) with the same chart shown using 28-tick bars (Figure 12.12). Looking at the KAR lines, we see that on average the risks in both scenarios are identical, that is, right around 3.25 cents per bushel. Thus, we have a similar global risk environment. Again we emphasize that the 3.25 cents is the average risk.

FIGURE 12.11 FIFTEEN-MINUTE WH7 WHEAT—AVERAGE RISK AT 3.25 CENTS.

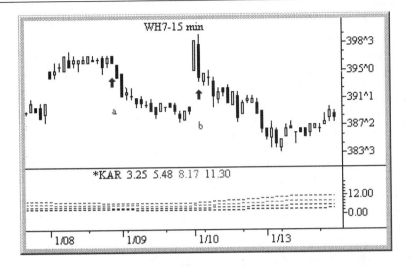

Although global risk is similar, the tick chart offers more information. Compare point **a** on both charts. At point **a** on the tick chart, we see a hanging man followed by four down candles. On the time chart, we simply have three down candles. This does not give us the same amount of warning or chance to enter on the short side that the more elongated price activity on the tick chart provides.

Similarly, at point **b** on the tick chart, we have a Harami line and star followed by a bearish engulfing line, very similar to a modified evening star formation. On the

FIGURE 12.12 TWENTY-EIGHT TICK WH7 WHEAT—AVERAGE RISK AT 3.22 CENTS.

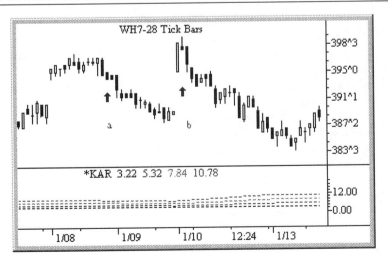

15-minute chart, we simply get a closing point reversal. Thus, we get a high degree of warning that a reversal may be coming with the Harami line and star on the tick chart. On the 15-minute chart, we get no warning of a reversal until after the closing point reversal is complete with a lower close, and the market already headed down.

Quantitatively, tick charts offer less risk. When comparing Figures 12.11 and 12.12, we can see as we scan across the average risk line that the first standard deviation over the mean is higher on the 15-minute chart. At the second and third stop levels, we see the same pattern of slightly higher risk to where we have almost a half-cent more risk on the 15-minute chart than on the tick chart. This pattern is consistent not only on these charts but on all markets in general. Our research has shown that, on average, we can expect a reduction in risk by something along the order of 15 percent to 20 percent using tick charts. While this may not be significant to a trader on an individual trade, a 15 percent to 20 percent savings in losses consistently throughout years of trading will add up and become significant. Thus, when trading intraday bars, certainly of a third of a day or less, tick bars provide a superior trading vehicle.

When setting tick volume bars, we recommend using a Fibonacci number (such as 8 ticks per bar, or 34 ticks per bar) or the average of two consecutive Fibonacci numbers (such as 28 ticks per bar) to meet risk criteria. For a time-based chart, we recommend that on average the number of bars per day be equivalent to a Fibonacci number as well.

MULTIPLE TIME FRAME TRADING

Scaling Up in Time

Since risk is related to the time frame or bar length we trade, then it stands to reason that the lower the bar length, the less the risk. Even if we are willing to trade a longer time frame, the risks associated with that time frame may be more than it is necessary for us to bear. Also, the longer the time frame, the less frequently we will see trends. For example, if we are trading a 5-minute chart, we might get a "trend" two or three times a week. If we are trading a daily chart, we might only get a trend once or twice a year that lasts sufficiently long for us to trade it.

"Scaling up in time" means to increase the number of bars we would see in a day's worth of trading. By scaling up in time, we see dramatic risk reduction and an increase in our chances of catching a trend. So we advise initiating trades on the shortest time frame that is practical, for example, 15-minute bars. Assuming the trade is not stopped out and then confirmed in a larger time frame, we move to the larger time frame, for example, 45-minute bars. If we are not stopped out in this intermediate time frame and get a confirming signal in even a larger time frame (e.g., daily bars), then we can move to the larger time frame and manage the trade from there.

Three charts are shown in Figure 12.13. This is again the March Wheat chart, showing a trade in November 1996. We can see on the 15-minute chart on November

6 at noon, a crossover that puts us long at about $3.66. For the purposes of our example, we are using the Kase DevStop© exit technique. Moving now to the 45-minute chart, we see that approximately two days later at 12:45 P.M., the moving averages cross at approximately $3.70. The trade moves up, then, to the 45-minute chart. If not stopped out, we monitor the daily chart, where, on November 14 we have an upward crossover at $3.90. Now we move to manage this trade on the daily chart. Later, on November 29, we are stopped out at approximately $3.81. Thus, by using very simple techniques of a moving average crossover and risk management, the trade made approximately $0.15, less slippage and commissions. Had we been trading on the daily only, this would have resulted in a loss of just under 9 points. So we have turned a losing trade into a winning trade through this technique.

Higher Time Frame Screens

When screening in a higher time frame, it stands to reason that it is best to confine our trading in the direction of the major trend. This is a technique which, to the best of the author's knowledge, was introduced by Dr. Alexander Elder, called the "Triple Screen Trading Method." We have taken this method a few steps further.

Simply put, moving averages, as we have seen, lag and therefore are not the best type of instrument to use as a screening tool. Thus, we would normally move to a momentum indicator such as the stochastic. The stochastic, however, still has the problem of lagging to some degree. For example, if we are trading a daily chart and screening with the weekly, we will only get our confirmation on the stochastic once a week on Fridays.

We have overcome these problems by redefining the upper time frame to end at every bar. For example, an hourly bar on a 15-minute chart would end every 15 minutes; that is, we have a moving hourly window.

FIGURE 12.13 WH7 (WHEAT FUTURES) SHOWN IN 15-MINUTE, 45-MINUTE, AND DAILY CHARTS.

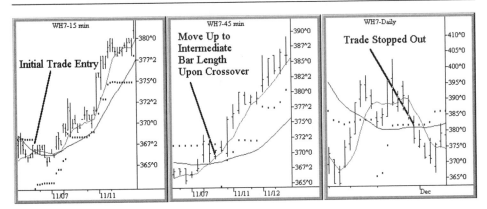

We further simplify the process by designing a number of rules to give us "permission to go long" or "permission to go short."[2] For example, when the %K stochastic indicator is below the %D in the neutral area between nominally 15 percent and 85 percent, we have permission to go short. The 15-minute chart in Figure 12.14 shows a whipsaw trade. The period when we have permission to go short is shown as a dotted histogram, and the period where we have permission to go long is shown as a solid histogram.

We can see that from January 9 through January 14 we only have permission to go short on our longer time frame filter. Therefore, the whipsaw reversal that takes place on January 10 is avoided and we continue only in the short direction. This technique is very helpful for avoiding those whipsaws associated with wave 2 and 4 corrections or the b portion of a clean ABC correction.

FIGURE 12.14 A 15-MINUTE WHEAT CHART WITH PERMISSION REGIONS DETERMINED BY RULES USING 75-MINUTE STOCHASTICS. PRODUCED USING TRADESTATION, A REGISTERED TRADEMARK OF OMEGA RESEARCH INC. USED BY PERMISSION.

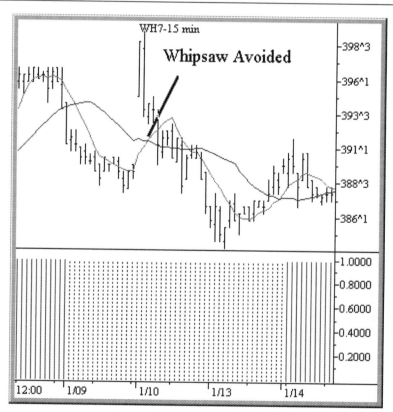

CONCLUSION

This chapter describes how to improve trading strategies by diversifying in time, understanding the relationship between time and risk, modifying our approach from time to volume, scaling up, and screening techniques.

ENDNOTES

1. The DevStop© methods are described in detail in my book, *Trading with the Odds,* Irwin Professional Publishers, 1996 as well as in the following articles I have written for *Futures* magazine: "Walking Through a Trade," June 1996, "Multi-Dimensional Trading," May 1996, "Putting the Odds on Your Side," April, 1996, and "New High-Probability Indicators—Metals," *Nymex Metals in the News,* Spring, 1996.

2. All the mathematics and rules for this method, the Kase Permission Stochastic© and the Kase Permission Screen© are provided in complete detail in *Trading with the Odds.*

CHAPTER 13

System Portfolio Optimization

GARY S. ANTONACCI

Portfolio theory principles and practices have important potential benefits with respect to computerized trading. Chief among these benefits is the value gained from careful and proper diversification. In fact, *the closest thing to a free lunch in the world of investing is the performance-enhancing benefit from a well-designed diversification strategy.* Nowhere is this more evident than in futures trading, where the ability to trade in unrelated markets can lead to significant reductions in overall portfolio volatility. This kind of diversification naturally takes place on the output side of our analysis. Here the investor determines which trading systems to use, as well as how many and which markets to trade. Yet diversification can take place on the input side, too, regarding the factors that make up computerized trading systems themselves.

INPUT DIVERSIFICATION

Many traders prefer to concentrate their efforts in trading a single market, such as the Standard & Poor's (S&P) 500. These investors may receive some benefits by diversifying their system's input. The idea here is to gain value by trying to incorporate as much information as possible. If testing reveals the extra information has no value at all, then the investor can exclude it from use. Thus, traders can only gain by trying to incorporate as much information as possible.

In the academic world, building models is known as data mining, and in the world of practitioners it is usually called curve fitting. Criticism that is sometimes brought against the approach of seeking as much input as possible (and, in fact, against all forms of sophisticated model building) is that it can lead to overspecification and selection bias in one's model. This outcome is also referred to as overmining the data, and overfitting the curve.

Data overmining or curve overfitting is like shooting thousands of arrows at the side of a barn and then drawing a target around where many of the arrows land close together. This kind of questionable target practice has almost no value, since it is unlikely anyone will be able to hit the same target next time out. Similarly, when investors throw lots of factors at their trading models, some are likely to stick solely by chance but they have little or no predictive power.

A way around this potential problem is to start with a simple and effective core trading model. This model should "make sense" by being in tune with what one already knows about the market(s) that are traded. Any parameters that need to be optimized (and there should be few at this point), must be robust and stable. This means that they should perform well over a range of values. Otherwise, attractive looking results may be spurious. Most important, back-testing data should be split into in-sample optimization and out-of-sample validation sections. Parameter values optimized over in-sample model development data must hold up well when applied to out-of-sample validation data. It is relatively easy to develop models that give a good fit to past data. Books and commercial trading systems are full of attractive looking results based on doing just this. But the replication of attractive results on out-of-sample validation data is much harder to come by.

Once the investor develops a satisfactory core model in the manner previously described, then he or she can add model factors one at a time in a stepwise manner continuing with the same procedure as described earlier: each additional input should be in tune with what is known about each market. Parameters being optimized should be stable and robust; and, finally, each additional input must hold up under out-of-sample validation, as well as in-sample optimization.

I have used the preceding approach to effectively build and improve basic trading models through the addition of entry filters and alternative exit strategies. I have also found value in incorporating nonprice information, such as volume, open interest, calendar anomalies, and intermarket price relationships into many of my trading models by using the same approach.

By being careful and conscientious in model construction, traders can safely build elaborate and sophisticated models from valid, simpler approaches. This is how to add value using a "portfolio approach" toward informational inputs.

OUTPUT DIVERSIFICATION

What distinguishes futures trading from other forms of investment is the unique opportunity available to enhance system performance by diversifying in many different non-correlated markets. This is in contrast to trading in equities where cross-correlations, or tendencies to move together, between securities are quite high. In such cases, the benefits of diversification are not as great as with futures trading, since the overriding risk of the stock market itself cannot be diversified away.

Portfolio theory still extols the virtues of diversifying away nonmarket risk by holding well-diversified portfolios of securities. In fact, international diversification has gained importance in recent years primarily because of its diversification value in reducing overall portfolio risk, since foreign securities are less highly correlated to domestic securities than are other domestic securities. Yet nondiversifiable market risk still accounts for a substantial amount of volatility given the high correlations between individual equities.

In contrast, there is very little correlation, or comovement, between futures groups as diverse as energies, currencies, interest rate instruments, grains, or meats. To see how this can work to our advantage, let us contrast two examples. In the first, we hold a portfolio of securities where the correlation between them explains, on average, about two-thirds of their composite movement up or down. If each security has an expected annual return of 10 percent and an expected maximum drawdown of 20 percent, then an equal asset allocation among these securities would give an expected return of 10 percent (their average) and an expected maximum drawdown of perhaps 15 percent. The reason this is not 20 percent is because although most of our portfolio holdings would be down at the same time, it is unlikely they will all be down the *maximum amount* at the same time.

Holding an equally weighted portfolio of unrelated futures contracts, in which the expected cross correlations between them is close to zero, would also give an expected return equal to an average of their respective returns. This is no different from the stock portfolio. Yet the maximum expected drawdown of the futures portfolio would be much lower than the average individual futures drawdowns. This would occur because when some futures markets are down significantly, others could be up significantly, while others might be unchanged.

Of course, futures themselves might be more volatile than equities. However, this apparent volatility is a function mainly of the leverage inherent in futures contracts. Commodities in and of themselves are often less volatile than equities. Traders can modify the leverage of futures simply by adjusting the amount of funding used as collateral for futures trading. Institutional investors, for example, who wanted to participate in futures trading without any leverage at all, could place into their trading account the full value of each futures contract.

OTHER FORMS OF DIVERSIFICATION

Not all the benefits of diversification come into play with respect to the diversity of markets available for trading. Trading the same markets using different frames of reference can also provide some of the benefits from diversification. For example, investors might trade bonds using systems based on daily, weekly, and intraday price patterns. Likewise, different kinds of trading systems can be applied to the same markets using the same time frames. The application of both different trading systems and different time frames means that market entries and exits are phased in and out, which often smooths out the ups and downs of performance in accordance with diversification principles.

Most traders, including professional trading advisers, ignore these other forms of diversification, preferring instead to trade all markets the same way using a singular method and/or time frame. The benefits of these additional forms are there for the taking; however, they entail much more research effort. A problematic aspect of this broad-based approach to trading is that the trader is forced to look at systems and methods developed by others to cover all bases. In doing so, the same principles of careful, methodical system selection and validation are just as important as in developing one's own trading systems.

According to the Sturgeon principle, 90 percent of everything ever developed is totally worthless. After years of evaluating, developing and refining trading systems, I can safely state that in the trading system design arena, Sturgeon was too optimistic. Much of my time is spent testing and trying to improve commercial trading systems, or systems and ideas in books, magazines, or newsletters. I can honestly say that less than 1 percent of everything I have examined has proven to be worthwhile.

EFFICIENT PORTFOLIOS

Once several promising trading methods have been identified and developed, the question then arises of how best to incorporate and balance these approaches into a single overall system portfolio. Many traders, even professional ones, simply trade all systems and markets the same way. Others try to adjust for volatility by attempting to risk the same dollar amount on each trade. They then adjust each position size accordingly. Traders following these two approaches are hoping that diversification benefits will come into play automatically because of the different markets that are being traded. To some extent this is true, but there is a more scientific way to properly construct and balance system portfolios.

Treating all markets and systems alike is the same as admitting that we know nothing about the relative value of our systems and methods other than that they all have some merit. Adjusting position sizes to conform to market volatility goes a step further by assuming that past volatility will remain constant into the future. But beyond that, it still assumes that we know nothing more about the expected future performance of the markets and of the systems we use to trade them.

Modern Portfolio Theory (MPT), first developed by Nobel laureate Harry Markowitz in the 1950s, takes a different approach.[1] Under MPT, we first gather what we know about the past returns, volatilities, and cross-correlations of the systems that we trade. We then apply a computer-based optimization model to this information that examines all possible ways of allocating trading capital. This computer model maps out all portfolios offering the highest expected return at every level of expected risk, or, conversely, those portfolios offering the lowest expected risk at each specified level of return. These are known as efficient portfolios, since they offer the best possible reward/risk characteristics based on past performance data. The set of all such efficient portfolios is known as the efficient frontier. It is then a simple matter to choose whatever portfolio we want along the efficient frontier. Often this is the portfolio offering the best overall reward-to-risk or Sharpe ratio.*

---

*The Sharpe ratio measures risk-adjusted rate of returns. The formula is (AAR-NR)/SAR, where AR is the system's average annualized percentage rate of return, NR is the annualized rate of return of a no-risk investment (e.g., 5% yield on 90-day T-bills), and SAR is the standard deviation of the system's annual rates of returns. (Editor)

The investor may, alternatively, select a portfolio that offers the highest expected geometric growth rate of capital, or some other appropriate objective function.

MODERN PORTFOLIO THEORY IN PRACTICE

When I first started applying MPT models to futures trading in the early 1980s, there were no commercially available software programs of this kind. I therefore had to develop my own. Now, however, at least several low-cost commercial programs are available that will do MPT calculations. A recent issue of the *Journal of Finance* had advertisements for two such programs. There is also an add-on module for commonly used Omega, Computrac, and MetaStock programs that will easily export the appropriate data from these programs to an MPT optimizer.[2] MPT software can also be obtained as an inexpensive add-on disk to a portfolio theory textbook.[3]

Before looking on the application of MPT principles as a trading panacea, however, traders should be aware of its limitations. Like any form of modeling, MPT optimization relies heavily on the assumption that future conditions will be similar to those of the past. This is always a dangerous assumption, especially when it involves optimized system performance with its attendant estimation risk and selection bias problems. It may also be problematic relying on model assumptions such as constant price variance, stationary (fixed) underlying return distributions, and serial independence of trading results.

One way to partially overcome some of these problems is to use as much data as possible for portfolio optimization. Many markets go through long active and quiet periods. Therefore, the more data traders have to work with, the greater is the likelihood of capturing an accurate representation of expected long-term performance. It may also make sense to take all system cross-correlations that are calculated as less than zero and set them back to zero. A cross-correlation of zero means that there is no relationship at all between the performance of one system and the performance of another. This is a reasonable assumption given that we are now dealing with trading system results rather than prices themselves. Cross-correlations that are less than zero imply that gains from one system are associated with losses from the other, and vice versa. I can see no reason for this to be true, unless one system is designed as a hedge to the other. Negative cross-correlations are therefore most likely spurious results due to randomness in the data, and setting them to zero seems appropriate.

Correlations that are too high may also create problems for MPT analysis because they may lead to model instability and "confusion." This problem can be avoided by dropping the least desirable of the highly correlated systems or markets. Little should be lost by doing this, since the remaining system or market will capture most of what is worthwhile from both, given its high correlation with the other.

Finally, the true state of affairs probably exists somewhere between MPT modeling, with its attendant estimation risks, and a naive strategy that calls for equal allocations of capital among all investment opportunities. A methodology known as

Bayesian statistics can be useful for this purpose, but it goes well beyond the scope of this chapter.[4]

CONCLUSION

Diversification in unrelated markets and the application of different trading approaches can add considerable value. Portfolio theory concepts can help us capture much of this value. But modeling has its limitations and can only approximate reality. In this uncertain world, where past performance is indeed not necessarily indicative of future results, portfolio optimization combined with common sense is the best combination for investment success.

ENDNOTES

1. Markowitz, Harry, *Portfolio Selection: Efficient Diversification of Investments,* New York: John Wiley & Sons, 1959.
2. Portfolio Manager. Ralph Vince, 46 Chagrin Plaza #110, Chagrin Falls, Ohio 44022
3. Haugen, Robert, *Modern Investment Theory,* Englewood Cliffs, NJ: Prentice Hall, 1996.
4. Bawa, Vijay, Brown, Stephen and Klein, Roger, *Estimation Risk and Optimal Portfolio Choice,* New York: North Holland, 1979.

Psychology

- System trading is perfectly designed for proactive trading. You can establish specific trading objectives and criteria, pay close attention to the marketplace, and measure your performance objectively. But in the final analysis, you have to call the trade, and decide when to place your order. You have to take responsibility for missing a trade, or the slippage in executing a trade.

- Systems do not entirely insulate you from your own emotional reactivity to the success and failure of your trades. Realize that all trading is influenced by life-long beliefs and habits that are operating for you when you trade. To the extent that your trading is dominated by long-standing life principles, you may not be maximizing your opportunities. Instead, you may be limited or stopped by your underlying assumptions of the world.

- You must learn to separate trading events from your emotional reactions so that you can see any habitual behavior that leads to compulsive and inconsistent trading.

- Record your trades and after the session has ended, review the facts and how you responded. This way you can see how emotions may have clouded your performance, leaving your mind clear for the next trading day.

- Enter into a meditative state of consciousness to reduce anxiety and tension and decrease the impact of distracting stimuli. It helps you distance yourself from the sequence of emotional responses and negative interpretations of stressful and unsuccessful trades that trigger panic, denial, rationalization, and avoidance—all of which perpetuate the circle of failure.

- Make a conscious commitment to a financial objective greater than you are accustomed to achieving. This means relinquishing any inclination to trade in terms of comfort and safety, and to allow your choice of price, volatility, and size of positions to be guided by parameters commensurate with your goals. This will help you overcome a natural fear of change.

- Do you have what it takes to succeed? Ask yourself these questions:

  —You will need to develop market intuition, which only comes from trading experience and a fair amount of reading. Your initial investment combined with initial losses while trading may easily exceed $5,000. You may need to wait a year or so before you break even. Do you have the financial resources and are you patient enough to prevail?

  —Proper system development will take longer than you want it to. Develop-test-develop-test . . . Can you afford the time to do a proper job and are you patient enough to avoid premature risk taking?

  —You will need to be fluent in handling hardware and software bugs and break-downs (e.g., database corruption, incompatible software, hard drive failure).

Can you afford the time to learn all this and are you patient enough to learn frustrating tasks?

Risk—Exposure

- Select exposure duration that's best for you. Although position trading (holding your position overnight) typically yields more profit than day trading (exiting your position at the end of each day), it is more important for you to select the method you can live with in terms of stress, risk, required skills, and required capital, than to make a choice based on expected annual profit.
- You can control risk by working in a time frame whose average risk, as measured by the KAR or VAR method, is just under the maximum risk you are willing to accept. For example, consider wheat futures, where 1 cent is equivalent to $50 risk exposure. A 7 cents average risk translates to $350 of exposure per contract.
- By shortening the chart's time frame, risk through price action drops but commission costs per trade increase in importance. One way to handle this balancing act is to initiate trades using a short time frame, a 15-minute bar chart for example, and then lengthen the time frame while in the market.
- When day trading, tick volume bars are superior to time bars in most cases because they form more quickly during periods of high activity and more slowly in periods of quiet activity. This produces visually cleaner signals.
- A more obscure aspect to risk control is the notion of "time in the market." It is better to be exposed to the market briefly than for extended periods of time. With all other factors the same, I prefer a system that has me holding positions (exposed to the market) for the least amount of time, because while I am out of one market, I can invest the money elsewhere.

Risk—Diversification

- Portfolio theory extols the virtues of lowering risk by holding well-diversified portfolios of securities or by trading in unrelated futures markets. Although futures are more leveraged than equities, diversification reduces risk faster with futures because unrelated futures markets are less cross-correlated than unrelated equities.
- Diversification can also be attained through multiple systems, each running in a different time frame, or a different set of indicators.
- To construct your optimal portfolio, first remove all contenders that deliver poor reward/risk performance as measured by the Sharpe ratio or by the gain/drawdown ratio. Create a return matrix and covariance matrix and feed them into a mean variance optimization program.*

---

* There are several low-cost, stand-alone software packages available to do this. For example, Ralph Vince offers Portfolio Manager. More general-purpose mathematics products like SAS and MATLAB can also perform this task.

Risk—Miscellaneous

- Risk is directly proportional to volatility. You can control risk by placing stops above or below the mean price action by an amount that is scaled to the standard deviation of either the bar-to-bar true range or the bar-to-bar change in closing prices.

- Get comfortable with all the mechanics of trading, including finding the right broker, data vendor, and so on. Then as your performance improves (hopefully), you may want to increase your risk with larger lots, leveraged trades, and volatile markets.

- A winning streak or losing streak can readily change your perception of your system's capabilities, possibly leading to over- or underconfidence. Either way, your system has not changed, you have. To help you stay neutral, analyze your system's winning and losing streak tendencies. If your system is showing consistent losses unlike you have seen while testing, then stop trading and examine the nature of your system's losing streak.

Charting

- "Zone analysis" quantifies how a market has behaved while an indicator was in various zones. Typical zone labels may include "bullish," "bearish," or "neutral." This approach may require additional analysis based on whether the indicator was rising or falling within a zone.

- "Subsequent performance" analysis gauges market performance over specific time periods following a specified condition. This approach is applicable to indicators with signals that are most effective for a limited time, after which they lose their relevance.

- Consider using primary indicators to time your trades and secondary indicators to screen or filter your zones of trading opportunities.

System Development

- Once you develop a satisfactory core trading system, you can add factors one at a time in a stepwise manner. During this process, each additional input should be in tune with what in known about each market. Parameters being optimized should be stable and robust; and, finally, each additional input must hold up under out-of-sample validation, as well as in-sample optimization.

- If you believe your system is making poor decisions, exit the market, stop trading, and rework the system until it once again meets your expectations. On the other hand, avoid being stuck for years developing a system at the expense of real trading experience. You need both.

- Your historical data should be clean and contain as much history as possible. When it comes to data, more is better. If it's inaccurate or incomplete, it can do

more harm than good. Because market behavior changes over time, your indicators should be robust enough to stand the test of time.

- Test your system on at least 5,000 bars of data. A good rule of thumb is 1,000
  bars of data per adjustable parameter. Reject any system whose test results produced less than a statistically significant number of trades, typically 100.

PART IV

Advanced Indicators and Forecasting

You have seen how to apply indicators, enter and exit the market, test and evaluate your systems, select the proper time frames, diversify, become focused and handle stress. Now you are ready for even more exciting and potentially rewarding techniques.

Much of the classical view of market behavior resulted from the mathematical tools available decades ago and has remained nearly constant ever since. However, the rush of newly available technologies is allowing individuals and institutions to pry open and exploit virgin inefficiencies in the market. These new technologies include fuzzy logic, neural networks, genetic algorithms, and data mining.

The authors in Part IV will guide you through the fundamental issues inherent in advanced modeling technologies.

Chapter 14 begins this discussion with the principles of advanced system development, including data collection and system complexity. The power of intermarket analysis is also illustrated with a simple, yet effective, trading strategy.

Since many of the world's traders are still using incorrect assumptions, you can make a profit by arbitraging the difference between systems that use correct and incorrect assumptions. Chapter 15 compares the classical and modern ideas about market action, and underscores the importance of working with correct assumptions about market behavior.

Building advanced models without proper data preprocessing is foolhardy. It typically produces overly complex systems with poor performance. Chapter 16 discusses the numerous ways you can preprocess data and why it is so important for proper data pattern recognition and price forecasting.

Chapter 17 discusses how to select the right input and target values for modeling your data. Modeling tools are compared, and a data-mining technology is chosen because it very quickly configures a model's size and shape, automatically. To verify its effectiveness, an example trading system is produced and evaluated.

Chapter 18 shows how to build a trading system where technology is not used to forecast price action, but rather to detect useful price patterns, such as the head-and-shoulder pattern. Classical rules are then constructed to make trading decisions.

CHAPTER 14

Developing a Trading System Using Intermarket Analysis

AVERILL J. STRASSER

The study of a time series of financial data involves the analysis of a stream of market prices over time, in an effort to create a model that describes its behavior. Once the model is quantified, it can be utilized in the prediction of future values.

Intermarket analysis involves the study of a second data stream, to attempt to determine whether it can provide information that will assist in predicting the first.

The ultimate goal of the technical trader is to develop a system that has a high statistical probability of success. This can be accomplished by using readily available tools to improve the odds beyond random results.

In this chapter, we will explore the theoretical and practical aspects of intermarket analysis of time series data. We will use as an example, the development of a trading system that predicts the future value of the S&P 500 Index based on an analysis of the S&P itself, and on an intermarket analysis with the Treasury bond market.

A study of past S&P market prices alone can provide some information that allows us to forecast future prices with better than random accuracy. That market has exhibited a consistent trend over the years, and many simple technical analysis indicators, such as moving averages and oscillators, will have strong predictive value.

However, if an additional filter is imposed whereby trades in conformance with the prediction are only made if they are preceded by a signal from the T-bond market, much greater forecasting accuracy can be achieved.

In developing a trading system, careful attention must be paid to issues such as system complexity and data adequacy. Consideration of these factors improves the likelihood that the system will perform well in the future.

DEVELOPING AN APPROACH

The field of statistics involves the numerical description of large sets of data. Beyond the description, one can create inferences about the data. For example, one can determine the moving average of a time series of data. One can then infer that if prices are above the moving average, there is an upward trend; if prices are below the moving average, there is a downward trend.

The statistical analysis of a data stream allows us not only to extract useful information from the data, but also to determine the accuracy of the inferences we may derive from this data.

Statistical tools, such as linear regression, multiple regression, and statistical modeling, have been with us for a long time, and are used by many market analysts. However, their use requires substantial expertise in two fields: (1) technical expertise in the properties of the markets in question, and (2) expertise in the interpretation of multivariate statistics.

In using statistical tools, the market expert must first interpret market behavior. He or she must then analyze and manipulate the data, and preprocess it into a more meaningful form. Mistakes in any of these choices or processes will result in an invalid analysis.

Furthermore, a detailed knowledge of statistical analysis is required. Decisions must be made as to what type of model will adequately portray the data, and what analysis tools are to be used. Then, the results must be interpreted to determine their statistical significance.

With the use of modern technical analysis software, traders can now easily design technical trading systems, and optimize and backtest them. The programs are powerful tools that can complement financial knowledge and statistical expertise. They allow for easy interpretation of the value of a statistical model by measuring the bottom line, which is the profitability of a trading strategy based on the model.

MODELING THE DATA

The development of every trading system should start with a rational observation about market behavior. The software should pick out isolated profitable patterns from even random data, so care must be taken in developing and understanding relationships that are meaningful. If the significance of a particular pattern is understood, and can be verbalized, the pattern is more significant and more likely to be repeated into the future.

To try to predict future values in a time series, we use the principle of modeling. Simply stated, this involves trying to find variables that can describe the data, and then determining how the variables are related.

One common model of the value of a time series, such as a stock or commodity price, over time is:

$$Y_1 = T_1 + C_1 + S_1 + R_1$$

where

$$Y_1 = \text{Market price}$$
$$T_1 = \text{Long-term trend or secular trend}$$
$$C_1 = \text{Cyclical effect}$$
$$S_1 = \text{Seasonal effect}$$
$$R_1 = \text{Residual effect}$$

The long-term trend, T, is a time series that describes the long-term movements of Y, or price. For example, the long-term trend of the stock market for the past 50 years has been upward for that period. This does not mean that the month-to-month or year-to-year values were always rising, but rather that there has been a long-term trend upward.

The cyclical effect, C, describes fluctuations of the value of Y about the long-term trend that can be attributed to business and economic factors. Although there has been a generally increasing long-term upward trend in stock prices, during times of recession prices fall below the long-term trend, and during general economic expansion they rise above this trend.

The seasonal effect, S, describes the fluctuations in the time series that recur during specific portions of each year. For example, energy prices may vary during specific times of the year due to weather and growing patterns.

The residual effect, R, is what remains after all the other components have been removed. The residual effect results from unpredictable events, such as natural disasters, political events, and unforeseen circumstances.

It will be necessary to look to the markets in question, to determine which of these factors will be useful in the model.

LOOKING AT THE MARKETS

The Standard & Poor's 500 Index, commonly known as the S&P Index or the S&P, is a weighted index made up of the prices of 500 stocks. The S&P futures contract size is the value of the S&P Index times $500. The contract is traded at the Chicago Mercantile Exchange. The minimum fluctuation is .05, which is equal to $25.

The S&P has obvious properties, which can be seen graphically in Figure 14.1. The long-term and consistent uptrend, from the inception of this contract to 1997, is visible by even a cursory look at the chart.

On top of the long-term trend, there may be cycles, which may be political or economic in nature. For example, there may be a 4-year presidential cycle, or there may be rhythmic periods of economic financial expansion and contraction.

Treasury bonds, commonly known as the T-bonds, are long-term U.S. government debt instruments with maturities of more than 7 years. They are fixed income assets that pay interest semiannually.

FIGURE 14.1 STANDARD & POOR'S INDEX.

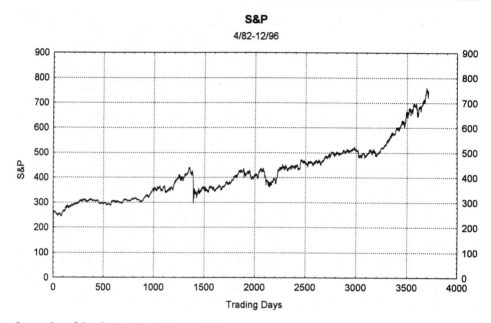

S&P
4/82-12/96

Source: Statsoft Inc. Statistica. Permission received.

The T-bond futures contract is traded at the Chicago Board of Trade. The contract size is $100,000, at 8 percent interest, with trading equivalent to the 30-year bond price. When interest rates rise, T-bond prices fall. This is because the existing lower interest debt instruments are less valuable. Prices are quoted as a percentage of par, and the minimum fluctuation is ½₂ of a point, or $31.25.

The T-bond market is well known to be strongly correlated with the S&P. Generally, the two markets move in the same direction, and confirm each other. When they move in opposite directions, it is a significant event.

It is often stated the T-bond market usually turns first—it is a leading indicator. This hypothesis is subject to interpretation, and investigation. There are a number of factors that could rationally explain such a relationship. It is well known that long-term interest rates have a powerful effect on stock market prices. Generally a bullish bond market implies rising stock prices, and vice versa. Bonds are an alternative investment for stock market investors. The public routinely moves money into the perceived safety of bonds when they have economic fears, and moves them into stocks when the economy is expanding.

Thirty-year bond yields (which are the inverse of interest rates) are influenced by inflation expectations, as opposed to short-term interest rate products, which are affected by monetary policies of the Federal Reserve Bank. Inflation expectations reflect expectations of future monetary policy, fiscal policy, and the economy. Thus, the bond yield combines much of the core information that affects future stock prices into a single number.

Once there is an understanding of the nature of the relationship between the two data streams, it is a simple process to determine which one leads the other and by how much. This will allow us to take advantage of the relationship, by looking for divergence between the trends that describe each.

For the studies done in this chapter, we will use continuous contracts constructed from futures contract data from Genesis Financial Data Services. The continuous contracts are constructed using the roll-forward, back-adjust method, with the rollover date five trading days before the last trading day. This creates a data stream containing prices that did not actually occur, but this method maintains relative price continuity.

STUDYING THE TARGET MARKET BY ITSELF

The design of a specific model or indicator, or of an entire trading system, involves the concept of statistical inference. In such a design, we draw conclusions about populations based on sample observations. Samples are observed directly, and serve as approximations to the true population characteristics.

To study the market, it is often useful to transform data by using a smoothing technique to filter out random noise. For example, a simple moving average, calculated by adding up the prices of a specific number of bars, dividing that sum by the number of bars, and plotting the average on the study bar, has a smoother appearance than a line drawn through each closing price. The greater the number of bars used, the smoother the curve, as any individual price has a smaller and smaller effect on the average.

Other filtering techniques would be exponential or weighted moving averages, in which more weight is given to recent prices than remote prices. Similarly, taking the logarithm of each value or a ratio of values may help smooth the data.

In developing a model for time series data, it is often helpful to view the data graphically, and see what conclusions may be drawn from the visual pattern. With the S&P, it is clear that there has been a continuous steady long-term upward trend. However, any cyclical or seasonal patterns are not readily discernible to the eye.

For such a market, it is useful to subtract out the trend and try to determine whether there is a clear reason for the daily variation of price over time. Some of it may be cyclical or seasonal, and the rest may be random error. A first choice for a model of this data series might be as simple as a straight line, connecting the beginning and ending points, or some other simple fitting technique.

The general formula for a straight line is

$$Y_L = a + bX$$

In this formula, *a* represents the intercept of the line with the Y axis, and *b* represents the slope of the line. A straight line can be drawn through a set of data points that visually approximates the best fit.

A detrended version of the original Y data points can be created by subtracting out the line that represents the trend:

$$Y_t = Y - Y_L = Y - (a + bX)$$

where Y_t is the transformed (detrended) value of Y.

The trend can be determined in a number of ways. A generally accepted approach is to draw a two-dimensional linear regression line, using the least squares approach. This is designed to minimize the error measured from the squares of the distances of the data points from the trend line.

If there are large errors from this approach, it is necessary to smooth the data using averaging, logarithms, or some other transformation. The data we are studying appears to be very linear, and lends itself, as a first approximation, to representation as a linear trend.

When we proceed to subtract the trend, a new data stream is created. The transformed data stream oscillates around the zero axis, making it easier to pick out other cycles that may exist.

In its transformed version, it is also possible to identify price shocks, which show up as sudden aberrations of the price data. Price shocks may be caused by political, economic, or social events, as well as natural and environmental occurrences. They are worthy of study, and should be considered in any system design.

A determination must be made whether there is any occurrence in the time period studied, which would make it beneficial to divide the data into different parts and analyze each part separately. Several statistical studies, such as ARIMA analysis, are designed for an interrupted time series.

STATISTICA™ is a statistical analysis program that allows for the ready analysis of time series data. Using STATISTICA™, we can statistically evaluate the S&P time series data, using trend subtraction. By eliminating the long-term trend, we can focus in on deviations from the trend.

In Figure 14.2, we transform the data to a time series that oscillates above and below the horizontal "zero" line. This transformation was attained by subtracting price from the trend line, which was determined through linear regression. Using this methodology, it is found that

$$Y_{transformed} = 240.3 + 0.0953 \times t$$

where $Y_{transformed}$ is the transformed value of the S&P, and t (time) is the number of data bars from the starting point.

Different values for the coefficients may be obtained if different starting and ending points are chosen, or if the continuous contract used for study is constructed differently.

FIGURE 14.2 TRANSFORMED S&P WITH TREND SUBTRACTED.

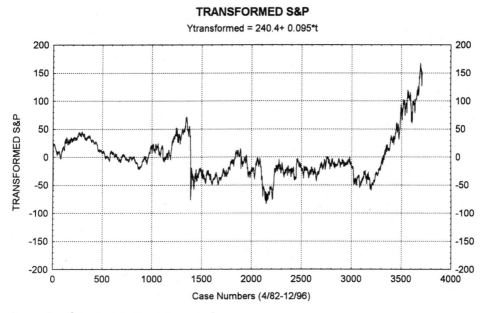

TRANSFORMED S&P

Ytransformed = 240.4+ 0.095*t

Source: Statsoft Inc. Statistica. Permission received.

The accuracy of this model can be demonstrated by designing and developing a trading system, and then evaluating its financial performance. For a development platform, we use TradeStation®, by Omega Research, Inc. The PowerEditor™ of TradeStation® allowed us to determine whether the transformed S&P prices have predictive value. TradeStation® is a registered trademark and PowerEditor™ is a trademark of Omega Research, Inc.

Figure 14.3 shows the system, called S&P Crossover Buy. It sets Y to be the transformed S&P indicator. If Y crosses above the closing price of the S&P, a buy is signaled. If it crosses below the S&P, the long position is liquidated.

Figure 14.4 shows the performance summary for the S&P Crossover Buy system. In analyzing it, we see that this simple system yields 100 percent profitable trades. This is a significant result and shows that we are working with a promising model. By comparison, a buy-and-hold strategy over the same time period would have yielded similar profit results, but would have experienced much larger drawdowns along the way.

This is not a tradable system. It is based on the slope and intercept of the trendline through the data points. This information could not have been available at the time the hypothetical trades were entered. This is the extreme example of a totally curve-fit system, where the result is known, and data is manipulated to reach the result.

FIGURE 14.3 SYSTEM: S&P CROSSOVER BUY.

Page 1

Type   : System
Name   : SP Crossover Buy
Notes   : Buy when linear regression crosses price.

Last Update : 02/10/97 11:05am
Printed on : 02/10/97 11:06am
Verified   : YES

{Data1 is S&P}
Var: Y(0);

Y =240.4 + .095 * BarNumber;   {Transformed S&P}

If Y crosses above Close of Data1 then Buy;
If Y crosses below Close of Data1 then ExitLong;

Source: Printed using TradeStation PowerEditor by Omega Research Version 4.02.15-Jul < 09 1996.

Logically, the data points will move back and forth across the trendline in back-testing, since the trend was established by the best fit. Thus, the trendline for the S&P leads the S&P. This has no practical value, but it does provide us with a confirmation that the straight line may be a useful modeling tool. It also provides us with an idea for system development that we will use when we begin to look at intermarket relationships.

FIGURE 14.4 PERFORMANCE SUMMARY: S&P CROSSOVER BUY.

```
S&P Crossover Buy   S&P 500 Index - CME-Daily    04/21/82 - 12/19/96

                    Performance Summary:   All Trades

Total net profit      $ 205350.00   Open position P/L      $       0.00
Gross profit          $ 205350.00   Gross loss             $       0.00

Total # of trades             42    Percent profitable          100%
Number winning trades         42    Number losing trades           0

Largest winning trade $  58900.00   Largest losing trade   $       0.00
Average winning trade $   4889.29   Average losing trade   $       0.00
Ratio avg win/avg loss     100.00   Avg trade(win & loss)  $    4889.29

Max consec. winners           42    Max consec. losers             0
Avg # bars in winners         51    Avg # bars in losers           0

Max intraday drawdown $ -36900.00
Profit factor              100.00   Max # contracts held           1
Account size required $  36900.00   Return on account           557%
```

Source: Printed using TradeStation by Omega Research Version 4.02.15-Jul < 09 1996.

PROVING THAT T-BONDS LEAD THE S&P

Once we have examined the first data stream, it is valuable to look at the second correlated data stream to determine the nature of the relationship. To determine the correlation between the S&P and T-bonds, a cross-correlation analysis is performed using STATISTICA™. As seen in Figure 14.5, the cross-correlation with 0 lag is .9135, which is highly significant.

A more difficult question is whether one is a leading indicator of the other, and by how much. It is seen that this data is highly correlated, with positive or negative lags of almost any amount showing a high correlation. With T-bonds leading the S&P by 90 days, the correlation is still .8646. With T-bonds lagging the S&P, the correlation is .7810. The slower degradation of the correlation when T-bonds led the S&P shows that the leading variable is T-bonds.

A simple visual graphical interpretation provides a rough confirmation of the correlation and an understanding of which market leads the other, and by how much. The S&P and T-bonds are plotted on the same chart, with different scales. In Figure 14.6, the S&P is shown by a scale on the left of the chart, and T-bonds are shown by a scale on the right. It is constructed by mathematically matching the slope of the trendlines of

FIGURE 14.5 CROSS-CORRELATION: S&P AND T-BONDS.

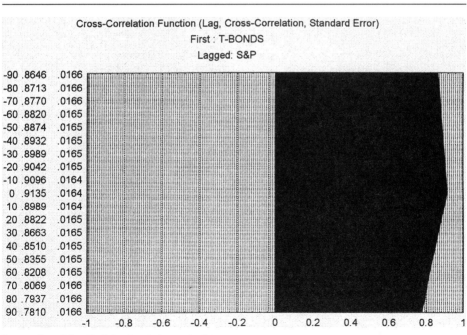

Source: Statsoft Inc. Statistica. Permission received.

FIGURE 14.6 CROSS-CORRELATION: S&P AND T-BONDS.

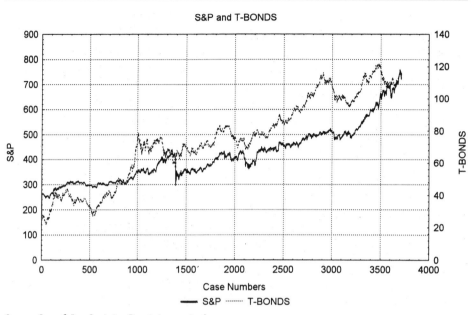

Source: Statsoft Inc. Statistica. Permission received.

the two data streams. It is evident that T-bond prices reach peaks and bottoms before the S&P prices.

The 9/81 bottom in bonds preceded the stock market bottom in 8/82 by 11 months. The 4/87 breakdown in bonds preceded the 8/87 stock market top by 4 months. From this observation, it is easy to make a simple system to determine conclusively whether T-bonds lead the S&P. We can do this with a simple trading system written in TradeStation whereby buy-and-sell signals are triggered by leading movements in T-bond prices. We can then measure the profitability of the trading strategy and use the results to confirm the hypothesis about market interaction.

The Intermarket Moving Average system, shown in Figure 14.7, generates a buy signal for the S&P when the closing price of T-bonds crosses over its own moving average. Similarly, a sell signal for the S&P is generated when the closing price of T-bonds crosses below its own moving average.

N is the number of bars to use in the T-bond moving average. In running the Optimization routine of TradeStation, it is found that *every* moving average between 20 and 40 days yields a substantial profit. For example, Figure 14.8 shows results for the top 10 values of N.

By contrast, a comparable one-line moving average system based on a close of the S&P above or below a moving average of S&P prices would prove to be grossly unprofitable for *all* values of N. This clearly shows that T-bond prices lead S&P prices.

FIGURE 14.7 SYSTEM: INTERMARKET MOVING AVERAGE.

Page 1

Type   : System
Name   : Intermarket Mov Avg
Notes   :

Last Update : 02/07/97 10:02am
Printed on : 02/07/97 10:16am
Verified   : YES

{Data1 is theS&P. Data2 is T-Bonds. This system generates trading signals for the S&P based on a close of T-Bonds above or below its moving average. Almost any value for N develops significant profits, which points to T-Bonds being a leading indicator for the S&P}

Input: N(27);

If Close Data2 crosses above Average(Close of Data2,N)
then Buy {the S&P} on Open;

If Close Data2 crosses below Average(Close of Data2, N)
then Sell {the S&P} on Open;

Source: Printed using TradeStation PowerEditor by Omega Research Version 4.02.15-Jul < 09 1996.

FIGURE 14.8 OPTIMIZATION: INTERMARKET MOVING AVERAGE.

Optimization: Intermarket Moving Average
Optimize N = 27 to N = 36. Subtract Commisions = $25, Slippage = $50

N	Net Profit	PFact	Max DD	ROA	#Trds	%Prft	AvgTrd
28.00	148250.00	1.35	-68875.00	215.25	302	44	490.89
27.00	139200.00	1.31	-75425.00	184.55	320	44	435.00
34.00	138625.00	1.36	-49375.00	280.76	246	42	563.52
33.00	137875.00	1.35	-56175.00	245.44	254	43	542.81
35.00	136725.00	1.36	-49375.00	276.91	244	42	560.35
29.00	135775.00	1.32	-71175.00	190.76	296	44	458.70
36.00	135125.00	1.35	-54200.00	249.31	236	42	572.56
31.00	131225.00	1.32	-65075.00	201.65	270	46	486.02
30.00	130475.00	1.31	-66275.00	196.87	292	45	446.83
32.00	123625.00	1.30	-65075.00	189.97	264	45	468.28

Source: Printed using TradeStation by Omega Research Version 4.02.15-Jul < 09 1996.

The system is much too simple to use as a trading system. Although it generates significant profits in backtesting, it also has large drawdowns. Before we begin to develop a usable trading system, it is worthwhile to consider some important concepts in system design.

CONSIDERING COMPLEXITY IN THE DESIGN AND TESTING OF SYSTEMS

System design and development utilizes past data to develop rules that will assist in the prediction of the future. In considering a data time series, such as market prices, we seek to develop a formula that adequately quantifies a series of discrete historical points, and use that formula to predict where future points will be.

An indicator, and a system using the indicator, can be designed to any level of complexity, by adding more and more variables. Generally, the more complex the system, the better it will fit historical data. But, how complex should our systems be? If an expert system has too few variables, the data is not sufficiently represented by a line through the points. There is too much distance from the data point to the line for the predictive value to be useful to the trader.

As seen previously, the formula for a straight line is:

$$Y = a + bX$$

If we desire to draw a curve through the data, additional variables must be added to the equation. If we add a third variable, c, to the equation, we have a parabola, which is represented by the formula:

$$Y = a + bX + cX^2$$

If we add more terms, the curve can move up and down, closely following the data points over time. The more terms that are added, the better the curve will fit the sample data.

For a polynomial, we measure the flexibility of a formula by noting its degrees of freedom, or DOF. This is defined as the number of variables in the formula. For a parabola, for example, there are three coefficients, a, b, and c. Thus the degrees of freedom is three.

If the DOF is high, the model tries to track each specific data point. Thus, a curve through the data may accurately describe the data that was used in finding the values of the coefficients. However, if the curve is carried forward (or backward) to a different data set, it will likely not adequately represent the new data.

The development of a rule-based technical trading system usually begins with the use of an indicator that presents data in a different form. This may be a graphical presentation, such as a moving average or an oscillator, or the identification of an occurrence, such as the highest high in 10 days. The indicator can then be used to design the rule-based system. The system consists of a series of IF . . . THEN, or IF . . . THEN . . . ELSE statements. For example, a simple system is:

> Entry:
> IF the *close today* is *above today's 10-day moving average* of the *close*, THEN *buy tomorrow* at the *open*.
>
> Exit:
> IF there is an open long position, THEN *exit* at the *close*.

This appears to be a very simple system, consisting of only one indicator, an entry rule, and an exit rule. However, as simple and basic as it appears to be, it must be recognized that it already has a high level of complexity. The italic words are terms that can be changed. There are already 10 variable terms for the buy rule alone. If we add a second indicator, if we allow for multiple contacts, if we hold the trade for more than a day, or if we add stop loss rules, the system then becomes vastly more complex.

A trading system increases in complexity as each new indicator, stop, or rule is added. In designing our system, we should strive for the simplest system that yields good results. In that way, our system has a better chance of having ongoing predictive value.

CONSIDERING DATA ADEQUACY IN THE DESIGN OF A SYSTEM

It stands to reason that if a system is optimized and backtested using inadequate data, the results cannot be relied on. A perfectly good system may be discarded because of seemingly poor results, or a mediocre system may be adopted based on good results.

Data adequacy involves issues of quality and quantity. With respect to quality, only accurate data should be used. Accurate data is exchange data, which has been verified and corrected for bad ticks. This means that traders should not use data that they have collected, but rather data purchased from a reliable vendor.

A standardized methodology should be used for data management. This should include, for example, how holidays or shortened sessions are handled, or whether evening trading sessions should be included in the data.

In addition, to allow for comparison of systems, standard methods should be adopted for creating continuous contracts from the contract data. Consideration should be given to the method for adjusting prices and the dates of rollover.

Data should be purchased from a single data vendor, since the software of each vendor for creating continuous contracts handles the task differently. Since prices in continuous contracts may not have actually occurred in the real world, the results of testing a system with data from different vendors may not be comparable.

Finally, the trader should consider how to handle outliers, which are data points that are more than a predetermined distance, such as three standard deviations, from an expected value.

For a system that utilizes multiple data streams, consideration must be given to the mutual correlation of data. If one data stream is very much like the other, we may be adding system complexity, but providing no new information.

If one data stream leads the other, that is useful additional information. The additional data stream can be used if a method is found to decorrelate the data. Basically, we are trying to mathematically eliminate the similarity, and accentuate the difference. Traders can do this with statistical analysis software. In a situation where one data stream leads the other, we designate the leading indicator as the independent variable, and the market we wish to trade as the dependent variable. We then identify the amount by which one leads the other.

Data adequacy also involves the quantity of the data used. Enough data must be used so that the results are statistically relevant. For example, the results derived from flipping a coin 10 times give us little information, and cannot be relied on, since any pattern can show up with such a small sample. However, if we flip a coin 100 times, it is likely that a close to even distribution of heads and tails will develop, assuming an evenly balanced coin.

If not enough data has been utilized to determine the coefficients of the polynomial equation, it is said that the model is underconstrained. In this case, there may be many combinations of variables that define the model, some of which may be accurate, and some of which are grossly inaccurate.

In practice, this should not present a problem to traders, since generally a large amount of data is available, and they should use all that is available. It may, however, become a problem if traders try to develop their model on a recently issued stock or a new commodity contract.

The amount of data used should also cover enough time to be representative of the market we are trying to model. For example, if the data used does not encompass a number of the short-term or seasonal cycles, or business cycles, it cannot be expected to handle unseen data.

System complexity and data adequacy must be kept in mind when developing any trading system. In developing a system as an example, we will take these factors into consideration at each step.

DEVELOPING A SIMPLE SYSTEM BASED ON A PREMISE

We start to design a trading system based on our perceptions of the market. We have shown that a straight line may create a usable model for the data. We have also shown that a change of trend of the T-bond market can be used to signal a trading opportunity in the S&P. If we transform the T-bond prices to mirror those reflected by the trend of the S&P, we can use that to directly predict a change in S&P prices.

The transformation of a T-bond price to an equivalent S&P price is akin to transforming degrees Centigrade to degrees Fahrenheit. The former scale goes from a freezing temperature of 0 degrees to a boiling temperature of 100 degrees. The latter goes from a freezing temperature of 32 degrees to a boiling temperature of 212 degrees. The formula for this temperature transformation is

$$F = 32 + C \times 9/5$$

where C is the temperature in degrees Centigrade, and F is the temperature in degrees Fahrenheit.

In the system Intermarket One, shown in Figure 14.9, we first transform T-bond prices to the equivalent S&P prices. This is done at each bar, so we are not

---

FIGURE 14.9 SYSTEM: INTERMARKET ONE.

Page 1

Type   : System
Name   : Intermarket One
Notes   :

Last Update : 01/20/97 05:33pm
Printed on : 02/07/97 10:19am
Verified   : YES

{Data1 is S&P. Data2 is T-Bonds. This system mathematically transforms T-Bond prices to S&P prices. It generates a trading signal when the Transformed T-Bond line crosses the S&P line. It is a simple system with no inputs, and is shown for development purposes.}

Var: Y(0), b(0), begSP(0), begTR(0), g(0), j(0), m(0), n(0);

If CurrentBar = 1 then begin
    begSP = Close of Data1;
    begTR = Close of Data2;
End;

If CurrentBar > 1 then begin
    m = AbsValue(Close of Data1 - begSP);
    n = AbsValue(Close of Data2 - begTR);
    If n<>0 then b = m /n;
    g = b * begTR;
    j = begSP - g;
    Y = j + b * Close[1] of Data2;   {This is the transformed T-Bond line.}
End;

If Y crosses above Close of Data1
then Buy {the S&P} on Open;

If Y crosses below Close of Data1
then Sell {the S&P}on Open;

Source: Printed using TradeStation PowerEditor by Omega Research Version 4.02.15-Jul < 09 1996.

relying on unknown information. Then, we utilize a crossover of the transformed T-bond line over the S&P line to signal a buy or a sell.

The results, at first glance, are poor. As shown in Figure 14.10, net profit is $155,075. Although 52 percent of the trades are profitable, the system developed a maximum intraday drawdown of $65,450.

The poor performance stems in part from the fact that Intermarket One is too simple a system. Stated another way, the formula for the indicator is a very crude interpretation of the data series. More complexity is required to better fit the data.

Moreover, the system generates a large number of trades, and transaction costs weigh heavily on the results. Improvement can be obtained by adding a filter.

IMPROVING THE SYSTEM WITH A MEANINGFUL FILTER, OR SETUP

Most simple systems are improved by adding a filter to the system, to reduce the number of trades and improve accuracy. This filter can be thought of as a setup, a condition precedent to executing a trade. It would be analogous to the cocking of a gun to get it ready, before you can pull the trigger to bring about the action.

Momentum is traditionally used in technical analysis as an oscillator, or overbought and oversold indicator. If momentum gets too high, prices have risen too fast, and it is time to sell. If momentum gets too low, a reversal to the upside is indicated.

Momentum, which is the change in price over time, is calculated by subtracting the price N bars ago from the current price, and plotting the point at the current point in time. If momentum is positive, prices are increasing; if momentum is negative, prices

FIGURE 14.10 PERFORMANCE SUMMARY: INTERMARKET ONE.

```
Intermarket One   S&P 500 Index - CME-Daily   04/21/82 - 12/19/96

                      Performance Summary:  All Trades

Total net profit      $ 155075.00   Open position P/L     $  14225.00
Gross profit          $1376500.00   Gross loss            $-1221425.00

Total # of trades           1776    Percent profitable          52%
Number winning trades        919    Number losing trades        857

Largest winning trade $  16425.00   Largest losing trade  $ -30725.00
Average winning trade $   1497.82   Average losing trade  $  -1425.23
Ratio avg win/avg loss        1.05   Avg trade(win & loss) $      87.32

Max consec. winners            9    Max consec. losers          13
Avg # bars in winners          2    Avg # bars in losers         2

Max intraday drawdown $ -65450.00
Profit factor                 1.13   Max # contracts held         1
Account size required $  65450.00   Return on account         237%
```

Source: Printed using TradeStation by Omega Research Version 4.02.15-Jul < 09 1996.

are decreasing. Used in this way, we can construct a filter, such that we will only consider buying the S&P if the momentum of T-bonds is positive, and selling the S&P if the momentum of T-bonds is negative. System: Intermarket 2 is shown in Figure 14.11.

Intermarket Two adds momentum to Intermarket One. Len1 represents the number of bars we go back for the momentum calculation. Figure 14.12 shows system performance across numerous values of Len1. For most values of Len1, there is a significant improvement in performance results with the addition of the filter.

Note that for Len1 = 3, net profit is $306,350. However, for the values of Len1 immediately preceding and following, performance falls off drastically. Furthermore, there is no stability in the drawdown figures. The system is not robust because neighboring input values give poor results. A slight change in future market conditions would result in a large decrease in system performance.

FIGURE 14.11 SYSTEM: INTERMARKET TWO.

Page 1

Type   : System
Name   : Intermarket Two
Notes   :

Last Update : 02/07/97 10:38am
Printed on : 02/07/97 10:40am
Verified   : YES

{Data1 is S&P. Data2 is T-Bonds. This system adds a momentum filter to Intermarket One.}

```
Var:  Y(0), b(0), begSP(0), begTR(0), g(0), j(0), m(0), n(0);
Input: Len1(3);

If CurrentBar = 1 then begin
     begSP = Close of Data1;
     begTR = Close of Data2;
End;

If CurrentBar > 1 then begin
     m = AbsValue(Close of Data1 - begSP);
     n = AbsValue(Close of Data2 - begTR);
     If n<>0 then b = m /n;
     g = b * begTR;
     j = begSP - g;
     Y = j + b * Close[1] of Data2;        {This is the transformed T-Bond line.}
End;

If Y crosses above Close of Data1 and Momentum(Close, Len1) of Data2 > 0
then Buy on Open;

If Y crosses below Close of Data1 and Momentum(Close, Len1) of Data2 < 0
then Sell on Open;
```

Source: Printed using TradeStation PowerEditor by Omega Research Version 4.02.15-Jul < 09 1996.

Figure 14.12 Optimization: Intermarket two.

Optimization: Intermarket Two
Optimize Len1= 3 to 10. Subtract Commissions = $25, Slippage = $50

Len1	Net Profit	PFact	MaxDD	ROA	#Trds	%Prft	AvgTrd
3.00	306350.00	1.55	-65925.00	464.69	535	52	572.62
5.00	249700.00	1.48	-44200.00	564.93	419	53	595.94
6.00	233350.00	1.50	-56800.00	410.83	369	50	632.38
8.00	209850.00	1.49	-59975.00	349.90	299	50	701.84
7.00	202850.00	1.46	-55900.00	362.88	343	52	591.40
4.00	180300.00	1.32	-83650.00	215.54	467	51	386.08
9.00	137550.00	1.30	-85400.00	161.07	279	47	493.01

Source: Printed using TradeStation by Omega Research Version 4.02.15-Jul < 09 1996.

ADDING ANOTHER FILTER TO IMPROVE THE SYSTEM

In system Intermarket Three, shown in Figure 14.13, we add another momentum filter to Intermarket Two. We will buy the S&P only if T-bond momentum is positive, while the S&P momentum is negative. This creates a situation whereby the T-bond momentum actually leads a change in the S&P. We look for a divergence in the momentum indicators and trade in the direction of T-bonds.

By adding a second input, we are making the system more complex. However, it is still a relatively simple system. If we optimize the two input values, we can see if performance holds up over wide ranges of inputs.

Figure 14.14 is an optimization table, sorted by net profit, showing all combinations of input values between 2 and 10. It is seen that all combinations are profitable, and a great many are very profitable.

We need to stop at this point to make sure we are heading toward a robust system, and to decide what input values we would consider using. We can then consider adding an artificial stop, such as a money management stop or a trailing stop.

BUILDING A ROBUST SYSTEM

A robust system is one that will stand up over time. It is designed based on data collected in the past, and expected to continue to generate profits into the future. Since the future will not be exactly like the past, a system's robustness is a measure of how different the future can be from the past and still yield good results.

FIGURE 14.13 SYSTEM: INTERMARKET THREE.

Page 1

Type   : System
Name   : Intermarket Three
Notes   : Uses two momentum indicators.

Last Update : 02/07/97 11:12am
Printed on : 02/07/97 11:13am
Verified   : YES

{Data1 is S&P. Data2 is T-Bonds. This system mathematically transforms T-Bond prices to S&P prices. It generates a trading signal when the Transformed T-Bond line crosses the S&P line, but only when the momentum of T-Bonds is positive while the momentum of S&P is negative.. It is a simple system with two inputs, and is shown for development purposes.}

Var: Y(0), b(0), begSP(0), begTR(0), g(0), j(0), m(0), n(0);
Input: Len1(3), Len2(10);

If CurrentBar = 1 then begin
    begSP = Close of Data1;
    begTR = Close of Data2;
End;

If CurrentBar > 1 then begin
    m = AbsValue(Close of Data1 - begSP);
    n = AbsValue(Close of Data2 - begTR);
    If n<>0 then b = m /n;
    g = b * begTR;
    j = begSP - g;
    Y = j + b * Close[1] of Data2;   {This is the transformed T-Bond line.}
End;

If Y crosses above Close of Data1 and Momentum(Close, Len1) of Data2 > 0
and Momentum(Close, Len2) of Data1 < 0   {This is the additional filter}
then Buy {the S&P} on Open;

If Y crosses below Close of Data1 and Momentum(Close, Len1) of Data2 < 0
and Momentum(Close, Len2) of Data1 > 0   {This is the additional filter}
then Sell {the S&P}on Open;

Source: Printed using TradeStation PowerEditor by Omega Research Version 4.02.15-Jul < 09 1996.

In building a trading model, we must first strive to design our system in a way that is likely to be robust. This involves principles previously discussed, such as minimizing system complexity and assuring data adequacy.

However, all the factors that lead to robustness cannot be specifically verbalized or quantified. A necessary part of system development is to test each system for robustness. This can be done by carefully and exhaustively evaluating the performance that each system achieves through backtesting, before beginning to trade it.

FIGURE 14.14 OPTIMIZATION: INTERMARKET THREE.

Optimization: Intermarket Three
Optimize Len1 = 2 to 10, Len2 = 2 to 10. Subtract Commissions=$25, Slippage=$50

Len1	Len2	Net Profit	PFact	MaxDD	ROA	#Trds	%Prft	AvgTrd
3.00	9.00	404025.00	2.79	-40050.00	1008.8	190	71	2126.45
3.00	10.00	392025.00	2.57	-41500.00	944.64	194	69	2020.75
3.00	8.00	367150.00	2.52	-38350.00	957.37	175	71	2098.00
3.00	3.00	320975.00	2.36	-56925.00	563.86	176	67	1823.72
2.00	5.00	315750.00	2.11	-92425.00	341.63	180	64	1754.17
3.00	7.00	312650.00	2.16	-45325.00	689.80	187	67	1671.93
2.00	6.00	297650.00	2.08	-72925.00	408.16	178	66	1672.19
4.00	10.00	295700.00	2.13	-35500.00	832.96	181	64	1633.70
2.00	9.00	294400.00	2.13	-88625.00	332.19	178	67	1653.93
2.00	8.00	285150.00	2.07	-78275.00	364.29	170	69	1677.35
5.00	9.00	283025.00	2.28	-43250.00	654.39	170	66	1664.85
3.00	6.00	281900.00	2.06	-53875.00	523.25	191	69	1475.92
5.00	10.00	273700.00	2.04	-56350.00	485.71	167	66	1638.92
2.00	7.00	261550.00	1.94	-81625.00	320.43	172	68	1520.64
3.00	4.00	261175.00	1.91	-57400.00	455.01	188	62	1389.23
5.00	7.00	258850.00	2.11	-55425.00	467.03	157	66	1648.73
4.00	9.00	257925.00	1.99	-43500.00	592.93	186	66	1386.69
4.00	7.00	249200.00	1.92	-67200.00	370.83	179	69	1392.18
7.00	3.00	247100.00	1.83	-75625.00	326.74	187	63	1321.39
9.00	8.00	246750.00	2.40	-45950.00	537.00	104	74	2372.60
6.00	2.00	245150.00	1.84	-53750.00	456.09	189	61	1297.09
7.00	4.00	244925.00	1.89	-65125.00	376.08	162	65	1511.88
6.00	8.00	244250.00	2.10	-62675.00	389.71	137	64	1782.85
7.00	2.00	241650.00	1.83	-32700.00	738.99	189	59	1278.57
3.00	5.00	241225.00	1.92	-51550.00	467.94	180	65	1340.14
10.00	8.00	239550.00	2.33	-44900.00	533.52	108	69	2218.06
2.00	4.00	238650.00	1.76	-66500.00	358.87	176	64	1355.97
4.00	8.00	234350.00	1.86	-61300.00	382.30	169	68	1386.69
8.00	3.00	234100.00	1.77	-90825.00	257.75	181	62	1293.37
10.00	9.00	232625.00	2.27	-39150.00	594.19	110	66	2114.77
9.00	3.00	232600.00	1.90	-81450.00	285.57	147	56	1582.31
2.00	3.00	232300.00	1.78	-70900.00	327.64	178	65	1305.06
7.00	7.00	230550.00	2.05	-44800.00	514.62	125	70	1844.40
7.00	8.00	228900.00	2.08	-62625.00	365.51	127	73	1802.36
5.00	8.00	228250.00	1.83	-49525.00	460.88	155	66	1472.58
9.00	9.00	224625.00	2.29	-45950.00	488.85	108	71	2079.86
2.00	2.00	217300.00	1.76	-68600.00	316.76	175	65	1241.71
10.00	10.00	217200.00	2.24	-38575.00	563.06	99	68	2193.94
8.00	9.00	216675.00	2.04	-35425.00	611.64	130	65	1666.73
9.00	10.00	210100.00	2.15	-50825.00	413.38	105	64	2000.95

FIGURE 14.14 OPTIMIZATION: INTERMARKET THREE CONT'D.

Len1	Len2	Net Profit	PFact	MaxDD	ROA	#Trds	%Prft	AvgTrd
7.00	9.00	208975.00	1.95	-51275.00	407.56	140	70	1492.68
6.00	3.00	208400.00	1.64	-90450.00	230.40	179	60	1164.25
3.00	2.00	207850.00	1.61	-73150.00	284.14	199	62	1044.47
8.00	8.00	205000.00	2.04	-51225.00	400.20	108	64	1898.15
4.00	6.00	203800.00	1.76	-72725.00	280.23	168	67	1213.10
2.00	10.00	203200.00	1.67	-88625.00	229.28	178	65	1141.57
7.00	6.00	202400.00	1.85	-59200.00	341.89	129	68	1568.99
6.00	9.00	201525.00	1.85	-43250.00	465.95	146	67	1380.31
6.00	4.00	199875.00	1.64	-87250.00	229.08	162	65	1233.80
9.00	7.00	199275.00	1.97	-56925.00	350.07	104	64	1916.11
8.00	4.00	198625.00	1.67	-66625.00	298.12	151	58	1315.40
9.00	2.00	191900.00	1.64	-55900.00	343.29	163	54	1177.30
4.00	3.00	190825.00	1.67	-56450.00	338.04	176	60	1084.23
5.00	6.00	190800.00	1.71	-100350.00	190.13	147	69	1297.96
9.00	4.00	190375.00	1.75	-63650.00	299.10	125	58	1523.00
10.00	7.00	189050.00	1.91	-51500.00	367.09	112	65	1687.95
5.00	2.00	187850.00	1.55	-88650.00	211.90	215	60	873.72
7.00	10.00	186650.00	1.75	-60475.00	308.64	137	66	1362.41
8.00	10.00	186500.00	1.82	-52175.00	357.45	127	63	1468.50
4.00	4.00	184675.00	1.61	-88625.00	208.38	166	59	1112.50
5.00	4.00	184475.00	1.57	-83025.00	222.19	170	63	1085.15
8.00	7.00	181500.00	1.79	-52575.00	345.22	120	63	1512.50
6.00	10.00	174250.00	1.66	-69675.00	250.09	145	61	1201.72
8.00	2.00	174100.00	1.55	-57425.00	303.18	171	56	1018.13
7.00	5.00	170000.00	1.63	-89000.00	191.01	141	65	1205.67
4.00	5.00	164650.00	1.60	-89725.00	183.51	164	63	1003.96
6.00	7.00	160800.00	1.63	-73975.00	217.37	129	61	1246.51
5.00	3.00	154250.00	1.46	-92350.00	167.03	189	59	816.14
9.00	6.00	152425.00	1.64	-48975.00	311.23	110	60	1385.68
5.00	5.00	149600.00	1.58	-87400.00	171.17	141	62	1060.99
8.00	6.00	149500.00	1.62	-43375.00	344.67	118	64	1266.95
6.00	6.00	138650.00	1.49	-81350.00	170.44	133	63	1042.48
10.00	2.00	137100.00	1.44	-56625.00	242.12	153	53	896.08
6.00	5.00	130800.00	1.44	-86850.00	150.60	139	63	941.01
10.00	4.00	130475.00	1.44	-79050.00	165.05	127	55	1027.36
8.00	5.00	116450.00	1.41	-99450.00	117.09	126	61	924.21
10.00	3.00	111450.00	1.33	-108825.00	102.41	151	52	738.08
4.00	2.00	104250.00	1.28	-69150.00	150.76	201	59	518.66
10.00	6.00	98400.00	1.39	-39625.00	248.33	104	53	946.15

Source: Printed using TradeStation by Omega Research Version 4.02.15-July 09 1996.

For a system to be robust, there must be broad ranges of variables that yield similarly profitable results. When a system is optimized, and the inputs chosen for the system to be traded, the results for neighboring combinations of variables should not be drastically dissimilar.

For a simple system, with two inputs, three-dimensional graphing gives a visual interpretation of system profitability. The system contour itself should have few deep valleys. The input combination should be surrounded by other combinations that also yield good results. The drop-off from there should be mild. Figure 14.15 shows the three-dimensional graph for the net profit of Intermarket Three. We see that there are many values around the combination of Len1 = 3 and Len2 = 9 that yield stable results.

FIGURE 14.15 THREE-DIMENSIONAL GRAPH: INTERMARKET THREE—NET PROFIT.

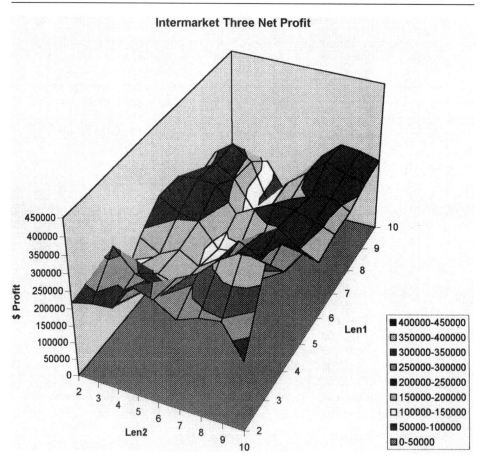

A similar three-dimensional graph, showing the drawdown resulting from the combinations of input values for Intermarket Three, is seen in Figure 14.16. This also shows low drawdown for the area Len1 = 3 and Len2 = 9.

The best trading systems are those that generate entry and exit signals based on market activity, rather than pure money management techniques. However, the performance of many systems, especially with respect to drawdown, is often improved by adding simple stops. If nothing else, the system becomes easier to trade because of the reduced drawdown and the psychological benefit of limiting losses.

FIGURE 14.16 THREE-DIMENSIONAL GRAPH: INTERMARKET THREE—DRAWDOWN.

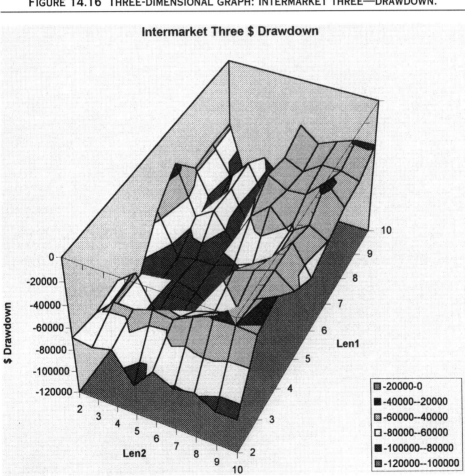

Source: Microsoft Excel. Permission received.

ADDING STOPS

To make Intermarket Three a more usable trading system, we should try to reduce drawdown. We can do this by experimenting with various stops, including profit targets, breakeven stops, money management stops, and trailing stops. For this example, we will use a trailing stop, to try to keep drawdown low while locking in profits from trades that are going well.

Figure 14.17 is an optimization table for every trailing stop from $2,000 to $20,000 at intervals of $1,000. All the lower trailing stops, those under $4,000, keep drawdown under $28,000. Excessive drawdown is the major factor that scares traders into abandoning a trading system. For that reason, many traders would have peace of mind in trading a system such as this with a small stop. However, the smaller stops greatly affect system performance figures.

The larger trailing stops, say from $15,000 up, maintain system performance, but at the expense of drawdown. The larger stops affect only a few trades over time, and results stay consistent, no matter what stop is used. Trading with such a large stop may provide some protection in the event of a market catastrophe, and for many people, it adds a measure of psychological security.

Thus, the addition of yet another optimized input, the trailing stop, increases complexity, but still does not greatly deteriorate the system. The decision whether to

FIGURE 14.17 OPTIMIZATION: INTERMARKET THREE.

Optimization: Intermarket Three
Len1 = 3 Len2 = 9. Optimize Trailing Stop $2,000 - $20,000. Subtract Commissions=$25, Slippage=$50

$Tr Stop	Net Profit	PFactor	Max DDown	ROA	#Tra	%Prof	Avg Tr
17000.00	408675.00	2.85	-37600.00	1086.90	195	71	2095.77
18000.00	406000.00	2.80	-37600.00	1079.79	195	71	2082.05
20000.00	400450.00	2.73	-37600.00	1065.03	194	71	2064.18
19000.00	400000.00	2.74	-37600.00	1063.83	195	71	2051.28
16000.00	393000.00	2.59	-40500.00	970.37	199	70	1974.87
15000.00	384375.00	2.43	-42500.00	904.41	203	70	1893.47
9000.00	369075.00	2.16	-34550.00	1068.23	229	66	1611.68
7000.00	364300.00	2.04	-42850.00	850.18	252	62	1445.63
14000.00	360425.00	2.23	-40500.00	889.94	205	69	1758.17
8000.00	350525.00	2.03	-40400.00	867.64	241	65	1454.46
10000.00	350275.00	2.08	-34850.00	1005.09	222	65	1577.82
6000.00	346575.00	1.97	-40350.00	858.92	266	59	1302.91
11000.00	337550.00	2.04	-36550.00	923.53	218	67	1548.39
13000.00	330525.00	2.08	-39625.00	834.13	210	68	1573.93
12000.00	327050.00	2.03	-37875.00	863.50	214	67	1528.27
5000.00	276000.00	1.73	-32775.00	842.11	291	56	948.45
4000.00	272950.00	1.79	-27825.00	980.95	316	55	863.77
3000.00	236775.00	1.76	-26975.00	877.76	347	50	682.35
2000.00	202350.00	1.79	-26950.00	750.83	381	44	531.10

Source: Printed using TradeStation by Omega Research Version 4.02.15-July 09 1996.

utilize a stop, and, if so, what type and at what value, is a personal one. In this example, the trade-offs can be easily seen. The choice depends on the trader's evaluation of the factors of maximizing profitability and minimizing risk.

EVALUATING THE SYSTEM

For the purpose of further analysis, we will choose the values of 3 and 9 for Len1 and Len2 respectively, and $17,000 as the trailing stop. We will deduct $75 per trade for commissions and slippage. For the evaluation, and the graphs that follow, we will use Performance Summary Plus (PSP), by RINA Systems, Inc. The results are shown in Figure 14.18.

The performance factors of net profit and percent profitable allow for a ready comparison of systems. In this case, profit statistics of $408,675, with 70.77 percent profitable trades, are favorable. However, the ratio of the average win divided by average loss is only 1.18, which is low.

The profit factor, which is the gross profit divided by the gross loss, shows how much money was made for every dollar lost. A good system has a profit factor of 3 or more. Our example, with a profit factor of 2.85, approaches that figure.

Return on maximum drawdown, otherwise known as return on account, is calculated as the net profit divided by maximum drawdown. A good system has this number at 150 percent per year. Since our test was for 14.6 years, the 2,153.67 percent return on account averages about 148 percent per year, which is not bad.

The average trade is calculated as the net profit divided by the number of trades. With the stop we have chosen, the average trade is an excellent $2,095.77.

To get a better idea of how this system performs, it is necessary to look at how its trades deviate from the average. This can be seen in a graph of the total trades, as shown in Figure 14.19.

It stands to reason that the closer the trades are to this profitable average, the more consistent and better the system. If we add and subtract one standard deviation from the average trade, we are able to see the range within which 64 percent of the trades reside. Here, the range is from $8,462.95 to −$4,271.42.

The coefficient of variation is calculated by expressing one standard deviation as a percentage of the average trade. The smaller the percentage, the more stable and consistent is the system. Our example system showed a coefficient of variation of 303.81 percent. This is quite high as a good system would have this figure at 200 percent or less.

A good analysis of a system focuses on drawdown. The maximum drawdown is the largest intraday drawdown experienced by the system. The $37,600 drawdown of this system is somewhat high, even for a contract such as the S&P, which has a value in excess of $350,000.

The maximum drawdown does not tell us the whole picture about drawdown, since it may have only occurred once in the many years of history. The average drawdown is a very important figure. This is the average maximum loss potential of all trades. It gives you an idea of what can normally be expected during trading. Here,

FIGURE 14.18 PSP PERFORMANCE SUMMARY: INTERMARKET THREE.

Intermarket Three S&P 500 Index - CME-Daily 04/21/82 - 12/19/96

System Analysis

Net Profit	$408,675.00	Open Position	$5,225.22
Gross Profit	$629,975.00		
Gross Loss	($221,300.00)		
Percent profitable	70.77%	Profit factor	2.85
Ratio avg. win/loss	1.18		
Return on Max. Drawdown	2153.67%		

Total Trade Analysis

Number of total trades	195	Total stopped trades	7
Average trade	$2,095.77	Avg. trade ± 1 STDEV	$8,462.95 / ($4,271.42)
1 Std. Deviation (STDEV)	$6,367.19	Coefficient of variation	303.81%

Drawdown

Maximum Drawdown	($37,600.00)		
Average Drawdown	($3,491.55)	Avg. trade ± 1 STDEV	$615.43 / ($7,598.53)
1 Std. Deviation (STDEV)	$4,106.98	Coefficient of variation	117.63%

Reward/Risk Ratios

Largest Loss Ratio	24.28

Outlier Trades	Total Trades	Profit/Loss
Positive outliers	1	$47,025.00
Negative outliers	1	($17,050.00)
Total outlier	2	$29,975.00

Source: RINA Systems, Inc. Used by permission.

FIGURE 14.19 TOTAL TRADES: INTERMARKET THREE.

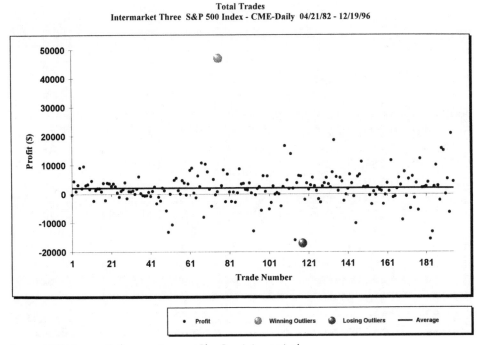

Total Trades
Intermarket Three S&P 500 Index - CME-Daily 04/21/82 - 12/19/96

Source: RINA Systems Performance Summary Plus. Permission received.

the average drawdown was $3,491.55. Since this is a system based on end-of-day prices, with a very big stop, this figure is not too bad.

The rewards to be expected by a system must always be considered as they relate to the risks incurred. The return on account, discussed earlier, relates average profit to maximum drawdown. Another measure of reward/risk is the largest loss ratio, which is calculated by dividing the net profit by the largest losing trade. Here, the ratio is 24.28, which is quite good.

A consideration of outliers points to how much of the system performance comes from a few isolated trades. If a large percentage of the system profits or losses come from these outliers, the system cannot be expected to perform well in the future, since these rare occurrences cannot be counted on. Because of this, some traders prefer to ignore the one or two extreme wins and losses in comparing systems.

For a system to remain robust, it must yield consistent performance results over time. The profits for each year should be similar to those of other years. A review of the annual trading results is shown in Figure 14.20. It is seen that there were just two losing years, only one of which was a significant loss. Furthermore, the system has continued to perform well in recent years.

FIGURE 14.20 ANNUAL TRADING SUMMARY: INTERMARKET THREE.

Annual

Annual Trading Summary

Annual Analysis (Mark-To-Market):

Period	Net Profit	Profit Factor	# Trades	% Profitable
YTD	$50,277.13	2.81	13	69.23%
12 month	$55,875.00	3.60	12	75.00%
95	$29,701.27	2.39	14	64.29%
94	$9,600.45	1.53	13	53.85%
93	$34,626.33	9.45	14	78.57%
92	$15,875.64	2.12	12	66.67%
91	$51,627.09	3.23	19	78.95%
90	$30,301.19	2.91	9	88.89%
89	($3,525.06)	0.87	16	56.25%
88	$20,750.84	2.77	15	73.33%
87	$84,678.41	7.50	13	69.23%
86	$37,226.56	3.59	17	76.47%
85	($18,725.69)	0.27	10	40.00%
84	$14,250.66	5.07	16	68.75%
83	$26,401.00	5.96	17	82.35%
82	$40,251.69	269.35	11	90.91%

Source: RINA Systems, Inc. Used by permission.

Another evaluation is the rolling period analysis, shown in Figure 14.21. This allows one to evaluate results from any time in the past to the present. It shows the ability of a system to remain consistently profitable no matter when in the time series the trader may have started to trade. It smooths out measures of profitability, such as profit factor and percent profitable.

The equity curve, calculated by showing cumulative equity, allows for a ready graphical analysis of overall performance. The trader looks for a steady upward-sloping line, with a minimum number of valleys. As seen in Figure 14.22, this system performs well.

It is worthwhile to consider the time between peaks on the equity curve. During trending periods, there probably will be large distances between peaks. During periods when the market is choppy, new peaks should be hit more frequently.

FIGURE 14.21 ROLLING PERIOD ANALYSIS: INTERMARKET THREE.

Annual

Annual Rolling Period Analysis (Mark-To-Market):

Period	Net Profit	% Gain	Profit Factor	# Trades	% Profitable
96	$50,277.13	12.78%	2.81	13	69.23%
95-96	$79,978.39	22.25%	2.63	27	66.67%
94-96	$89,578.84	25.90%	2.33	40	62.50%
93-96	$124,205.20	38.28%	2.74	54	66.67%
92-96	$140,080.80	50.10%	2.64	66	66.67%
91-96	$191,707.90	77.66%	2.76	85	69.41%
90-96	$222,009.10	102.25%	2.78	94	71.28%
89-96	$218,484.00	96.04%	2.45	110	69.09%
88-96	$239,234.90	117.30%	2.47	125	69.60%
87-96	$323,913.30	266.05%	2.85	138	69.57%
86-96	$361,139.80	430.44%	2.90	155	70.32%
85-96	$342,414.20	333.49%	2.59	165	68.49%
84-96	$356,664.80	400.07%	2.63	181	68.51%
83-96	$383,065.80	617.85%	2.71	198	69.70%
82-96	$423,317.50	1693.27%	2.88	209	70.81%

Source: RINA Systems, Inc. Used by permission.

PSP allows for the consideration of many more important factors of system performance. Although time consuming, it is beneficial to look at each system from as many aspects as possible to determine whether the rewards of implementing the system into a trading plan is worth the risk involved.

WHERE DO WE GO FROM HERE?

The system we have analyzed is an oversimplified system, shown for demonstration purposes. With not too much effort, much better systems can be devised, with better results.

We showed that additional filters, rationally chosen based on sound principles, improved the system. Can we keep adding filters? With each succeeding addition, we were generally able to improve most measures of performance. We have an infinite number of filters we can try, ranging from other moving averages to other oscillators, to volatility breakout triggers. However, without the addition of a new concept, we may have come close to the maximum benefits that can be derived.

FIGURE 14.22 EQUITY CURVE: INTERMARKET THREE.

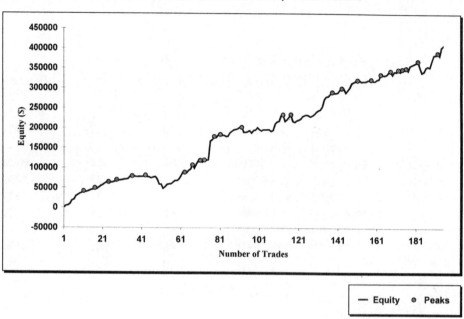

Intermarket Three S&P 500 Index - CME-Daily 04/21/82 - 12/19/96

One reason is that many technical analysis indicators merely explain the same thing in different ways. Therefore, we are adding indicators that are so highly correlated with each other that they duplicate each other. Furthermore, additional filters may start to be contradictory to the existing filters. This would lead to fewer trades, but worse results.

This system averages about one trade per month. If more filters cut the number of trades down substantially, some practical problems may result. The most obvious one is that the historical data may not yield sufficient trades for the system's performance to be statistically valid.

In addition, we may be aiming toward the ultimate example of curve fitting. We can see that the S&P has gone up for the entire history at a relatively constant slope. Once we know this, a system that trades very little will be expected to do very well in backtesting, but may not hold up under different conditions.

In this example, we chose a very simple linear model of the data. Future efforts, designed toward improving upon these results, or toward investigating other intermarket relationships, can use a somewhat more complex approach. The tools of linear regression or multiple regression can be effectively used. The data can be better preprocessed by using, for example, ratios, logarithms, weighted or exponential averages, or myriad other approaches.

CONCLUSION

We have shown by example the development of a simple system utilizing intermarket analysis. The concepts presented can easily be adapted to help traders develop trading systems that will improve their probability of success.

REFERENCES

Box, George E. P., Hunter, William J., and Hunter, J. Stuart, *Statistics for Experimenters—An Introduction to Design, Data Analysis and Model Building,* New York: John Wiley & Sons, 1978.

Deming, W. Edwards, *Statistical Adjustment of Data,* New York: Dover Publications, 1938, 1943.

Farnum, Nicholas R., and Stanton, LaVerne W., *Quantitative Forecasting Methods,* Boston: PWS-Kent Publishing, 1989.

Jurik, Mark G., "Developing Indicators for Financial Trading," in Jess Lederman and Robert A. Klein (Eds.), *Virtual Trading,* Chicago: Probus Publishing, 1995.

Keeping, E. S., *Introduction to Statistical Inference,* New York: Dover Publications, 1995.

Mandel, John, *The Statistical Analysis of Experimental Data,* New York: Dover Publications, 1964.

Vince, Ralph, *The Mathematics of Money Management,* New York: John Wiley & Sons, 1992.

CHAPTER 15

Complex Indicators: Nonlinear Pricing and Reflexivity

CHRISTOPHER THOMAS MAY

The purpose of this chapter is to give potential investors an overview of the need for using nonlinear pricing technology. In the financial market, especially, we see how well the components of this technology work in concert. Nonlinear pricing affects asset allocation, stock selection, option pricing, and risk management.

BACKGROUND

Some of the best minds, both academician and practitioner, are heralding a fundamental change in economic thinking. The practical implications are far reaching and raise two important questions: How can we quickly improve our understanding of market behavior? How have we been misled in decades past? We will begin with the latter question.

A common approach to market analysis is to assume that large price changes are usually traceable to well-determined causes that should be eliminated before attempting a stochastic model of the remainder. Such preliminary censorship brings any distribution of price changes closer to resembling the popular and better understood Gaussian curve. The distinction between the causal and random areas is sharp in the normal (Gaussian) case and very diffuse in the stable (Paretian) case. The difference between these two distributions may allow for arbitrage opportunities as it changes a fundamental assumption in financial theory. More on that later (see Figure 15.1).

The very practice of fitting linear (e.g., regression) models, particularly those involving trended variables, acted to filter out low-frequency variance and outliers, thereby making real distributions appear "normal." But they are not normal at all. The appearance is just an artifact of a shotgun wedding of deterministic theory with "random shocks." Although the motivation is to have this filtered data fit current linear theory, it is not a scientific approach.

Why does this motivation for linear models exist? John Holland, father of the genetic algorithm said, "It is little known outside the world of mathematics that most

FIGURE 15.1 A NORMAL DISTRIBUTION CURVE OF PRICE CHANGES
AND A STABLE DISTRIBUTION CURVE. THE HORIZONTAL AXIS REPRESENTS
HE SPREAD OF POSSIBLE FUTURE PRICES OF AN UNDERLYING SECURITY,
WITH THE CENTER OF THE CURVE REPRESENTING TODAY'S PRICE.

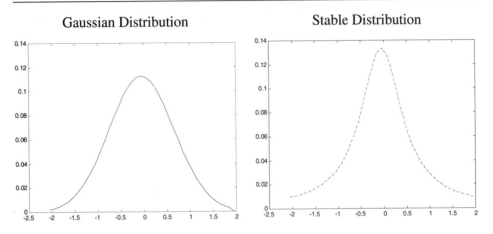

Gaussian Distribution   Stable Distribution

of our mathematical tools, from simple arithmetic through differential calculus to algebraic topology, rely on the assumption of linearity." In short, we don't have a sufficient set of well-understood tools for nonlinear analysis. Fortunately, this is changing.

In 1995, famed investor George Soros wrote:

> There has been a recent development in science, variously called the science of complexity, evolutionary systems theory, or chaos theory. To understand historical processes, this approach is much more useful than the traditional approach, which is analytical. Unfortunately, our view of the world has been shaped by analytical science to a greater extent than is good for us. Economics seeks to be an analytical science. But all historical processes, including financial markets, are complex and cannot be understood on the basis of analytical science. We need a whole new approach and my theory of reflexivity is just the first step in this direction.[1]

The very existence of changing interest rates, business and political cycles runs contrary to standard financial theory. These cycles mathematically imply that the dynamics of the market are changing with time, and thus exhibit nonlinear behavior.

Murray Gell-Mann, Nobel laureate in physics, adds:

> Some dogmatic neoclassical economists had kept claiming that fluctuations around so-called fundamentals in financial markets amounted to a random walk, and they produced some evidence to support their assertion. But in the last few years, it has been shown—I believe quite convincingly—that, in fact, various markets show fluctuations that are not entirely random. They are pseudo-random and that pseudo-randomness can be exploited.[2]

How can this new understanding be exploited? Here's an example from personal experience.

Years ago, I was a derivative arbitrageur hedging Japanese warrants against their underlying equities at Baring Securities in Tokyo. A warrant is a long dated call option on an equity. The call option and its equity are equivalent, though not identical. Their relationship is intuitive; if the price of an equity rises, then one would correctly expect the call option to increase as well and vice versa. The relationship between the two instruments is measured statistically using the popular Black-Scholes option pricing model.

We encountered a problem though. Warrants typically have a three- to five-year life and the Black-Scholes model becomes very inaccurate after about 90 days. In the simplest terms, if reality and current theory are not congruent, then an arbitrage opportunity exists. Implementing new techniques that more accurately depicted reality led to an arbitrage between the pattern nonlinear pricing can detect and the market, which is less informed. The next question is, can the arbitrage be systematically and profitably exploited? I believe the answer is yes.

Wall Street's View

The language of mathematics may be arbitrarily divided into two camps: the linear or the additive and the nonlinear or the nonadditive. Historically, linear mathematics is the type with which we are most familiar.

For example, if a candy bar costs one dollar, a linear or additive relationship means that three candy bars costs three dollars. Another example of linear addition is $2 + 2 = 4$. Linear relationships are not time dependent: $2 + 2 = 4$ will remain true tomorrow as well as today and yesterday. Deterministic *systems,* where the relationships in time are fixed, are linear. Car washes and soda vending machines are good examples: money in and 5 seconds later soda out, *ad infinitum.* It is easy to understand this simple deterministic or linear relationship, which has been the dominant paradigm for scientific interpretation of phenomena in the West.

The linear view persisted probably because of practical necessity, since technology was not advanced enough to detect modeling errors. Basic laws of physics were simple, widely accepted, and did not allow for the small changes—the nonlinearities—and without the technology to measure them practically, the linear or deterministic viewpoint became dominant.

Like their predecessors, economists borrowed from existing lines of linear thought. Even though the theories may not always have been accurate in the eyes of the practitioner, they fit together neatly in terms of linear math. Probability theory and the partial differential equations of equilibrium physics are the root of classical economics.

When applying classical economic theory and the portfolio theory of the 1970s, we need to make assumptions about the future behavior of asset prices and how the returns of assets are distributed. In keeping with the linear mind-set, theoreticians assumed that the movement in time of any traded asset was random and that its returns were normally (Gaussian) distributed. While this is still the prevailing view, it is wrong.

Why? Trend and momentum are two concepts in technical analysis that are most common to Wall Street. They have their basis in linear math (e.g., $2 + 2 = 4$, where the relationship is not time dependent). Unlike momentum, persistence is the *tendency* of a time series to continue its current direction (up or down) and antipersistence is the tendency of a time series to reverse itself rather than to continue its current direction. Momentum cannot characterize time series that are antipersistent. Persistence is also *not* trend. Trend is a perspective in the present that looks back in time. Persistence is a perspective in the present that looks forward in time to give a likelihood of future price movements.

The problem with the prevailing view is that the time series of financial markets are complex affairs that do not lend themselves to simple interpretations of trend and momentum. Nor are they random most of the time. Most of the time, traded asset prices persist or antipersist. That is, they have the tendency to follow their current path or reverse themselves. Therefore, stock price movements are dependent, in part, on past action and time. The goal, then, is to model this dependency using nonlinear techniques.

NONLINEARITY

Modeling Phenomena

In terms of modeling phenomena, one may visualize three basic states of the world: predictable, unpredictable, and partially predictable. Table 15.1 summarizes some nomenclature and concepts in terms of those three states. Various terms in the table will be explained throughout this chapter.

The bulk of Western thinking on economics, science, and mathematics is linear and is depicted in the center column and the columns at either extreme. But the reader's reward will come from considering the columns in between.

Picture a lit cigar. For the first three inches or so above the ash, the smoke is smooth or laminar. It then gets a little twisted and about three to five inches up it bends into curlicues. Parallels exist between cigar smoke and dynamic system behavior. Nonlinear mathematics better depicts dynamical systems or systems that change with time. Orbits, behavior, and cigar smoke are dynamical systems. So are markets. Mathematically, nonlinearity means that results are nonadditive. A small difference today can become a bigger difference tomorrow. Results are time dependent.

The laminar flow of smoke approximates a linear relationship—by looking at the smoke particles, you can estimate where they will be a moment or two later.

The curlicues are turbulence. Mathematically, these flows are unpredictable. Knowing the position of any given particle tells you nothing about where it may be in the next instant. Unpredictable systems are out of control because no relationship in time exists. A chaotic system is, in the long term, unpredictable.

Oddly enough, we define linearity by those conditions that are either completely random or perfectly correlated (either positively or negatively) in time. All conditions not at either extreme are a special mixture of persistence or antipersistence

TABLE 15.1 COMPARISONS OF PREDICTABLE, UNPREDICTABLE, AND
PARTIALLY PREDICTABLE PHENOMENA

Predictability	Predictable	Partially Predictable	Unpredictable	Partially Predictable	Predictable
Comments	Exactly the opposite as predicted		Completely random		Exactly as predicted
Mathematics	Linear	Nonlinear	Linear	Nonlinear	Linear
Correlation	−1		0		+1
Brownian Motion H		Fractional H < 0.5	H = 0.5	Fractional H > 0.5	
Time series persistence		Antipersistent	Independent	Persistent	
Equilibrium states			None	Partial	Perfect
Finance		New reality	Old assumption	New reality	
Behavior	A 3-year-old child		Person with Alzheimer's	General public	Robot
Cigar smoke pattern			Curlicues	Twisted spiral	Laminar
Orbits			Multiple moons (3 body problem)	Typical orbit	Earth's moon

and randomness. They are nonlinear. By this definition, standard financial theory assumes linearity because it assumes that asset prices follow a completely random walk, referred to in the scientific literature as Brownian motion (Bm).

The twisted flow, as a simple physical model and as a nonlinear relationship, lies between linearity and chaos and best depicts the reality of everyday markets. They are in a kind of equilibrium that is dynamic and changing in time. Twisted flows are partially predictable although predictability decreases the more it becomes disordered over time.

Any order within a system bears redundancy or patterns that can be exploited. Imagine a word partially represented by "B__ddh__." What's the full word? If you guessed Buddha, you are correct. With ⅔ of the information you received 100 percent of the message. Patterns in traded assets are no different. Yet, standard financial theory assumes that no patterns exist (i.e., the movements in time are random). This is where nonlinear pricing comes into play.

Nonlinear Pricing

As a recognized leader in the field of nonlinearity, Kriya, Inc, has proffered the following definition: Nonlinear pricing is any technological trading aid that acknowledges the nonlinearities exhibited by markets to more accurately characterize patterns exhibited by traded assets. Nonlinear pricing comprises new technologies such as chaos theory, abductive logic, fuzzy logic, genetic algorithms, and neural nets to model the new paradigm of evolution or adaptation. Soros' theory of reflexivity is congruent with nonlinear pricing.

Nonlinear pricing assumes the markets are adaptive and its goal is to quantify the relationship in time between asset price movements, to gain some degree of predictability over probable future prices. Nonlinear pricing has been used successfully since July 1994.

The opportunity to profit is the arbitrage between the pattern depicted by nonlinear pricing and the market's inability to detect the pattern just as accurately. Moreover, this opportunity is unlikely to be arbitraged away because of the number of variables involved, the varying investment horizons, the technology gap, and the fact that the dissemination of Black-Scholes built the derivatives industry on a foundation of linear assumptions.

For a comparison, consider that Wall Street typically makes investment decisions, especially on equities, in one or a combination of three ways: fundamental analysis, technical analysis, and via the "whisper circuit." In a fundamental valuation, consistent earnings are a plus and in classical analysis, its effect on price is heuristically or subjectively interpreted. In contrast, nonlinear pricing actually quantifies this concept, modeling the dynamics of how those fundamentals interact in time and their effect on price.

Measurements

When adopting the nonlinear paradigm, new measurable aspects of time series become available. Some of the more popular concepts are presented in this section.

Persistence and the Hurst Exponent

The basic process is to identify when an equity's price has persistence (the "what"). Then attribute a business reason (the "why") to that behavior. For example, strong price persistence may be reliably detected during strong earnings. Invest when the "what" and "why" agree. Monitor the position and remove when they do not agree. Looking at factors that affect price instead of at price itself makes for more sophisticated relationships.

Cutland et al. found[3] that, statistically, random walks occur only part of the time and there is a relationship between variables in time and that relationship changes over time. Peters[4] identified the relationship in time using the Hurst exponent H.

The Hurst coefficient, H, is a scaling factor in time. If we were to view a time-series at a faster than normal rate, in hypertime, like using fast-forward on our VCR, H would be an acceleration factor. H tells us something about the function's behavior. Using H is like putting time in fast-forward to discern something about the stock's future tendencies. Mathematically, it looks like the following formula where the equality sign means "equal in distribution," and not "equal point for point along the time series":

$$X(t) = 1/aH \times X(at)$$

where

$X(t)$ is a function in time,
$1/aH$ is the scaling factor,
$X(at)$ is the process $X(t)$ speeded up by a factor of a

When a time series is a Bm, H = 0.5. When H is greater or less than 0.5, the time series is persistent or antipersistent, respectively. If a time series' H = 0.7, then it may be said that the time series has a greater probability of continuing its current direction and a lesser probability of reversing itself. The converse is true for H < 0.5 (an antipersistent time series). Rescaled range is one way to measure the Hurst coefficient.[5]

One of the underlying premises of the portfolio theory of the 1970s is that the movements in time of all traded assets are random 100 percent of the time. In contrast, our research shows that U.S. equities are random only about 10 percent of the time at transient points. In other words, classical theory is inaccurate about 90 percent of the time in its assumption that a financial time series is Bm.

For example, in Figure 15.2, begin at the left-hand side of the graph with the line intersecting H = 0.8. This line measures the Hurst coefficient for the US equity Conseco (NYSE: CNC). If standard financial theory accurately depicted reality, the line intersecting the left-hand side of the graph at 0.8 would have been a constant 0.5. But as we see, from 12 April to 1 October, most of the time the stock price was either persistent or antipersistent—not random.

In simple terms, this graph crystallizes the disagreement between academics and practitioners about the assumption of randomness of stock prices. Practitioners quickly learn that linearity is an inaccurate paradigm. Straight lines are not good forecasting tools, nor are completely random walks. Based on a continuum from randomness (i.e., no relationship in time) to predictability (i.e., perfect relationship in time) many natural phenomena, as well as market behavior, exist most of the time between the two extremes.

Reflexivity

In many important respects, nonlinear pricing is a practical implementation of Soros' theory of reflexivity, which he first wrote about in 1987.[6] The theory of reflexivity holds that equilibrium—the assumed norm in classical economics—is but a

FIGURE 15.2 HURST EXPONENT VERSUS TIME FOR CNC.

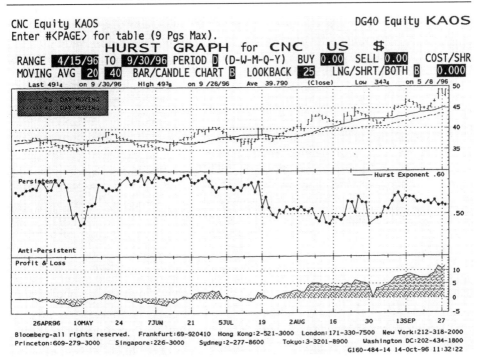

Source: Bloomberg Financial Markets. Used by permission.

special case of the more common dis-equilibrium state in markets and of the more in-frequent far-from-equilibrium state (e.g., crashes).

Reflexivity goes one step further, in describing the warp and woof of market activity. It states that practitioners' expectations can actually influence the markets themselves. Because you and your competitors have the same information, you have to *anticipate.* If several firms do large trades, their collective views and resultant action will have a real but temporary effect on the market. For example, when views of a widely followed spread affect the market, and views of the market affect the spread, reflexivity is easily demonstrated. When reflexivity occurs, nonlinear pricing models have the advantage over linear pricing models.

Fractal Dimension

Fractal is a *property,* just like mass, or hardness. A fractal consists of self-similarity and a fractal dimension. A graphic example of scaling self-similarity is the fern leaf, where a small leaf is geometrically similar to a larger leaf. Some price time series exhibit statistical self-similarity. That is, when viewed without labels, the minute, daily, weekly, and monthly time series look alike.

A fractal dimension is a non-integer dimension. A typical price time series drawn on a sheet of paper is somewhere between a straight line (1D) and a solid plane (2D). A random time series (Brownian motion or Bm) has a fractal dimension of 1.5D. A persistent time-series is closer in resemblance to a line and conversely, an antipersistent time series is closer to a solid plane. Persistent and antipersistent time series are fractional Brownian motion (fBm).[7]

Wavelets

Spectral analysis searches for periodicity and the system's characteristic scale. The cyclic behavior in time series is most commonly measured by using a fast calculating version of Fourier Analysis, called the FFT. It is based on the assumption that a time series captured within a window (a piece of a time series) repeats itself outside the window forever and that the segment within the window can be analyzed into constituent sine and cosine waves. Sine and cosine terms assume stationary (fixed) periodicities over time and do not do well for financial time series that are aperiodic or nonstationary.

Wavelet theory is a more suitable form of analysis and is now over a decade old.[8] Wavelets may be likened to a formless lycra garment. The garment fits many similar body contours and derives its form from whatever it fits. Wavelets can be made to "fit" data in a window by means of translation and dilation, decomposing the original time series into component parts. These parts can be used to reconstruct the same time series. In part because of its flexible windowing capability, wavelets can be used to analyze multiple scales of fractal time series. Sometimes, feeding wavelet coefficients into a nonlinear pricing model is superior to feeding the prices themselves.

Unlike Fourier analysis, which is given to stationary data, time-frequency (e.g., Grossman-Morlet) wavelets are suited for quasi-stationary signals and time-scale wavelets are given to fractal structures. Figure 15.3 is an example of a wavelet generated using the least asymmetric Daubechies filters of order 11 in Mathematica 3.0™.[9]

Applications

The following are some applications based on nonlinear pricing.

Asset Allocation

Asset allocation is potentially one of the most promising and least explored applications of nonlinear pricing. Rotating between asset classes or even evaluating fund managers are well within the purview of nonlinear pricing.

Conceptually, asset allocation is very similar to stock selection. Suppose we wish to rotate between equities, bonds, and cash. If each asset class is represented by an index, then the balancing between indices is much like looking at patterns in different equities.

FIGURE 15.3 A SAMPLE WAVELET GENERATED USING MATHEMATICA'S
FUNCTION "LEASTASYMMETRICFILTER" TO GENERATE FILTER COEFFICIENTS,
AND THE FUNCTION "WAVELET" TO RECONSTRUCT THE ORIGINAL "MOTHER" WAVELET.

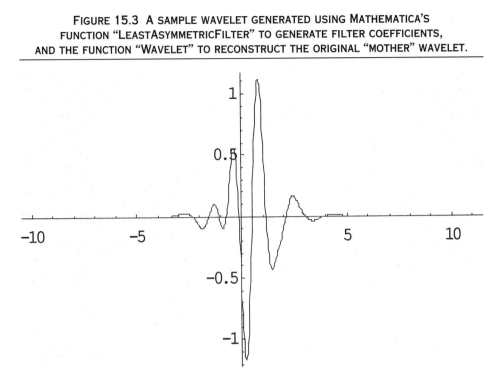

Source: Wolfram Mathematic Research 3.0. Used by permission.

Options

Each equity poses a unique probability distribution that may be expressed as a probability density function (PDF). To assume that the returns of all equities have the same PDF—in this case, a Gaussian or normal bell shape curve—is tantamount to saying that all men wear the same size suit, or that all companies should be valued by the same methods, or that the loss distributions from one line of insurance, such as commercial automobile collision, may be used to price another line, such as flood insurance. And as with insurance underwriting, accurate risk pricing is the central issue of sustained profitability.

Improper modeling can lead to mispricing. To illustrate this effect, we will consider stock option pricing. A stock option is the right to buy or sell a particular stock at a certain price for a limited period of time. The price at which the stock may be bought or sold is called the strike price. The option's intrinsic value is the difference between the agreed strike price and price of the underlying security.

An option's market price is based on the public's perception of the option's potential future intrinsic value, and therefore, to a large degree, on the perceived future price of the underlying security. One way for mispricing to occur is to misjudge likely future price changes of the underlying security.

In general, a PDF of the log of price ratios p_{t+1}/p_t is nearly normally distributed, and so the popular Black-Scholes pricing formula assumes price movement is log-normally distributed. However, this assumption is not totally accurate, as it implies yesterday's price changes are wholly unrelated to today's price changes. This assumption is appropriate for a time series that is 100 percent random (e.g., Brownian motion). If, however, the price time series for a traded asset is not random 100 percent of the time—and it is not—then the normal distribution hypothesis is inappropriate.

The difference between linear and nonlinear assumptions can be visualized as the difference between two probability distributions. The former, in the case of Black-Scholes, is the assumed normal distribution and the latter, in the case of the actual underlying equity, is the empirical and more stable distribution. Table 15.2 summarizes these features.

A comparison of these two curves is illustrated in Figure 15.1. With regard to the relative likelihood of how an underlying security's price may change, we see a normal (Gaussian) distribution curve, a stable (real-world) distribution curve, and an overlay of both curves. Note the stable distribution is narrower, but has larger values as it tails. The overlay shows shaded regions where the two curves differ.

To examine how this affects pricing, look at the curve's tails at the extreme right of the overlay (region A) in Figure 15.4. Because the Gaussian tail is lower than the stable tail, classical pricing formulas expect a smaller frequency of occurrence of very large positive price changes than you would find in the real world. It also expects a *larger* frequency of occurrence of moderately positive price changes than there really are in regions B and C. To correct this problem, we would need to move a portion of classical model's expected occurrences from region B to region A, as shown by the arrow. However, because Gaussian models produce a bias toward smaller positive price changes than reality calls for in the A-B regions of the chart, the underlying security will tend to be underpriced in this region. Consequently, call options with a strike price within this region will tend to be underpriced and put options overpriced.

A similar argument can be made for regions C and D but with the opposite effect. Because the Gaussian curve is higher than the stable curve in region C, classical pricing formulas expect a larger frequency of occurrence of moderately positive price changes than you would find in the real world. It also expects a *smaller* frequency of occurrence of tiny positive price changes than there really are in region D. To correct this problem, we would need to move a portion of model's expected occurrences from region C to region D, as shown by the arrow. However, because Gaussian models produce a bias toward larger positive price changes than reality calls for in the C-D regions

TABLE 15.2 RELATION OF TIME SERIES AND
CORRESPONDING ASSUMPTIONS AND DISTRIBUTION TYPE

Time Series Type	Assumptions	Model	Distribution
Brownian motion	Linear	Black-Scholes	Normal
Persistent	Nonlinear		Stable

FIGURE 15.4 A NORMAL DISTRIBUTION CURVE OF PRICE CHANGES, A STABLE
DISTRIBUTION CURVE, AND AN OVERLAY OF BOTH. THE HORIZONTAL AXIS
REPRESENTS THE SPREAD OF POSSIBLE FUTURE PRICES OF AN UNDERLYING
SECURITY, WITH THE CENTER OF THE CURVE REPRESENTING TODAY'S
PRICE. THE DIFFERENCE BETWEEN THESE TWO DISTRIBUTIONS MAY ALLOW
FOR ARBITRAGE OPPORTUNITIES AS IT CHANGES, A FUNDAMENTAL
ASSUMPTION IN OPTION AND RISK PRICING AS WELL AS FINANCIAL THEORY.

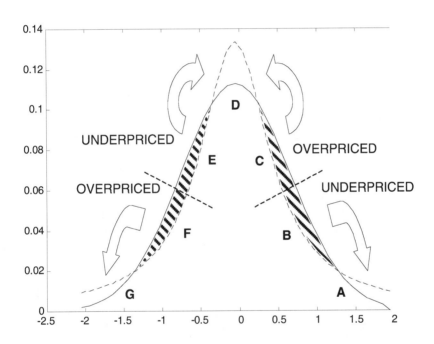

of the chart, the underlying security will tend to be overpriced in this region. Consequently, call options with a strike price within this region will tend to be overpriced and put options underpriced.

Similarly, Gaussian models will tend to *underprice* underlying securities in the small-to-medium negative price change regions (D-E) and *overprice* underlying securities in the medium-to-large negative price change regions (F-G).

Remember that nonlinear pricing applies to *any traded asset,* not just to options, and almost any time frame: minute bars, daily bars, monthly, and so on. However, it is folly to use just one valuation method (nonlinear pricing included) mechanistically, since reality is far more complex than any one model can depict.

Because current mispricing is based on the overly restrictive assumption of Gaussian returns used by Black-Scholes to model PDFs, it stands to reason that information regarding the unique PDF of each equity would enable a superior way to value an option. However, there are shortcomings. For example, no clear link exists between probability and a stable time series with Hurst exponent H < 0.5. By definition, these series are antipersistent. To a mathematician then, positing certain nonlinear arguments may lack rigor because theory is incomplete.

MODELING TOOLS

The previous section discussed various measurements of a time series suitable for nonlinear pricing. The following section presents software technology that can process these variables and model their relationships in nonlinear ways. They include fuzzy logic, genetic algorithms, and neural networks.

Fuzzy Logic

Because the markets are extremely nonlinear, multidimensional, and time varying, attempts to simplify analysis by using fewer dimensions and standard econometric and portfolio analysis offers little help. What is needed is a practical way for users to devise models in low-dimensional space and transfer their knowledge about the subject matter to a mathematical function that yields nonfuzzy results. Fuzzy logic provides that capability.[10]

Fuzzy logic (FL) is a universal approximator. FL offers a way to both capture human knowledge mathematically and perform logical operations on it that makes intuitive sense. It is ideal for processing statements of reality that are neither 100 percent true or 100 percent false.

A simple way to picture the power of FL is to visualize the thermostat and air conditioner (AC) in your office. Although the thermometer gradually moves through its normal range, the AC is either off or on full force. When the temperature rises above 78 degrees F, the AC comes on full force until the temperature drops. It would be more effective to design a FL-based system with the two rules "If it is a little warm, then the AC comes on a little bit" and "if it is a lot warm, then the AC comes on a lot." The concept of a little bit warm and a little bit of AC is similar to the concept of a financial instrument being a little bit cheap or expensive, or to buy or sell a little bit more.

FL has some great advantages: it is fast and it is auditable. Unlike neural nets where the relative weightings between variables are hidden, with FL you can actually see the input-output relationship. This should give fund managers and investors an additional degree of comfort.

Figure 15.5 is an example of a fuzzy logic model's response to two variables: Risk as a function of Volatility (V) and the Hurst coefficient (W). Input values W and V trigger a graded risk response called "Grade." Note that if this were a plain "yes/no" or "on/off" response map, then the peaks would not have sloped sides.

This chart was created with Mathematica's Fuzzy Logic™ toolbox. The Mathworks also provides a Fuzzy Logic Toolbox™ for MATLAB users.

FIGURE 15.5 RESPONSE MAP OF A SET OF FUZZY LOGIC
RULES TO INPUT VARIABLES W AND V.

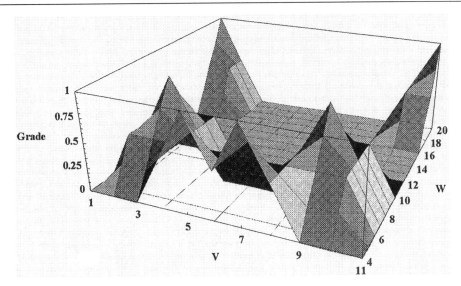

Genetic Algorithms

Genetic algorithms (GAs) offer a way to optimize complex systems. Inspired by Darwin's theories of evolution, GAs create a solution with the optimal mix of variables the same way nature "creates" a well-adapted animal for a given environment by allowing the fittest to pass along their good genes to a new generation. GAs create a virtual population of possible solutions and let the fittest survive to create offspring solutions. This process continues until the best solution evolves. Elegant in their simplicity, GAs are now being used by over half the Fortune 500 companies in scheduling, distribution, management, and any other problems that involve optimizing models with many interacting solutions.

GAs can optimize performance based on historical trading decisions and are applied to problems assuming that some a priori solution exists, such as finding optimal portfolios. For example, determining optimal weighting for a portfolio is analogous to the topographical problem of determining the highest mountain in a range where clouds cover many of the peaks. Rather than examine every mountain peak in search for the highest one, GAs jump through the cloud layer and take a repetitive sample of many peaks, yielding the correct answer relatively quickly. Money managers look to GAs to handle cases when stocks close at 54 and open at 48 the next morning limit down. Designing an algorithm to handle such jump-discontinuities is no trivial feat, yet GAs have an innate ability in this area as they naturally jump to possibly correct solutions.

Neural Nets

When modeling a financial instrument, we require a powerful tool that can process several independent (input) variables. Rule-based models were found insufficiently adaptive to deal with the market's nonstationary nature. Neural networks are more suitable because they are inherently nonlinear and adaptive.

The neural net is a modeling device that takes data regarding a previously solved example and learns to make new forecasts by modifying interconnections between processing elements, called "neurons" or "cells," analogous to the way the human brain connects neurons. There are numerous types of neural net architectures and learning paradigms. One popular architecture, the "Perceptron" net, has three or more layers of processing elements, and cells in one layer feed their output to cells in the next layer. The first layer receives input data and the last layer produces the model's output.

Neural nets are "trained" to mimic the input-output performance of some target model. Training involves feeding a representative data set of previously solved examples and adjusting the weights or strengths of the cells' interconnections to improve the net's performance. This process continues until the neural net's weights have either stabilized and will not change in any significant manner or the desired input-output performance is attained, whichever comes first. Once the net is trained, new predictions are feasible.

The problems that best lend themselves to this type of processing require "pattern recognition" and involve fuzzy variables. Modeled on the structure of the synapses of the human brain, neural nets attempt to ascertain patterns in the relationship between various kinds of data. Money managers do this intuitively when they attempt to distill meaning from the relationship between interest rates, bond yields, equity indices, gold and oil prices, and so on.

Neural networks can be trained to yield new types of indicators. They can combine not only historical data from the current financial instrument, but also cross-market indicators, which singly or together can predict buy-sell signals.

A neural net may be too brittle if it is either over trained or the training data is not sufficiently representative of what could actually occur (e.g., a crash).[11, 12]

CONCLUSION

Some popular assumptions used in today's financial models are in error. Asset prices are linear and random for only a fraction of the time, and are mostly persistent and nonlinear. This says that, statistically, random walks occur only part of the time and there is a relationship between variables in time and that relationship changes over time. Because nonlinear pricing more accurately predicts empirical data, it has created an opportunity for arbitrage whereby the vigorish is the difference between the assumption of randomness (i.e., $H = 0.5$) and empirical results.

When adopting the nonlinear paradigm, which is more consistent with reality, new measurable aspects of time series become available. This chapter discussed persistence, Hurst coefficient, wavelet coefficients, fractal dimension, and reflexivity. Modern nonlinear techniques are also available: genetic algorithms for optimization, fuzzy logic for representing human concepts on a "gray scale," and neural nets for function approximation. The growing number of investors that incorporate chaos, genetic algorithms, neural nets, and fuzzy logic is an indication of their success.

The reader is encouraged to consider using nonlinear pricing techniques. Two simple examples of patterns can be profitably exploited. One is the difference between the assumption of randomness and persistence (or antipersistence) in an equity time series (Figure 15.2) and the other is in the difference between the assumption of a normal distribution and stable distribution for an option (Figure 15.4).

We have entered an era where biology, which allows for the messiness of reality via chance and mutation, may be a more accurate paradigm for financial economics than one that assumes constituent variables do not change in statistical behavior. One wonders why investors have not exhibited, up to now, greater discomfort using linear mathematics in a clearly nonlinear environment.

Further advancement in financial modeling lies not only in looking further within the discipline of financial analysis, but also in seeking descriptions of phenomena from other fields. This should be a priority of all who renounce the arrogance of certainty. In that spirit, much remains to be described in light of a new interpretation. For a more complete treatment of nonlinear pricing, see May.[13]

REFERENCES

May, C.T., *Nonlinear Pricing*, New York: John Wiley & Sons, 1998.

May, C.T., "An Introduction to Nonlinear Pricing," *Asia Risk Manager*, pp. 45–50.

May, C.T., "Nonlinear Pricing: A New Investment Category," *Private Asset Management*, p. 8.

May, C.T., "An Introduction to Nontraditional Pricing," *J. Hedge Fund Review*, pp. 20–30.

Mirowski, P. "From Mandelbrot to Chaos in Economic Theory," *Southern Economic Journal*, pp. 289–307.

Mirowski, P. "Tis a Pity Econometrics Isn't an Empirical Endeavor: Mandelbrot, Chaos, and the Noah and Joseph Effects," *Ricerche Economiche*, pp. 76–99.

Shiller, R. *Market Volatility*, Cambridge, MA: MIT Press, 1994.

Vaga, T. *Profiting from Chaos*, New York: McGraw Hill, 1994.

ENDNOTES

1. Soros, G., *Soros on Soros*, John Wiley & Sons, 1995; Soros, G. *The Alchemy of Finance*, (2nd ed.).

2. Brockman, J., *The Third Culture*, New York: Simon & Schuster, 1995.

3. Cutland, N., Kopp, P., & Willinger, W., "Stock Price Returns and the Joseph Effect: Fractional Version of the Black-Scholes Model," in *Mathematics Research Reports*, December 1993, Hull: Univ. Hull.

4. Peters, E., *Chaos and Order in the Capital Markets*, (2nd ed.), New York: John Wiley & Sons, 1995. Peters, E., *Fractal Market Analysis*, New York: John Wiley & Sons, 1994.

5. The Hurst coefficient for a time series can be seen on Bloomberg by typing IBM <equity> KAOS <go>. It can be calculated using the RS function found in the Wolfram Research MathSource repository at http://www.mathsource.com/cgibin/MathSource/Publications /Periodicals/TheMathematicaJournal/0205-692.

6. See Soros, G., "The Theory of Reflexivity," Address to the MIT Department of Economics, *World Economy Laboratory Conference,* Washington, DC, April 26, 1994.

7. For more information on fractals, see Schroeder, M., *Fractals, Chaos and Power Laws,* New York: W. H. Freeman, 1993.

8. Meyer, Y., *Wavelets, Algorithms and Applications,* Philadelphia: SIAM, 1993, offers a good introduction.

9. I wish to thank Rolf Carlson of Wolfram Research for his illustrations and expertise with Mathematica 3.0™.

10. For a good introduction on fuzzy logic, see Cox, E., *Fuzzy Logic for Business and Industry,* Rockland, MA: Charles River Media, 1995.

11. A WWW site for exploring neural networks with Mathematica™ and for exploring with MATLAB™ is *Error! Bookmark not defined.* A neural net add-in module to MS Excel also can be found at *Error! Bookmark not defined.*

12. For an introduction to neural nets, see Caudill, M., and Butler, C., *Naturally Intelligent Systems,* MIT Press. For a unified view of neural net architectures, see Jurik, M., "Understanding Neural Networks," in *Neural Networks and Financial Forecasting,* Aptos, CA: Jurik Research, 1996. Neural nets can be explored using Mathematica™, MATLAB™, or many other commercially available software products.

13. May, C.T., *Nonlinear Pricing,* New York: John Wiley & Sons, 1998.

CHAPTER 16

Making Profits with Data Preprocessing

CASIMIR C. "CASEY" KLIMASAUSKAS

The primary motivation for preprocessing data is to build better models, where "better" means more consistently profitable. To this end, there are three reasons to preprocess data:

1. To extract key features that a human analyst might use, simplifying the structure of the model.
2. To reduce model dependency on specific signal levels, improving the performance of models as markets enter new trading ranges.
3. To reshape the distribution of the data enhancing the performance of the neural or statistical modeling techniques used to develop the models.

Each of these transformations increases the number of candidate input variables. This often has an adverse effect on model performance, particularly in financial applications. Though some modeling techniques have been developed for effectively dealing with large numbers of highly correlated inputs and noisy data, they are not readily available. As such, whenever using transformations, it is always essential to select a handful of inputs from all the candidates prior to building the model.

MOTIVATION AND ISSUES IN PREPROCESSING

When one of our customers needs to hire a statistician, they place an ad in the local paper. Everyone who responds is required to take a test prior to an interview. The test consists of 1,000 rows by 51 columns of numbers. The objective of the test is to determine what relationships, if any, exist between the first column and the last 50 columns. The applicants have their choice of computer and statistical package to use. There is no specific time limit on the test.

Most individuals who take the test find some relationship between the first column and the last 50. All the data is random, however, and any relationships they discover are spurious. This example illustrates one of the issues that arise when using relatively small amounts of data in high-dimensional spaces.

This is exactly analogous to the problem of pulling faint signals out of noisy financial data. The relationships we want to find may be hidden by spurious correlations in the flood of data available. To effectively pull these signals out, it is essential to find ways to transform the data so that we enhance the signals we want.

As an example of one of the problems with small amounts of data in high-dimensional spaces, Table 16.1 shows the kind of correlations and models that can be created with random data. You can replicate this experiment in Microsoft Excel® by filling 16 columns and 100 rows with random data (=rand()). Then copy the entire area and use "paste special," to paste only the values. Use the "correl()" function to compute the correlation (R) between the dependent values (first column) and each of the independent variables. This is the "Linear Correlation Coefficient" shown in Table 16.1. Finally, use "linest()" (the linear regression function) to perform linear regression from the dependent variables to the independent variables. Read the documentation on "linest()" carefully. It swaps coefficients with the first one last and vice versa. This is the "Linear Regression Coefficient" in Table 16.1. (If you decide to write a program to test this, DO NOT USE the ANSI standard random number generator found in the math library of many compilers. Instead, select one from those described in a professional

TABLE 16.1 COEFFICIENTS FROM LINEAR REGRESSION AND
LINEAR CORRELATION COEFFICIENT FOR A PROBLEM WITH
FIFTEEN DEPENDENT VARIABLES AND ONE INDEPENDENT VARIABLE

	Linear Regression Coefficient	Linear Correlation Coefficient (R)
Y-Correlation (R)	0.394	0.382
X1	0.01	−0.03
X2	0.05	0.05
X3	−0.04	0.02
X4	0.11	0.09
X5	−0.04	−0.01
X6	0.28	0.28
X7	−0.04	−0.01
X8	−0.03	−0.04
X9	−0.03	−0.06
X10	0.17	0.10
X11	0.04	0.05
X12	0.05	0.04
X13	0.12	0.11
X14	0.10	0.08
X15	−0.08	−0.08

The first row of the table shows the linear correlation of the resulting formula with the dependent variable.

reference.)[1] You will find that the correlations and coefficients you get will be different, but the same concepts apply.

The most striking feature of this table is that these formulas seem to have discovered a relationship that is somewhat predictive! The largest correlation of any input with respect to the dependent variable is 0.28. When combined with the other inputs, the result is an R value of 0.39. All these correlations are spurious, the result of a combination of chance and too few examples in a high dimensional space.

One key to successful data preprocessing is to develop a method for sifting through the myriad possible inputs to find that handful of candidate inputs with consistent predictive power. Networks with more than 5 or 10 inputs almost always wind up modeling spurious correlations in the noise.

Another issue faced by anyone using neural networks is how the network interprets the data. Often, without additional constraints, a neural network will find alias solutions that appear to fit the data as well as possible, yet fail to effectively capture essential relationships. This is the motivation for transformations that enhance the information in the data and can potentially reduce the number of inputs to a network. A few well-chosen transformations yield much better models than many poorly selected ones.

To illustrate the problem of alias solutions, Table 16.2 summarizes the training set for a neural network. One example has been included to test the trained network. Figure 16.1 shows this data graphically. The problem consists of two inputs that form a saddle shape. Look at Figure 16.1 a moment and consider what value you would expect the network to predict for the point labeled "T"?

Figure 16.2 shows the neural network solutions to this problem. Notice that all three solutions shown in Figure 16.2 fit the data perfectly. After running several simulations, solutions 2(a) and 2(b) each occur about 40 percent of the time. Solution 2(c) occurs approximately 20 percent of the time. All three solutions utilize three hidden units in a standard fully connected feed forward configuration. Which of these is

TABLE 16.2 NINE TRAINING RECORDS AND
ONE TEST RECORD USED TO ILLUSTRATE ISSUES IN DEVELOPING NEURAL MODELS

$X1$	$X2$	Y
0.0	0.0	1
0.0	0.5	0
0.0	1.0	1
0.5	0.0	1
0.5	**0.25**	**T**
0.5	0.5	1
0.5	1.0	1
1.0	0.0	0
1.0	0.5	1
1.0	1.0	0

FIGURE 16.1 GRAPHICAL DEPICTION OF DATA IN TABLE 16.2. NETWORK HAS
TWO INPUTS, X_1 AND X_2, EACH HAVING THREE TRAINING VALUES.
THIS YIELDS NINE TRAINING COMBINATIONS. THERE IS ALSO ONE TEST CASE.

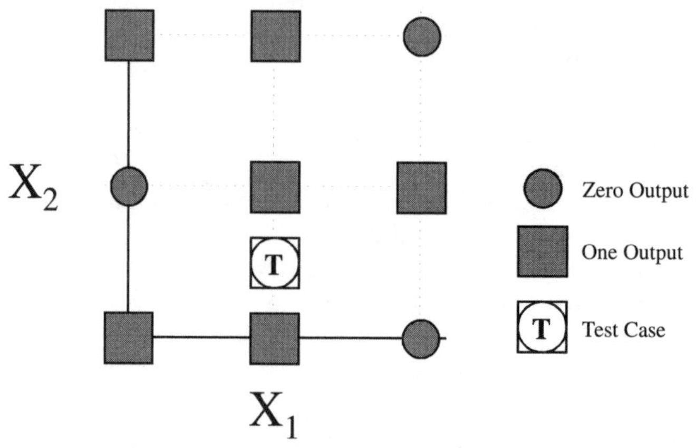

preferable? When asked to choose, most individuals find solution 2(c) most appealing. It is the only solution that preserves a sense of "rationality." It is the only one of the three that meets the smoothness criterion: if a point lies between two others, its value should be between the value of the points it is between. Solutions 2(a) and 2(b) violate this assumption. In a real problem, solutions 2(a) and 2(b) would not generalize as well as 2(c).

Tying this back to preprocessing, neural networks often find "lazy" solutions that fit the data, missing more fundamental relationships. In general, to the extent that the raw data can be transformed in ways that pull out and extract more subtle relationships, the model will have fewer inputs and typically perform better on a validation set.

Data preprocessing enhances subtle relationships and sifts through candidate variables to select a few synergistic inputs for a model. The net result is simpler models that generalize better.

FEATURE EXTRACTION

The fundamental assumption underlying the application of neural and other modeling technologies applied to financial problems is that there is some predictable signal for making better than random decisions. One explanation for this is the "Financial Ponzi Scheme" hypothesis of Meir Statman.[2] This hypothesis leads to a strategy for identifying potentially good transformations on data.

FIGURE 16.2 THREE POSSIBLE SOLUTIONS TO THE DATA IN TABLE 16.2.
THESE SOLUTIONS USE BACKPROPAGATION TO TRAIN PERCEPTRON NETWORKS
WITH TWO INPUTS, THREE HIDDEN UNITS, AND ONE OUTPUT UNIT. INPUTS
RE FULLY CONNECTED TO THE HIDDEN AND OUTPUT LAYERS, AND HIDDEN
LAYER IS FULLY CONNECTED TO THE OUTPUT LAYER. ALL HIDDEN AND
OUTPUT UNITS ALSO HAVE A BIAS INPUT.

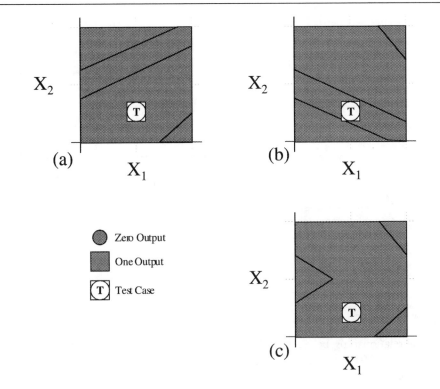

The basic idea behind the financial ponzi (pyramid) scheme is that there are four types of people, as shown in Figure 16.3. Insiders with inside information cannot play. Risk-adverse individuals hold indices. Information traders use statistics to determine when to buy or sell. Three classes of noise traders provide liquidity and price changes used by the information traders to make money. Noise traders input information and make decisions that change prices. Information traders anticipate this behavior to make money. Predicting prices in this context is a problem of predicting human behavior.

If we accept this hypothesis, what we want to predict is the effects of the noise traders' behavior. To predict the effects of their behavior, we need access to the same stimuli that they have. For many traders, the most common stimulus is some form of technical analysis. Both noise traders and information traders may use technical analysis. What distinguishes them is how they use it. Information traders collect statistics on

FIGURE 16.3 THE FINANCIAL PONZI SCHEME. MARKETS ARE CREATED
AS INFORMATION-BASED TRADERS INTERACT WITH VARIOUS TYPES OF NOISE
TRADERS. THE KINDS OF INFORMATION USED BY NOISE TRADERS TO MAKE DECISIONS
LEADS TO CHANGES IN PRICES. THESE CHANGES ARE ANTICIPATED BY
INFORMATION-BASED TRADERS AND APPLIED WITH PROFITABLE RESULTS.

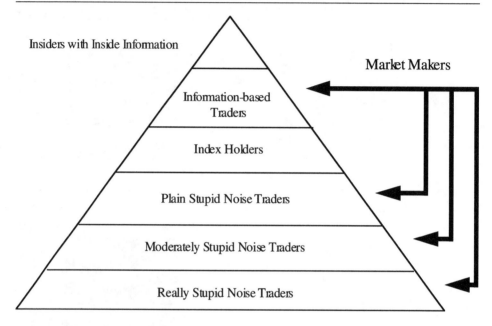

historical relationships between technical indicators and future market conditions. They use this information to trade regardless of what they feel. Noise traders, to various degrees, are distinguished by "rules of thumb" that are inconsistently applied.

Lane's Stochastic

As an example of this, consider a popular indicator, Lane's Stochastic. (*Note:* Contrary to its use in mathematics, the "stochastic" in Lane's Stochastic has nothing to do with random numbers.) The formula for a stochastic is:

$$S(p) = (C - Lp) / (Hp - Lp) \times 100$$

where

        $S(p)$ is the stochastic with period p (p > 1)
        C is the closing price at the current time
        Lp is the lowest low over p prior periods (between now t, and $t - p + 1$)
        Hp is the highest high over p prior periods (between now t, and $t - p + 1$)[3]

There are many ways in which to use stochastics, and the rules for how to use them can become complex. Typically, they are combined in different ways to create a series of rules for when to go long, short, or exit a market. Noise traders often use simple rules of thumb to decide when to buy or sell based on stochastics. Furthermore, these rules of thumb are often violated in favor of "gut" feel, panic, or greed.

The following example illustrates how an information trader uses stochastics. It constructs a system for estimating the minimum, maximum, and expected return given the 5-period and 14-period stochastics for the S&P 500. The system uses several of these simplistic statistically based estimators as input to a network that decides the degree to which it can believe any one of them. Each of the estimators uses statistics from a different overlapping window of data or a different type of indicator. In this way, each estimator becomes specialized to a particular market. By deciding which estimator to believe, the network is deciding the type of the current market.

The inputs to this network may consist of technical or broad market indicators or other data such as the prediction error for each of the specialized feature extractors. The market selector network is a soft-max* backpropagation† network trained on a 1-of-N code to select the best prediction of the future price change. This network learns the probability that a particular output is correct. These probabilities are multiplied by the market estimates to produce a single final output. The final output is used in a rule-based system to determine how to trade based on the estimated risk-reward and investor's preferences.

The first step in building our stochastic trader is to collect some statistics. Table 16.3 shows statistics for the S&P 500 for March through December 1991 and 1992. First, compute the 5-day forward change in the S&P 500 for each trading day for the years 1991 through 1992. Compute the 5-day and 14-day stochastics for this same period. Divide each of the ranges for the 5-day and 14-day stochastics into uniform-size bins, five in this instance. For each day in the target range March through December 1991, determine which "bin" that day belongs to based on the value of the 5-day and 14-day stochastics. Update the minimum, maximum, average, and count for that bin. When done, you will have a table similar to Table 16.3. The center point of each bin is used to label the rows and columns in the table.

The period over which data is collected must be sufficiently long to ensure that most of the bins have data in them. Using more bins requires more data. Fewer bins require less data. It may be necessary to experiment somewhat to find a balance between the number of bins and the amount of data.

---

*With regard to the nonlinear transformation occurring in a neural net's cells (neurons), a "hard-limit" transformation forces the cell's output to be within a fixed range, typically from −1 to +1. A soft-max transformation has no fixed bounds, but makes large deviations from a mean value very difficult to attain. (Editor)

†For many years, backpropagation was the most popular training algorithm applied to Perceptron based neural networks. Its mathematics is based on error reduction by gradient descent and is relatively simple to code. (Editor)

TABLE 16.3 EXPECTED VALUE, MIN, MAX, AND COUNTS OF THE FIVE-DAY FORWARD CHANGE IN THE S&P 500 ARE SHOWN FOR A COMBINATION OF A 5-DAY AND 14-DAY STOCHASTIC

		3/1/91–12/31/91						3/1/92–12/31/92			
Max	10	30	50	70	90	Max	10	30	50	70	90
10	17.38	3.52	3	0	0	10	21.77	13.55	1.85	5.46	0
30	2.86	13.63	5.1	0.22	11.37	30	11.3	12.62	15.4	4.45	9.04
50	17.3	6.2	6.25	12	6.61	50	7.86	7.73	2.09	3.52	6.3
70	22.32	7.44	5.44	5.43	12.34	70	8.52	6.82	4.44	−0.21	11.75
90	−0.5	0	1.57	16.59	19.42	90	4.73	5.76	8.19	6.23	6.84
Min	10	30	50	70	90	Min	10	30	50	70	90
10	−9.9	−7.94	0.14	0	0	10	−7.81	−9.73	−8.54	5.46	0
30	−5.7	2.41	−6.59	−9.19	−3.32	30	−5.3	−2.18	−9.62	3.05	−13.55
50	−7.29	−9.94	−2.28	−2.37	−5.06	50	−7.36	−3.44	−7.24	2.5	−10.02
70	−8.44	−11.55	0.27	−6.92	0.02	70	−5.96	−7.34	−8.57	−5.52	−4.96
90	−0.5	0	1.57	−11.46	−18.88	90	−5.96	−6.91	−4.06	−5.46	−7.8
EV	10	30	50	70	90	EV	10	30	50	70	90
10	3.4767	−2.535	1.5475	0	0	10	1.9572	−0.07	−3.345	5.46	0
30	−0.515	5.96	0.0525	−4.485	1.669	30	1.2056	5.9471	−0.91	3.75	0.1175
50	4.1975	−2.138	2.8775	4.815	0.4214	50	0.5989	1.8	−2.575	3.01	−0.323
70	0.6573	−2.708	4.03	−2.533	5.1837	70	0.1157	−0.592	−1.223	−2.533	1.26
90	−0.5	0	1.57	−1.199	−0.367	90	0.5625	−1.737	1.64	1.424	−0.359
Count	10	30	50	70	90	Count	10	30	50	70	90
10	33	4	4	0	0	10	29	7	2	1	0
30	8	4	4	2	10	30	9	7	6	2	8
50	16	5	4	2	7	50	19	6	2	2	11
70	11	4	4	3	8	70	14	6	4	3	11
90	1	0	1	17	67	90	4	3	3	5	56

The x-coordinate is the 14-day stochastic, the y-coordinate is the 5-day stochastic. For example, in 1991 when the 14-day stochastic is around 90, and the 5-day stochastic is around 70, the expected value of the change in the S&P 500 over the next five days is 5.18.

Use Table 16.3 to compute the expected value of what will happen in the next five days. The following formulas show how. Assume that the data is in the following format as shown under expected value (EV) in Table 16.3:

$$
\begin{array}{cccccc}
 & & c_{21} & c_{22} & L & c_{2m} \\
 & c_{11} & e_{11} & e_{12} & L & e_{1m} \\
 & c_{12} & e_{21} & & & \\
 & M & & & O & \\
 & c_{1n} & c_{n1} & & & e_{nm}
\end{array}
$$

Compute the expected value of the change in the S&P 500 over the next five days as:

$$
E(X_1, X_2) = \frac{\displaystyle\sum_{i=1}^{n}\sum_{j=1}^{m} e_{ij} \times \min\left\{\begin{array}{l}\max(0,\ 1-k_1\times|x_1-c_{1i}|) \\ \max(0,\ 1-k_2\times|x_2-c_{2j}|)\end{array}\right\}}{\displaystyle\sum_{i=1}^{n}\sum_{j=1}^{m} \min\left\{\begin{array}{l}\max(0,\ 1-k_1\times|x_1-c_{1i}|) \\ \max(0,\ 1-k_2\times|x_2-c_{2j}|)\end{array}\right\}}
$$

where

x_1 is the 5-day stochastic

x_2 is the 14-day stochastic

$E(x_1,x_2)$ is the expected change in the S&P 500 over the next five days

c_{1i} is the center of the i-th bin of the 5-day stochastic

c_{2j} is the center of the j-th bin of the 14-day stochastic

e_{ij} is the expected value (or min or max) of the 5-day forward change in the S&P 500

k_1 is the slope of the fuzzy membership sets for the 5-day stochastic. Assuming equal spacing between the center of each bin, $1/(c_{12}-c_{11}) > = k_1 > 0$. Typically, $k_1 = 0.5/(c_{12}-c_{11})$.

k_2 is the slope of the fuzzy membership sets for the 14-day stochastic. Assuming equal spacing between the center of each bin, $1/(c_{22}-c_{21}) > = k_2 > 0$. Typically, $k_2 = 0.5/(c_{22}-c_{21})$.

This formula uses fuzzy logic to do the computations. Other techniques like the Generalized Regression Neural Network (GRNN) or kernel density regression can be used as well.

By way of explanation of the formula, the degree of membership of x_1, DOM(x_1), in the ith triangular fuzzy membership centered at c_{1i} is: DOM$(x_1) = \max(0,\ 1 - k_1 \times |x_1 - c_{1i}|)$. Similarly for x_2. The complete matrix formed by generating the set of fuzzy rules of the form: "If x_1 is c_{1i} and x_2 is c_{2j}, Then, E is e_{ij}." is evaluated for all i and j (the numerator). The result is defuzzified by dividing by the total area under the fuzzy antecedents (the denominator). The defuzzified result is the expected change in the S&P 500. The values for the slopes of the membership sets can be adjusted to enhance or limit smoothing as desired. When there are cells with no data, it is best to use the suggested smoothing factors.

Exponential Moving Average

Another popular transform is the exponential moving average (EMA). This is used to smooth data series and construct oscillators for identifying trends. (An oscillator is the difference of two indicators of the same type, but computed over different time windows.) The most popular oscillator of this type is the Exponential Moving

Average Convergence Divergence (EMACD) oscillator. It is constructed by taking the difference of two exponentially smoothed moving averages.

The exponential moving average (EMA) is computed recursively. The formula for an n-period EMA is:

$$EMA_n(t) = k_n \times X_t + (1 - k_n) \times EMA_n(t - 1)$$

where

$k_n = 1/(n + 1)$, the smoothing coefficient
X_t is the value of the time series at time t
$EMA_n(t)$ is the value of the n-period EMA at time t

To start the process, the value of the EMA is set to the n-period simple average of the prior n values of data. Some programs simply assume that the first value of x is approximately equal to the average. This formula is called an exponential average, because it can be written as a series expansion of the form:

$$EMA_n(t) = k_n \sum_{i=0}^{\infty} (1 - k_n)^i x_{t-1}$$

This formulation highlights one of the problems with starting up an EMA that can be troublesome with automated systems. When we start the EMA, we are truncating this exponential series. Table 16.4 shows the impact of this. There are three solutions to the truncation problem. The first is simply to use substantial quantities of data. This works well if we have an essentially infinite supply of data without gaps

TABLE 16.4 TRUNCATING AN EXPONENTIAL SERIES

	Period (n)			
Window (p)	3	5	10	15
10	5.6%	16.2%	38.6%	na
20	0.3	2.6	14.9	27.5%
30	0.2	1.8	12.3	24.2
40	0.0	0.3	4.7	12.7
50	0.0	0.0	0.9	4.0
60	0.0	0.0	0.3	2.1
70	0.0	0.0	0.1	1.1
80	0.0	0.0	0.0	0.6
90	0.0	0.0	0.0	0.3
100	0.0	0.0	0.0	0.2

The maximum error is shown in computing an n-period EMA when truncating the series at different points. Each row represents a different number (p) of examples over which the EMA was computed. Each column represents a different smoothing period (n). Typical errors are less than those in the table.

for both training and execution of the model. The second is to avoid exponential moving averages, and use a simple moving average instead. The third is to compute an exponentially weighted moving average (EWMA), which eliminates the error. This approach can be used to replace the EMA itself as well as when applying an EMA smoothing to an indicator.

The n-period EWMA over p data examples is computed using the following formula. Notice that this formula requires the prior p values of the data for each computation. If you are writing your own technical indicators, this corrected or EWMA will often improve the performance and consistency of your system. At present, I am not aware of any commercially available systems that implement this:

$$EWMA_{n,p}(t) = \frac{\sum_{i=0}^{p-1}(1-k_n)^i x_{t-1}}{\sum_{i=0}^{p-1}(1-k_n)^1}$$

where

> n is the smoothing period
>
> p is the window over which the exponential average is computed
>
> $k_n = 1/(n+1)$ is the smoothing coefficient
>
> x_t is the value of the time series at time t
>
> $EWMA_{n,p}(t)$ is the n-period EWMA evaluated at time t over p data points

One of the most popular uses of the EMA is in an EMACD oscillator. To construct an EMACD oscillator, compute the difference of a "fast" and "slow" EMA. The formula for the EMACD oscillator is:

$$EMACD_{f,s}(t) = EMA_f(t) - EMA_s(t)$$

where

> f is the fast period, for example 3
>
> s is the slow period, for example 14
>
> $EMACD_{f,s}(t)$ is the result

The basic idea behind this is that when the time series is rising, the fast oscillator will respond more quickly than the slow one, and the result is positive. When a time series starts to fall, the fast again responds more quickly than the slow one and the result is negative. This difference is coupled with other logic to decide when to enter or exit a market.

Other technical indicators can be used to generate candidate inputs to a trading model. Examples include the Relative Strength Index (RSI), On-Balance Volume (OBV), directional movement indicators (PDI, MDI, DX, ADX, ADR). Two good references for examples of technical indicators are Colby[4] and Eng.[5] The monthly magazine *Technical Analysis of Stocks & Commodities* also has good articles on technical indicators and their characteristics.

Trend Information

Trend information can be derived from a time series by use of statistical trends. Continuous wavelets have been helpful in identifying shapes such as double peaks. Several other mathematical tools are available for doing shape-based analysis.

In many situations, intermarket indicators are important. A variety of techniques can be used to extract this information. One of the easiest transformations is to compute the linear correlation between two time series using a moving window. Linear correlation, sometimes called Pearson's-R is computed as follows:

$$R_p(u,v,t) = \frac{\sum_{i=0}^{p-1}(u_{t-i}-\bar{u}_{p,t})\,(v_{t-i}-\bar{v}_{p,t})}{\left(\sum_{i=0}^{p-1}(u_{t-i}-\bar{u}_{p,t})^2\sum_{i=0}^{p-1}(v_{t-i}-\bar{v}_{p,t})^2\right)^{1/2}}$$

$$\bar{u}_{p,t} = \frac{1}{p}\sum_{i=0}^{p-1}u_{t-i}$$

$$\bar{v}_{p,t} = \frac{1}{p}\sum_{i=0}^{p-1}v_{t-i}$$

where

$R_p(u,v,t)$ is the linear correlation over a window of p examples between time series u and v at end-time t

u is the first time series with data points $u_t, u_{t-1}, \ldots, u_{t-p}$

v is the second time series with data points $v_t, v_{t-1}, \ldots, v_{t-p}$

t is the current time

p is the period or window over which to compute the correlation

Applications such as long-term (12 months +) stock picking may use more long-term indicators such as key ratios based on financial statements. When using long-term information, it is important to address the issue of when the information is available to make a decision. For example, quarterly sales and earnings reports are often delayed at least one and sometimes two or more quarters. Moreover, when using historical databases, this information is sometimes retrospectively updated. When using this type of information, it is essential to understand inherent delays and make allowances accordingly. Some companies have gone to the effort of actually taking weekly or monthly snapshots of fundamental data from data providers to create a simulation environment that is as realistic as possible.

PREPROCESSING FOR NONSTATIONARITY

At a conference, I asked a trader about his firm's use of neural networks, and their effectiveness in the bull market of 1994–1995. His answer was that the company was badly burned by signals from their neural networks, and they no longer use them. Probing further, I discovered that the networks they were using had started giving "short" signals as the market moved up, and despite retraining continued to do so. After losing a fair amount of money, they simply gave up on the networks.

What happened?

The networks were based on price data as input. When prices trended strongly upward, the networks saturated, and as they were pushed beyond the edges, the output went down rather than up. The resulting "short" signals were disastrous. Neural networks do not predict trending markets well.

When a time series trends strongly, it is said to be nonstationary. A stationary time series has a constant long-term average. In a nonstationary or trending time series, the long-term average moves significantly. Neural networks have demonstrated their ability to effectively predict stationary (nontrending) time series. They perform very poorly on nonstationary (trending) time series. There are several approaches to solving this problem. All of them involve converting the problem into one that is stationary.

When we remove level dependence from the inputs to a network, it will often generalize well even when the market reaches record highs. The new highs are not what it is looking at, but rather the relative shape and relationships between recent activities.

Even when price level is important, for such things as resistance levels, this can be transformed into a price-independent form. For example, a new indicator may be created that indicates the degree to which the price is close to a resistance or support level. Fuzzy membership sets are a convenient way of doing this.

Many technical transformations are level independent. Examples of level-independent technical indicators include stochastics, relative strength, and the directional-movement indicators. Price differences expressed as a percentage are also level independent. One issue to be aware of when applying certain technical transformations is the effect of missing data on the value of the indicator. Missing data can be caused by holidays, for example. The best way to handle this, either copying the last known value or eliminating the day, depends on the specific type of technical transformation.

Moving averages and exponential moving averages can be made price relative by dividing them by a longer moving average. For example, dividing all the moving averages by a 100-period moving average will not substantively affect the relationship between current values, but will create a general level independence. An MACD or EMACD oscillator can be made level independent by dividing it by the slower of the two moving averages.

A variant on this is to compute a rolling trendline. This is subtracted from all the prices to produce "detrended" prices. The trendline is added back into any price predictions to produce an adjusted trended price.

Another approach to achieving level independence is to use a broad market measure as the base and transform all prices as a ratio to the current market measure or a moving average of it.

In certain cases, magnitude may be important. For example, some levels of sales are strongly correlated to bond rating. In such instances, the problem may be subdivided into three or four broad subproblems based on sales level. Alternatively, the sales level may be encoded into a series of fuzzy membership sets as input to the network.

In general, transforming input data into a form that is level independent results in models that generalize better and will perform well in trading as well as trending markets.

STATISTICAL PREPROCESSING

Most neural networks are constructed to minimize a sum of squared error or regression criteria. As a practical matter, the net result is that they work best when all the data is normally distributed, having zero mean and unit variance.

An example of this type of transformation commonly used to express price changes is $\log(p_{t+1}/p_t)$. Though the raw distribution of price changes (p_{t+1}/pt) is leptokurtotic (has a long tail), the $\log(p_{t+1}/p_t)$ is more nearly normally distributed. This is what is meant by the expression, "returns are log normal."

The log transformation is one example of a variety of transformations that do distribution shaping. (A reasonably readable treatment of this is found in Chatterjee.[6]) The basic idea is as follows. While examining one input variable, select a univariate transformation $f(x)$ that maintains monotonicity (i.e., If $x_i < x_j$, then $f(x_i) < f(x_j)$) and has a distribution that is most similar to the desired distribution.

One strategy for accomplishing this has been implemented in Aspen Technology's Neural Simulator™. A series of transformations are tested of the form $g(a_0 + a_1 x)$. The transforms tested include $\log(x)$, $\log(\log(x))$, $\exp(x)$, $\exp(\exp(x))$, $1/x$, $1/x^2$, $1/x^4$, x^2, x^4, $1/x^{0.5}$, $1/x^{0.25}$, $x^{0.5}$, $x^{0.25}$, $\tanh(x)$, $\ln(x/(1-x))$. The values a_0 and a_1 are determined using a directed random search procedure, and include both negative and positive values for a_1. The distribution of the transformed data is compared with a normal (or any arbitrary distribution) using the Kolomogorov-Smirnov statistic[7]. The transformation and values for a_0 and a_1 that produce the best fit to the target distribution are used to transform the data. Even when transforming the data with a technique like this, it is useful to retain the raw nontransformed data as a candidate input.

SCALING DATA

Candidate inputs should all be scaled into the range −1 to +1 with zero mean. This is what is expected for any statistical technique, including linear and neural regression. Use the following formula to compute the linear scale (a_1) and offset (a_0):

$$a_1 = \frac{1}{\max(x_{max} - x_{avg}, x_{avg} - x_{min})}$$

$$a_0 = -a_1 x_{avg}$$

where

x_{max} is the maximum value of x
x_{min} is the minimum value of x
x_{avg} is the average value of x

Data is transformed using the following formula: $x_{new} = a_0 + a_1 \times x_{old}$. The new values have zero mean and lie in the range $[-1..+1]$.

SELECTING DATA FOR TRAINING

How you select training data depends on what kind of network your are planning to use.

If you have carefully selected a handful (less than 5 to 8) candidate inputs, kernel-based networks, such as Generalized Regression Neural Network (GRNN) can be trained almost instantly and often will produce good results. In this instance, the output of the GRNN is the expected value of whatever you are predicting. Fuzzy rulebases are equally effective in this application.

When there are more than a handful of inputs, or a backpropagation trained Perceptron network is used, subselecting training examples is important. The reason for this is that the backpropagation algorithm minimizes the sum of the squared errors between the estimated output and the observed output. This objective function is data distribution dependent. Figure 16.4 illustrates this issue. When substantial amounts of data are concentrated in one portion of the space, they tend to dominate the solution to the exclusion of the more sparse examples. Though the regression line shown is optimal in terms of minimizing sum of the squared errors, it fails to capture infrequent events. In financial applications, it is often the infrequent events that are the most important in terms of profit.

The solution to this is to find a way to uniformly select data so that it covers the input space. Unfortunately, with many candidate inputs, this is not possible. However, under certain assumptions, we can create an approximation of a uniform covering of the input space by selecting a uniform subset of examples based on their outcomes.

Here is how the procedure works. Divide the output range into a series of equal width non-overlapping bins. Assign each example in the training set to a bin based on its outcome. Begin with the first bin and select an example from it at random. Put the example in the output training set. Proceed to the next bin and continue this process in a round-robin fashion until the desired number of examples have been selected. Use the new data set to do variable selection and train the network.

FIGURE 16.4 LINEAR REGRESSION. THIS EXAMPLE ILLUSTRATES THE
EFFECTS OF DATA DISTRIBUTION. THE LINE SHOWN MINIMIZES THE SUM
OF THE SQUARED ERROR BETWEEN THE INPUT (X-AXIS) AND
OBSERVED VALUES (Y-AXIS) FOR THE 100 POINTS.

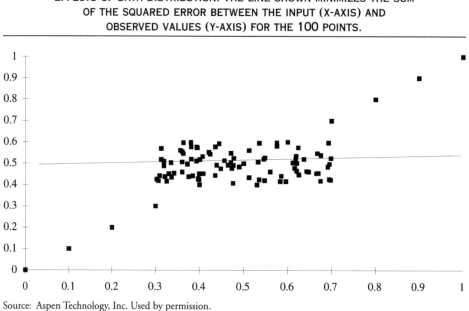

Source: Aspen Technology, Inc. Used by permission.

Does it work? Figure 16.5 shows the cumulative equity curves on a validation set for trading the S&P 500. Each curve represents a network trained on different fractions of the available data. Each network was trained to predict the five-day forward change in price using nine inputs selected by prior experiments. If the output of the network was greater than 0.1, take or maintain a long position. If the output of the network was less than −0.1, take or maintain a short position. Of the data available for training, 40 percent was set aside as a test set in a train/test methodology. All networks were trained using Aspen Technology's Neural Simulator.™* Table 16.5 shows summary data for both the train/test data as well as the validation set. Note, that even with perfect information the trading strategy resulted in 94 percent win ratio on the train/test set and 89 percent ratio on the validation set. This is due to a mismatch between the prediction horizon and the trading strategy. This problem can be eliminated by using a more complex trading strategy.

In general, less data resulted in better generalization (more profit) up to a point at which the data was insufficient to fill the space. At that point (30%), performance decreased rapidly from overfitting a network trained on very few examples.

---

*Predict contains many of the preprocessing features described in this chapter. (Editor)

FIGURE 16.5 EQUITY CURVES OVER THE VALIDATION PERIOD FOR EACH
OF THE NETWORKS. THE PERCENTAGES AT THE RIGHT IDENTIFY THE
PORTION OF RAW DATA USED TO TRAIN THE NETWORK.

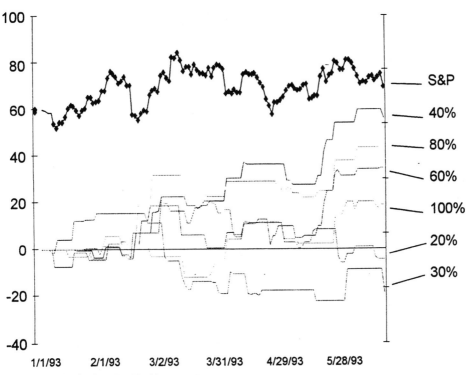

Source: Aspen Technology, Inc. Used by permission.

TABLE 16.5 PERFORMANCE OF NETWORKS WITH DIFFERING SIZES OF
WORKING SET SELECTED UNIFORMLY FROM THE TRAINING DATA

Network	Nodes	12/31/90 to 12/31/92 Train / Test Set					1/1/93 to 6/18/93 Validation Set				
		R	P/L	Win	Lose	Ratio	R	P/L	Win	Lose	Ratio
Perfect	N/A	1.00	581	85	5	94%	1.00	116	16	2	89%
100%	3	0.52	210	55	29	65	0.09	18	14	13	52
80%	1	0.49	143	53	31	63	0.21	44	11	8	58
60%	3	0.49	213	56	29	66	0.11	35	19	12	61
40%	4	0.49	289	80	34	70	0.25	56	14	11	56
30%	4	0.40	205	47	37	56	−0.10	−17	11	19	37
20%	6	0.44	267	57	29	66	0.20	−2	15	18	45

The portion of the data selected for the working set is shown under the Network heading. The number of hidden units in the final network is shown under Nodes. The range 1/1/93 through 6/18/93 was set aside as a validation set. It was not used at all for developing the model.

A FEW GOOD INPUTS

The prior discussions on preprocessing described how to create additional candidate inputs to a model. Many of those inputs are colinear. That is, they have a high degree of correlation between them. In general, networks trained on this type of data often find idiosyncratic solutions as shown in Figure 16.2. The solution to this problem is to find a way to select a synergistic subset of candidate inputs that best solve the problem.

Several approaches to this problem of variable selection have been developed. Most work well on clean data where relationships are strong. I have found only one that works well on noisy data of the type found in financial modeling problems: Genetic Variable Selection.

As part of developing a stock picking system for managing an equity portfolio, several techniques for selecting variables were tested. These included simplistic through esoteric approaches. None but genetic algorithms proved effective. The methods tested were:

- Candidate inputs with the highest correlation to the target output.
- Stepwise linear regression inputs with largest coefficients.
- Selecting the most predictive variables from a particular level of Hierarchical Cluster Analysis applied to the inputs.
- Principal component extraction.
- Training a network and picking the variables with the highest sensitivity.
- Training a network and measuring the effect of leaving out one variable.
- Iteratively training and pruning network inputs with the lowest sensitivity.
- Causal data analysis to identify fundamental causal inputs.
- Genetic variable selection.

Though many of these approaches work well on clean data such as found in physical processes, even there they often prove suboptimal. As an example, an analytic formula of a chemical reaction was constructed with two inputs and one output. Each of the independent inputs was transformed into four new inputs for a total of eight inputs. These transformations were selected based on prior analysis. The input space was rotated (detrended) to remove the principal components that were modeled as a linear trend. A network was trained on the residual and added to the trend. The result was a 8–5–1 network with a linear correlation of 0.93 and a normalized rms error of 0.1.* When a network was trained on the data without rotating the input space, the result was a 8–2–1 network with a linear correlation of 0.99 and a normalized rms error of 0.02. In both instances, dozens of networks were trained. The results represent the best network in each test. It is not intuitively obvious why rotating the

---

*RMS (root mean square) error is the square root of the average squared error. (Editor)

combined input and output space should make the problem so much harder for a neural network to solve. This is an area that requires more research. A lesson to be learned from this is that you cannot rely on "theoretical" arguments to predict the best way to preprocess data. The only effective method is to take the time to compare a new approach to other proven methods on real data sets.

Genetic variable selection is the best overall approach that was tested. It was implemented as a binary chromosome in which each bit represented the presence (1) or absence (0) of a candidate input. The subset of inputs represented by a chromosome is used to train a network. The performance of the network on the test set is its measure of fitness. Standard bit-mutation and uniform crossover operators are used.

In initial tests, the final population of the genetic algorithm contained several sets of candidate variables all with similar rankings. When a network was trained on the union of the top five sets of variables, the resulting network performed *worse* than networks trained on any of the subsets. These subsets were definitely synergistic. The situation appears to be that certain variables mask the more subtle and at times more powerful predictive nature of other variables when they are all together. Only the genetic variable selection approach was able to identify these subsets.

When an application starts with 50 or more candidate variables, even genetic variable selection may have problems. A solution to this is to cascade the variable selection process. In cascade variable selection, genetic selection is repeatedly performed. Each selection is limited to a small number of generations so that the resulting populations are still quite diverse. The frequency of occurrence of each variable in the top 10 percent of each population is computed. Those with a low frequency of occurrence are dropped from future consideration. The remaining variables are retained and the process repeated until a stable set of candidate variables remains. Cascade variable selection, a feature in NeuralWorks Predict™, has been successfully used on a problem with over 3,500 candidate input variables.

The primary benefits of effective variable selection are better performance and better generalization. Table 16.6 shows the impact of variable selection on the performance of networks trained to predict the S&P 500. Reducing the number of inputs from 65 to 5 resulted in substantially better generalization from the training to test to validation sets. Notice that the network was able to find an almost perfect solution on the training set using 65 inputs. However, performance degraded rapidly on the test

TABLE 16.6 THE EFFECT OF VARIABLE SELECTION ON GENERALIZATION

Data Set	Run 1	Run 2
Training set	0.976	0.573
Test set	0.329	0.433
Validation set	0.182	0.499

Run 1 used 65 inputs to predict the five-day forward change in the S&P 500. Run 2 used 5 inputs selected by genetic algorithm to make the same prediction. All other conditions were maintained constant. Performance measure is linear correlation coefficient.

and validation sets. In Run 2 with five inputs, performance was relatively consistent across the three data sets.

In my experience, variable selection consistently ranks as the number one factor in enhancing generalization. If you have more than a handful of variables as input to your model, you have too many. As a side benefit, the performance of a series of networks trained on a reduced data set is often much more consistent. This is comforting in terms of predicting the performance of a deployed system.

CONFLICTING DATA AND EXPECTED VALUES

Local minima are one of the problems often faced in training a neural network, particularly on financial data.* One of the causes of local minima is conflicting data. When two training examples have nearly identical input values, but substantively different output values, this induces a small ripple or local minima in the objective surface. Though most of these are small enough that they do not adversely affect training, they can cause problems.

If the number of inputs have been reduced to a sufficiently small number (5 to 10), it is often possible to eliminate conflicting inputs by computing expected values in local neighborhoods and using those prototypes as training vectors. This process also tends to reduce data distribution effects on network training.

The process is simple. Divide the range of each input into a small number of bins, typically 5 to 10. For each example, construct a "key" that consists of a series of digits. Each digit corresponds to the bin to which the input field belongs. Sort all the data based on this key. If two or more examples have the same key, replace all of them with a new prototype that is the average of all the examples with the same key. Use this reduced set of data for training the network. You are now assured that no two data vectors will conflict.

Eliminating conflicting data results in smaller training sets, reduces the dependence of the model on data distribution, and eliminates the likelihood that a model will get stuck in a local minima.

CONCLUSION

Data preprocessing involves several steps. Some of them are simply mechanical; others require a certain degree of expertise. Use the following seven-step process to prepare raw data for network training:

---

*A local minima or maxima refers to the parameter settings of a function, so optimized that any small changes made to any of the parameters would degrade the function's performance, as rated by some score. A local minima is produced when the optimal score is at its lowest, and a local maxima is produced when the optimal score is at its highest. (Editor)

1. Identify domain specific transformations that may enhance the signals in the data or make a good solution more obvious. This typically involves technical transformations, financial ratios, correlations, or shape detectors.

2. Convert the problem into a stationary prediction problem. Modify or scale transformations as required.

3. Further modify data by applying distribution-shaping transformations. Continue to maintain transformations from Step 2 as part of the candidate inputs.

4. Extract a subset of data for performing variable selection and training the network that uniformly covers the input space.

5. Select small synergistic sets of variables for network training.

6. Eliminate conflicting data by converting "conflicting" examples to expected values.

You are now ready to train a network or develop any other kind of model-based system. Data preprocessing is a tedious and unglamorous process. Often it is easier to simply use raw data and let the neural network do its "magic." However, as discussed, the time and effort to effectively preprocess data often leads to substantially more profitable models. It is worth it.

ENDNOTES

1. Press, William H., Teukolsky, Saul A., Vetterling, William T., & Flannery, Brain P., *Numerical Recipes in C* (2nd ed.), Cambridge, UK: Cambridge University Press, 1992.

2. Statman, Meir, (Leavey School of Business, Santa Clara College), "Behavioral Finance" presentation at Chicago Quantitative Alliance annual conference, September 13–14, 1995.

3. Colby, Robert W. & Meyers, Thomas A., *Encyclopedia of Technical Market Indicators,* Homewood, Il: Business One Irwin, 1988.

4. Ibid.

5. Eng, William F., *The Technical Analysis of Stocks, Options and Futures,* Chicago: Probus Publishing, 1988.

6. Chatterjee, Samprit & Price, Bertram, *Regression Analysis by Example* (2nd ed.), New York: John Wiley & Sons, 1991, p. 31f.

7. See Note 1.

Modeling the Markets Using Statistical Network Data Mining

KEITH C. DRAKE AND DALE E. NELSON

WHAT IS THE MARKET AND WHAT SHOULD WE MODEL?

When we first begin to think about the markets and think about modeling them, we must ask some salient questions. First, what determines the price of a stock (or the value of an index)? Is it the book value? No. If that were true, stocks would sell at no more than book value. We have all seen stocks selling above or below that value. Is it the amount of profit a company is making? No. There are companies that have been losing money for years and yet their stock prices have increased. On the other hand, there are very profitable companies whose stock has decreased in value. Why then, do stock prices go up or down? It is simply the perception by investors that the price of the stock will increase or decrease! The investors will make the appropriate choice based on this.

When using the computer to try to influence our investing decisions, what we are really trying to do is develop some sort of model of the market of interest (see Figure 17.1). In engineering, the method often uses first principles of the process at

FIGURE 17.1 MARKET MODELING PARADIGM.

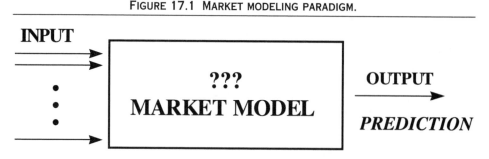

hand. For example, in electrical circuits we use the differential equations that describe how components interact. By piecing together various components and solving a system of differential equations, we can determine how a circuit will operate. This works, in theory. In reality, we have made many assumptions as to how components operate, the purity of materials, and often linearity assumptions just to permit us to solve the equations. This means that the prediction of performance needs to be verified by actually building and testing the circuit. This error-prone process has been perfected through the years and adjustments made so that engineers can do a fairly good job designing circuits. When applied to market analysis, the processes involved are many times more complex than in circuit design.

Can we ever hope to develop a model of the market? Through the years, we have seen experts evolve who make some good predictions and make a lot of money. They develop a reputation, and often a newsletter providing advice. For awhile, they are quite successful, but then for some reason, their predictions stop being as good, and their performance becomes lackluster. What has happened is that they have clued in to some highly influential parameter that is a good predictor of the market. But, because the market is highly dynamic, that particular indicator is no longer a reliable predictor and they are no longer very successful at predictions. However, their reputation continues.

For a long time, investors have used linear statistics to develop strategies to determine when to invest and when to divest. Moving averages and variance lines are just some examples of this method. The problem with linear statistics is that the underlying market that is providing the data is not linear. Therefore, any method based on linearity assumptions is at best inaccurate and at worst, just plain wrong. When neural networks were introduced to the investment community they were thought to be a panacea. They could handle nonlinearity. As Dr. Steve Gustafson, senior research physicist at the University of Dayton Research Institute, said, "Neural networks are statistics for the uninitiated." This means that someone not trained in the mathematics of statistics could use neural networks to do nonlinear statistical analysis of the markets and make money. Wrong!

What, exactly, are we trying to model? If stock prices go up and down based on investors' perceptions, perhaps we should try to model an investor. This would be an impossible task. Since we cannot gather sufficient data on an individual investor, we cannot develop a model. It is far easier to gather data on what all investors are doing. This is usually represented as an index such as the Dow Jones Industrial Average (DJIA). Perhaps we should model the price fluctuations of the shares in various companies. If the goal is to predict a single stock, we have a more difficult problem. If the goal is to predict a broad market index, we are more likely to be successful.

How can we develop a model of many investors and their perceptions in order to make money? Investors are influenced by factors that we can measure. Their perceptions are influenced and reflected by what is happening in the various markets (other than the one we are trying to model) and in reported data. For example, if the price of gold is rising, this may indicate investors are becoming worried about inflation. If the M1, a broad-based U.S. money supply index, is increasing rapidly, this too may be a harbinger of inflation. Some investors believe that if the Dow Jones Transportation Index is increasing it means that industry is delivering more goods and will be more profitable; therefore, a good time to invest. These are just some of the many possible indicators that could be used. Some of them may be precursors to market moves in one direction or the other. In any reading of the *Wall Street Journal* financial section, you can find hundreds upon hundreds of such indicators and can then use them to generate a model.

Our goal is to find a way to predict the future so that we can use this prediction to make money. We have been discussing this approach with the idea that we will create a model of some process. Figure 17.1 illustrates what it is that we are trying to accomplish. In examining this figure, we are led to a logical way to discuss this area of modeling. The breakdown is in three separate areas: input, output, and the model itself.

In regression, or curve fitting, the point that is emphasized is that it is important to have a cause-and-effect relationship between the independent and dependent variables. Even if the results of the regression analysis show that there is a perfect fit to the data, there still must be a cause-and-effect relationship. Suppose I have data that shows that two times the age of my father equals the price of ground beef for the past 75 years. I could use this as a model to predict the price of ground beef in the future. It is obvious, however, that here is no cause-and-effect relationship and therefore the prediction should be suspect. What we are advocating is creating a model using data that may be an influencing factor on the output of the model. The data involved may or may not be obviously related to the model. We are, therefore, loosely interpreting the cause-and-effect relationship in the methodology proposed.

MODEL INPUT: WHAT SHOULD WE USE TO MEASURE THE MARKET?

When developing a model of a market, we want to use as many indicators as possible for the input to avoid missing the important ones. It is important to note that an indicator may have made its influencing change at some time in the past. For example, a move in the price of gold in January may not be reflected in a movement of the DJIA until March. Or is it better to use gold's move in December or February? Perhaps we need three consecutive values. Or is it two or four?

Another point to consider when gathering and choosing input for a model is the relative range of the data. A neural network type model that is using as inputs the price of gold ($400–$450) and the inflation rate (3%–5%) as inputs influencing the DJIA (6,000–8,000) is going to have trouble. It is difficult for an input variable with a small range of 0.03 to 0.05 to have as much influence on its internal cell calculations as an input variable with a much larger range of 400 to 450. Consequently, a neural network would probably ignore the inflation rate. Therefore, the two most important issues, when using neural networks to model a market, are the normalization and transformation of the input.

After considering the input transformations and normalization, we need to consider exactly how we will use these inputs. We can use each one as an individual input, or we can develop models to predict these values at some point in the future and use the output of these models as input to subsequent models. Often investors must make this decision through intuition or experiments.

Technical market analysts have developed many tools to aid in the task of predicting the market. Many of these use the concept of moving windows (creating a small data series) and then compute salient statistics of that window to use as an input or decision value. As we consider this methodology, we must answer several questions. How wide is the window? What statistic(s) should be computed? What is the proper lag for the value? When does the value influence the DJIA, one week, one month, or more in the future? If we try to use all possible choices, the number of input values becomes unmanageable. One way to reduce the number of inputs is to use the market modeler's intuition and experience. Another approach is to use automated methods to eliminate ineffectual inputs.

There are other considerations in developing a market model. Assume that we want to model the DJIA with the goal of predicting what the closing DJIA will be two weeks from now. Takens' theorem[1] says that we can use past values as input to create a multidimensional input space for predicting future values of the series. While this should work (in theory), market pundits will tell you that the market has no history. While past values may give us a trend, there is no good reason to suppose that the previous values of the DJIA are necessarily influencing the future values. However, since the DJIA only moves up or down within a small range daily, an investor could argue that past values do have an influence. In any case, we should consider other input.

The simplest approach, for the modeler, is to model the market of interest directly. This means using past values, as input, to predict future values. Although this is simple for the modeler, it relies on rather complex mathematical theory, Takens theorem. Therefore, we can use past history information to develop a multidimensional model of the Dow Jones Industrial Average (DJIA). In theory, this should work. However, how many time-lagged inputs are used? Which ones? Are there exogenous events that will affect the developed model? These are all valid questions that the modeler must ask and answer.

Input to the model and the transforms of this data are the most important area for accurate modeling. In summary, the modeler must chose the inputs for the model and the transformations on these values. Then these values must be normalized. If the goal is direct market modeling, using past values to predict future values, the number of inputs to be used must be determined. Often, the only way to do this is trial and error. However, if a model using many different inputs is being developed, there are other considerations. The input variables chosen should be influencing factors. If windows of data are to be used, the size of the window, the window statistic, how many windows, and how far to lag the window must all be decided. This can be by hand or, as we will present later, there are automated methods that will help.

MODEL OUTPUT: WHAT PARAMETERS SHOULD WE PREDICT?

Another question that arises when building a model is, "What is the output?" The answer depends on what we are trying to accomplish with the model. Sometimes the answer may be the value of an index or a stock price forecast. Other times, it may be best for the output to be a rate of change in the current price. This has the advantage of detrending the data, an important consideration.

Obviously, we want to predict the future, but how far into the future? There are basically two answers to this question. Since we know by intuition that a prediction of something tomorrow is more accurate than something a month from now, a short prediction is best. However, the daily movements of the DJIA contain a large degree of noise, through which the daily trend of the market may be difficult to determine.

What, then, are our choices? We can develop models that predict for a short time in the future. These values can then be used as input to the same networks to predict the next-time step in the future. This process, known as iterated prediction, can continue until a prediction is made sufficiently far in the future. The problem is that any error made in any of the predictions will be magnified many times in this process. If the prediction point is significantly far away, the prediction may have little resemblance to reality.

Another approach is simply to develop a model that predicts as far in the future as you desire. This avoids the problem of magnifying small errors, but is likely to be inaccurate due to higher variability. The only way to really determine what is best is to do both: compare results, then choose.

NEURAL NETWORKS: A SEMIAUTOMATED MODELING APPROACH

Many years ago, a new technology burst on the scene—neural networks. It was originally thought that this technology would solve all the world's problems. It could learn, and within just a few years with the speed of computers and the large, perfect memory, computer scientists would be able to emulate the human brain and thought processes. In fact, it was thought that they might be able to do even better. What was soon discovered and reported by Minsky and Pappert,[2] was that single-layered neural networks, based on the Perceptron, could not solve even the simple XOR problem.* Werbos, in his dissertation, showed that multiple-layered neural networks using Perceptrons, connected together in a network and trained through the use of backpropagation, the XOR problem could be solved. In fact, it was found that neural networks could handle the separation of highly nonlinear spaces through the creation of hyperplanes in a multidimensional space.[3]

---

*This tested whether or not the neural net could detect if two binary inputs were the same or different.

Determining whether to buy or sell stocks is akin to the military target recognition problem. Is predicting the markets a target recognition problem? Yes. We are trying to recognize if the time is right to buy, sell, or hold. These three are our targets and this problem is posed as a discrete space with three decisions.

Early neural net users thought that they could just throw all possible data at the network and let it figure out what is important and what is not important. Important values will have large weights associated with that input and unimportant inputs will have associated weights close to zero. What was not considered is that as the number of inputs increases so too does the complexity of the network and the required training time. This approach also does not consider who it is that will gather and enter all this data.

Once the input and its transformations have been chosen and normalized and the proper output chosen for the appropriate prediction period, then the network topology must be selected with traditional neural networks. The topology consists of the number of nodes per layer, the number of layers, and the transfer functions (squashing functions) to be used. Kolmogorov[4] and Cybenko[5] have proven that any function can be represented by a neural network consisting of three layers (input, hidden, and output) using any transfer function provided it is not an even polynomial. In essence, a neural network is nothing more than a complicated, nonlinear equation with many adjustable coefficients. In fact, a sufficiently complex equation with all the input variables represented, a copious number of coefficients, and an appropriate algorithm to adjust the coefficients, could perform the same job as a neural network.

Conventional wisdom suggests the following approach for applying traditional neural networks: use the sigmoid as the transfer function (since this can represent any function), one hidden layer (since this is sufficient to represent any function), and twice the number of hidden layer nodes as in the input layer. This may or may not work. We must remember several points when selecting the topology. If there are too few hidden nodes, there may not be sufficient degrees of freedom for the network to model the underlying process adequately. If there are too many hidden nodes, the network may just "memorize" the training data and will be unable to generalize. During memorization, the network models all the noise and inaccuracies in the input data. It will be unable to do a good job of extrapolating, predicting outside the range of the input data or it may be a poor performer at interpolating, predicting data within the input data range. In addition, the selection of too many hidden nodes will require vastly more time to train. Why should we consider more than one hidden layer? Kolmogorov and Cybenko both showed that one is sufficient (although neither tells us how to construct the network, only that one exists). However, training time may be less and there may be fewer problems with local minima if more layers are used.

When training a neural network, proper selection must be made of starting values of the node weights (normally randomly selected) and learning rates. Frequently, the neural network will become "stuck" in a local minimum and will not perform the desired prediction task. When this happens, reinitializing and retraining will generally solve the problem.

What have we determined so far? The topology must be selected to promote fast training while having sufficient complexity to model the underlying process. Many topologies must be examined to select the right one. In practice, these decisions are made using a trial-and-error approach (along with intuition) to develop the model. Considering all the possibilities, it would probably take forever to train and select the final network model, even on the most high-powered computers available. Further, the network needs to be retrained frequently to model the changing dynamics of the market. Is there any hope? Is there an easier way? There is; the technology is known as ontogenic statistical networks, models that can generate their own topology during training.

ONTOGENIC STATISTICAL NETWORKS—A TRULY AUTOMATED AND INTELLIGENT MODELING APPROACH

To address the problems that backpropagation neural networks present, a new class of neural networks has been developed, called ontogenic statistical networks. The name comes from the word *ontogenesis* meaning the history of the organism. An ontogenic network develops its own topology during training. No longer does the developer need to decide, a priori, how many layers, what transfer functions, or how many nodes. Depending on the specific ontogenic network technology chosen, unimportant inputs may also be eliminated. A particular class of ontogenic networks—statistical networks—is presented here with modeling results.

Some researchers would class algorithms that start with many nodes in a hidden layer and then prune (or eliminate) nodes that have little influence as ontogenic neural networks. We specifically exclude these methods from this class. The reason is that the large network must be trained to determine what nodes to prune. This can require a lot of time. Further, the pruned network must also be trained, requiring even more time. It makes much more sense to start small and grow to the correct size.

Another approach taken in some algorithms is to eliminate the concept of backpropagation of the error. In other words, develop a very fast method to train a fixed network. Using this method, many network topologies can be evaluated very quickly. However, an evaluation criterion must be used that is sensitive to how well the training data is modeled and to the complexity of the model itself.

Cascade Correlation

One of the best known ontogenic networks is Cascade Correlation developed by Fahlman and Lebiere.[6] They discovered that the reason many networks require long training times was that two or more nodes in the hidden layer were "fighting" to recognize a certain input pattern. Often this would take many training cycles to resolve. They reasoned that this process could be hastened if the network is built one node at a time. This would also result in a network that could not get stuck in a local minimum. When a new node is added, so too is an additional dimension that allows movement toward the global minimum. They also believed that some problems are linearly separable and this would be a good place to start.

It is not the goal of this section to give a complete description of the Cascade Correlation algorithm. Rather, it is to show some of the strengths and weaknesses of this methodology. The first step in Cascade Correlation is to determine a linear fit to the training data. This is best illustrated in Figure 17.2a. The three input nodes are shown on the left and the output nodes are on the upper right. The intersection of the lines represents the weights. After the initial training, if the problem is linearly separable, the problem is solved. If there is residual error, then hidden nodes must be added (one at a time) to reduce the error to acceptable levels. A pool of potential hidden nodes is created using random initial weights. All nodes are trained until either the maximum number of training cycles is reached or there is no more progress toward maximizing the correlation (really the covariance). The winning node is selected and inserted into the network, its input weights frozen, and all the output node weights are trained (Figure 17.2b). This is a very fast process. If there is remaining residual error, another hidden node is added using the same process (Figure 17.2c).

Several things should be noted about the Cascade Correlation algorithm. First, as a node is added, its input includes all the original input plus the output of all previously added hidden nodes. What this is really creating is a network of many layers consisting of one node each. Each added node has also become a feature detector. The node is chosen to detect a specific pattern in the input and it is the only node doing that job. Thus, the hidden nodes no longer have to compete to become a feature detector. Second, notice that the input weights to the node, when it is added to the network, are frozen. They will not change at any time in the future. This means that backpropagation of the model's output error is not needed. This leads to fast training. This also permits the existing network to be trained if new data is added to the training set while not requiring the relearning of the earlier data. Third, any transfer function may be added to the node. All node types may train and compete to be added to the network. Because the training is uncomplicated, this facilitates the construction of complex networks.

Why would we want to have a transfer function other than the sigmoid? Simply because our data may be better represented by another function. For example, if we

FIGURE 17.2 EXAMPLE CASCADE CORRELATION NETWORK GROWTH.

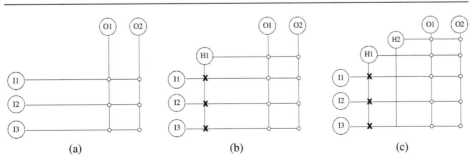

(a)   (b)   (c)

use a sine as the transfer function, it may represent a cyclic market. Using a sine as a transfer function means we are performing a pseudo Fourier analysis of the data.

For all its good points, Cascade Correlation does have problems. The first is seen in Figure 17.3. Assume that our data is a perfect sine wave and we want to model this using Cascade Correlation and a sine as the node's transfer function. With one hidden node, we should be able to exactly model this data. However, Cascade Correlation cannot do this. Remember that the first step was to do a linear fit and then model the residual error with the hidden nodes. The straight line in Figure 17.3 represents the linear fit. Once this linear fit is accomplished, the hidden nodes must model the residual error. Since this is no longer a pure sine wave, it becomes a difficult task.

In experiments using Cascade Correlation to model the Mackey-Glass equation (a time delay chaotic function), we found that Cascade Correlation would sometimes do a good job and other times a poor job.[7] The problem lies in specifying when to quit. The more complicated the network, that is, the more nodes in the network, the worse its performance was. Networks that quit training with around 30 nodes did best, while networks of 60 nodes were notoriously bad.

FIGURE 17.3 CASCADE CORRELATION LIMITATION EXAMPLE.

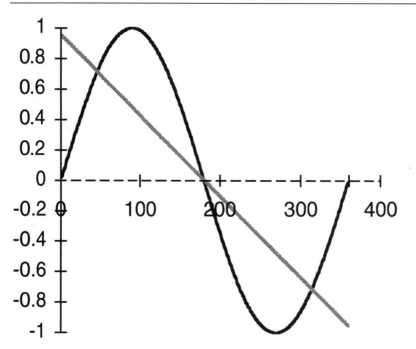

Probabilistic Neural Networks

Another example of an ontogenic network is the Probabilistic Neural Network (PNN) developed by Donald Specht.[8] This network has some very interesting properties that should be considered when deciding which methodology to use in building your model. First and foremost, this network is very fast in its training. Specht claims it to be almost instantaneous. Second, it has the feature that under some easily met conditions, the decision surfaces approach the Bayes optimal decision surface. Basically, this is the theoretical limit of how good a classification can be done. Specht also claims that this network is able to perform function approximation. This means that we can use the PNN to either forecast the future or help us make a trading decision.

What then, is a PNN? A PNN consists of four layers, Figure 17.4. The first layer, the input layer, is fully connected to the next layer and is just used to distribute the input components to each node in the next layer.

The second layer has nodes, also called pattern nodes, where each node represents one training example. This means that the more training examples you have, the more nodes and thus more storage is required. With the memory capacity of current personnel computers, plus the ever diminishing cost of memory, this should not be a consideration if this is the kind of network that you feel would be best. The

FIGURE 17.4 PROBABILISTIC NEURAL NETWORKS ARCHITECTURE.

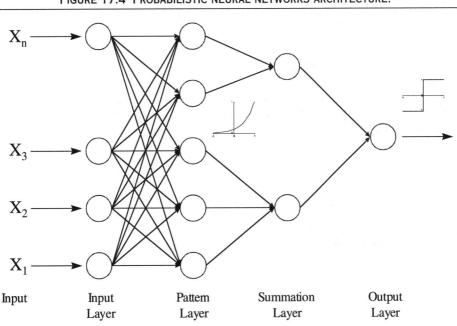

| Input | Input Layer | Pattern Layer | Summation Layer | Output Layer |

second-layer nodes have a transfer function that can be one of several different functions. The choice is left to the user. The most typical function used is

$$\exp[(Z_i - 1) \, \sigma^2]$$

where

Z$_i$ is the result of matching pattern$_i$ to the input $Z_i \leq 1$

σ is a user-defined smoothing parameter

The σ parameter has the effect of smoothing or lumping the training examples. Small values of σ tend to make each training point distinct, whereas larger values will force a greater degree of interpolation between the training points. Small values mean that the probability density function is close to that of the training examples. Large values of σ would force the probability density function to be Gaussian even if the underlying function is not.

The third layer in Figure 17.4 has one node for each class of output. Each cell sums only the output of the pattern nodes in the second layer that correspond to its class. This result is then passed to the fourth layer consisting of output nodes. Output nodes take into consideration a priori probabilities as well a bias factor representing losses associated with wrong predictions. These nodes then use a hard limiter to produce a binary output.

Reports have shown PNN to be as good as or better than conventional backpropagation neural networks. While requiring more memory than a backpropagation neural network, they train many orders of magnitude faster. The drawbacks concern the use of the biasing factor in the third layer and the smoothing factor, σ, in the pattern layer. These must be chosen through trial and error. Because they train so fast, this is not a problem.

These networks have been used successfully by other researchers for short-term stock prediction. We recommend that you read Specht and other references available on the Web site before embarking on the use of these networks. Versions of the PNN written for MATLAB are available free on the World Wide Web at http://chem1.nrl.navy.mil/~shaffer/pnn.html. At this same Web site is a good list of references on PNNs.

STATISTICAL NETWORK™ DATA MINING TECHNOLOGY

Here, we discuss an ontogenic network algorithm that has been successfully applied to stock market data mining. We first discuss the Statistical Network data mining algorithm, and then present a specific approach and corresponding results for a particular stock market modeling application.

As presented earlier, *analytical* development of trading algorithms is an extremely difficult task. For many fundamental and practical reasons, an in-depth understanding of the complex set of interactions among the plethora of prices, indicators, and other variables (including human psychology) required for precise mathematical models typically does not exist. Further complicating this task is the high degree of noise (i.e., price movements that cannot be explained by existing variables and indicators) that typically exists in these applications.

As presented, modeling of complex dynamic systems (i.e., financial markets) from *examples* of behavior—rather than from a fundamental understanding of the system—is often a more successful strategy. Statistical Networks offer a practical ontogenic network modeling approach that can learn complex relationships from example data.

Statistical Network Algorithm

Statistical Networks produce relational models (those relating a set of inputs or observations to a desired parameter estimate) that learn inductively from empirical evidence. Relationships that potentially represent a complex process or environment are hypothesized and "scored" according to some criterion that minimizes error. On the basis of the performance of the hypothesized relational model, several refinements and adjustments are made. Traditional statistical regression and neural network approaches offer some utility, but suffer from practical limitations.

Statistical Networks process information with complex mathematical functions.[9] Functions are attractive because they capture a large number of complex relationships in a compact and rapidly executable form. The Statistical Network learning algorithm produces a network of functional nodes, each containing a multiple-term polynomial relationship. Polynomial nodes are an extremely powerful method for performing complex reasoning tasks—they are the basis of traditional neural networks and other modeling techniques. They process one, two, or three inputs to compute an output value; and contain a bias or constant term (w_o), and linear, quadratic, cubic, and cross terms. A linear node processes several inputs and contains only the linear and bias terms. The equations for each node type are:

$$\text{Single} = w_o + w_1 x_1 + w_2 x_1^2 + w_3 x_1^3$$

$$\text{Double} = w_o + w_1 x_1 + w_2 x_1^2 + w_3 x_1^3 + w_4 x_2 + w_5 x_2^2 + w_6 x_2^3 + w_7 x_1 x_2 + w_8 x_1 x_2^2 + w_9 x_1^2 x_2$$

$$\begin{aligned}\text{Triple} = {} & w_o + w_1 x_1 + w_2 x_2 + w_3 x_3 + w_4 x_1^2 + w_5 x_2^2 + w_6 x_3^2 + w_7 x_1^3 + w_8 x_2^3 + w_9 x_3^3 + w_{10} x_1 x_2 \\ & + w_{11} x_1 x_3 + w_{12} x_2 x_3 + w_{13} x_1 x_2 x_3 + w_{14} x_1 x_2^2 + w_{15} x_1^2 x_2 + w_{16} x_1 x_3^2 + w_{17} x_1^2 x_3 \\ & + w_{18} x_2 x_3^2 + w_{19} x_2^2 x_3 \end{aligned}$$

$$\text{Linear} = w_o + w_1 x_1 + w_2 x_2 + \ldots + w_n x_n$$

An example Statistical Network is shown in Figure 17.5. It is a feed-forward network of polynomial nodes processing information from left to right. Each node produces intermediate information that is used as inputs for subsequent nodes. This networking strategy segments the overall relationship being modeled into more manageable components, and simplifies the learning process. Functional networks are

FIGURE 17.5 EXAMPLE STATISTICAL NETWORK. INPUT VALUES
PROPAGATE THROUGH A SERIES OF FUNCTIONAL NODES THAT ARE
RAINED AUTOMATICALLY BY THE DATA MINING ALGORITHM.

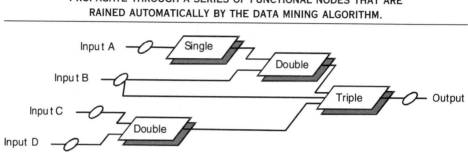

synthesized automatically from a flat file database where each column is an input or
output parameter (i.e., a variable), and each row contains an example set of the parameters. A hypothesize and test strategy finds the network that best represents the relationships contained in the database.

While individual nodes only allow up to three inputs and are limited to third
order terms, using them in the networking strategy shown in Figure 17.5 allows the
overall network to accept any number of inputs. In addition, because a specific node
can contain a third order term, a two-layer network can model a ninth-order relationship. An additional layer allows the modeling of up to 27th order relationships, and so
on. Therefore, networking relatively simple node types creates a powerful knowledge
representation.

The Statistical Network learning process produces networks of functional elements that more effectively "learn" complex relationships among features than is
often practical with other methods. The key to any machine learning strategy is the
learning algorithm itself. It must be able to *generalize* from, and not *memorize,* numerical examples of a problem domain. It must be able to automatically discover relationships to produce a model that performs well for not only training data but also
independent (i.e., real-world) data. The driving reason for this crucial requirement is
that *all data contain uncertainty.* Noisy, missing, conflicting, and erroneous data are all
manifestations of uncertainty in numerical examples.

An effective machine learning algorithm *must learn relationships and avoid mem-
orizing noise in an automated manner.* Statistical Networks achieve this through the
use of intelligent search heuristics to find the optimal network architecture and a
modeling criterion to ensure generalization. What follows is a top-level summary of
the Statistical Network learning algorithm (outlined in Figure 17.6).

Step 1

Several statistical measures are computed for each database variable such as their
mean and standard deviation. The values for each variable are normalized so that they

FIGURE 17.6 STATISTICAL NETWORK LEARNING ALGORITHM. THIS
AUTOMATED PROCESS FINDS THE BEST NETWORK ARCHITECTURE, THE
NODE EQUATION, AND GUARDS AGAINST OVERFITTING THE TRAINING DATA.

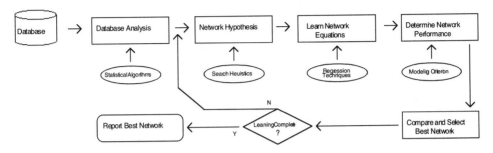

exhibit a mean of zero and a standard deviation of unity, greatly enhancing node regression performed in Step 3.

Step 2

Candidate network architectures are hypothesized using graph-tree network search heuristics. The heuristics employ a survival of the fittest strategy—similar to the underlying concept of genetic algorithms—by hypothesizing more refined versions of networks that have already exhibited promise. Initially, very simple network models are hypothesized (i.e., those that contain only one node). The best of these simple models (as scored by the modeling criterion in Step 4) are then used with the original input parameters as building blocks to hypothesize more complex networks. Search heuristics determine the best manner of combining simpler networks to form more complex ones. This process is repeated (automatically) several times, each providing an additional network layer.

Step 3

For each hypothesized network, each node's coefficients and their respective values are determined using advanced regression algorithms. In each node, the coefficients are

$$w_0, w_1, w_2, \ldots, w_n.$$

Step 4

Each network is "scored" with the Predicted Squared Error (PSE) modeling criterion, shown in Figure 17.7. The PSE was developed at Stanford University in the early 1980s specifically as a modeling criterion for statistical learning.[9] The network

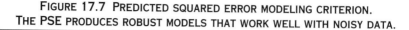

FIGURE 17.7 PREDICTED SQUARED ERROR MODELING CRITERION.
THE PSE PRODUCES ROBUST MODELS THAT WORK WELL WITH NOISY DATA.

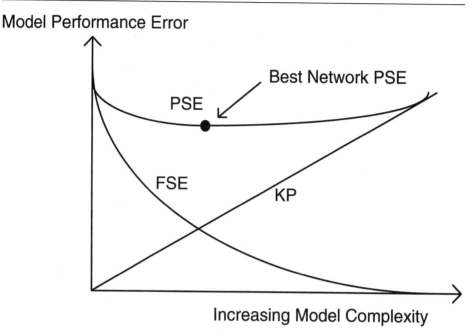

with the best (i.e., least) score is selected as the best for a particular database. The PSE performs a trade-off between network complexity and accuracy to find the simplest network that best models training *and* independent data. It gives an analytic estimate of the network for independent data. The PSE is:

$$PSE = FSE + KP = FSE + CPM \ [(2K/N) \cdot s_p^2]$$

where

FSE is the fitting squared error of the network on the training data

KP penalizes more complex networks, as they are more likely to overfit training data and therefore not perform well on independent data

CPM is a Complexity Penalty Multiplier, used to vary the emphasis of the KP term

K is the total number of network coefficients in the network model

N is the number of training observations

s_p^2 is an a priori estimate of the optimal model's error variance

The PSE produces networks that avoid modeling noise and overfitting training data. The network synthesis process begins at the left of the PSE curve shown in Figure 17.7. As the complexity of hypothesized networks increases, the PSE of those networks decreases until the network with the minimum PSE is found. The learning process ends when certain "stopping criteria" are met (see Figure 17.7). These criteria include heuristics that recognize when the learning process is taking place on the upward slope of the PSE curve, indicating the best network has already been found.

Statistical Network Advantages

While Statistical Networks are parametric at the node level, the hypothesis heuristics and modeling criterion at the network level create an *automated* nonparametric process. Therefore, the modeler is *not* required to be an integral part of the learning algorithm as *is* required by other approaches. This allows the modeler to focus limited resources on other issues, such as data collection, problem analysis, approach design, model evaluation, and trading system development. Compared with traditional neural network technology, Statistical Networks excel at estimating continuous parameters and are much more practical to develop. Because the process is nonparametric, resulting models generally outperform those developed with linear regression.

EXAMPLE OF A STATISTICAL NETWORK TRADING APPLICATION

To demonstrate the application of Statistical Network's data mining to market modeling, we chose to model daily price and volume data from the Dow Jones 30 Industrials (DJIA) as of January 31, 1997. We used High, Low, Open, Close, and Volume data from the period January 1, 1987, to January 31, 1997, which includes 2,548 trading days. Our goal was to create a model that accurately produces Buy and Sell indicators.

Technical Indicator Descriptions

One of the distinct advantages of Statistical Networks is that inputs that do not provide useful information for modeling the output variables will not be used in the final network produced by the Statistical Network learning algorithm. This ontogenic characteristic allows considerable freedom in selecting input variables; it allows one to include any and all variables that may contain useful information. The Statistical Network learning algorithm will automatically determine which variables should be used, and in what way.

For this problem, we chose a diverse set of technical indicators.[10] Each is a function of Open, High, Low, Close, and/or Volume data. We did not use indicators that are functions of broad market indicators such as indices, new Highs/Lows, Put/Call ratios, and Up/Down Volume.

Each technical indicator is useful for characterizing certain market characteristics. The challenge is determining how to combine the many different characterizations

TABLE 17.1 TECHNICAL INDICATOR DESCRIPTIONS

Indicator Name	Abbreviation	Time Windows
Open, High, Low, Close, Volume	Open, High, Low, Close, Vol.	None

Description

Daily Open, High, Low, and Close prices, and the trading Volume of the issue on a particular day.

Accumulationion/Distribution	Accumulation/Distribution	None

Description

A cumulative momentum indicator which associates changes in price and volume.

Average True Range	TrueRangeXX	5, 10, 14, 20, 30, 60, 90, 180

Description

The moving window average (typically 14 days) of the True Range, providing a measure of volatility.

Chaikin Oscillator	ChaikinOscXX1–XX2	3/10, 5/10, 3/15, 10/30, 10/45, 30/90

Description

An oscillator based on a function of two exponential moving averages of the Accumulation/Distribution indicator.

Chaikin's Volatility	ChaikinVolatilityXX1–XX2	3/10, 3/15, 5/10, 10/20, 10/30, 10/45, 30/90

Description

A quantification of the spread between High and Low price, involving a function of the percentage change over a time period (X1) of a moving average of period (X2).

Ease of Movement	EaseofMovement	None

Description

Characterizes the relationship between price and volume changes; showing how much volume is required to move price.

Exponential Moving Average	ExponMWAXXX	5, 9, 12, 14, 20, 21, 26, 30, 45, 90

Description

A moving average that places more emphasis on recent prices.

Negative Volume Index	NegVolIndex	None

Description

Indicates when volume decreases, presumes "smart money" takes positions when volume decreases.

On Balance Volume	OnBalanceVolume	None

Description

A momentum indicator relating price and volume change.

Positive Volume Index	PosVolIndex	None

Description

Indicates when volume increases, premised on the hypothesis that the "crowd" takes positions when volume increases.

Price Oscillator	PriceOscXX1–XX2	10/30, 12/26

TABLE 17.1 CONT'D.

Indicator Name	Abbreviation	Time Windows
Description		
The difference of two moving averages of the price of a security.		
Price Rate-Of-Change	PriceRateChangeXX	5, 10, 15, 20, 30, 45, 90
Description		
The difference in current price and the price XX time periods ago, expressed in percent.		
Price and Volume Trend	PriceVolumeTrend	None
Description		
A cumulative total of volume, weighted by changes in closing price.		
TRIX	TRIX–XX	5, 9, 12, 14, 20, 21, 26, 30, 45, 90
Description		
A momentum indicator involving a triple exponential average.		
Typical Price	TypicalPrice	None
Description		
An average of the High, Low, and Close of each day's price.		
Vertical Horizontal Filter	VerticalHorizontalFilterXX	28
Description		
Indicates whether prices are trending or congested.		
Volume Oscillator	VolumeOscXX1–XX2	3/10, 3/15, 5/10, 10/20, 10/30, 10/45, 30/90
Description		
The difference between two moving averages of a security's volume.		
Volume Rate-Of-Change	VolumeRateChangeXX	5, 10, 15, 20, 30, 45, 90
Description		
The difference in current price and the price XX time periods ago, expressed in percent.		
Williams' %R	WilliamsR–XX	5, 10, 15, 20, 30, 45, 90
Description		
A momentum indicator measuring overbought/oversold conditions.		

A variety of technical indicators were used as input variables to model Buy/Sell conditions.

these indicators provide into a useful model. This is accomplished automatically by the Statistical Network.

The technical indicators, their abbreviation, and a brief description are listed in Table 17.1. Many of these indicators require specification of a time window, and may therefore result in many different actual input variables depending on the time windows selected. In these cases, the set of time windows for each are also listed, and are designated by an "XX" in the variable abbreviation (e.g., ExponMWA_XX where XX = 30 is the 30-day Exponential Moving Window Average). This results in a set of 86 input variables for our problem.

Performance Target Selection

To define the Buy and Sell indicators, it was necessary to choose "performances targets." Ideally, we want the Buy/Sell indicators to tell us when the value of a particular stock will change more than predefined thresholds; that is, when it will rise a certain percentage or more and when it will fall another certain percentage or less. These performance targets form the basis of our Buy/Sell indicators.

We chose an annual gain of 35 percent and an annual loss of −15 percent as our performance targets. These were scaled to the time periods shown in Table 17.2. The goal is to select the best time period yielding the most accurate Buy/Sell Indicators. Note that other performance targets may be used, and with potentially better results than reported here.

To produce the actual Buy/Sell indicators, we first calculated the percentage gain or loss over the time periods indicated of the stock's closing price. We then determined whether these percentages exceeded the Gain/Loss thresholds listed in Table 17.2. If so, a value of "1" was assigned to the indicator, else a value of "0" was assigned.

Selection of Predictive Time Period

Four subsets of the data (A, B, C, and D) each containing approximately 4,000 observations were selected at random from the entire set of approximately 72,000 data. For each of the 10 Buy/Sell indicators (i.e., 5 Buy indicators and 5 Sell indicators), two Statistical Networks were synthesized using subsets A and B, for a total of 20 networks. Testing was performed on subsets C and D. Table 17.3 shows the performance of each Statistical Network model, ranked by Average Absolute Error.

Here, it is obvious that longer periods produce better results. Therefore, the remainder of our modeling was performed using time periods of 90 days and the corresponding Buy/Sell indicators. Note that the networks ideally output values of "0" and "1." The average errors of these networks range from 0.34 to 0.48; in all cases this is better than "guessing," which has an average error of 0.5.

TABLE 17.2 PERFORMANCE TARGETS

Period	Calendar Days	Trading Days	Scaled Performance Targets Gain (%)	Loss (%)
One week	7	5	0.673	−0.287
One-half month	15	11	1.458	−0.625
One month	30	22	2.917	−1.250
One-half quarter	46	33	4.375	−1.875
One quarter	91	65	8.750	−3.750

Several time periods were chosen, each with an annual gain of 35 percent and an annual loss of −15 percent.

TABLE 17.3 PERFORMANCE OF INITIAL BUY/SELL INDICATOR NETWORKS

Buy/Sell	Time Period	Train/Test Subset	Ave. Abs. Error	Buy/Sell	Time Period	Train/Test Subset	Ave. Abs. Error
Sell	90	B/C	0.340	Buy	30	A/D	0.460
Sell	90	A/D	0.352	Buy	30	B/C	0.463
Buy	90	A/D	0.399	Sell	15	A/D	0.470
Buy	90	B/C	0.408	Sell	15	B/C	0.477
Sell	45	B/C	0.410	Buy	15	B/C	0.478
Sell	45	A/D	0.422	Buy	15	A/D	0.480
Sell	30	B/C	0.443	Buy	5	A/D	0.485
Buy	45	A/D	0.446	Buy	5	B/C	0.485
Sell	30	A/D	0.447	Sell	5	B/C	0.485
Buy	45	B/C	0.453	Sell	5	A/D	0.486

Longer time periods showed a clear superiority for indicating buy and sell conditions.

Information Content Analysis

Typically, for large input sets such as that used here, it is useful to reduce the number of inputs considered to allow better focus on the input variables used. A particularly useful method for this is *Information Content Analysis*™.[11] Here, we take advantage of the fact that Statistical Networks synthesized at higher values of CPM are more "discriminating" and will therefore retain only the input variables that contain a high information content.

The information content of a set of input variables is quantified by synthesizing a set of Statistical Networks over a range of CPM values, and weighting the frequency of occurrence of each input over the set of networks to emphasize the inputs retained at higher CPM values. The key advantage to the ICA is that not only will useful input variables be identified, but also valuable *combinations* of inputs, because Statistical Network nodes can mathematically combine two or three inputs.

We performed an ICA for each of the four data subsets described for both the 90-day Buy and 90-day Sell indicators, and averaged the results. Typically, most of the input variables will have a zero information content—they will not appear in any of the synthesized networks. Table 17.4 shows the normalized information content of each technical indicator for both Buy/Sell indicators. Only input variables with an information content greater than 0.100 were used for subsequent modeling. Also, only a subset of all input variables has non-zero information content.

Baseline Models

To produce a set of baseline results, four subsets of the data (E, F, G, and H), each containing approximately 16,000 observations, were selected at random from the entire set of data. For the two Buy/Sell indicators, a Statistical Network was

TABLE 17.4 INFORMATION CONTENT ANALYSIS

Information Content for Buy Input Variables

TRIX90	1.000	High	0.177	ExponMWA30	0.064
Accumulation/Distribution	0.849	TrueRange10	0.166	WilliamsR20	0.051
TRIX30	0.752	ChaikinVolitility30–90	0.163	EaseofMovement	0.049
ChaikinOsc30–90	0.570	PriceRateChange30	0.163	TrueRange5	0.036
PriceVolumeTrend	0.563	ExponMWA45	0.120	TRIX26	0.032
VolumeOsc30–90	0.560	TrueRange90	0.120	WilliamsR15	0.032
Close	0.446	TRIX45	0.094	PriceOsc10–30	0.020
ExponMWA90	0.412	VolumeRateChange15	0.084	PriceRateChange20	0.016
VerticalHorizontalFilter28	0.337	ChaikinVolitility3–15	0.081	TrueRange45	0.003
PriceRateChange90	0.283	TrueRange14	0.081	TrueRange60	0.003
TrueRange180	0.283	PriceRateChange15	0.072	TrueRange20	0.003
TrueRange30	0.206	TypicalPrice	0.067		
Open	0.193	Low	0.065		

Information Content for Sell Input Variables

TRIX90	1.000	ChaikinVolitility10–30	0.177	TypicalPrice	0.042
TRIX45	0.753	TrueRange10	0.172	ChaikinVolitility30–90	0.039
Accumulation/Distribution	0.629	ExponMWA21	0.142	ExponMWA45	0.039
ChaikinOsc30–90	0.605	VolumeOsc10–45	0.138	ExponMWA14	0.038
TRIX30	0.419	TrueRange30	0.130	Open	0.031
TRIX26	0.351	PriceRateChange90	0.098	ChaikinVolitility10–45	0.020
Close	0.315	PriceRateChange15	0.086	ChaikinVolitility10–20	0.012
TrueRange14	0.260	TRIX21	0.075	ExponMWA26	0.012
VerticalHorizontalFilter28	0.256	High	0.060	TrueRange20	0.003
TrueRange5	0.218	ExponMWA5	0.055		
Low	0.192	ExponMWA20	0.050		

The normalized information content of each buy and sell type technical indicator is shown.

synthesized using subsets E and F; both networks for each Buy/Sell indicator were tested using subsets G and H. This resulted in eight sets of performance results, as shown in Table 17.5. The data shows that predicting Sell indicators (defined by our annual performance target selection and future time period) is somewhat easier than predicting Buy indicators.

Network Optimization

Typically, the default CPM value of 1.00 does not result in the best performing network model. Therefore, we employed an optimization routine that automatically finds the best CPM value for a specific database and set of input variables, using a search optimization algorithm.[12]

TABLE 17.5 PERFORMANCE OF BASELINE MODELS

Buy/Sell	Train/Test Subset	Average Absolute Error
Sell	E/H	0.347
Sell	E/G	0.347
Sell	F/G	0.349
Sell	F/H	0.349
Buy	F/H	0.399
Buy	F/G	0.399
Buy	E/G	0.400
Buy	E/H	0.401

Two statistical networks were synthesized for the buy and sell indicators; each of the four networks was evaluated on two independent data subsets. Rightmost column shows the network's average absolute error for each scenario.

Table 17.6 shows the results of optimizing for CPM. Here, data subset E was used for training, subset G was used to evaluate each network during optimization, and subset H was used for independent testing. In each case, optimization only slightly increases network performance.

Trading Strategy and Results

While the statistical performances of these models show promise, their real benefit can only be demonstrated in an actual trading environment to determine whether they actually make money. Each network was used to process the technical indicators for a number of stocks over the 10-year period. Here, we present the results for AT&T and IBM; the results for other companies are comparable.

Each model—the Buy network and the Sell network—produces simultaneous indicator signals on the continuous range $0.00 \leq output \leq 1.00$ for each trading day. Both networks can potentially output any value on this range at the same time. We smoothed the outputs with a three-day moving average and defined activation thresholds for each. The result is either a value of "0" (inactive) or "1" (active) for each indicator on each day ("0" when the signal lies below threshold, and "1" when it is above). Once an indicator begins to activate, it typically remain activated for several days.

TABLE 17.6 CPM OPTIMIZATION RESULTS

Buy/Sell	Train/Evaluate/ Test Subset	Average Absolute Error
Sell	E/G/H	0.346
Buy	E/G/H	0.399

Optimizing the statistical network only improves results slightly.

For our trading strategy, we defined the following rules:

- If no signal is currently present and either the Buy or Sell indicator activates, take the appropriate action.
- Only take action (Buy/Sell) on the first day the indicator signal becomes active; ignore subsequent identical signals until there is a change.
- If one signal is present and the other activates, ignore the second signal while both are on.
- If both signals are present and one deactivates, then take the action of the remaining signal.
- "No Signal" gaps of one day's duration are ignored, that is, two "strings" of Buy indicators with a single day of no signal in the middle is treated as a single string of Buy indicators.

In addition, because we allow both long and short positions, we include the following rules:

- Long positions are closed out by a Sell signal.
- Short positions are closed out by a Buy signal, and a new long position is also established at the same Buy price.

Finally, each position was closed out at the end of the 10-year period. Note that there are many methods to interpret the indicators produced by this approach by establishing different sets of rules. Here, we merely present one of many.

FIGURE 17.8 BUY/SELL INDICATOR PERIODS FOR AT&T.

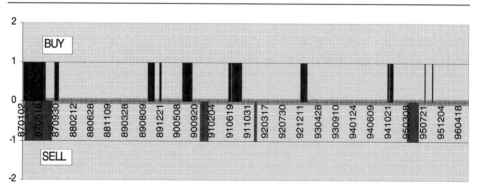

Source: Microsoft Excel.

FIGURE 17.9 PRICE DATA AND CORRESPONDING BUY/SELL INDICATORS FOR AT&T.

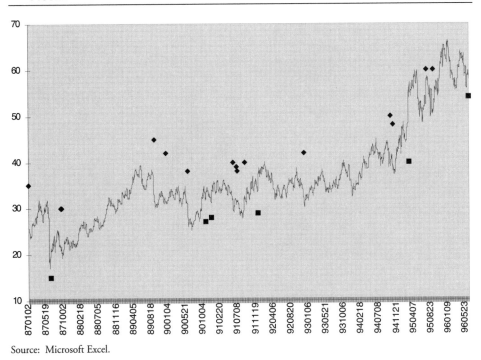

Source: Microsoft Excel.

Figure 17.8 shows the Buy (above the *x*-axis) and Sell (below the *x*-axis) indicators for AT&T over the 10-year period as defined by the preceding trading strategy. Figure 17.9 shows the closing price of AT&T during this period, with the Buy and Sell indicators plotted. Buy indicators appear as diamonds above the price curve; Sell indicators appear as squares below the price curve.

Table 17.7 shows the results of the individual trades resulting from this approach. During the 10-year period of consideration, 16 trades were made for an average gain of 21.2 percent per trade. The average annual gain of each trade was 33.6 percent. With the exception of trade number one, all trades produce a positive return. For short positions, we simply calculate the return as the percentage gain between the Buy and Sell price.

Figure 17.10 shows similar chart analysis for IBM. Table 17.8 shows the performance results of the individual trades. During the 10-year period of consideration, 20 trades were made for an average gain of 34.3 percent per trade. The average annual gain of each trade was 33.5 percent.

TABLE 17.7 TRADING RESULTS FOR AT&T

Trade #	Establish Position	Price	Date	Close Position	Price	Date	Number of Trading Days	% Gain	Annualized % Gain
1	Buy	$25.750	870106				121	−16.23	−35.01
				Sell	$21.571	870626			
2	Buy	$21.440	870911				787	49.25	16.33
3	Buy	$21.125	870921				781	51.48	17.20
4	Buy	$31.875	890914				279	0.39	0.37
5	Buy	$31.000	891213				216	3.23	3.90
6	Buy	$29.875	900604				98	7.11	18.94
				Sell	$32.000	901019			
7	Sell	$32.696	901206				120	10.11	21.99
				Buy	$29.695	910529			
8	Buy	$29.695	910529				136	25.67	49.27
9	Buy	$30.944	910620				121	20.60	44.44
10	Buy	$31.324	910628				114	19.14	43.82
11	Buy	$32.000	910826				74	16.62	58.63
				Sell	$37.319	911209			
12	Buy	$31.441	921127				571	73.34	33.52
13	Buy	$39.000	941003				105	39.74	98.79
14	Buy	$38.000	941021				91	43.42	124.54
				Sell	$54.500	950302			
15	Buy	$52.500	950714				237	14.05	15.47
16	Buy	$50.375	950908				198	18.86	24.86
				Sell	$59.875	960619			
						Average:	253.1	21.2	33.6

FIGURE 17.10 PRICE DATA AND CORRESPONDING BUY/SELL INDICATORS FOR IBM.

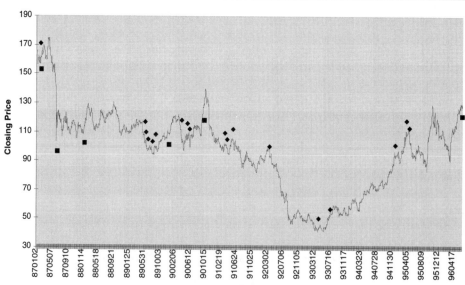

TABLE 17.8 TRADING RESULTS FOR IBM

Trade #	Establish Position	Price	Date	Close Position	Price	Date	Number of Trading Days	% Gain	Annualized % Gain
1	Buy	$156.625	870204				5	2.71	141.64
				Sell	$160.875	970210			
2	Sell	$118.000	870623				500	15.97	8.34
3	Sell	$116.625	880201				346	14.62	11.03
				Buy	$101.750	890613			
4	Buy	$101.75	890613				133	5.53	10.86
5	Buy	$100.75	890621				127	6.58	13.52
6	Buy	$97.375	870706				117	10.27	22.92
7	Buy	$94.625	890815				89	13.48	39.53
8	Buy	$99.000	890901				76	8.46	29.07
				Sell	$107.375	891219			
9	Buy	$103.88	900329				130	23.70	47.58
10	Buy	$106.38	900518				95	20.79	57.13
11	Buy	$100.25	900607				82	28.18	89.69
				Sell	$128.500	901002			
12	Buy	$101.38	910321				1328	25.76	5.06
13	Buy	$98.500	910409				1316	29.44	5.84
14	Buy	$103.63	910523				1284	23.03	4.68
15	Buy	$92.875	920312				1081	37.28	9.00
16	Buy	$42.750	930413				807	198.25	64.12
17	Buy	$51.875	930716				741	145.78	51.35
18	Buy	$92.875	941222				377	37.28	25.81
19	Buy	$107.500	950327				313	18.60	15.51
20	Buy	$106.750	950413				300	19.44	16.91
				Sell	$127.500	960619			
						Average:	462.4	34.3	33.5

CONCLUSION

Statistical Network data mining provides a highly automated ontogenic approach to interpreting technical indicators for daily price data. It allows creativity in defining a robust set of input indicators, and flexibility in defining different trading strategies. The results shown here demonstrate the validity of this approach.

ENDNOTES

1. Takens, F., "Detecting Strange Attractor in Turbulence," *Lecture Notes in Mathematics*, D. Rand, L. Young (Ed.), Berlin: Springer, 1981.
2. Minsky, M., and Papert, S., *Perceptrons*, Cambridge, MA: MIT Press, 1969.

3. Werbos, P. J., "Beyond Regression: New Tools for Prediction and Analysis in the Behavioral Sciences," Doctoral Dissertation, Harvard University, 1974.

4. Kolmogorov, A. N., "On the Representation of Continuous Functions of Many Variables by Superposition of Continuous Functions of One Variable and Addition" [in Russian], Dokl. Akad. Nauk USSR, 114, 1957, 953–956.

5. Cybenko, G., "Approximation by Superpositions of a Sigmoidal Function," *Mathematics of Control, Signals, and Systems,* Vol. 2, No. 4, 1989, pp. 303–314.

6. Fahlman, S. E., and Lebiere, C., "The Cascade Correlation Architecture," in *Advances in Neural Information Processing Systems,* Vol. 2, D. S. Touretzky (Ed.), 1990, pp. 524–532, Morgan Kauffman, San Mateo.

7. Ensley, D. D., & Nelson, D. E., "Extrapolation of Mackey-Glass Data Using Cascade Correlation," *Simulation,* May 1992, pp. 333–339.

8. Specht, D. F., "Probabilistic Neural Networks," *Neural Networks,* January 1990, pp. 109–118.

9. Montgomery, Gerard J., & Drake, Keith C., "Abductive Reasoning Networks," *Neurocomputing— An International Journal,* June 1991, pp. 97–104; Farlow, S. J. (Ed.), *Self-Organizing Methods in Modeling: GMDH Type Algorithms,* New York: Marcel-Dekker, 1984.

10. Achelis, Steven B., *Technical Analysis from A to Z,* Irwin Professional Publishing, 1995; Myers, Thomas A., *The Technical Analysis Course,* Irwin Professional Publishing, 1994; and Murphy Jr., Joseph E., *Stock Market Probability,* Irwin Professional Publishing, 1994.

11. Drake, Keith C., Richard Y. Kim, & Jeff Xu, "Ontogenic Avionics Time Signal Modeling Tool and Application," *Final Report,* contract F33615-94-C-1548, WL/AAAT-1, Wright Patterson Air Force Base, Ohio, July, 1995.

12. Ibid.

CHAPTER 18

Case Study: Building an Advanced Trading System

JEFFREY OWEN KATZ, PH.D., AND DONNA L. MCCORMICK

In this chapter, we are going to develop a fully mechanized, rule-based trading system using a component-based approach to neural network technology that also brings the human brain into the loop.[1] Essentially, we will be conducting an experiment: We want to determine whether a pattern in a given market, which can be visually detected and marked on charts by the developer, can be learned and identified by a neural network.

A series of neural networks will be developed, each of which shall be responsible for identifying a specific pattern in the market's behavior. A set of rules will then be coded to provide the system with the criteria necessary for it to evaluate the information furnished by the networks' outputs in the generation of trading signals. This approach (which we call the "Katz Click-And-Train Approach" or KCATA) is intended to take the subjectivity out of visual recognition of chart patterns, while still maintaining the human element in a fully mechanized system. The approach is also unique in that it uses neural networks in a way that capitalizes on the power of the technology by applying it in a manner consistent with its capabilities. This differs from traditional applications of this technology (what we have come to call the "neural newbie" approach) as well as other common methods of applying neural networks to trading. All charts and tables were produced on TradeStation®, version 3.5, a product of Omega Research,™ Inc. TradeStation® is a registered trademark of Omega Research, Inc.

TRADITIONAL APPROACHES

The "Neural Newbie" Approach

By "neural newbie" we mean a newcomer ("newbie") to neural networks who takes a neural network, throws a lot of mildly preprocessed data at it, and hopes that the technology itself comes up with something useful. Back in the late 1980s, we were all neural newbies because the technology itself was so new and we did not know how to apply it most appropriately.

We have learned from much experience that the neural newbie approach does not work well with current-day markets, although it may have had some success in the past. What may account for the change is that, when the technology was new, few traders were using it. In those days, there were still inefficiencies in the markets relative to simple neural network models that were not being taken advantage of by traders. The neural newbie approach could, therefore, detect and generate signals from these market inefficiencies. However, once neural network tools became the rage, everyone began using them and simple models were tried first. As more and more people traded simple neural network models, the patterns that neural networks could detect were "traded away."

Certain market inefficiencies can still be found by using this approach but, for the most part, they are not tradable (e.g., they produce too small a net return, if not a loss, after slippage and commissions are factored in). The failures developers had experienced with their application of neural network technology is most probably the cause of the technology's loss of popularity among traders. However, it is a mistake to blame such failure on the technology itself; blame should be placed on the ways in which the technology was applied. Other potentially profitable inefficiencies still exist in the markets, but more effort and more unique approaches to their discovery are required, as are more appropriate applications of the available technology.

Other Common Approaches

Over the years, we have experimented with many commonly known approaches that use neural technology and that are slightly more advanced than the neural newbie approach. For example, we have explored various kinds of inputs: used more heavily preprocessed data, the slopes of adaptive moving averages, wave sampling, Fourier transforms. We have also used inputs consisting of such kinds of data as the Commitment of Traders' (COT) Reports, fundamental data, data bearing on intermarket relationships.

In addition, we experimented with different kinds of forecasting targets: Instead of trying to predict price change over the next several bars, we tried to predict simply whether a bottom or a top (defined in some simple, direct manner) would occur. We have tried to predict indicator values, as well as the future slope of moving averages.

None of these approaches produced a system with stunning performance; in fact, most of the time, the performance of such systems was fairly poor. We do not know why we never achieved complete success using these methods—perhaps, as happened with neural newbie models, such approaches simply became worse over time (we never bothered to investigate them from their inception onward); perhaps they never really worked at all. Apparently, these techniques are inadequate for capturing the inefficiencies that remain in today's markets.

BEYOND TRADITION

Because of our lack of success with traditional approaches, we backed off entirely from the idea of trying to use neural technology to predict the market in any direct way, shape, or form. Initially, we focused our efforts on the development of systems that consisted entirely of rules, including rules that attempted to describe the kinds of patterns we were subjectively recognizing. However, we soon discovered that this use of rules was not as feasible as we expected.

One pattern that we recognized on the S&P 500 occurs when the stochastic oscillator has a particular kind of double bottom; this seems to foreshadow a very short-term move. However, when we tried to cast this pattern into simple rules (e.g., the bottom is defined as when the price before and the price after are higher), the rules did not properly represent the concept because the pattern is not perfectly smooth and there may be jiggles. When we tried to generate such rules to represent what we were subjectively identifying as a pattern, the rules caused a lot of wrong patterns to be marked, which we would not have marked ourselves if we were looking at the chart. So, in many cases, even though we are quite competent at disentangling a set of concepts into rules to differentiate and define features, many ambiguities had to be considered when trying to write rules to express subjective knowledge, even if it is in the form of a pattern that is very easy to detect visually. It was after the experimentation with using rules to detect patterns that we decided to attempt to have neural networks recognize patterns that exist in data within their view.

While experience has shown that neural networks cannot identify useful patterns if they are just given relatively raw data and told to find anything that is predictively useful, they can be excellent pattern recognizers, if handled in the right way. So, rather than directly training a neural network on raw market data to generate buy and sell signals, we decided to train nets to emulate a successful trader, that is, to identify the same patterns that a trader would identify on charts and use in trading. If we can subjectively mark the terminations of things like head-and-shoulders patterns, double bottoms, and stochastic hooks, perhaps we can train neural networks to accurately recognize such patterns in their window of view and to perform that same function in the future (identify patterns that we can identify by eye on charts).

Such thinking is what contributed to our decision to use the brain as the instrument that initially decides on the kinds of patterns that may be tradable, and to then use neural networks as a tool to objectively identify instances of those patterns when they occur. In essence, we are allowing the brain to serve as a trainer for the neural networks. Best of all, this keeps the objectivity in the trading system; anything that is subjective is transferred into the machine through use of neural networks.

In the procedure we are proposing, a person subjectively recognizes a useful pattern, for example, Pattern X, and identifies the instances of Pattern X on a chart. While Pattern X is considered to be a single pattern, it will have variations and, while the task set before the neural network may appear simple because it has only one pattern to learn, the task is still complex because of these *variations*. For example, Pattern X might be a particular kind of double-bottom pattern but, in some instances of its occurrence, the bottoms may be spread further apart, be closer together, one bottom might be higher than the other yet, subjectively, it is still the same pattern. In this way, the net may still have a fairly difficult job in learning Pattern X and all its variations, but the complexity of the job is a lot simpler than having the network find any and all patterns in all the many patterns that exist that are useful to the prediction objective.

Subjective knowledge is brought into the equation and the networks are used to capture that knowledge in a computerized form. In this way, the trader is brought into the loop.

Our preliminary efforts using this approach provided much better results than those we obtained when applying neural networks in more traditional manners to the same type of problem. Nets trained a lot more reliably, faster, and better, and generalized well with respect to the particular patterns they were trained to detect. If the pattern that was subjectively thought useful is really useful, then the system may be quite effective. If the pattern is not a useful one after all, the net may still generalize (i.e., it will always detect that pattern since it has learned to do so, and it will continue to detect it reliably into the future); its detection of that pattern will not necessarily be predictively useful, but that is through no fault of the net, and the net is still useful in that now the pattern can be put to an objective test.

WHAT CAN GO WRONG?

If the approach does not work, two factors may be responsible for failure. The factors involve the accuracy of our observations of the patterns, and their predictive value. We may simply be wrong about these things.

One of the questions we are trying to answer is whether a neural network can detect a subjectively identified pattern when an experienced researcher is developing the system. If we can get a net to recognize a subjective pattern, at least we have made some statement about the usefulness of AI technology and about how one can go about detecting patterns that are hard to define in rules. Knowing that, if some patterns prove to be useless, we can sift through them with objective tests to find those that really work and are useful in trading.

Even if the patterns themselves are not predictively useful, we will have shown that a neural network can be trained to accurately detect a visually or subjectively recognized pattern consistently, which makes that pattern objectively testable without such factors as hindsight, which make backtesting by eye less reliable. So, even if the patterns themselves are not predictively useful, there is still the advance of having mechanized the detection system successfully.

Now that we have discussed how we came upon this approach, why we believe it is a feasible one, and what can go wrong, we will outline the exact methodology, apply it, and examine the results.

STEPS INVOLVED IN TRAINING NETWORKS

The intention is to get a neural network to emulate a trader who marks a chart for each occurrence of some specific pattern. We are going to carry through this procedure for a number of different kinds of patterns, the terminations of which can be identified and marked on a chart. We are going to build what we call "pattern detection components"; in this case, the components are networks trained using the KCAT approach. The patterns are all based on subjective brain work, or outside analysis, so the person doing this needs to have some knowledge about the market being modeled, as well as some ability to recognize and mark specific patterns on charts. We are then going to use the components we develop to construct a full trading system.

These are the basic steps of the KCAT approach:

1. Identify a number of potentially useful patterns.
2. Mark those patterns on a long chart to find as many instances of each pattern as possible.
3. Train a number of neural networks, each of which will be tasked to recognize one of the patterns identified.
4. Evaluate the networks to determine whether they can provide good pattern recognition capability.
5. If they can, then integrate those components (the networks) into a rule-based system that will use the information provided by the outputs of the networks to generate trading instructions.

DESCRIBING THE PATTERNS TO THE NETWORK

How do you describe a pattern to a neural network? This is a simple process, assuming that the right tools are available. You need a tool that can generate charts (bar charts, candlestick charts, whatever your preference), and that can plot as many variables as desired (and you will probably want to plot some intermarket variables as well as price and other indicators); TradeStation® works quite well for this job (this is what we are using). In addition, we needed a capability to record the exact date and time anywhere one indicates or "clicks" on the chart. This capability is crucial and is one we have had to custom program (we call it "TradeMarker™"). One of the functions of Trade-Marker™ is to allow a user to mark the pattern that he or she wants the neural network to learn to recognize. For example, if we want to train a network to recognize a double-bottom pattern (Pattern X), we would take the following five steps:

1. Pull up a chart.
2. Go through the chart looking for the end of every instance of Pattern X and click on that end. Every time we click on an instance of Pattern X, TradeMarker™ will write to a file the date and time of the particular bar on which we clicked. We should point out that when you "click" to mark where the pattern ends on the chart, you should use some kind of objective determination of the pattern's end (e.g., an end marker for the stochastic may be where it crosses its moving average); this will provide a standard end-point. Although the signal pattern that came before the mark will shift about a bit (e.g., some are longer, some are shorter), one part of the pattern will always be anchored in an objective way. After clicking on all instances of the pattern we could identify, we will have a "mark file," each line of which will contain a date and a time for a critical bar.

3. Having prepared the mark file, it is now necessary to prepare what we call a "pseudo-fact file," which is the fact file that we are actually going to use. Rather than having *real* targets (consisting of whether or not there was a mark), it will have the *date and time* for each bar as two targets. To create this pseudo-fact file, TradeStation® code is set up so that it does all the input preprocessing and a file is written that contains the inputs, the date, and the time for each bar.

4. The next step is to locate on the pseudo-fact file the date and time of each pattern specified in the mark file. For every date and time successfully located, TradeMarker™ will insert a 1 as the new target (substituting that for the date and time); then, for every bar in the fact file where the pattern was not recognized (i.e., where there was no corresponding date and time in the mark file), it will insert a 0 as the new target. What we now have is a fact file with inputs and target, where the target is a 1 if the pattern was recognized (marked) at that bar, or 0 if the pattern was not recognized (not marked).

5. The neural network will then examine the inputs and determine whether there is a 1 or a 0 in the target, for example, whether it was judged as a pattern or not. It will attempt to learn to use the inputs to discriminate the presence or absence of the marked pattern. This is standard network training: We choose a training and testing sample, train on the training sample, then test the network on the out-of-sample testing data.

Assuming we have a network that accurately captures the subjectively detected and marked pattern, it is necessary to write some rules in TradeStation® which will make use of that network. If the network works fairly well, a typical rule for using the network's output to generate a trading signal might be written as follows:

If Value1 > N_threshold then Buy at Market.

Where Value1 is a value returned from the neural net.

Here are some tips for using the KCAT approach:

- Make sure that you have indeed identified a recurrent market pattern.
- When marking the chart, be sure to mark the patterns in a consistent manner.
- The longer the data period over which you can generate the marks and the more marks you have, the better the results will be; too few marks provide less statistical stability.
- Keep the networks simple. Do not overoptimize.

APPLYING THE KCAT APPROACH

Our first step was to decide on a market. We wanted an end-of-day trading system for the S&P 500 that would hold trades for somewhere between 1 to 10 days, that would be highly profitable, and that would have a high percentage of winning trades.

For this experiment, we decided to include three basic patterns in the final system: pull-backs-in-trends, multiple bottoms and tops, and head-and-shoulders patterns. We considered both the long (upward) and short (downward) varieties of each pattern, which yielded six patterns in total.

A "pull-back-in-trend" is a situation in which a trend in the movement of the market has clearly been established, but the market reverses for a short time before continuing in the direction of the trend. The key is to jump in at the extreme of the pull-back. There may be several pull-backs along the way to a major top or bottom. As such, pull-backs-in-trends provide favorable entry points in the direction of the overall trend. On the long side of this pattern, there were 194 marks; 140 instances were identified for the shorts.

The "multiple bottoms and tops" pattern occurs when there are clear-cut bottoms or tops that are *not* pull-backs in trends, with an emphasis on double- or triple-bottoms or tops. No definite trend has to be present for this pattern to occur; in fact, we are looking for the end of a major trend or where there is no trend, as in market consolidation periods, to differentiate the multiple bottoms and tops pattern from a pull-back in trend pattern. There were 150 instances for the longs, 145 for the shorts.

The "head-and-shoulders" pattern is when the market forms a sort of hump (a rise followed by a decline), pulls back a bit, forms a higher hump (usually with some noise in it), pulls back again, and finally forms another smaller hump (relative to the second one), at which point the market drops off. When marking this pattern, we would click on the chart a little after the peak of the rightmost hump, which would indicate a good place to sell. There were fewer markings for this pattern than for the multiple bottoms or tops pattern: only 48 on the long side, 19 on the short.

We used our neural network development tool, N-TRAIN®, to train one neural network for each of the six patterns. All six nets had the same structure: 25 inputs in the first layer, 6 middle layer cells, 1 output. The output was what we wanted the network to predict—whether or not the chart pattern was present. They were essentially simple, unadjusted networks; in fact, the networks were trained using mostly default settings of N-TRAIN®.

All the networks had the same parameters. In all cases, the inputs to the networks were the same. Input data is examined by the networks to determine whether a pattern is present. While, we cannot fully disclose the precise nature of the input signals because of their proprietary nature, we can say that they consisted of the slopes of several moving averages of different periods (for trend information), as well as specially normalized price change values.

The data sample used for this study consisted of the period from 1/3/83 through 5/3/96; there are 3,322 bars in this sample. Bars 10 through 2,599 were used to train all six networks; bars 2,600 through 3,322 were used as the out-of-sample test data for all six systems.

The neural networks were all trained until correlations between their output and the target had reached a plateau with the in-sample data set. This usually occurred by 200 training runs for each network. After each net was trained, it was then "polished" with a very small learning rate for about 20 runs. Training for the in-sample runs ranged between 0.20 and 0.60; in the out-of-sample runs, they ranged between 0.08 and 0.50. In most cases, there was reasonably good generalization.

After the networks were trained and tested, we entered TradeStation® and wrote the trading rules for each of the six networks, which constituted six systems. The entry rule for all six systems was the same, with the exception of a threshold parameter, which varied somewhat from net to net. Thresholds were adjusted for each system to get a reasonable number of trades from each system. As it turned out, the threshold was not too critical for most of the patterns: If it was too low, there would be more signals than would be expected based on the marking procedure and the profits would drop; if the threshold was set too high, it would not necessarily hurt individual trade performance, there would just be fewer trades (e.g., there might be 100% wins, but only with 10 trades). We, therefore, set the thresholds to a middle range, a value that would provide a number of trades roughly equal to the number of instances of the pattern we had marked on the chart, and would also provide an acceptable profit.

The entry rule was "If the network's output is greater than the threshold, then buy/sell next bar." The exit rule was based on a proprietary, "quasi-parabolic" ratcheting stop: Basically, the stop would start out (for the long side) some multiple of the average range below the entry price, and it would go up with the market, becoming like a moving average pulling toward the market as the market rose; in this way, the stop would rise along with the market to lock in profits. Aside from the threshold parameter, the stop acceleration was the only factor that varied across the systems (in a couple of the short patterns, we needed to alter the acceleration factor to prevent market volatility from causing stops to be hit too quickly).

We combined the six systems into one integrated system. We ran the integrated system with a money management stop of $7,500, and a profit target of $2,000. A money management stop is designed to exit a trading position when the trade's net loss exceeds a specified amount, in this case $7,500. A profit target is designed to lock in profits by exiting the trade as soon as the trade's net profit reaches a specified amount, in this case $2,000.

A NOTE ABOUT THE FIGURES AND TABLES

The charts are standard bar charts, with opens and closes marked for each bar. Several kinds of signals are generated by the systems on the out-of-sample data, which extended from 2/26/93 to 5/3/96:

- An arrow pointing upward with a 1 indicates a long entry signal.
- An arrow with a −1, pointing downward, indicates a short entry signal.
- An arrow with a 0 and a horizontal bar at the top or at the bottom indicates an exit from the trade.

RESULTS FOR THE
PULL-BACK-IN-TRENDS PATTERN

Long Positions

Figure 18.1 is the chart for the long side of the pull-backs-in-trends pattern. An upward trend is occurring in the market during this time period. With the exception of the second entry signal (mid October), all entry signals are very close to the kinds of pull-backs-in-trends we marked by hand using the KCAT approach.

Table 18.1 is the performance summary for this pattern, which produced 84 percent profitable trades. There was a net profit of $62,375; a gross profit of $109,550. The drawdown was $10,175, higher than we would like. The system was in the market for an average of 3 days for winning trades, with a maximum number of 15 consecutive winners; losing trades were in the market for an average of 6 days, with only 1 consecutive losing trade at a time. The average trade was $974.61.

This system could be traded on its own. It took 64 trades in the three-year out-of-sample period, which suggests some degree of statistical stability.

FIGURE 18.1 THE LONG POSITIONS OF THE PULL-BACKS-IN-TRENDS PATTERN.

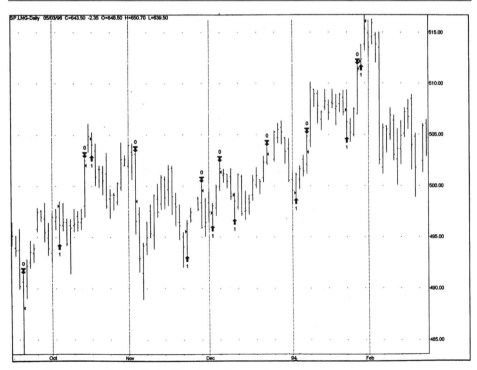

Source: Chart created with TradeStation® by Omega Research, Inc.

TABLE 18.1 TRADING PERFORMANCE SUMMARY USING THE PATTERN IN FIGURE 18.1

Performance Summary: All Trades (Long)			
Total net profit	$ 62375.00	Open position P/L	$ 0.00
Gross profit	$109550.00	Gross loss	$–47175.00
Total # of trades	64	Percent profitable	84%
Number winning trades	54	Number losing trades	10
Largest winning trade	$ 2450.00	Largest losing trade	$ –6500.00
Average winning trade	$ 2028.70	Average losing trade	$ –4717.50
Ratio avg win/avg loss	0.43	Avg trade (win & loss)	$ 974.61
Max consec. winners	15	Max consec. losers	1
Avg # bars in winners	3	Avg # bars in losers	6
Max intraday drawdown	$–10175.00		
Profit factor	2.32	Max # contracts held	1
Account size required	$ 10175.00	Return on account	613%

Short Positions

Figure 18.2 illustrates the short positions for pull-backs-in-trends. These signals are not necessarily exactly where we would have placed them by hand, but they are fairly close and illustrative of the pattern; the first short signal is perhaps the closest to the kind we marked.

Table 18.2 presents the performance summary for this pattern. There were fewer trades taken for the shorts (only 26) than the longs; 81 percent were wins. The drawdown was a little lower than that for the longs: $8,975, which is a little on the high side for a net profit of $20,425. The basic behavior of the two systems was similar; however, we would not feel comfortable trading this system on its own because of the small number of trades taken over the three-year period.

RESULTS FOR THE
MULTIPLE-BOTTOMS AND MULTIPLE-TOPS PATTERNS

Bottoms (Long) Positions

Figure 18.3 is the chart for the multiple-bottoms pattern (long positions). This chart clearly illustrates the multiple-bottoms pattern and, in many cases, the network marked the bottoms almost exactly where we would have by hand.

Table 18.3 provides the performance summary for this pattern. This system did very well: 95 percent (or 18 out of the 19 trades taken) were winners. Again, the drawdown ($12,025) is a little high for the net profit ($29,500). The number of trades is smaller than we would like for statistical reasons.

FIGURE 18.2 THE SHORT POSITIONS OF THE PULL-BACKS-IN-TRENDS PATTERN.

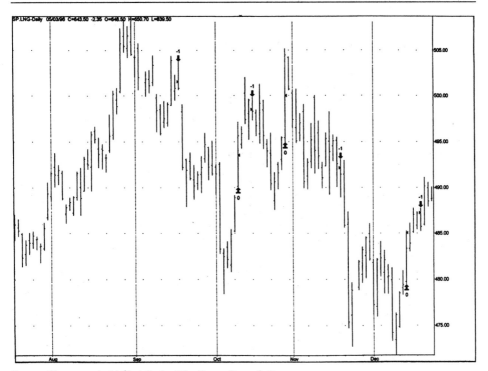

Source: Chart created with TradeStation® by Omega Research, Inc.

TABLE 18.2 TRADING PERFORMANCE SUMMARY USING THE PATTERN IN FIGURE 18.2

Performance Summary: All Trades (Short)			
Total net profit	$ 20425.00	Open position P/L	$ 0.00
Gross profit	$ 42225.00	Gross loss	$−21800.00
Total # of trades	26	Percent profitable	81%
Number winning trades	21	Number losing trades	5
Largest winning trade	$ 2225.00	Largest losing trade	$ −6500.00
Average winning trade	$ 2010.71	Average losing trade	$ −4360.00
Ratio avg win/avg loss	0.46	Avg trade (win & loss)	$ 785.58
Max consec. winners	9	Max consec. losers	2
Avg # bars in winners	2	Avg # bars in losers	8
Max intraday drawdown	$ −8975.00		
Profit factor	1.94	Max # contracts held	1
Account size required	$ 8975.00	Return on account	228%

FIGURE 18.3 THE LONG POSITIONS OF THE MULTIPLE-BOTTOMS PATTERN.

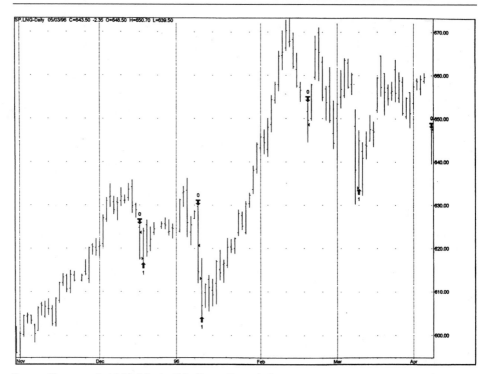

Source: Chart created with TradeStation® by Omega Research, Inc.

TABLE 18.3 TRADING PERFORMANCE SUMMARY USING THE PATTERN IN FIGURE 18.3

Performance Summary: All Trades (Long)			
Total net profit	$ 29500.00	Open position P/L	$ 0.00
Gross profit	$ 36000.00	Gross loss	$ -6500.00
Total # of trades	19	Percent profitable	95%
Number winning trades	18	Number losing trades	1
Largest winning trade	$ 2000.00	Largest losing trade	$ -6500.00
Average winning trade	$ 2000.00	Average losing trade	$ -6500.00
Ratio avg win/avg loss	0.31	Avg trade (win & loss)	$ 1552.63
Max consec. winners	13	Max consec. losers	1
Avg # bars in winners	2	Avg # bars in losers	2
Max intraday drawdown	$-12025.00		
Profit factor	5.54	Max # contracts held	1
Account size required	$ 12025.00	Return on account	245%

FIGURE 18.4 THE SHORT POSITIONS OF THE MULTIPLE-TOPS PATTERN.

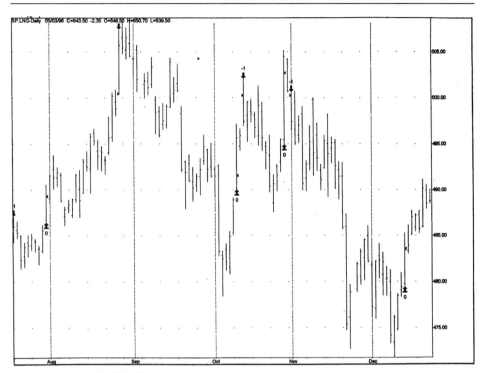

Source: Chart created with TradeStation® by Omega Research, Inc.

TABLE 18.4 TRADING PERFORMANCE SUMMARY USING THE PATTERN IN FIGURE 18.4

Performance Summary: All Trades (Short)			
Total net profit	$ 26050.00	Open position P/L	$ 0.00
Gross profit	$ 60275.00	Gross loss	$−34225.00
Total # of trades	35	Percent profitable	80%
Number winning trades	28	Number losing trades	7
Largest winning trade	$ 4650.00	Largest losing trade	$ −6500.00
Average winning trade	$ 2152.68	Average losing trade	$ −4889.29
Ratio avg win/avg loss	0.44	Avg trade (win & loss)	$ 744.29
Max consec. winners	10	Max consec. losers	2
Avg # bars in winners	4	Avg # bars in losers	7
Max intraday drawdown	$−15300.00		
Profit factor	1.76	Max # contracts held	1
Account size required	$ 15300.00	Return on account	170%

Tops (Short) Positions

Figure 18.4 illustrates the multiple-tops pattern (short positions). A good example of the kind of multiple tops we would have marked by hand can be seen as the first signal in October.

The performance summary for this pattern can be found in Table 18.4. The system took 80 percent wins, not quite as good as the longs, with a larger drawdown of $15,300 and a smaller net profit of $26,050.

RESULTS FOR THE
HEAD-AND-SHOULDERS PATTERN

Long Positions

Figure 18.5 is the chart for the long signals of the (inverted) head-and-shoulders pattern. The only entry signal on this chart presents an illustration of a little head-and-shoulders pattern: The system bought in at the pull-back after the neckline of the pattern was broken.

The performance summary in Table 18.5 shows that only 13 instances of this pattern were identified by the neural network during the three year period. However, it was 77 percent profitable. The drawdown was $7,600. The system took $14,275 net profit, with the average winning trade being $2067.50.

Short Positions

The chart for the short side of the head-and-shoulders pattern is presented in Figure 18.6. Again, the signal appeared after the neckline of the pattern was broken, which is close to where we would have marked it by hand. However, on the trade illustrated, the system chose an exit which drew some profit, but it could have been better.

Table 18.6 contains the performance summary for this pattern, which drew the least profit ($10,000), because of the very small number of trades (5); however, it had 100 percent winning trades. The drawdown was also the lowest of all the systems: only $2,250. While this is certainly impressive, it is not a system that one would trust due to the small number of trades, an insufficient number to give us any statistical sense of how the system might perform in the future.

RESULTS OF THE INTEGRATED SYSTEM

Figure 18.7 illustrates the performance of the integrated system (i.e., it contains all the signals from all six patterns). The preponderance of signals derive from the pull-back-in-trends patterns, which were the most frequent to occur, especially during the upward move prior to September ("S," on the chart). From September until October

FIGURE 18.5 LONG POSITIONS OF THE (INVERTED) HEAD-AND-SHOULDERS PATTERN.

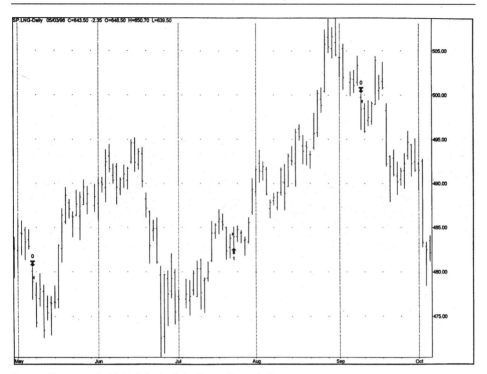

Source: Chart created with TradeStation® by Omega Research, Inc.

TABLE 18.5 TRADING PERFORMANCE SUMMARY USING THE PATTERN IN FIGURE 18.5

Performance Summary: All Trades (Long)			
Total net profit	$ 14275.00	Open position P/L	$ 0.00
Gross profit	$ 20675.00	Gross loss	$ −6400.00
Total # of trades	13	Percent profitable	77%
Number winning trades	10	Number losing trades	3
Largest winning trade	$ 2675.00	Largest losing trade	$ −2950.00
Average winning trade	$ 2067.50	Average losing trade	$ −2133.33
Ratio avg win/avg loss	0.97	Avg trade (win & loss)	$ 1098.08
Max consec. winners	9	Max consec. losers	3
Avg # bars in winners	3	Avg # bars in losers	4
Max intraday drawdown	$ −7600.00		
Profit factor	3.23	Max # contracts held	1
Account size required	$ 7600.00	Return on account	188%

FIGURE 18.6 SHORT POSITIONS OF THE HEAD-AND-SHOULDERS PATTERN.

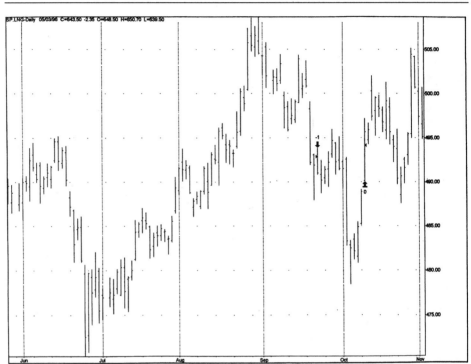

Source: Chart created with TradeStation® by Omega Research, Inc.

TABLE 18.6 TRADING PERFORMANCE SUMMARY USING THE PATTERN IN FIGURE 18.6

Performance Summary: All Trades (Short)			
Total net profit	$ 10000.00	Open position P/L	$ 0.00
Gross profit	$ 10000.00	Gross loss	$ 0.00
Total # of trades	5	Percent profitable	100%
Number winning trades	5	Number losing trades	0
Largest winning trade	$ 2000.00	Largest losing trade	$ 0.00
Average winning trade	$ 2000.00	Average losing trade	$ 0.00
Ratio avg win/avg loss	100.00	Avg trade (win & loss)	$ 2000.00
Max consec. winners	5	Max consec. losers	0
Avg # bars in winners	0	Avg # bars in losers	0
Max intraday drawdown	$ −2250.00		
Profit factor	100.00	Max # contracts held	1
Account size required	$ 2250.00	Return on account	444%

FIGURE 18.7 SIGNALS OF A SYSTEM USING ALL SIX PATTERNS.

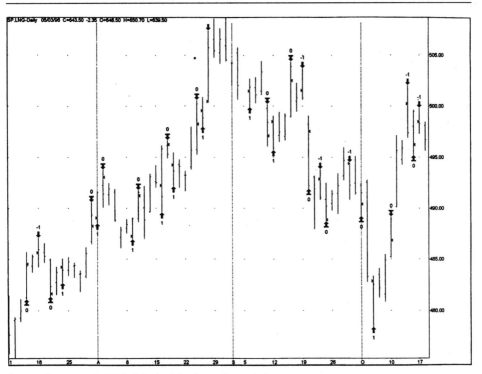

Source: Chart created with TradeStation® by Omega Research, Inc.

("O"), there were a lot of down signals, again, mostly of the pull-backs-in-trends type. There was a clear multiple bottom buy in the beginning of October.

The integrated system produced good simulated trading results, as can be seen in Table 18.7. The drawdown ($15,000) is a little higher than what we would prefer, but the system made a 765 percent return on the account in three years ($117,050 net profit); 75 percent of the 164 trades were profitable. The average trade was $713.72, with some trades that were quite a bit more profitable than that (e.g., a trade on 3/1/96–3/4/96 took in $2,450; 3/6/96, exiting the same day, took $2,000). The maximum number of consecutive wins was 17, with an average of two days in the market. The maximum number of consecutive losers was 2, with an average time in the market of 4 days; it only had one loss between 3/1/96 and 5/2/96. It is also a fairly active trading system (e.g., it took five trades in April 1996).

The integrated system performed well over both the longs and shorts: $77,350 profit on the longs, $39,700 profit on the shorts. The drawdown was roughly the same on both and both were highly profitable: 78 percent wins on the longs, 71 percent on the shorts.

TABLE 18.7 TRADING PERFORMANCE SUMMARY USING THE PATTERNS IN FIGURE 18.7

Performance Summary: All Trades			
Total net profit	$117050.00	Open position P/L	$ 0.00
Gross profit	$222525.00	Gross loss	$−105475.00
Total # of trades	164	Percent profitable	75%
Number winning trades	123	Number losing trades	41
Largest winning trade	$ 4650.00	Largest losing trade	$ −7500.00
Average winning trade	$ 1809.15	Average losing trade	$ −2572.56
Ratio avg win/avg loss	0.70	Avg trade (win & loss)	$ 713.72
Max consec. winners	17	Max consec. losers	2
Avg # bars in winners	2	Avg # bars in losers	4
Max intraday drawdown	$−15300.00		
Profit factor	2.11	Max # contracts held	1
Account size required	$ 15300.00	Return on account	765%

On its own, the integrated system would probably be tradable. This might even be truer if the system were traded with options, as the options would cushion the large drawdown. And, with a profit target, if options were purchased that were somewhat in the money, it would not weaken the profits too greatly due to premium expansion.

WHY DOES THE KCAT APPROACH WORK?

Why the KCAT approach works so reliably is a complicated question that does not have any definitive answer. One issue might be synchronization. Consider the analogy between the rather crude method of trying to predict price change over the next two or three bars and an attempt to trace a signal on an oscilloscope. If you do not have a fixed point on an oscilloscope, at which you start tracing the signal each time, you will not be able to see the signal clearly: you will have a jumble of superimposed traces; however, if you always start the scan at a certain point in the signal curve, each time it scanned the curve could appear in roughly the same place. When you are asking the network to predict the change on the next few bars, it is like jiggling the point at which you start the trace on the oscilloscope (i.e., the patterns the network is viewing in the data being presented to it are in every possible position; the network basically has to deal with the patterns being all over the place, not synchronized or located the same way each time. This makes the network's recognition of the pattern a much more complex problem because it is almost as if more patterns are present.

When we use the KCAT approach, by marking the position of the pattern on the chart, we are providing the network with a "synch-lock" point. The network is only being asked to find one pattern that is positioned in a certain way within the window of data it is looking at; it is a much easier problem for the net to solve—to find one pattern that is synchronized so that its end occurs at a rightmost part of the window that the network is examining. Rather than asking the network to see an "A" and moving the "A" all around a grid of pixels, we are positioning the "A" so that its rightmost part is always aligned with one line and its topmost part is always aligned with another line; it is a much easier job for the network to recognize an "A" when the "A" is consistently positioned in the same location. Using the KCAT approach, we are always making sure that the network is looking for a pattern that has its rightmost edge at the edge of the window of data that the net is examining.

The KCAT approach only requires the network to recognize a pattern, not to predict; the network is just learning a pattern that existed in the past and being asked to determine whether or not it is currently recognized. The network is not being required to recognize every single pattern that exists in the data; its job is just to recognize one pattern. There are enough variations of the one pattern to still make the task somewhat difficult (e.g., there are all kinds of shapes to pull-backs-in-trends), but at least the net is only having to deal with the multiplicity of subpatterns for that one pattern.

A neural network can, conceivably, deal with recognizing a large number of patterns, but it is then going to need many more neurons in its middle layer, many more inputs, and such a complex net will cause the loss of many degrees of freedom, which means that a hundred times more data will be needed to train the network and achieve consistency. With our method, because one particular pattern is being imposed on the network a priori, the world that the network has to examine is greatly constricted, as is the number of patterns that the network has to deal with. This drastically simplifies the task; imposing such constraint conserves degrees of freedom and lessens the amount of data needed to train the network. This is analogous to doing an experiment where you have an a priori hypothesis and seek either a "yes" or "no" answer versus an experiment wherein you try every possible solution to find the one solution that works; in the latter instance, the result will not necessarily generalize as it could be taking advantage of chance.

These reasons possibly are why neural networks train much better and are much more stable than when we try to use them to develop predictive models based on price change, for example.

CONCLUSION

Through use of the KCAT approach, together with proprietary input preprocessing, we have developed, for both ourselves and our clients, highly successful systems that trade different markets and different time frames, and that can be traded directly on futures without having to cushion drawdowns using options.

The key to using the KCAT approach is in being able to detect by eye, recurrent, recognizable patterns in the market and then being able to consistently mark those patterns on a chart of as long of a time period as possible—a rather labor-intensive task, to say the least. Processing the inputs to the networks is also a critical factor in this development process (neural newbies should stay away), as is skill in handling exit stops (such expertise can turn a losing system into a winner). Lastly, it is important to have good neural networks and other tools, as well as the knowledge of how to use them appropriately.

Our experiment has illustrated that it is indeed possible, and potentially highly profitable, to develop fully mechanized, rule-based trading systems that make use of advanced neural technology in conjunction with subjective knowledge.

ENDNOTE

1. We have written in greater detail on this topic and recommend you read the following:
    "Introduction to Artificial Intelligence" and "Neural Networks in Trading" in Lederman, Jess, and Klein, Robert A., *Virtual Trading*, Chicago: Probus Publishing, 1995.
    Three articles that appeared in *Technical Analysis of Stocks & Commodities:* "On Developing Trading Systems," November, 1996; "A Rule-Based Approach to Trading, Part I," December, 1996; and "A Rule-Based Approach to Trading, Part II," January, 1997.

SUMMARY

Market Analysis

- The development of every trading system should start with a rational observation about market behavior. You must take care in developing and understanding relationships that are meaningful so as not to rely on random patterns. Statistical analysis will help you determine the accuracy of the inferences you may derive from data.
- Your first attempt should be to break down a price time series into these components: long-term trend, cyclical effects, seasonal effects, and residual effects. It may be easier to preprocess or model each component separately.
- Examine cross-market interactions and measure cross-correlation effects. Once you understand the relationship between two data streams, it is a simple process to determine which one leads the other and by how much. This will allow you to take advantage of the relationship, by looking for divergence between the trends that describe each.
- Classical economic theory is based on linear, Gaussian, and stationary (non-time-varying) assumptions about market behavior. Nonlinear pricing (NP) is based on nonlinear, non-Gaussian, and nonstationary assumptions. In addition to relying on market relationships, NP assumes the strengths of these relationships may change over time, and quantifies these changes as well.
- NP practitioners quickly learn that sometimes linearity is an inaccurate paradigm. Straight lines are not good forecasting tools, nor are completely random walks. Most of the time traded asset price actions are not random; instead they persist or antipersist. That is, they have the tendency to follow their current path or reverse themselves.
- Persistence is not trend. Trend is a perspective in the present that looks back in time. It is easy for a random walk to appear trending. Persistence is a perspective in the present that looks forward in time to give a "likelihood" of future price movements. It is therefore useful to measure price's persistence over time.
- An opportunity to profit is to arbitrage between the pattern depicted by NP and the market's inability to detect the pattern just as accurately. Moreover, this efficiency is unlikely to be arbitraged away because of the number of variables involved, the varying investment horizons, and the technology gap.

Data Representation and Preprocessing

- There are three reasons to preprocess your data prior to modeling.
  1. To reshape the distribution of the data.
  2. To extract key features that a human analyst might use, simplifying the structure of the model.

3. To reduce model dependency on specific signal levels, improving the performance of models as markets enter new trading ranges.

- A common preprocessing method is to detrend your data. If you do so, your model will often generalize well even when the market reaches record highs because detrended data focuses on the relative shape and relationships between recent activities.

- If you intend to include a spectral analysis of a time series in your advanced system, consider using wavelets instead of Fourier coefficients. Unlike Fourier analysis, which is given to stationary data, time-frequency wavelets are suited for quasi-stationary signals and time-scale wavelets are given to fractal structures.

- You can attain a uniform distribution of input values by separating the input records into bins and selecting an equal number of records from each bin. By doing so, you can frequently build systems using only a fraction of the data set. This leaves you with more data cases to test your system.

- Complex, overoptimized systems may work well on in-sample data but will likely fail miserably on out-of-sample data. The more complex your system is, the more data you will need to develop and test it. But because the financial markets are nonstationary (statistical characteristics change over time), distant historical data may be unusable. Therefore, keep your systems simple. Simple models are often more accurate than sophisticated models.

- One way to simplify your system is to reduce the number of input variables feeding it. There are many ways to do this. Theoretically, the perfect way is to try all possible combinations of input variables and see which collection works best. But for large numbers of variables, this is far too time consuming. Acceptable alternatives are listed in Appendix C.

- If the number of inputs have been reduced to a sufficiently small number (5 to 10), it is often possible to eliminate conflicting inputs by computing expected values in local neighborhoods and using those prototypes as training vectors. This process also tends to reduce data distribution effects on network training.

Forecasting

- The first task in building a forecasting model is to evaluate the optimal forecast distance into the future. One method for obtaining this estimate is described in *Neural Networks and Financial Forecasting* (Jurik Research, 1996).

- Neural networks (NN) are more powerful than classical (linear) regression methods. Neural networks are divided into two classes: those that employ non-linear regression modeling (Perceptron cells) and those that build a library of examples (template cells). The former class is constructed in such a way as to minimize a sum of squared error or regression criteria. As a practical matter, this class works best when all input data is normally distributed and has zero mean and unit variance.

- Fuzzy logic (FL) is a technique that offers a practical way to transfer the value judgments and wisdom of the user to a quantitative model. The user need not know the math to create, tune, or use a set of fuzzy rules. In some cases, the user can program rules in words or sentences.

- Genetic algorithms (GAs) offer a way to optimize extremely complex systems. This compares favorably to most traditional optimization methods, such as "hill-climbing" techniques, because these cannot handle discontinuities typically present in complex systems.

- Use NN, FL, and GA technology to either forecast price action and/or detect patterns in the data stream.

  - When using them for forecasting, it is best to make your target data as stationary as possible, over the entire training set. Forget about predicting price; price has no stable mean, it wanders all over. Instead, consider the percent rate of change (PROC) of price, or the PROC of the highest high (and lowest low) of the next N price bars. The latter gives you a stable price channel forecast.

  - When using them for pattern recognition, you will get best results training one model per price pattern. Use an equal number of "pattern found" and "pattern not found" examples. Vary the size and shape of the pattern to be detected. Use features to describe the price pattern that will remain unaffected when volatility or price is either high or low. Finding good invariant features is a difficult skill to master. I suggest you hire a professional for this task; overall you will save yourself time and money. For an up-to-date list of Software Consultants, see Appendix C.

- Verify your system's parameters are robust by determining how well performance is maintained when the parameters are adjusted up or down by 10 percent. A fragile (and therefore unworkable) system will quickly lose performance under less than optimal parameter settings.

- There may be occasions when you do not have thousands of data points for model testing. For this situation, consider using resampling, leave-out testing, and bootstrap methods. For additional information on these methods, see *Computer Systems That Learn* (Weiss & Kulikowski, 1991, Morgan-Kaufmann Publishing).

Epilogue

Trading the market is like no other experience you've ever had. It's as challenging as driving a taxi in Katmandu. There you have adults, children, buses, taxis, bicycles, dogs, cows, and yaks all moving in a semi-chaotic manner, yet getting where they want to go. Just when you think you know what's going to happen next, someone accidentally hits a cow and all hell breaks loose. To a Westerner, the entire "system" is both amazing and nerve-wracking. To the locals, it's part of their daily routine. Likewise, the financial market is so dynamic and competitive that just when you think you know what's going to happen next, it doesn't. This places strong demands on any trading strategy.

To help you improve as a trader, I prepared a collection of one-liners, some extracted from this book and some from other accomplished traders. There are 31 of them; one for each day of the longest month. I like to read one each morning and contemplate how my techniques can be further improved:

1. If you want profits, you must become better than the crowd. It's that simple and it's that difficult.
2. Resist the temptation to purchase prebuilt trading systems. That's what the crowd does.
3. Read many books on various aspects of trading. There's no point in reinventing the wheel.
4. Buy a good charting program, especially one that lets you devise and test your own strategies.
5. Look for patterns that stack the odds in your favor. If you don't have an edge, don't trade.
6. Consider using fundamentals to find your "prey," and technicals to get in and out. (Good tools for evaluating stocks both fundamentally and technically are available at http://www.VectorVest.com.)
7. Determine what and when to trade yourself; don't ask others. The public is generally wrong.
8. If the trading style does not suit you psychologically, replace it. There's no need to fan your fears.
9. Keep your strategy simple and test the crap out of it. Literally. Crappy rules will cost you.

10. Backtesting doesn't guarantee winners, but it sure picks out losers.

11. A backtested system over-optimized to perfection is almost surely useless.

12. Paper trading lets you test, without emotional involvement, your strategies on lots of markets.

13. Trade with a simulated broker to test everything, including your timing and ability to handle stress. (A good simulated broker is available at http://www.auditrack.com.)

14. It's better to capture half a trend with low risk than bottoms and tops with high risk.

15. Exchanges are imperfect, and unlike online trading, human brokers can help resolve discrepancies.

16. Treat your broker with respect and he will go the extra mile to get your orders filled.

17. A novice should start slowly, trade end of day, in small lots, and in medium volatility markets.

18. Never assume your trades and stops were executed. Get confirmation.

19. Control losses by managing your risk with stops and appropriate trade size.

20. Only trade what you are willing to lose; otherwise your risk analysis will be distorted.

21. Limit your loss on any trade. Don't be afraid to cut loose from a sinking ship.

22. Be constant. After a few good trades, you'll want to begin doubling your exposure. Don't.

23. Faithfully follow your fully tested strategy, unless you really know what you are doing.

24. Internalize the way your system works and note when and how discretionary intervention would help.

25. The market is always changing and so should you. Endeavor to keep ahead with better strategies.

26. Stay in top physical shape. You'll feel, think, trade, and handle stress better.

27. Believe you deserve to win. The market will punish self-doubters.

28. Being "in the zone" means your mind is confident, alert, calm, eager for engagement, and automatic.

29. Intuitive, discretionary trading requires you to be "in the zone." When not, don't trade.

30. To control your emotions, meditate. It is simple, free, and has worked for thousands of years.

31. It's you against "them." Make friends or else the loneliness of trading may get to you.

FINAL WORDS

All fired up? I'm now going to offer a word or two of caution.

Nothing can ensure that your strategy will make profits in the future. You can only hope that your strategy will work almost as well into the future as it did in the past. If you are a novice and want to trade because you *need* the money, forget it. You're lost before you even begin. If you don't have the right mental makeup, life as a trader will be miserable.

On the other hand, if you accept the challenge, it can be intellectually and financially rewarding. Because your experiences and beliefs in life are unique, your path to the top will also be unique. A book, conference, audio tape, or any other tutorial course that works for someone else may not work for you. Just as with any other worthwhile endeavor, you will have to put in your time and pay your dues to develop the necessary skills. You can't just buy them.

Your challenge will be to see what works for you. You'll discover that no one system works all of the time. So, to progress, you will have to start slowly and push yourself into the unknown to gain an understanding of both the market and yourself. It will be scary and exciting to strike out on your own, confront your own demons, and discover more of who you are. You'll also learn to weight, analyze, compromise, and underneath it all, develop an appreciation that without risk, there's no reward.

Now, . . . roll up your sleeves and get to work!

Appendices

Now it is time to get started. You are getting ready to spend money. To succeed in this game, you will need the best data and software tools you can afford. The money you save with pennywise (mis)management is insignificant to the increase in risk exposure poor tools may induce. Plan a budget to spend money on a fast computer, solid software, hardware, data, and technical support. Appendices A, B, and C can help you in these matters.

Lastly, before you spend a dime, read Appendix D. It is a real treat—a rollicking true story about my trials and tribulations in developing an options trading system right next to the exchange pits years ago. It has some important lessons pertinent to building your own system. The lessons I learned are as relevant today as they were back then.

ACQUIRING MARKET DATA

First, you will need data, and lots of it. You can't do anything without it. Luckily, for system testing, historical financial data is inexpensive and numerous vendors offer it. However, not all vendors supply the same quality data. Ticks may be missing and prices may be inaccurate. So what's a trader to do?

Decide what type of data you need. Appendix A will help you figure out what price level is best for you and includes lists of data vendors to choose from. But before you close a deal, it is wise to be a smart consumer and pump the vendors with hard-hitting questions. Otherwise, *you* may get hit hard instead. To help you prepare the right questions, Appendix B provides detailed "behind the scenes" insight into the entire life cycle of a price quote: from its birth, all the way to your computer. The more you know how vendors collect, process, and transmit data, the smarter your questions will become and the more you know what to expect and demand. After all, *you* are the paying customer and it is *your* money they want.

As for receiving the data, unless you live north of the Arctic Circle or in a valley surrounded by tall mountains, consider getting a satellite feed. This technology is getting cheaper all the time and can handle enormous data rates. Eventually, it will have to compete with the low cost of Internet communications, but only when the latter becomes more reliable.

ACQUIRING MARKET KNOWLEDGE

There are some very smart people out there. To learn what they have to offer, read good books. Not that you will find the Holy Grail inside a paperback, but that little by little, you will be accumulating wisdom. There are many good books on the market covering fundamental and technical analysis, as well as market and personal psychology. To save you time, check out my compiled list of books recommended *by real traders,* in Appendix C. If you discover just one good idea that works for you, it is worth it.

An inexpensive way to get and give information is through several very good moderated forums on the Internet. They are listed in the Preface.

If you want to attend seminars or purchase a tutorial course, be sure the method taught can be applied by someone with your account size, data access, and computer software. Also, demand to see account statements that were directly attained by trading the same system to be taught in the course. Remember, you are the customer. If the instructor is hesitant, don't consider him.

Consumers have rights. Whenever you suspect you have been a victim of disreputable or illegal actions, consult the appropriate authorities. There are numerous agencies chartered to protect you and your investments, and their services are generally free. See Appendix C for a list of consumer protection Web sites.

Appendix A

Financial Data Sources

Kevin Marder

You have done your homework. You have read a ton of books, subscribed to various newsletters, listened to countless gurus, and perhaps picked up a new computer with all the latest high-tech gadgetry. And, after seemingly endless deliberation, you have armed yourself with great software for building a trading system. The next piece in the trading puzzle will be to choose a data provider.

Although data is usually looked on as an afterthought in the process of devising a trading system, once you begin to test the multitude of ideas pulsating through your brain, data assumes the importance of a powerful weapon. With it, you have the potential to win the battle for investment survival, and without it, you have nothing.

Data has come a long way from the days when aspiring traders leafed through scores of yellowed newspapers searching for historical securities prices. An increasing number of enterprising firms have developed state-of-the-art content and retrieval; all at prices that resemble the chart of a glamour stock in a bear market. Convenience, reliability, breadth of coverage and affordability, then, combine to give the individual trader data that was once reserved for Wall Street professionals.

REAL-TIME DATA

Securities data falls into two categories: real-time and end-of-day. Real-time data, also known as tick data, represents a continuous stream of prices corresponding to each trade that takes place in a security. Thus, it is possible to follow a security's every trade throughout the market day. This type of data is necessary for the trader who will be making intraday (within the day) market moves. As the Information Age matures, market developments occur with startling speed. The result is that market moves that used to take days now take hours. And those that used to take hours now take minutes.

An interesting yarn illustrates just how much more efficient the markets have become in reacting to new information. A gray-haired salesman for a Wall Street brokerage house used to mail his firm's research reports to his clients, most of whom were portfolio managers. The salesman would follow up each mailing with a phone call to determine what interest the client might have in buying the stocks that were the subject of the research reports. Twenty years ago, a portfolio manager's typical response would be that a decision would have to wait until the firm's monthly strategy meeting. Ten years ago, the money manager would reply that he would need the weekend to pore over all the research that had piled up on his desk during the week. Today, the salesman quips that he simply telephones his portfolio manager clients, who usually give him an order over the telephone without having seen any research report about the stock in question.

There are three general classes of real-time data. The distinction between the three is made by cost and services provided. The so-called upper tier is intended for use by institutional traders and portfolio managers, and brokerage firm salespeople and analysts. The medium tier attracts the individual investor and independent trader. The lower tier is designed for the budget-conscious.

END-OF-DAY DATA

End-of-day (EOD) data consists of information summarizing a security's activity for one day. The market participant who has a longer-term horizon and/or needs to understand the long-term trend will benefit from this data type. EOD data is used by traders and investors to construct price charts with the help of charting software. As the name implies, the minimum time interval on a price chart using end-of-day data consists of one day. Typically, the data is downloaded from the vendor's database, either via a telephone call or an Internet connection. The data fields themselves are fairly standard—open, high, low, close, and volume. An open interest data field is added for futures.

Each data vendor uses one or more file formats with the ASCII format being popular. Various financial software packages may also have their own proprietary data format. Pick a software application that accepts a large variety of data formats. You never know in what format some critical piece of data may be available.

End-of-day data is usually available for downloading anywhere from 1 to 2 hours after the market's close.

DATA SOURCES

Real-Time Data, Premium Class

In the equity arena, the primary vendors of these premium products are ADP, ILX Systems, Bridge, and Quotron. In the fixed-income sector, the dominant providers are Bloomberg, Bridge, and Reuters.

Some of these products overlap and provide quotes on some or all security types. Others specialize in just one area. Each product comes with a slew of optional third-party add-on modules. For example, if you want to stay abreast of breaking news, these offerings will allow for a subscription to a newswire service. If you need to keep up with earnings reports, this, too, is possible through a subscription to one of the three dominant providers of corporate earnings data: First Call, IBES, and Zacks Research. If you require a quality research service to augment your trading, chances are a premium provider will be able to deliver the goods here as well.

For the most part, these quotation services are not able to connect with real-time charting software such as Omega Research's TradeStation® (TradeStation is a registered trademark of Omega Research, Inc.) or Equis MetaStock RT. This is a major disadvantage as these two real-time charting software packages are the most popular among traders.

Table A.1 lists various premium real-time data vendors and their products.

Real-Time Data, Medium Class

There are four predominant services in this category of real-time data. Far and away the most popular is Data Broadcasting Corporation's (DBC) product called Signal. The other three are DBC's datafeed called BMI (Bonneville Market Information), Standard & Poor's ComStock, and FutureSource.

For several reasons, the medium class appeals most to serious individual investors and traders. First, many of these market participants are seeking real-time quotes, and nothing but. Therefore, it makes little sense to subscribe to a premium service that offers quotes as well as a multitude of less important features at a price several times that of a medium-class real-time data service.

Second, the two most popular real-time charting programs, TradeStation by Omega Research, Inc., and Equis MetaStock RT, operate mostly with data generated from medium-class data vendors.

A third reason medium-class real-time data services are the preferred choice of traders concerns the plethora of third-party software products that are intended to work in conjunction with TradeStation and, to a lesser extent, MetaStock RT, and the many smaller software developers whose products will only function with real-time data generated from one of the leading medium-class providers.

Finally, most medium-class data services offer at least two and, in some cases, four different means of transmission. Depending on where the trader resides, there exist one or more of these distribution mediums: FM radio, satellite, TV cable, leased line, or Internet. Selection should be based on cost, convenience, speed, and accuracy (see Appendix B for details).

The serious trader, then, who is desirous of nothing but tick data for real-time charting purposes, will undoubtedly find the medium class of data provider to be just what the doctor ordered.

Table A.2 lists various medium-class real-time data vendors and their products.

Real-Time Data, Budget Class

The budget-conscious market participant is being catered to more and more as technology opens new frontiers. The low cost of distributing data over the Internet, in

TABLE A.1 PREMIUM REAL-TIME DATA VENDORS AND THEIR PRODUCTS—PREMIUM CLASS

Data Provider	Distribution Medium	Securities
ADP* 201 E. Park Drive Mount Laurel, NJ 08054 800-367-9447 www.fis.adp.com	Leased line Modem	**ALL VENDORS OFFER ALL THE FOLLOWING MARKETS:**
Bloomberg Financial Markets 499 Park Avenue New York, NY 10022 212-318-2300 www.bloomberg.com	Leased line Satellite	Stocks Mutual Funds Bonds
Bridge Information Systems 3 World Financial Center, 27th Floor New York, NY 10285 212-372-7100/800-927-2734 www.bridge.com	Leased line Satellite	Commodities Options Futures Indices Foreign Exchange
Dow Jones Markets, Inc.* Harborside Finl Center 600 Plaza Two Jersey City, NJ 07311 201-938-4000/800-334-3813 www.djmarkets.com	Leased line Modem	
ILX Systems 111 Fulton Street New York, NY 10038 212-964-1199 www.ilx.com	Leased line Satellite	
Quotron 40 E. 52 Street New York, NY 10022 212-426-4770	Leased line Modem	
Reuters 40 E. 52 Street New York, NY 10022 212-593-5500 www.reuters.com	Leased line Satellite	
Telekurs USA Inc. 3 River Bend Center Stamford, CT 06907 1-888-Telekurs www.tkusa.com	Leased	

*ADP and Dow Jones Markets were purchased by Bridge, yet they maintain their own product line and web sites.

TABLE A.2 MEDIUM-CLASS REAL-TIME DATA VENDORS AND THEIR PRODUCTS

Data Provider	Distribution Medium	Securities
CQG 201 Centennial Street Glenwood Springs, CO 81601 800-525-7082 www.cqg.com	Leased line Satellite	S,C,O,F,I,X
S&P ComStock 600 Mamaronek Avenue Harrison, NY 10523 914-381-7000/800-431-2602 www.spcomstock.com	Satellite Leased Line Cable Internet	S,M,B,C,O,F,I,X
Data Broadcasting (BMI) 3 Triad Center, Suite 100 Salt Lake City, UT 84180-1201 801-532-3400/800-255-7374 www.dbc.com	Satellite Cable WWW	S,M,B,C,O,F,I,X
Data Broadcasting (Signal) 1900 South Norfolk Street San Mateo, CA 94403 800-833-1228/800-367-4670 www.dbc.com (for Signal) cbs.marketwatch.com (for DBC Online)	FM, Cable Satellite WWW (real time)	S,M,B,C,O,F,I,X
Data Transmission Network 9110 West Dodge Road Omaha, NE 68114 402-390-2328/800-475-4755 www.dtn.com	Satellite Cable Leased Lines Modem WWW (delayed)	S,M,B,C,O,F,I
FutureSource 955 Parkview Boulevard Lombard, IL 60148 708-792-2001/800-621-2628 www.futuresource.com	Leased Line Satellite Cable	F,O,I,X,C,B
Global Market Information (Track/OnLine) 56 Pine Street New York, NY 10005 800-367-5968	Modem	S,M,B,C,O,F,I,X
North American Quotations 1900 Hyde Park Road London, Ontario N6H 5L9 Canada 800-465-4300 www.naq.com	Modem Satellite Leased WWW	S,C,F,O

TABLE A.2 CONT'D.

Data Provider	Distribution Medium	Securities
Paragon Software (InterQuote) 10509 50th Avenue Kenosha, WI 53142 414-697-7770/800-311-1516 www.interquote.com	Modem WWW	S,M,F,O,I,X
PC Quote 300 South Wacker Drive, Suite 300 Chicago, IL 60606 312-913-2800/800-225-5657 www.pcquote.com	Satellite Leased Line Modem WWW (real time + delayed)	S,M,B,C,O,F,I
Quote.com, Inc. 850 North Shoreline Boulevard Mountain View, CA 94043-1931 415-930-1000 www.quote.com	WWW (real time + delayed)	S,M,B,C,O,F,I
SmartServ Online One Station Place Stamford, CT 06902 888-467-3783 www.smartserv.com	WWW (real time)	S,M,B,O,I
Telescan (TIPnet) 5959 Corporate Drive, Suite 2000 Houston, TX 77036 800-324-8246 www.tipnet.com www.telescan.com	Modem WWW (delayed)	S,M,B,C,O,F,I
World Wide Quote 1111 11th Street, Suite 405 Calgary, Alberta D2R 0G5 Canada 403-209-2089 www.wwquote.com	WWW (real time)	S,M,B,C,O,I,X
Legend:	S: Stocks M: Mutual Funds B: Bonds C: Commodities O: Options F: Futures I: Indices X: Foreign Exchange	

particular, has allowed data providers to offer prices so low as to be unheard of just a few years ago. The result has been that increasing numbers of market participants, who previously could not afford tick data, are now able to go real time. This has no doubt contributed to the heightened efficiency and volatility inherent in today's markets.

Many Internet sites offer delayed quotes, but far fewer provide real-time data. Some of these services offer news and analysis as well as basic charting capabilities.

Although the price of budget class data is but a fraction of medium- and premium-class services, using budget-priced data comes with a catch—it is not easy to feed data into any of the popular real-time charting programs. This is a major disadvantage since the serious trader usually relies heavily on real-time charts. And the basic charts currently provided by Internet-based services are downright Neanderthal: one or just a few technical indicators (e.g., a simple moving average) are all that is offered. However, technology is changing rapidly, with an ever increasing number of Internet sites providing real-time feeds, and companies producing new Internet feed server software. These are exciting times.

Another drawback with budget-priced data is that you must rely on the vagaries of the Internet, with all its delays, server problems, outages, and so on. Many traders would rather pay more for quotes than place their trading accounts at the mercy of the almighty Web.

Also included in the budget category are services providing tick data with a 15-minute delay. Although technically this data cannot be considered real-time, it does serve a purpose in the system-testing regimen of the trader. Specifically, the trader can accumulate tick data, albeit delayed, on any number of securities: stocks, bonds, commodities, currencies, or options. The data may then be used in designing and testing trading systems. The advantage is one of cost—delayed tick data is but a fraction of the price of its real-time counterpart.

The medium-priced data provider, then, with all of its advantages, is the most logical source of real-time data for the serious computerized trader or investor.

End-of-Day Data

The principal purveyors of end-of-day data are Dial Data, a division of Global Market Information, Telescan, and Worden Brothers. The presence of many smaller firms has lowered prices to the point where this type of data is now considered a commodity.

An interesting wrinkle exists with respect to historical data. More and more vendors are offering this so-called back data on compact disk. This is of great benefit to the trader/investor who must have discovered by now the primary disadvantage of maintaining historical data: Gobs of hard disk space are a necessary evil. However, through modern technology, it is possible to store 25 years or more worth of back data on a CD.

The first companies to embrace this method of storage technology with respect to securities data were Omega Research and Dial Data in the mid-1990s. The latter created a CD containing data going back to 1970 that seamlessly merges with a few months of more current data stored on a hard drive. This current data can be accumulated, each day, a few hours after the market close. This downloaded data sits on the user's hard drive to be seamlessly merged with the historical CD data to produce price charts at the snap of a mouse button.

Some data vendors also offer bimonthly or quarterly CD updates which, on installation, automatically remove the last two or three months worth of redundant data from one's hard drive. This automatic removal feature may be unwanted if it deletes data you had carefully cleaned of any bad values and replaces it with data that has not been as well scrubbed. Further details on data accuracy are described in the next section.

With respect to end-of-day data, the two means of product differentiation lie in price and file format. The general price range for daily downloading of an unlimited number of quotes runs between $20 and $50 per month.

Almost all vendors produce data files in ASCII format. Some produce data in Metastock's proprietary file format. For the user of Omega Research's SuperCharts®, (SuperCharts® is a registered trademark of Omega Research, Inc.) only Dial Data and Telescan offer the option of providing end-of-day data in the proprietary Omega format.

DATA RELIABILITY

Real-Time Data

For the futures trader with an intraday emphasis, it is always unnerving to encounter a bad tick. A program such as TradeStation has the necessary tool to correct such an error fairly quickly. Fortunately, a bad tick often stands out like a sore thumb on a real-time chart as shown in Figure A.1.

Another problem relates to the speed of data delivery. At some point, many traders, particularly those with an intraday orientation, will find that data timeliness becomes of paramount importance. There are two methods of determining the data speeds of each vendor. The first compares two different data feeds side by side. This is, in most cases, not possible. The second involves comparing one's current data feed with that of another vendor via a telephone call. The vendor on the phone can then announce each tick on a particular security and the trader may then compare this stream of data with that appearing on his or her computer screen. A variation on this is to get two vendors on different phone lines at the same time and then see whose ticks are more timely.

Also, some data providers end their trading day at midnight, instead of at the end of the floor session, as the exchanges do. The result is that the open, high, and low prices may be off substantially. This may prove critical to traders who rely on such information in their trading strategy.

In addition, certain providers do not correct their data errors after the fact. Some traders will not find this disarming, whereas others who value data accuracy for backtesting purposes will.

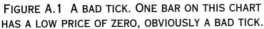

FIGURE A.1 A BAD TICK. ONE BAR ON THIS CHART
HAS A LOW PRICE OF ZERO, OBVIOUSLY A BAD TICK.

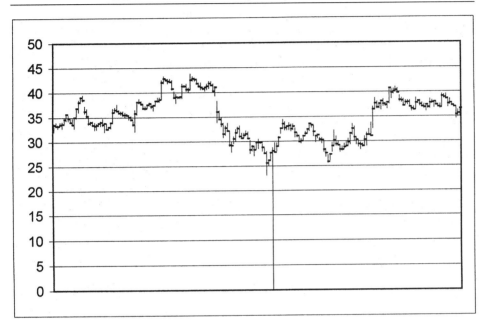

Further, due to bandwidth limitations, some data services will use "data queuing" methods so that data will not be lost when the incoming data rate exceeds the
available circuit bandwidth. Others will not and ticks may simply fail to reach your
computer.

End-of-Day Data

Providers of EOD data obtain their market information from the exchanges
themselves, or from other data providers. Most use two sources to double-check the
accuracy of their data. Nevertheless, faulty data manages to slip through the cracks
from time to time.

Typically, these data errors emanate from either a problem in the provider's tran-
scription process, or the inability on the part of the provider to detect a stock split. In
the case of the latter, some data services calculate the daily standard deviation of each
stock, and then flag any issue that substantially exceeds this range. This flagging alerts
a data clerk to the possibility of a stock split or an erroneous data set.

Some end-of-day providers employ a mechanism that, in the event an error is
detected after the day's data is made available for download, will automatically correct
a data set. Then when users download the next day's data for the security, they will un-
knowingly retrieve, as well, the newly corrected data for the previous day.

CONCLUSION

The vast majority of computerized traders will find medium class real-time data to be most suited to their needs. Such needs encompass the ability to interface with many software packages, reliability of transmission, and price. Neither premium- nor budget-priced data services fit this bill. The medium-class data service does.

For end-of-day data, the computerized trader will need to assess which data service accommodates the file format of the charting software to be used. The other principal consideration is whether the need for historical data on compact disk is essential. If so, it will be necessary to use a data service that will interface with such a disk.

EOD data is now considered a commodity. Even the price range of monthly download services among various vendors has narrowed. Consequently, the only other qualitative measure of value worth mentioning is accuracy.

Whether it is real-time or end-of-day, one thing is for certain: the computerized trader will surely appreciate the importance of a robust, accurate, and trouble-free securities database.

Finding the Best Data

Data is essential, and the more you have to analyze the better your chances of success. Well, up to a point. First, you will need historical data to test your systems. Then you will need timely and reliable data to trade. Both versions must be accurate and complete.

As data vendors begin to proliferate, on and off the Internet, you need to be very selective in choosing your supplier. Some offer extremely high quality at a price that only banks and institutions can afford. Some offer data so cheap and dirty that any money you might have saved buying it would likely be lost on the time you spend cleaning it up. Some offer a service that never fails to deliver, and some drop quotes like there's no tomorrow. You will need to select your vendor carefully; else you could be paying big time for large fees or large losses.

This appendix is not intended to be anything like a *Consumer's Report* on financial data. There are no tables of comparative numbers. Instead, it is written to educate you on most aspects of financial data creation, packaging, transmission, reception and processing. Once you have the big picture in mind, you can be a smarter consumer by asking the right questions and cutting the right deals.

The material in this appendix is divided into six parts: Data Production, Data Transmission, Data Reception, Data Storage, Data Analysis, and Other Considerations. The parts chronicle the life cycle of a price quote, from its creation at the exchange to its analysis by the user's charting software.

All material for Appendix B was obtained from various sources on the Internet, and almost exclusively from moderated forums listed in the Preface of this book. Forums tend to have more knowledgeable members than nonmoderated Usenet bulletin boards.

NOTICE: Futures trading is risky business. Prior to entering any contract, verify all information before relying on it. Although my sources for the material in this chapter were assumed reliable, financial information vending and its related technology is a fluid market and changes do occur. Therefore, I make no warranty of any kind regarding the material contained herein. In addition, all product and business names mentioned herein are copyrights and trademarks of their respective owners.

GLOSSARY

AMEX	American Stock Exchange
CBOE	Chicago Board Options Exchange

CBOT	Chicago Board of Trade
CBT	Chicago Board of Trade
CEC	Commodity Exchange Corporation
CME	Chicago Mercantile Exchange
CSE	Chicago Stock Exchange
EOD	End of day
FX	foreign exchange (generic)
GLOBEX	Global Exchange
IMM	International Monetary Market
MACE	Mid-America Commodity Exchange
NASDAQ	National Association Securities Dealers
NYFE	New York Futures Exchange
NYMEX	New York Mercantile Exchange
NYSE	New York Stock Exchange
OHLC	Open, High, Low, Close price bar
OPRA	AMEX+CBOE+NYSE+PSE+PE
PE	Pacific Exchange
PSE	Philadelphia Stock Exchange
Tick	a recorded transaction
WWW	World Wide Web

DATA PRODUCTION

The first stage in the life cycle of a price quote is its creation in the exchanges.

Price and Volume

All market data is the result of transactions taking place at exchanges. There are many exchanges throughout the world; some are listed in the preceding glossary. Each exchange broadcasts its market data on a medium called a *tape*. Each tape consists of reports of each *trade* (a quantity of shares or contracts exchanged at a specific price at a certain time) or each *quote* (a change in the bid or ask) taking place at the exchange.

Amazing as this may sound, not all transactions are necessarily reported by the exchanges. It is impossible for the humans typing the information into terminals to keep up, even if they could see every transaction that occurs, which often does not happen. Even more amazing is that many pits each have only one person typing in all their trades, even during a fast market!

A *data provider* is a company that makes a business of selling the data received from exchanges to subscribers. Data may be combined from several exchanges and broadcasts the information in the form of a *datafeed* to its subscribers. The datafeed can be delivered by phone line, satellite link, cable, radio, or the Internet, with various advantages to each medium.

Some data vendors make it their business to broadcast each and every transaction (trade or quote reported by exchanges) as packets, a *tick packet* or *data packet*. Other vendors will try to broadcast everything, but will occasionally drop changes to the bid/ask when the market is too "fast" moving. What practical consequence this has on traders depends on several factors. Does your trading strategy utilize volume analysis? If you are trading options, note that *"idle" options,* those that did not trade yesterday, are not reported for quote updates, even though they are for trade updates.

While daily securities volume is accurate at the end of each trading day, futures trading volume is only estimated and isn't officially released until the following day. The CME and IMM release true volume prior to the opening of the following day while the CBOT and NY markets release it mid-day. If you look in the *Wall Street Journal* at the futures page in section C, you will see "Estimated Volume" for the last trading day and "Final Volume" for the day before.

Some data vendors will transmit packets with the volume field set to zero whenever actual volume is unavailable. Some trading programs substitute the last available volume wherever volume arriving to your computer is quoted as zero.

Questions to Ask

Is a new tick created for each trade, or only when a trade causes a change in price?

When actual volume is unavailable, what is put into the volume field in a data packet?

How will the receiving software handle zero volume fields?

Will the charting software produce fixed-time bars when no ticks occur have occurred? If so, what OHLC prices will be used?

Time Stamping

Here comes another surprising fact. Individual packets come from the exchanges with no time stamps; they do not contain the exact time of the trade. This is because data flow rate is so high that every means is taken to reduce the amount of numbers coming from the exchanges. Even at the data-vendor level, individual real-time quotes are not time-stamped. Price quotes get time-stamped at the user's computer!

All securities and futures exchanges in the United States synchronize their clocks continuously with time signals derived from the National Institute of Standards and Technology (NIST) official time clocks in Fort Collins, Colorado. NIST coordinates international time reference with the International Bureau of Weights and Measures (BIPM) in Paris, jointly maintaining Coordinated Universal Time (UTC). The time synchronization normally is extremely accurate between exchanges, with differences not exceeding very small fractions of a second.

Data vendors send this precise time to their customers approximately once a minute, depending on data stream activity. They obtain their time from one of the exchanges, but not the same exchange in each case. Time synchronization systems sometimes fail. When that happens, there can be differences in the time transmitted by different datafeed services. *Time packets* contain the hour, minute, and second. Time-packet transmission has lower priority than quote and news-story transmission; so time packets sometimes are skipped for a while during periods of high activity.

It is the user's receiving software that time stamps each trade's tick as it arrives. Some software programs stamp the quotes with a time clock that's updated by the periodic time packets. Others use the computer clock time. Some software packages can be configured to set the local computer clock to datafeed time each minute when datafeed time packets are received.

It is possible for three traders, each using a different vendor, to receive the same quote and view them as having different time stamps. For example, one user's software would be stamping with his computer clock and the other two are using datafeed time from services that lost mutual synchronization. In addition, because time packets are spaced about one minute apart, it is also possible that individual quotes arriving very near time interval boundaries could fall in different one-minute intervals in different computers. Despite these imperfections, the process is not as bad as it sounds, just as long as your ticks arrive the right order! The bottom line is that you and a friend could both be using the same charting software, watching the same market, and have different one-minute bars on the screen, all because your data vendor is not the same as your friend's.

Question to Ask

What are the options available for configuring the data server software to time-stamp incoming packets?

Delayed Data

To increase availability of tick data to the public, quote data is offered in another type of service at much lower cost, but with one caveat: it is not guaranteed to arrive at your site within a specified period of time. This service is commonly referred to as *delayed data,* and typically arrives 10 to 20 minutes after the fact.

Curiously, there appears to be no uniform definition among the exchanges for "delayed data." In fact, they prefer not to use that term at all. To demonstrate the sensitivity with which some of the exchanges guard their position, questionnaires were sent out in connection with the construction of a data dictionary, soliciting their proposed definitions of "real-time data," and some exchanges refused to respond.

The exchanges want to avoid obligating themselves in delivering data with any guaranteed timeliness. The exchanges currently do not recognize the concept of "delayed-data." They will recognize a "time-interval" (that starts when data is received by their data-vendors) during which, if received by a subscriber, the exchange charges a fee because the data so received is "fee-liable"; if received after the end of that interval, they don't charge a fee because then the data is "non fee-liable."

This time interval, in minutes (identified in literature distributed by some vendors as "Optional Delay"), has been chosen differently by the membership of each exchange. Table B.1 is a list of delay times at various futures exchanges and Table B.2 is for stock exchanges.

TABLE B.1   FEE-LIABLE INTERVAL AT SEVERAL EXCHANGES

Minutes	Futures Exchanges	
15	BMF	Bolsa de Mercaderias & Futuros
15	CBOE	Chicago Board Options Exchange
10	CBOT	Chicago Board of Trade
30	CEC	Commodity Exchange Center
10	CME	Chicago Mercantile Exchange
30	COMX	Commodity Exchange
15	DTB	Deutsche Termin Bourse
15	HKFE	Hong Kong Futures Exchange
10	KCBT	Kansas City Board of Trade
15	LCE	London Commodity Exchange
10	LIFF	London Financial Exchange
15	LIPE	London International Petroleum Exchange
30	LMEX	London Metals Exchange
15	MATI	Marche a Terme Intl France
15	MEFF	MEFF Renta Fija Spain
10	MGE	Minneapolis Grain Exchange
10	MIDA	Mid-American Commodity Exchange
15	MONT	Montreal Exchange
30	NYMX	New York Mercantile Exchange
10	SFE	Sydney Futures Exchange-Australia
15	SIME	Singapore International Money Exchange
15	SOFX	Swiss Options-Futures Exchange
15	TORO	Toronto Futures Exchange
15	WCE	Winnipeg Commodity Exchange

These numbers may change. Before relying on this data, verify the current value for each relevant exchange.

TABLE B.2 FEE-LIABLE INTERVAL AT SEVERAL EXCHANGES

Minutes	Stock Exchanges	
20	AMEX	American Stock Exchange**
15	—	Deutsche Bourses
15	NASDAQ	National Association of Securities Dealers
20	NYSE	New York Stock Exchange**
15	PSX	Philadelphia Stock Exchange
15	PSE	Pacific Stock Exchange
15	OPRA	Options Price Reporting Authority
15	—	All Canadian Stock Exchanges

These numbers may change. Before relying on this data, verify the current value for each relevant exchange.
** Only last sale price and volume are delivered from these exchanges when delayed.

Questions to Ask

Which time frame do you prefer: real-time, delayed, or EOD?

What is the average transmission delay for the markets you want? Ask for real numbers, not what the sales department says it should be on a quiet market.

If the data always arrives at your site later than the *advertised* time of delay, can you cancel your subscription and be refunded for the unused portion of the contract. Any penalties?

Symbol Assignments

Whatever market you want to trade will have a unique identifying symbol, for example, an "IBM" security and a "JO" (frozen orange juice) contract. Some instruments are also traded in the evening and/or around the world (24 hours). With regard to trading the same market, some data vendors will retain the same symbol for trades after the day's session and some will assign a different symbol. This can be either desirable or undesirable, depending on the trader's needs. Investors preferring 24-hour continuous charts want the symbol unchanged, whereas others like to keep them separate because market behaviors in the after-day sessions (e.g., Globex) are uniquely different and they have a different system trading the evening and night sessions.

Data Broadcasting Corp. (DBC) has two feeds: BMI and Signal. BMI uses the same symbol for all sessions. Signal uses different symbols. Some other vendors are inconsistent in their treatment. For example, you may find GC and SI (gold and silver) retain the same symbol through the night sessions, although all the energies and currencies are renamed.

Finally, not all vendors use the same symbol for the same market during day trading. If data coming from multiple vendors have assigned dissimilar symbols, the receiving database software may have a problem combining them. Some software products (e.g., WINdoTRADEr) combine, if necessary, these separate symbols into one chart and let the user toggle between day only, and day/night trading.

Questions to Ask

Do any symbols differ between day, evening and GLOBEX sessions?

Can your data server and charting software handle the symbols properly?

If you determine that the server software is not processing symbols properly, can you get a refund? Request the refund be retroactive to the day you first called in with this problem. This way, there is no profit for the vendor in delaying your technical support.

Contract Rollover (for Futures and Commodities Trading)

Commodity contracts have a limited life span. After all, delivery has to occur sometime. Consequently, at any one time, contracts having any one of a number of expiration dates are being traded. Contracts for the same commodity on the same day may have different prices simply because their expiration dates differ. This is a big headache for system builders wanting to test their strategies with years of historical data. To produce a long series of historical futures prices that "roll over" from one contract to the next, one must "splice together" two time series by any sensible technique that might be considered continuous where the discontinuity at expiration has been dealt with to smooth the transition. Although there will likely be some absolute deviation of the continuous contract price from the actual price, the relative short-term tick-to-tick or bar-to-bar variations are largely preserved.

There apparently is no universal agreement regarding the definitions of and differences between "continuous" and "perpetual" contracts. Each vendor seems to have their own idea as to what those two words mean. I have not seen a definitive explanation of a perpetual rollover process.

To produce a database of continuous historical prices, some data suppliers will roll contracts using their own formula. For example, one vendor's continuous contract data is both back and forward adjusted. Continuous contract files are back adjusted up to January 31, 1995, and henceforth forward adjusted. The reason is probably because back-adjusting huge amounts of data consumes many hours of customer-computer processing time.

If you don't like the way a data vendor is rolling over contracts, you can "roll your own." There are numerous ways to do this. Some data suppliers offer contract-building software, of varying quality and flexibility. One user complained, *"The rollover software does not correctly create about half of the types of contracts it claims to do. Two of the choices, for example, create a continuous contract where the bar of the roll day has the same ohlc of the day prior to roll."* To avoid such bugs in the code, use one of the following methods:

- Roll-Your-Own Method 1 (Schwager method). Switch to the newer contract the day after the open interest of the front month contract falls below the succeeding contract for three consecutive trading days. Backward adjust historical prices. (Shift all the prices of all contracts prior to the new one upward or downward by some fixed amount to eliminate any price gap between the two joining contracts on the bar of the switchover.)
- Roll-Your-Own Method 2. Roll to next contract immediately when its volume exceeds the current month.
- Roll-Your-Own Method 3. Roll on a date relative to the beginning of a month. For example, you would roll on the 22nd of the month.
- Roll-Your-Own Method 4. Roll on a fixed number of days from month end. For example, seven days from the month's end would be Jan. 24, Feb. 21, and so on.

Whichever method you use, be aware that when producing a very long historical time series of futures prices, back adjustments could create early historical prices near or below zero. This would create big problems for certain indicators, such as price Rate-of-Change. A rate-of-change calculation with zero in the denominator would produce a "Divide by Zero" error fault. That why I have included two additional methods:

- Roll-Your-Own Method 5 (Raw method). Whenever you switch to the next contract, DO NOT backward adjust historical prices. When backtesting, set your trading system to trade as you would in the real world. That is, you sell on the close of one bar, and buy back on the open of the next bar using the newer contract. You will miss out on the overnight price change, but that's the problem with testing on only one time series.
- Roll-Your-Own Method 6 (Log method). Take the natural logarithm of all prices in all the futures contracts intended to be rolled together. When rolling, treat these new prices just as if they were the original prices and apply rollover method: 1, 2, 3, or 4. The negative values that may result are perfectly harmless. When the entire rollover process is completed, take the anti-log of all the prices in this new historical time series. You are now back in the domain of regular prices, but you are guaranteed all prices will be above zero and that all relative price movement (e.g., percent price change or any other indicator based on ratios) is completely accurate, from beginning to end.

Questions to Ask

How are historical futures contracts rolled over? What is the exact formula?

Is there a contract rollover software application compatible with your data format?

If you can verify the rollover software is producing incorrect results, can you get a refund? Will the vendor fix the bug and offer a free upgrade? If so, within what guaranteed time period (e.g., one week)?

Bad Ticks

All day long on the floor of each exchange many "prints" (official records of a trade) are inserted and many are taken out of the official database. Consequently, even though you think you never miss a tick, some of your prices may still be wrong. Your data will include ticks that have been taken out, and your data will be missing ticks that have been inserted. The CME will fax you an official copy of time and sales and you can see how well (or poorly) your ticks match the official ticks. Therefore, it is possible for the market to take out your stop and retreat while your datafeed fails to show the move.

NOTE: You should never assume your trade was executed. Whenever the market gets anywhere close to your stop, it is wise to call your broker and verify if, when, and where it traded.

As for accuracy, when traders at the exchange execute a trade at a new price, first they record the trade, and then they yell the price making certain that the price clerks have recorded the new trade. These prices are furiously entered on keyboards (laptops) by the clerks typing in prices as fast as they can. You can see them perched in pulpits above the pit. This manual process creates a large opportunity for bad entries, which propagate down to data vendors, brokers, and traders (you).

Questions to Ask

Does the vendor have bad tick detection and automatic cleanup? What, precisely, is the mechanism or formula applied?

Does the vendor offer automatic bad tick replacement at the end of the trading day? If so, when is it available (how soon after the day session has ended)?

DATA TRANSMISSION

The second stage in the life cycle of a price quote is its transmission from the vendor to your site.

Generic Issues

Timing your trades is important and, therefore, so is the promptness of your datafeed. In a fast market, S&P prices can move over 200 points per minute. Not all vendors are equipped to handle bursts of market activity. Upgrading datafeed technology is both expensive and time-consuming. It may take years to complete an equipment upgrade cycle (propose-plan-review-approve-upgrade-test). One year vendor A may be faster, the next year it is vendor B, but only because of decisions made years earlier. Now that the financial world and its needs are changing ever faster, the slow upgrade process is becoming painfully obvious. When the existing technology is not fast enough to handle sudden demands on throughput speed, data may get dropped, and the end user suffers.

Even though much delay is produced by having only one person for each market at an exchange typing in all the trades, the speed of a vendor's transmission to your receiver is also a significant factor. As much as a minute and a half difference between a signal at 9,600KB and at 38,400KB was found during fast markets. If you are day trading the S&P, this difference may significantly affect your system's performance.

To improve reliability, some vendors use *data buffering,* a procedure that stacks information on a queue when data production rates exceeds transmission rates. The hope is that the market will slow down soon enough to permit these buffers to unload. But if the market remains fast for too long, buffers fill and drop data. Curiously, there is a common complaint that European data vendors lose about 20 percent of all ticks on the S&P each day, despite their very fast data transmission rates. Somewhere along the line, buffers are overflowing.

Since it is likely that S&P activity correlates highly with stock activity, those feeds carrying everything (futures, stocks, options, news, etc.) are more likely to have data loss during fast markets than feeds dedicated to only one market. For example, FutureSource transmits quotes on futures and related options and indices. This permits very fast data throughput, especially by satellite, as its transmission is not bogged down with quotes on securities, mutual funds, baseball scores, and so on.

You can test your data feed timeliness simply by comparing tick arrival with another trader (using a different datafeed) over the phone. Another way is to set up a squawk box with the pits and compare what you hear with what you see. A squawk box is a speaker placed by your computer that plays the audio signal from a commentator at an exchange. In addition to comments, you also get to hear floor traders barking in the background. The sudden rise and fall of their overall noise level gives some indication as to what is happening on the floor. Make sure you do this when the market is quiet. In a fast market, the exchanges can be 20 seconds slower (with corresponding delays in the datafeed) than what the squawk box announces.

As an aside, only a small number of vendors create and release their own data: Reuters, Bridge, S&P Comstock, Bloomberg, PC Quote, and Telekurs. Vendors not producing their own data can be regarded as data "repackagers."

Questions to Ask

What is the data rate for transmission? Insist on at least 56KB.

Can you borrow a squawk box for a few days to check out the data's timeliness?

What time in the morning does the vendor begin transmitting real-time quotes on each market you are interested in?

Do EOD quotes include evening trades, or GLOBEX? (Hopefully not, unless you know what you are doing.)

Phone Line Transmission

Of the several media available, telephone lines provide the most elementary, easiest to set up, portable and often most reliable way to connect to a data provider. With the recent advent of the Internet and its escalating use by data providers, the telephone is often the *only* way to access some of these varieties of market data. The data providers offering service via telephone line typically allow a subscriber to either dial into their data server directly, or access the data via a Web site using an Internet connection. Generally, the user's target application for the data in some way dictates whether telephone access is practical, or even possible.

Line speed and data error rates are the key factors to consider when using a phone line to access market data. Several options are available, starting with the standard phone line connected to a residence or business. Generally, although it varies considerably by locality, it is possible to acquire data with minimum error rates at speeds up to 56Kb using a standard phone line (slower, however, is much more typical). The next better alternative is the ISDN line, more expensive (2–5 times the cost of a standard line) and not available in all locations, especially away from larger population centers. Finally, the direct T1 connection offers the subscriber very clean data at speeds up to 1.4 MB, at correspondingly higher fees and complexity of installation.

FM Transmission

FM transmission is the second oldest method of market data delivery, following telephone lines. Typically, the data provider leases bandwidth from one or several FM broadcast stations in a city or region, and supplies the data to the broadcaster via leased phone line. The broadcaster then multiplexes the data onto the broadcast FM signal, which is then received and de-multiplexed at the user's end. The output from this receiver is typically a serial data line that is then fed into the user's computer.

A limited amount of data can be delivered on the FM sideband via this method. Since most of the bandwidth available at the broadcast FM frequency is used by the radio station for its own programs, only a small amount remains for dedication to other purposes, the data provider in this case. As market data volumes have increased, less of that data, and in a less timely fashion, can be delivered via this medium.

As a result of the data delivery mechanism, data is received by the end user at a much slower baud rate than typically available via other media. There is constant criticism from the trading community about the data delays via FM. For example, DBC Signal's reporting of SP futures real-time via FM is reported by users to arrive several minutes behind a direct audio squawk box, and in fast markets, from 5 to 8 minutes late. Nonetheless, some users rely on FM as an emergency backup should their primary method (cable, satellite, etc.) fail.

Users have complained formally about the delays inherent in this medium, by bringing a class action lawsuit against DBC and its Signal subsidiary. The basis for this complaint is that Signal has historically advertised "real-time" quotes via this service, at a substantial increase in subscription rates over its delayed quote service. But due to the delays in this medium (and the slow baud rate of the receivers used to capture the data), data arrived with unacceptable delay.

Questions to Ask

If you purchase satellite or cable transmission, will the vendor provide you for free a means to receive FM as a backup measure?

Will the vendor guarantee a no-hassle refund if nondelayed data frequently arrives too late to be reliable?

Cable Transmission

Data arrives via cable in "packets" that are spaced apart in time. Technically, the vendor collects data and queues them prior to insertion into an analog TV signal. The data is transmitted in the *vertical blanking* interval space in the TV signal between video frames on a commercial cable broadcast channel. Data must be queued, because vertical intervals come only once every 1/60 of a second and last about 1 msec. In that interval, only about one-fifth is normally available for data transmission, even less when the interval is shared with other digital information. Therefore, incoming data must be queued at least until the next vertical interval, and, just as lines at banks grow very large on Friday afternoons (payday), the data queue grows longer during fast markets. Thus, both the signal's bandwidth (speed at which data can be pumped through the cable) and the queue process contribute to the cable's signal throughput speed, and the faster the signal's bandwidth, the less data queuing is needed.

The local cable station has the option of preempting the national feed for commercials, and when they do, the feed is disrupted for up to 60 seconds, or more. They have no fixed schedule for such interruptions, and so it can be difficult to forecast when this will happen. During that time all data that you would have received is lost until the interruption ceases. It is not delayed or stored. You will know when this is happening when the "data" light goes out on your receiver box. And of course if your TV is running on that station, you can also see when a commercial is running. Not all commercials cause a blackout, though. The national commercials are not likely to disrupt the feed; rather the local commercials sold and broadcast by the local cable TV station are the culprits.

Cable's unique advantage is that you can hook up and trade anyplace that receives any of the appropriate cable channels. On the other hand, cable has its own set of problems:

- There are blackout interruption periods, as just discussed.
- Service by the local cable company may be very poor. The cable signal can be down for days. (So can leased lines, for that matter.)
- Cable companies will, without warning, retune their amplifiers, corrupting the signal.
- The local cable channel may not allow the datafeed signal to travel over its network. For example, vendors are losing lines in many markets to closed captioning, and so on. This is bad news if all of a sudden your signal is gone for good and you took out a nonrefundable lease for your receiver box.

You can counter some of these problems:

- Ask your cable company about these issues. Insist on speaking to an engineer, not the first customer service representative who answers the phone.
- Some cable channels are more likely to insert blackouts than others are. Test all the available channels recommended by the vendor. Sometimes transmission is blocked during sports games only after trading hours. Nonetheless, this will still impact Globex trading.
- Try getting your cable signal by using a satellite dish. The DBC Signal International feed via private satellite hookup is purported to be a great method. Use the new small-footprint direct-TV type of dish.
- Place the receiver box in plain view so when the signal is cut off, you can detect the data light go out. Some software will alert you when there have been no data changes for an unusual period of time, even though the reception is good. Most software products do not.
- Employ the squawk box service from the S&P pit and the T-bond pit over the phone during such outages. When there is no outage, the telephone squawk box gives a good way to check the speed of your feed.

Questions to Ask

Vendors may not realize that closed captioning has blanked out your neighborhood's transmission of the datafeed. Ask that you be given a trial period so you can test all the available channels.

Ask if you can get the cable signal via a satellite dish, which will bypass the cable company's interference.

Satellite Transmission

The overall advantage with satellite transmission is that there is less to go wrong except for the weather. Advantages include avoiding blankouts by local commercial insertion, avoiding power blackouts at the cable company or at any intermediate amplifying station and simply avoiding anything else the cable company can do to mess up your signal. In that respect, satellite is more reliable.

Disadvantages include lack of convenient portability, sensitivity to meteorological conditions, local zoning ordinances, and condo restrictions. Heavy storms can cause the receiver to unlock off the carrier frequency causing data loss. Likewise, snowstorms can unlock the signal by building up snow on the dish. Also sunspots can cause blackouts. Twice a year, geostationary satellite transmissions are affected by the sun's energy due to their relative position between the earth and sun. This will affect receiver locations at various times of the day for 10 to 15 minutes, depending on your position on earth relative to the satellite.

Remember that a satellite operates in line of sight, and if there are mountains, buildings, or trees in the way (blocking line of site), it can be a problem, especially in northern latitudes. Lots of tinkering may be needed to align your dish to the satellite. You may even need to hire an installer to do it properly.

Questions to Ask

Is your latitude too high for direct line of sight?

Does it rain, thunderstorm, and snow a lot in your area? If so, you may want to consider a bigger dish or cable.

If reception is not strong enough, does the vendor have a bigger dish or a better amplifier? If so and you need to upgrade, what additional costs would you incur?

Internet Transmission

The newest development in data transmission is through the Internet. Advantages include portability and not needing to rent or buy a signal receiver box or satellite dish. You plug in wherever you are, in the office, at home, or on a trip.

Vendors offer real-time, delayed, EOD, or some combination on the WWW. Some require special software while others are pretty much open to universal servers.

As for speed, using Netscape and a 56 kbps modem through a local Internet service provider (ISP), one user reported his Internet feed was delivering data earlier than his cable feed! Another user reported data via the Internet arrives about the same time as data from S&P Comstock. On the other hand, one user said his Internet feed was behind cable all day on DJII, SPX, and NASDAQ. As cable speeds up to 56KB, this speed advantage of WWW over cable will likely disappear.

Disadvantages using an Internet feed include unreliable delivery rates because the Internet's throughput rate is so unpredictable one minute to the next. Reported one user:

Once when we pinged the connection, our test revealed that the signal was required to traverse 28 Internet hops before reaching my computer. Other tests have been as low as 7 and as high as 35. Each "hop" is another trip through a computer or router somewhere which takes time and is subject to [inducing additional] error.

Although Internet Services Digital Network (ISDN) lines make Internet communication faster than conventional lines, they are not much more reliable. You may not even be able to connect during very heavy trading, the time when you most need to.

You could also get disconnected abruptly from the WWW site if it is extremely busy. Your ISP may also have input/output (I/O) problems now and then. For example, incoming junk mail can be so voluminous that data processing at an ISP can temporarily grind to a halt, and during this time you will not receive any data.

Internet services fall into three categories whereby,

- Data is processed by a Java enabled Browser.
- Data is processed by a general purpose commercial application (e.g., MS Excel, Visual Basic, Delphi) that supports connection to the Internet.
- Data is processed by a custom stand-alone application that connects to the Internet, that in turn can pass data on to general-purpose commercial applications. Townsend Analytics is one such application. It connects to *www.spcomstock.com, www.pcquote.com, www.intersat.com, www.marketconnect.de*. If you want to use your own software, consider *www.interquote.com,* or *www.naq.com*.

Questions to Ask

Does the vendor offer real-time, delayed, or EOD?
Any special software required to process data from the Internet?

DATA RECEPTION

The third stage in the life cycle of a price quote is its processing at the receiving site.

Signal Translation

At the receiving end of FM, cable or satellite transmission, the signal passes through a receiver (black box) undergoing several transformations before entering into your computer. First the signal is demodulated, which extracts relevant data from the analog signal and converts it to a digital data stream.

Next, it is sent to a microprocessor and the processing performed on this data stream depends on the microprocessor's software. For example, DBC's receivers are driven by software called the *Receiver Operating System* (ROS), which is uploaded into the microprocessor's RAM type memory by a small program in the user's computer. Each of DBC's two data streams uses a fundamentally different ROS, each with advantages and disadvantages. In both cases, DBC's data dispatch center transmits all information (price quotes, news, etc.) in binary (compressed) format. The ROS selects (prefilters) only the type of information the user has paid to receive. Now here is where the two versions differ:

1. *DBC Signal.* The ROS converts the prefiltered information into ASCII text format and then relays to the computer only the price quotes whose symbols are in the user's portfolio. When only these data packets are sent to the user's computer, the computer's processing workload is fairly light. This version of the ROS also saves the most recently received price quotes for all the symbols in a portfolio in the microprocessor's RAM, so the server can request them and have current prices whenever it is restarted. A good backup feature.

2. *DBC BMI.* The ROS relays to the computer all the prefiltered information, still in binary format. This makes the computer's workload very high. This version of the ROS does not save specific prices in the microprocessor's RAM and so the backup feature is missing.

Dumping all the markets' data to your computer can create a very large workload. Data would include every tick of every contract month of every ticker of every subscribed exchange as well as all the options from your subscribed exchanges. Plus, it would include all the freebie indices and there are quite a few of them.

The bottom line here is that if the receiver is designed to send everything straight to your computer, charting and analysis performance will be heavily dependent on the speed and power of your computer. In this case, the easiest way is to get the fastest computer you can afford. A more serious procedure is to buy a second computer, whose sole purpose is to filter out all the quotes you are not interested in, then convert the remaining data to ASCII text and send it to the computer running your charting and analysis software. Don't laugh. I know several traders doing this.

Questions to Ask

Can the receiver prefilter for symbols exclusively in your portfolio?

Does the receiver send data to your computer in text or binary format?

Does the vendor have a developer's kit that explains the format of the data stream?

Time Clocks

Trading systems and related analysis rely heavily on the time associated with the trades being analyzed. As such, it is common (and necessary) for each trade to be timestamped with a notation of the time at which the trade was consummated. Some data providers deliver the time of the trade along with the trade report, which consumes considerable bandwidth in the datafeed. Most, however, rely on the user's software and computer to record the timestamp with the trade. Considering that a trade can be represented by a record of (1) the market, (2) the price, (3) the volume, and (4) the time, leaving out the time stamp can render a considerable savings in the space it would otherwise consume in the datafeed.

Most data providers broadcast a "current market time" on a periodic basis in the datafeed, typically every minute. Ordinarily, trading applications interpreting the datafeed set their "current time" based on this data. To gain access to the greater granularity of time increments than one minute, the trading application will typically set the computer's internal clock according to the value received from the datafeed. This setting could occur each time the "market time" is received, but more typically it is set either when the program is booted or on a daily basis. With the user's own computer clock thereby synchronized with the datafeed's reported market time, reading the clock on receipt of each trade and using that value for the time stamp of the trade, gives a crude (but best) approximation of the time that the trade actually occurred.

However, leaving it up to the user's application software to record the time stamp is by no means without its problems. First, some computer trivia. Computers have two clocks. They have a *hardware clock* that runs all the time, even when your computer power is switched off. They also have a *software clock* that runs only when the operating system (e.g., UNIX, DOS, Win95, WinNT, OS/2) is running. When the operating system, or "O/S," first starts, it initializes its internal software clock to match hardware clock time. Software clock initialization only has effect until the O/S is restarted. If you change the software clock time and then restart the operating system, the software clock time will be set back to hardware clock time.

Regarding the potential problems, it is obvious that if datafeed transmissions are late, the computer clock will be set wrong. If the user's computer is not synchronized with the true market time, the time of each trade will be misrecorded, causing even bigger problems with respect to the value of subsequent analysis. Even if the user's computer is correctly synchronized with the time of the market, data delays, especially in fast markets, mean that there can be some variance between the true time of the trade and the time it is delivered for recording at the user's site, even under ideal conditions.

A sometimes-confusing phenomenon occurs when your incoming data shows a time on your charting software that is different than the time shown by the computer operating system. This could happen when your data server is setting and reading the hardware clock while your O/S is reading the software clock. This has confused many users as they sit watching two different clock times on their computer screen.

Some software datafeed servers will ignore the "seconds" information in the time-of-day packets. This makes it impossible to create time-bars lasting less than 1 minute each.

Questions to Ask

Does the server software update the computer's hardware of software clock?

Does the server time-stamp data packets using the hardware or software clock?

Does the server include the "seconds" information when time-stamping a quote?

Buffer Overflow

There are two main causes of data loss or dropout at the receiver end: *buffer overflow* and signal corruption. You need to know when this occurring and why, otherwise you'll be trading merrily away without knowing what the market is really doing.

Assuming your receiver is picking up 100 percent of the data, your computer might fail to process it all simply because it is receiving more data than it can handle. Your receiver box and software package may not be designed to select (filter) from the enormous data throughput only those instruments you want to enter your symbol portfolio. Consequently, your computer's I/O buffer may get overwhelmed and new data will then simply have nowhere to go. They get dropped until the buffer empties out.

Computer manufacturers now implement a fast I/O chip (16550) for the COM port. This is generally fast enough for most purposes; however, if an overflow error occurred in the 16550 and the software properly triggered the "reset" flag, the port erroneously does not clear the flag. This would result in considerable lost data (a classic hardware bug). To work around this bug, some software products will set and then clear the flag when this error occurs. Even so, it is better to avoid overflowing the buffer altogether.

To lower the chances of buffer overflow, try a vendor that enables data filtering in the receiver box. Also, shut off news monitoring if you do not really need it. Shut off exchanges you are not interested in.

Another way to address the problem is to speed up I/O throughput. To do so, you need special hardware and software to replace the COM port on all computers. Some vendors, like FutureSource, have their own plug-in board so you don't need to use your computer's port. If that is not available, try a vendor whose receiver has a built-in buffer, and as far as buffers go, bigger is better. For example, DBC Signal's Plus box has a built-in buffer that can hold about 16K bytes.

More powerful buffering methods include installing T/Link software and a T/Port board. The T/Port has 16K bytes of input buffer whereas the modern 16650 so-called high-speed COM port has only 16 bytes. So the T/Port has 1,000 times the input buffer size of the modern 16650. T/Port and T/Link are available from Telcor Ltd (phone: 441-238-4970).

Even if your I/O is very fast, you can still lose data if your computer is too slow to handle the average data throughput. Eventually the T/Port buffer will overflow and you are still with the same problem. The T/Link software expands the 16K buffer to essentially unlimited size by using 200K of RAM and if that overflows it is sent to your hard disk.

Still, you need data on screen in a timely manner, not just buffered somewhere. Therefore, your computer needs to be fast, too. Speeding up your main processor means getting a fast Pentium, AMD, or Cyrix processor. A top-quality graphics board will also help prevent delays by updating screens very quickly.

Questions to Ask

When buffer overflow occurs, does the server software set *and clear* the "reset" flag in 16550 I/O chip?

Is the datafeed server compatible with Telcor's T/Link software and T/Port hardware?

Can you afford to buy a top-quality graphics board?

Bad Packets

A *bad packet* is a data packet that was received, but the data contained is only partially correct, due to signal corruption caused by a weak signal somewhere between the vendor and your computer.

To verify you are getting bad packets, most software provided by vendors offer a bad packet counter that you could inspect periodically. If the bad packet count is incrementing higher, you have the problem. The better products should distinguish between two types of error: dropout (some bytes were lost in a packet) and CRC error (some bytes values were corrupted). Some software charting products, like WINdoTRADEr, can do both.

In addition, your black box may *unlock,* from time to time, due to a weak or corrupted signal, or dirty cable connectors. All data reception is lost until the box regains a lock on the incoming signal.

Here are some potential remedies. Tighten all cable connectors. Verify your satellite dish is aimed properly. Get a larger dish. Reorient the dish. Spray a lubricant or wax over the dish to prevent snow buildup, make sure your satellite dish LNB has a noise figure no higher than 0.8dB. If not, get one with a lower noise rating. The LNB is a Low-Noise Block downconvertor, the electronic gizmo positioned by the three-strut support at the focal point of the dish. It detects, amplifies, and downconverts (shifts from GHz frequency down to MHz frequency), making the signal less vulnerable to noise and attenuation in the cable.

At times, the vendor may be the cause of bad packets, typically the result of power outages, crashed computer hard drives, and numerous other technical failures. According to Murphy's Law, the datafeed always seems to go down at the worst possible moment in your trading.

Questions to Ask

Does the receiver or software have a bad packet counter?

Does the receiver or software have a means of alerting the trader when excessive bad packets occur?

Can you swap a small dish for a larger one and pay only the difference in cost?

Can the vendor give you a higher quality LNB if the one you first receive is not strong enough?

Does the vendor have a fault-tolerant system? In what manner is it fault-tolerant?

- With disks running in image mode?
- With backup power generators in case of power outages or brownouts?
- With a redundant (secondary) system working as a backup?

Data Accumulation and Correction

Some vendors let you download data on the entire day's trades in a very short period of time after the trading session has ended. Typically, service becomes available 30 minutes after the market session closes and transmission is repeated (recycled) every few hours thereafter. This service lets you update your database in case your computer, for whatever reason, failed to collect and process some quotes in real time.

Exchanges and vendors sometimes release bad data, and most will make corrections if they are detected. Some vendors will retransmit the corrected information after the day's session and some software charting products use this information to automatically update bad ticks. Other vendors require you to access their database and download what you need, then manually paste the missing data into your database. The former method is the way of the future. For example, FutureSource (FS) automatically corrects all bad ticks, and if your computer goes down, FS automatically replaces the real-time data that you missed. The same is true with Reuters Trend DataLink.

As for detecting bad ticks, WINdoTRADEr has a sophisticated bad price filter that catches ticks in error by as little as four ticks. Detection is based on the kinds of errors typically made by the typist at each exchange pit.

Questions to Ask

Does the data vendor filter out bad quotes?

Does the datafeed server software filter out bad quotes?

Does the server software make it easy to detect and fix bad quotes as well as enter missing quotes?

Is the update process manual or automatic?

DATA STORAGE

Generic Issues

How do you plan to store large amounts of historical data? Some services that provide historical data expect you to store it on your hard drive. Make sure it can be set up in a format your trading software can read. Popular formats are MetaStock and

ASCII Text. Other vendors supply data on a CD and expect your software to be able to access it off the CD.

The CD disk is the upcoming trend for mass storage of financial data. Disks have large capacity and are cheap to manufacture. However, there are issues regarding accuracy and convenience of use. For example, would the software let you transfer data from the CD to your hard drive, so you can fix any bad ticks? If so, will the next CD upgrade search for your clean data and automatically delete it, thinking it is doing you a service by removing "redundant" data?

The data format on the CD may be incompatible with data stored on your disk, creating a problem for "on-the-fly" data integration. This issue will become more important over time as we connect data services to other software such as spreadsheets or homebrew software. Converting between these formats is time-consuming and error-prone. Since storage is so inexpensive now, there is less incentive to compress data than there has been in the past. In addition, NT offers compression built into the file system, simplifying storage and access in standard ASCII text format with good performance. So, why bother compressing data into proprietary formats? Isn't open access across applications more important than proprietary gains? As large vendors come to realize the power of open access and implement it (and they do), smaller vendors will likely follow suit.

Questions to Ask

What data formats (text, MetaStock, etc.) does the server support?

What data format will the historical data be in?

Can the software read data from a CD? If so, will it let you transfer data from the CD to your hard drive, so you can fix any bad ticks? If so, will the next CD upgrade search for your cleaned data on disk and automatically delete it, thinking it is doing you a service by removing redundant data? If so, can you disable that feature?

Can the server roll together contracts on the fly? If so, can the user specify that particular contracts in the default directory are to be replaced with "corrected" ones somewhere on the user's disk?

Does the server support "Open Access," whereby other applications can receive data from and send data to the server by means of DDE, OLE, or some other common I/O link?

DATA ANALYSIS

Generic Issues

One consideration when choosing your charting and analysis software is cost. For example, owning a copy of charting and trading software can cost up to $2,000 or more, a significant amount to a novice EOD trader trying to keep costs low and buying data at, say, $50 per month. However, the same $2,000 may seem insignificant when compared with the fees of real-time data services, some exceeding $1,500 per month.

Another software consideration is whether you can live with the limited features of the product. Which capabilities and features do you want (see "Questions to Ask" for this section)?

Trading the night session has unique requirements, besides a pot of coffee. Because you may find large spaces between bars on a time-base chart, you are almost forced to use tick-based charting software. You may experience difficulty trying to include the symbol of a new instrument into a commercial analysis software application. Sometimes the vendors are almost never accessible to solve these problems promptly, or blame the exchanges, or give their subscribers a runaround.

Questions to Ask

Is a payment plan available?

Which software features do you want? Here are a few to get you started:

Auto bad data detection	General programming language	User-definable trading systems
Charting	Graphics	Simulation trading
Auto alerts	General programming language	Real-time analysis
Auto stock picking	DLL, DDE, OLE connectivity	Portfolio management
Auto trade placement	Database management	System optimization
Auto bad data detection	Fast and reputable tech support	User-definable indicators
Internet user forum	Online tech support	User-definable trading systems

Homebrew Software

If you want to route the incoming data stream into your own software application, several approaches are available. For more information on the software mentioned here and their manufacturers, see Appendix C for a list of Web sites.

Plan A

Use a ready-made server designed to be open for easy communication to your own applications:

- The Universal Market Data Server (UMDS), by MarketStream Inc. is a real-time market data collection program for desktop computers running Microsoft Windows NT and Microsoft Windows 95. The server collects real-time data for all stocks, indices, futures, bonds, mutual funds, options, economic indicators, news, text services, fundamental data and other data provided by a real-time data vendor. It also allows multiple applications to access both real-time and historical data at the same time.

- Pal File Real Time, by Investment Engineering Corp. will generate a price text file and maintain it in real time. The text file contains Date, Time, Open, High, Low, Close for a specified chart and then posts updates to this file in real time. The file will have one line for each bar in your chart. The resulting ASCII file can easily be read into any other program such as Excel, Access, C++, etc. This allows the user to easily integrate the real-time datafeed into other programs.

Plan B

Use a charting package with a server that can communicate to your applications via Windows DDE or OLE protocol. Several commercial products that have this capability include:

- Townsend Analytics Server
- Omega Research TradeStation
- DBC Signal for Windows and BMI for Windows
- ILX System's Workstation
- Telekurs' FINVEST Workstation
- Dow Jones' Workstation

The receiving application (yours) needs to support "hot link" or "advisory" client DDE. Your receiving application can be either homebrew or a qualified commercial product, such as Microsoft Excel and The MathWorks MATLAB.

To help you part of the way, some vendors provide software development kits. For example, the Market Data Interface Library (MDIL) from ILX allows C programmers to build customized market data applications for the Internet. Likewise, North American Quotations also offers several products specifically for developers and webmasters.

Plan C

Code your own datafeed server.

If you develop your own, you can build in lots of data queuing to ensure incoming data is never lost. You can time-stamp incoming packets as they are received, so the time of receipt is saved correctly even if the storage system gets behind. You can save data files in any format or combination of formats you want. You can communicate to other application software any way you want. You can communicate to other computers any way you want. Lastly, you can build in all sorts of error trapping to let you know if anything is going wrong.

For example, one clever fellow wrote his own personal server by using a TV/Teletext/video capture board to extract prices from several different TV broadcasts via satellite in Europe. He then wrote a server that collects data from the Teletext pages and applies filtering to ensure the data is good. It then distributes prices as single items via DDE to MS Excel and has no performance problems. Data is saved as standard ASCII text files, which ultimately is processed by Omega Research's Super-Charts® (Supercharts® is a registered trademark of Omega Research, Inc.) charting software.

Questions to Ask

Can the server communicate by DDE or OLE to other applications?

Can other applications transmit data to the charting program?

Audio Commentary

You will probably gain more insight into what is going on the exchange floor from an *audio service* commentary (squawk box) than from any datafeed. With this service, you can hear a commentator describe the floor's activities. He makes no mention of sales or closes, rather comments almost exclusively in bids and offers. For example, you might hear, "50 bid at 60, 50 bid at 60, 60 at 70, 65 at 75, 70 bid at 80, 65 bid at 70." The commentary also includes comments from time to time about volume and who is trading. For example, you might hear, "little action now," "50s trading," "100s trading," "only 1s and 2s trading," "only occasional locals," "Merrill Lynch selling 100s," "outside paper coming in."

Experienced traders claim that an audiofeed helps them attain a "3-D" perspective of the market's activities. You can hear the outcry and emotional level rise and fall, and phones ringing in the background indicating new orders coming in. This feedback can certainly help you avoid trading in very fast and very slow markets, as both situations will likely produce bad fills from slippage.

In addition, the commentator will let you know who is driving the market, either the paper traders or the floor. You may wish to avoid trades when the floor is "running the stops" to clear out their books. For example, if the market has just made a new low and the commentator says, "There are no offers and the floor is in control," it is likely that you have just seen a retest of the low in which the floor did a run on stops. Price may likely rebound to the upside.

On the other hand, the market's high-strung tension can be contagious and stressful. It can also be humorous, as the commentator's expletives are not deleted when matters seem to get out of control.

Question to Ask

Does the vendor offer audio commentary? If not, check out Intersat's service (see Appendix C for Web link).

Customer Support

Good customer support is essential. If your datafeed is acting suspiciously, you need quick, intelligent help to resolve the problem. After all, it is your money that is at risk in the market. There are far too many complaints in this area; problems regarding responsiveness, overcharging, technical competence, timely bug fixing, refunds—and the list goes on.

A typical complaint about responsiveness reads:

Their phone is busy 85 percent of the day and my faxes are not answered for two to three days if at all. I cannot count how many times they have promised to return a call and not done so.

Another complaint said the vendor:

. . . seems to have plenty of people sitting idle in their offices. You should have seen the eyes of their salesman when I explained that I needed more than 10,000 ticks storage—they probably thought I was some nut trying to bad-mouth their product.

In complete contrast, some vendors give impeccable service. For example, here's one compliment heard on the Internet:

FutureSource (in London anyway) provides excellent backup. If I ever miss data they usually send it round on disk by courier. They have also sent me historical data if I start looking at a new market and haven't previously been collecting data for that symbol.

Before packing up your bags and moving to London, consider that support staffs of most vendors will provide correct answers, albeit, at times, not without a little extra effort on your part. You may have to insist on speaking to a supervisor or manager if the person on the other end of the phone cannot help you. They are more knowledgeable and are responsible for making things happen.

Beware of "Free Trial" offers, as some vendors have a different interpretation as to the meaning of "free." For example, one respondent complained that a vendor

. . . advertised a 30-day free trial. But I discovered it's only free if you *do not* continue with the service. Otherwise they charge you for the first 30 days.

Read your service contract carefully. One customer complained,

They get you to sign a 1 year contract without making it clear that (1) they will not let you out of the contract for any reason and (2) they won't even let you reduce the level of service below the initial dollar amount for any reason. I originally signed up for CME, NYSE, AMEX, and NASDAQ. When I wanted to remove the stocks, they said they would continue to charge me the surcharge for both futures and stocks.

Questions to Ask

Will the vendor correct quotes that traders call in to report as incorrect? If so, in what time period (24 hours?) do they guarantee fixing the error?

Does the vendor guarantee their data baud rate? That is, if you paid for 38.4K baud and the only way you can get reliable transmission is to lower your receiver down to a 19.2K service, can you cancel the contract without any penalties?

If you use cable or satellite and move to an area where that service is not available, can you get a refund?

Are there any trial offers? What are all the conditions for a free trial? Will you be billed for the trial period under any circumstances?

Can you make changes to the services you want after you opened your account? Any additional fees involved? Can fees be reduced if less service is requested during the year?

Does the vendor guarantee tech support will call back within X days of the customer calling in? If not, why not?

Does the vendor offer a refund if the software crashes more than X times during the first N weeks of use?

Ask the vendor to list all surcharges and fees that you might be subject to, for any reason.

Ask the vendor to fax or mail you a copy of the contract's termination clause and have the agent circle anything pertaining to extra fees imposed for early termination.

Historical Data Quality

When it comes to historical data, quality involves completeness and accuracy. If the numbers are not accurate, how can your system tests be meaningful? As for completeness, some databases for sale had gaping holes in them. For example, one user complained that a CD of historical data had places where an entire day (nonholiday) of trades was missing from all contracts and commodities, and a replacement from the vendor set still had 22 of 42 contracts missing one or more days.

Another unrelated complaint was that one vendor offered data with 537 days missing, while a second vendor had all of those days present for the very same markets.

Questions to Ask

If you find errors in the data, will the vendor supply you with a corrected database? How soon? Agree that if you have to wait more than N weeks for the new database, you may get a refund.

If any of the original reported errors are also in the "corrected database," will you get a refund?

OTHER CONSIDERATIONS

Exchange Fees

Data vendors' fees for their services include costs passed on to them by the exchanges. Legally, price quotes belong to the exchanges and they charge for the service of making their data publicly accessible. In 1994, the top eight exchanges collected over $5 billion in fee revenue.

Data providers sell data to the trading community on two bases: "real-time" in which the quotes are delivered as they are received from the exchanges, and "delayed," in which the data is delayed by some arbitrary (but consistent) amount of time, typically 15 minutes. The cost for real-time data is considerably more expensive than that for delayed data: one vendor (BMI) offers all exchanges on a delayed basis for a flat $60/month; but prices for real-time access start at $200/month. To offer "real-time" access, the data provider must also assess fees based on each exchange to which the user subscribes.

The exchanges distinguish between "professional" and "nonprofessional" traders, and price their fees accordingly. Exchange fees for equities quotes are relatively inexpensive for the nonprofessional trader: As of November 1997, they were less than $4.50 per month. Fees for options data are larger, hitting a maximum of $24 per month. Exchange fees for commodities quotes is something else altogether. First, an independent trader has to pay a fee to each exchange providing data. For example, if you want quotes from CME, CBOT, Nymex, and other New York futures exchanges, exchanges fees alone will exceed $300 per month. This is then added to your data vendor's fees.

The following list shows fees at various exchanges at time of publication. Fees may have changed. Consult relevant exchanges for current values.

AMEX	$ 3.25	CME	55.00
NASDAQ	4.00	NYMEX	55.00
NYSE	5.25	COMEX	55.00
OPRA	3.00	KCBT	12.50
Canadian Exchanges	6.00	MACE	7.50
CBOT	60.00	WCE	14.00

Foreign Exchange Data

Most vendors offer some sort of Foreign Exchange (FX) feed. However, the difference is that some feeds have very few contributing banks supplying information and others feeds have more. In other words, not all vendors use the same banks as their data source. To further complicate matters, FX is a nonregulated market and ticks from this market are "price indications" from banks. Believe it or not, the same bank can repeat the same price, sometimes very often. Therefore, not only is it possible that vendors may have very different FX tick volume on the same day, but a high tick number may not mean much at all.

The top three FX data vendors are considered to be Reuters, Dow Jones Markets, and Bridge.

Final Suggestions

Remember, these services want your business (i.e., your money). So, here are my suggested steps to take when seeking a data vendor.

- Ask all the questions you want, especially the questions proposed in this chapter. Make sure all fees are included (hookup, box rental, etc.).
- Write down the answers you get. Read them all back to the salesperson and verify all that was said. This will be your "attached list of conditions."
- Ask them to send you a written agreement. Write on the agreement that it is contingent on all the attached conditions that were described by the salesperson. Attach the list of conditions.
- Do not phone in your order. Make a copy of your agreement and mail in the original.

When you cancel a contract, return everything you are required to send in an *insured* package. Also, if you are canceling because the datafeed couldn't deliver properly, focus a video camera on the screen and keyboard to demonstrate the problem. Later, if you don't receive the refund you are entitled to, you will have evidence to support your claim.

May your data be delivered accurately and promptly.

Books, Consultants, Software

SELECTING THE BEST BOOKS

Getting educated first is as important when betting on markets as when betting on horses. Likewise, there are very good books as well as awful ones to choose from in both disciplines. To save you time and expenses, I compiled comments about financial books from experienced traders and organized only the most recommended books into categories. Browse through the reviews at my Web site and take notes on which ones you like the most. Afterwards, you can jump to one of several financial bookstores also on the Internet.

My list of recommended books with their up-to-date reviews is available at this Web location:

www.jurikres.com/faq/booklist.htm

Three online bookstores:

www.amazon.com	Amazon sells books on anything.
www.elder.com	Elder sells books on financial trading and investing.
www.traderspress.com	Traders Press sells books on financial trading and investing.

DATA FEEDS THROUGH THE INTERNET

You can actually receive financial market data through the Internet as vendors offer real-time, delayed, EOD, or some combination. Some require special software while others are pretty much open to universal servers. For an updated list of WWW sites providing these services, see my Web page

www.jurikres.com/cool/maincool.htm

For squawk-box service, digital audio and video services, data transmission and fax service, see the Web site

www.intersat.com

SOFTWARE CONSULTANTS FOR EASY LANGUAGE AND C PROGRAMMING

Owners of Omega Research products typically prefer developing their own mechanical trading systems. However, for many, there typically comes a point in time when the desired system is just too complicated to code by oneself. Professional help is needed. For an up-to-date list of available trustworthy, competent programmers and consultants willing to help you with data preprocessing and modeling, see my Web page

http://www.jurikres.com/faq/consult.htm

SOFTWARE WITH A DATA SERVER

If you want to route the incoming data feed into your own software applications, there are several approaches available. These approaches and the relevant software are mentioned in Appendix B. Below is a list of Web sites related to these software products:

The Universal Market Data Server (UMDS), by MarketStream Inc.	www.uniserv.com/umds.htm
Pal File Real Time, by Investment Engineering Corp.	www. InvestLabs.com
Townsend Analytics Server	www.taltrade.com
Omega Research TradeStation	www.omegaresearch.com
DBC Signal for Windows and BMI for Windows	www.dbc.com
ILX System's Workstation	www.ilx.com
Telekurs' FINVEST Workstation	www.tkusa.com
Dow Jones' Workstation	www.djmarkets.com
Microsoft Excel	www.microsoft.com
The MathWorks MATLAB	www.mathworks.com
Market Data Interface Library (MDIL) from ILX	www.ilx.com
North American Quotations	www.naq.com/partners.htm
TV/Teletext/video capture board	www.hauppauge.com
Omega Research's SuperCharts charting software	www.omegaresearch.com

RECOMMENDED SOFTWARE FOR FINANCIAL MODELING

By the time you feel you have exhausted the potential of classical technical indicators, you are ready to begin the next step in your journey: forecasting. After all, indicators that *lead* the market are certainly more useful than those that *lag* the market. Be cautioned, however. Creating leading indicators is not a trivial exercise. Probably the most difficult aspect of creating leading indicators is in selecting the correct inputs to feed your indicator. There is a world of data to choose from.

Here is my list of recommended software products, grouped by the manner in which they select the proper inputs to your desired leading indicator:

Genetic Algorithms

Genetic algorithms reduce the number of inputs by trying semirandom combinations, keeping those combinations of inputs that work the best, making new modifications from them, again keeping the best combinations, and so on. As the process repeats, the algorithm finds increasingly better combinations of inputs for your leading indicator.

- Neuralware's Neural Works Predict (www.neuralware.com), an add-in module for MS Excel.
- Biocomp's Neural Genetic Optimizer (www.bio-comp.com), a stand-alone program.

Systematic Elimination

Systematic elimination starts with all the inputs a user has collected, and eliminates the least useful, one by one. Eventually, only the most useful inputs remain. This procedure is more efficient than genetic algorithms when the task is strictly limited to making "Yes/No" decisions (e.g., the specific input is useful/not useful).

- Promised Land's Braincel (www.promland.com), an add-in module for MS Excel.

Ontogenic Statistical Selection

This heavy-duty method uses General Method Data Handling (GMDH), a mathematical procedure that models data by generating one or more layers of polynomial equations. The following software product combines this method with expert system and data mining technology into one powerful workhorse. Expensive.

- Abtech's ModelQuest Enterprise (www.abtech.com), a stand-alone application.

Decorrelated Dimension Reduction

Even after you have eliminated all useless input variables, those that remain may still be highly correlated with each other, and therefore, highly redundant. One method to attain further input reduction is to decorrelate the remaining input variables without throwing away any useful information they have to offer.

- Jurik Research's DDR (www.jurikres.com), an add-in module for TradeStation, SuperCharts, and MS Excel.

CONSUMER PROTECTION AGENCIES

Consumers have rights. Whenever you suspect you have been a victim of disreputable or illegal actions, consult the appropriate authorities. There are numerous agencies chartered to protect you and your investments, and their services are generally free. For a list of agencies accessible on the Web, go to the consumer protection section on the following Web page:

www.jurikres.com/cool/maincool.htm

For a short tutorial on how to recognize disreputable vendors of "super profitable" trading systems, go to this Web page:

www.jurikres.com/snake/main_oil.htm

TEST FLIGHT YOUR TRADING SYSTEM

Before placing real trades with your newly developed system, you may want to test your system with a simulated broker service. This way, you can gain experience placing trades over the phone, watch your trades perform in real time, and discover how fast slippage and commission expenses add up and eat into your profits. Here are some relevant Web pages:

www.auditrack.com
www.forex-trc.com
www.futuresnetwork.com
www.tradersnetwork.com
www.tradecomp.com
www.wallstreetstation.com
www.virtualstockexchange.com

Project Nimble: An Automated Equity Options Market Making System

JOSEPH ALOTTA

This is the account of an actual and profitable trading system and the ideas and events that came together in the summer of 1987 and through 1989. The persons mentioned are real people to whom the author owes a debt of gratitude for a very challenging and satisfying project experience.

Although some of the circumstances described here happened over a decade ago, the reader may draw on our collective experience for the implementation of new projects, which all share the same basic principles of having a real edge in the market and exploiting it in a way that minimizes the downside risk. Though the models have become more complex and the systems are faster and cheaper, trading is still about game theory and risk management.

ABOUT STEVE FOSSETT

I was introduced to Steve Fossett in March 1987. In addition to running a large trading organization, Steve had a number of sports exploits to his credit—swimming the English Channel, swimming the strait of Dardanelles, leading the Snowbird expedition to the top of Mount Everest, racing dogsleds in the Iditerod, running super marathons, skiing super marathons, holding the world record for the longest balloon flight (from Seoul, South Korea, to Vancouver, British Columbia), and most recently winning the Chicago to Mackinaw Island sailboat race, in a catamaran "Stars and Stripes," which won the Americas cup in Australia.

Fossett Corporation had about 350 market makers and about 20 staff persons. Some of the market makers traded with the firm's capital and some used their own capital and were essentially clearing customers. The largest part of the market makers worked on the Chicago Board Options Exchange (CBOE) trading equity options, a smaller part traded futures options on the Chicago Board of Trade (CBOT) or the Chicago Mercantile Exchange (MERC).

Steve Fossett has that determination, that super perseverance, that tough-it-out till you succeed attitude that is infectious; so when he asked me to build him a trading machine, I found myself saying "Yes" and then thinking about how to accomplish it. There existed one other machine in early development, the Timber Hill system, partially deployed at the time. Steve took me onto the floor of the CBOE to study this system, but all I could see were colored monitors and options prices, and they were not always on line. The inner workings of their operation were a highly proprietary secret.

THE SPX PIT

The pit designated by exchange authorities for automated systems was the SPX pit. This pit has European-style options on the S&P 500 index. The OEX was a much bigger and more active trading pit, containing American-style options on the S&P 100 index and I guess the motive was to increase the volume in the SPX pit, although it was still more active than all but the largest single stock option, IBM. Having European style options was an advantage to the systems designer; we could use the less computationally intensive Black-Scholes formula without having to worry about the binomial trees of the Cox-Ross-Rubenstein model.

SELECTION OF THE DATA FEED SERVICE

I quickly did some calling around, wanting to use the best datafeed available. Steve Schwartz had an option trading system that was popular upstairs at the Options Exchange called the Schwartz-a-tron. The market makers would eat their lunches and play backgammon to the yellowish glow of the Schwartz-a-tron.

We hired two team members in the first few days, Rob Davis Jr. and Pat Mac-Caulley. Together we analyzed alternative quote sources and we presented our findings to Steve Fossett. All vendors were expensive; the quality was difficult to determine, sometimes good, sometimes not.

This was the problem: SIAC was the only carrier able to get feeds directly from the exchanges; all other data vendors received their data from SIAC. Vendors would attempt to avoid problems of the feed during peak times, such as crashes, panics, opening rotation, and closing rotations, first by omitting option bids and offers, then by omitting underlying bids and offers and then finally by omitting option last sale prices. These were times we absolutely needed to be operating with full data.

We decided to go to SIAC ourselves directly, becoming our own data vendor. This was a very expensive prospect and Steve Fossett backed it 100 percent. We still did not have a design for the complete trading system, but we acted on faith, knowing that the best source of data would be crucial for its success. In the opinion of some of the team members, this would be the reason the system avoided big losses during the market break in 1989.

How a Development System Was Chosen

Computer salespersons visited me constantly—IBM, Stratus, Tandem, Data General. They kept saying only a minicomputer could handle a mainframe-oriented BYSNC feed. I decided to give a PC network a try. I was buying PC Limited's 286 computers for about $2,000 each (memory was dear at the time) and felt that we could get a long way toward the $200,000 to $350,000 a minicomputer would cost.

We had some PS/2's (we wanted to be ready when IBM decided to release the 386 chip), and we bought, Novell netware, on 3Com Ethernet and later Arcnet, when the 3Com drivers were delayed. We bought a dozen PC Limited 286's, now known as Dell Computer.

We had hired Cathy Huang and Belinda Chang to work on the feed problem. Cathy Huang worked on the BYSNC data reception, and Belinda Cheng worked on the protocol by which the feed handlers, data storage servers, backup feed handlers and backup servers would communicate and broadcast their status to each other. Rob Davis was working on the touch screen and character mappings to display fractions. Pat MacCaulley was using the option models to print out trading sheets for Fossett market makers.

The option models came right from the book. The Cox-Ross-Rubenstein book was pretty much incomprehensible. We used McMillian and Bookstaber, which even had BASIC code. Three years later, I was teaching and deriving options models at First Chicago Corp.

Hardware and Software Development Headaches

The data reception problem was a much harder challenge than first supposed. Cathy Huang wrote her own drivers in assembler for this purpose. She got it working. Later, an engineer at SIAC explained to me how it was not possible for it to work since there were circuitry design flaws in the PS/2 serial port. We did not know that, but luckily Cathy used different computers to test with and we found it worked on the PC Limited 286.

When using the data storage servers on the live feeds, we quickly ran out of memory under DOS. 640K basic memory, 384K extended and 2MB expanded. We used the expanded memory until we could convert the b-tree program to OS/2.

I kept trying to get 3Com to deliver drivers for their boards under OS/2. They kept delaying. Finally in desperation, I popped out the Ethernet and replaced it with a Standard MicroSystems Arcnet that had a fully functioning OS/2 driver and we segmented the topology into an Arcnet segment and an Ethernet segment. It worked, but it was not elegant. A few months later, I was still on the phone to the developers at 3Com trying to get their product shipped. The engineer told me that he could write the driver in one day, but his management had forbidden him to do so, since IBM was in the network business. I called him at home that night, and two days and $200 dollars later, I had the driver.

ENCOUNTERING A MINOR DELAY

The data was coming in full speed and the network was handling it. We powered down machines to check the fault recovery. The touch screen was operating, trading screens were being updated with real prices and our theoretical option prices, and the fun was about to start. We were preparing to get a station in the OEX pit. It was the October 1987.

After the initial terror, the introspection, the follies of some participants, and the makings of great stories in years to come, business had changed substantially and our efforts were needed elsewhere. The decision was made to put the project on hold temporarily, to keep improving various components in our spare time, and to move forward with other more timely endeavors. We concentrated our efforts on the quotation system, the risk management system, and the clearing systems.

Rob Davis Jr., our lead programmer, resigned shortly after the October panic. He made some comments about wanting to find an industry that is more stable where he could responsibly raise a family. To me, stability meant boredom, and to Steve Fossett's credit, no one was laid off at Fossett Corporation at the time.

PROJECT NIMBLE BEGINS

In March 1988, Steve Fossett expressed his desire to resume the project. He picked one of his best market makers, Jim Sauser to join the team. I picked two new software engineers to join the team, Evan Jones and Dave Lawson. The four of us moved into an office together and we brainstormed day and night. We thought of the name, Nimble, because that is what we would have to be on the floor of the exchange to escape harm. Then we designed the system, as shown in Figure D.1.

The Nimble system would be composed of three major and independent systems: the volatility monitor, the pricer, and the risk manager module. The volatility monitor would listen to the data feeds constantly and back out the implied volatilities for different expiry months and strike prices. It would always keep a current estimate of what the market thinks the volatility is.

The pricer would use the volatility and calculate the house theoretical value for each option, then apply a bias (to be discussed), and then issue the house price given the bids and offers of other firms. This is an important feature. For example, suppose our theoretical value was $1.50 but the best bid was $1.00. We would either bid with them at $1 or become best bid at $1 1/16, but we would never bid more.

FIGURE D.1 THE LAYOUT OF PROJECT NIMBLE.

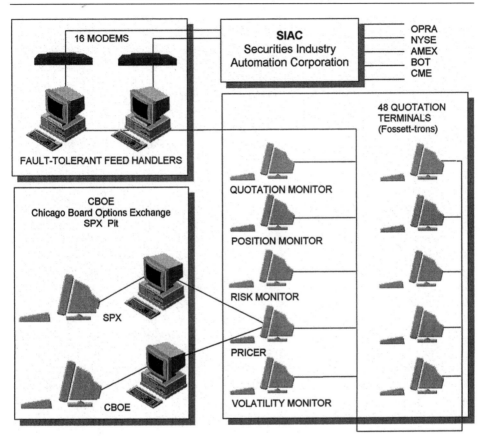

The risk module would keep track of all the options and hedges currently active in inventory. It would keep a live estimate of all the Greek letters. A clerk would sit by the screen and enter futures trades in the early days. Later, that was done from the trading floor.

The risk module would also be the generator of the bias parameters that the pricer would use. The bias would start to kick in to bias the pricer away from long options when our total delta was approaching our set limits and would bias the pricer away from buying options when our vega limits were approached. The delta limits would come down as a hedge was entered. We were looking at managing the gamma and theta limits as well, but early experience showed this was not necessary as they mainly took care of themselves, in such a large options book. However, we did display these values for the human traders to monitor.

THE SCREEN IN THE PIT

Getting a screen installed in the pit was no easy matter. Although it was in the next building from us, (we were in 440 S. LaSalle and the CBOE is at 400 S. LaSalle), turf issues kept us from wiring directly from our Telco closet to their Telco closet only six feet away!

We had to order a dedicated 9600 baud line from Illinois Bell that ran from the 440 building to the switching station on Wabash and back to the 400 building. While we were waiting for the installation, we split the pricer in half. One half would use a 386 PC to paint the screens down on the CBOE floor and the other half would listen to current markets on a 286 machine in our upstairs trading room. Thus traffic on the dedicated 9600 line would be kept to items by request only.

We had supposed that the 386 computer would be installed near where the monitors would be installed in the SPX pit. This was not the case. The CBOE had a separate computer room in the undercroft of the raised floor specifically for this purpose. It was about 30 feet away. The other trading firms used a computer that had the CPU built into the monitor, but we didn't want to do this because the built-in CPU was only a very slow 8088 and we needed the 286. To overcome the distance problem between the 386 and its monitors, I called around to the electronics supply houses and came up with a set of amplifiers. The manufacturer would not guarantee their use for monitors and the engineer thought it would only work for 20 feet. We tried it anyway and it worked fine. I took the opportunity to remove the floppy drive in the computer in the undercroft for security reasons. All file transfers were done remote via the 9600 baud line. I also taped a black trash bag to the ceiling to prevent dirt from falling through the above floor onto the computer. Two weeks after the line was installed, we were ready to test live on the floor.

THE COMPUTER SHARKS

The first week was fraught with system problems. In that week, we lost more money than all but one week of market vagaries. The crowd in the SPX pit was quick to pick up and capitalize on any computer glitch. It was a game to them akin to taking candy from a baby. It was a hard week for the programmers. They worked late into the night to make changes that were furiously tested the next day. In addition, we had not anticipated that some members of the crowd would stand right on top of us and scrutinize everything we did.

The terminal in the pit controlled the market quote screens. The human operator could control the spreads, best bid/offer, behind the best bid/offer, the bias, long or short, the amount of deltas, long or short, in essence, the bet size, which would cause the bias to be less and less as it got closer to the delta limits. I am not sure if we were able to control the other Greek letters. All this information had to be available to the human operator and to many of the members of the crowd as well. I remember standing behind Jim Sauser as another market maker explained to his buddy where the delta information was located on our screen, and so on. He said it in a matter-of-fact manner as if he was directing a newcomer to the restrooms. He generously gave us credit for things we had not yet implemented and probably would not.

To maintain some secrecy, we came up with a scheme to put all position information in one long number at the bottom of the screen. For example, character positions 3–5 would contain the delta and positions 10–12 would contain the bias. To hide the real information, additional numbers were added. These numbers would change based on a formula off of the real numbers. We tried using pure random numbers, but they would change when the others did not and the randomness became apparent to the crowd. Instead, we programmed a routine that would multiply the Greek letter by linear equations and put the result in the spare digits, and it would all move in sync together either up or down, but nobody else would know which was the real number. We also rotated the character position orders around a bit just to make sure. Before the trading day started, the human operators would go talk to the programmers to get the latest character location information as it usually was changed overnight.

Soon the computer failures decreased and the computer sharks laid off. We gradually got our nerves up, turning on the best/bid offer for a while and then turning it off when it got too hot. We played like this for a few weeks, in the market, out of the market, in the market, always getting braver, staying in the market longer, adding more bias, setting larger deltas, always getting better.

RISK MANAGEMENT

At the same time, work was progressing on the risk management side, which was located in the upstairs office. We added on-line position reports, smile charts, all the Greek letters, everything we could think about to measure our exposure. We also developed coded messages that could be sent down to the floor. These messages occupied a certain two-digit position. These were some of the messages:

- Everything OK.
- Check your screens—I think I see something.
- We are going to lunch.
- Don't feel well.
- Someone is giving me a hard time.
- Someone's coming downstairs to see you.
- The boss wants to see you.
- We are experiencing minor technical problems.
- We are experiencing more serious technical problems.
- Panic—pull the plug immediately.

Trading cards were made with all these codes translated and most of the staff kept them handy in their shirt pockets. My favorite message announced "We're eating donuts/bagels/muffins/pizza and they're going fast."

ENTER CARY GRANT

Cary Grant came on the scene about this time. Not *the* Cary Grant, the actor, but Cary Grant the famous technical trader. I never did find out if it was true, but Cary told me that he figured it was worth about $10,000 a year to him to have this name, in terms of people remembering his name, doors opening to him, and especially people not cashing checks he wrote. Cary later went on to become the head of the Third Market Corporation.

Cary was a successful SPU trader (pronounced "spooze," S&P 500 Index futures traded at the Chicago Mercantile exchange). He used a technique based on George Lane's stochastics, Elliott waves and Gann angles. He was using FutureSource to trade SPUs from his desk and doing quite well. Somehow, he knew Steve Fossett and was on very friendly terms. An idea came up at one of our staff meetings, and Steve immediately put us both together and we were totally enthusiastic about the idea.

The idea was this: Nimble up to this point was making money following the market up and down, making money on allowing the orders to come to us. Cary was making money predicting short-term movements of the S&P, splitting his profits with the market makers and the brokers. We would have Cary call the market and instead of picking up his phone to place his order, he would call the upstairs Nimble risk management desk and they would adjust the bias as if he had entered a position in the underlying. We then would be trading without commissions, gaining the bid/offer spread from each transaction, instead of giving it up.

This was easy to implement and success came quickly. The only drawback was that execution was slower than futures directly. Cary would enter an order and it would take a few minutes to become long, and more than a few minutes on a slow day. This didn't seem to affect his trading very much. He took it on faith that orders would be "filled" and when it took time, well, that was the price one had to pay to trade without friction.

Cary did very well and the Nimble team did its best to keep the system operating smoothly and the rest is history. It was like being a runner who trains with ankle weights and takes the weights off before an important race. Cary's trading ran hot and stayed hot, thanks to the buffer of accumulated spreads and commissions he did not need to pay.

HOW THE CROWD REACTED

Here we were with a successful trading system in the SPX pit and soon were one of the biggest market makers in the pit. We had expected more than the usual hostilities from the non-computer crowd, but their reaction surprised me. They liked the system; they liked us. We took some suggestions from the crowd for ways to make our screens better. Different color schemes, different groupings, lines, and cosmetic things like this. The roving brokers liked our screens also. These are the floor brokers or market makers who work more than one pit, usually going from one pit to the other to fill orders or to stay where the action is. Their response was overly positive. They liked to look at screens that were always up-to-date, without having to yell out.

TONY SALIBA AND THE SALIBA SYSTEM

We were not the first trading system in the pit and we were not the last. Tony Saliba gave it a try, and we would watch him daily. Burt Beckman was the programmer, systems manager for Tony. Their system came for a while, traded for a while, and then went without explanation. About six months after their monitors were taken down, I got a call from one of the marketing people of Tony's organization. He explained to me their now defunct system was for sale and asked if I was interested. I told him, I had one already, but that I would take a look at it. I tried to be humble and not rub in the fact that our system was still running.

Some of the other Fossett people joked with me about the value of an unsuccessful trading system. I was looking for system parts that might be useful. For example, our modem infrastructure would be outdated in just a few years and might be replaced with something faster. I went to their office and looked at their system. I was astounded! Only years later did I see a system as impressive, when I sat in the cockpit of a Boeing 767. It had a bewildering assortment of dials, meters, and other instruments filling 4 or more screens. I did not think I or anyone else I knew was smart enough to operate such a system. Jim Sauser said it early on, and it became a motto for the Nimble team, "Walk before you run, and crawl before you walk." This is a rule I have taken to heart and use constantly in my life. I do not know why the Saliba system failed, but I have a strong hunch it was all those dials.

LESSONS LEARNED IN DEVELOPING THIS SYSTEM

- Walk before you run, and crawl before you walk.
- Trade without paying brokerage or bid/offer if you can.
- Systems never are as easy to implement as you think they will be.
- Sometimes technology leads you to a dead end, but being able to switch technologies will often get you past snags.
- Never pay fair value, just pay what you need to pay to get the trade accomplished.

- Understand why a system should work logically. What is your edge, and why do you have it?
- Always be introspective about your trading.
- Ease yourself into the water slowly.
- Practice continuous, stepwise improvement.
- If an idea comes up, evaluate it fully, regardless of whose idea it is.
- If you want the freshest, get it from the source.
- Time and circumstance happen to us all.

APPENDIX E

About the Editor
and Contributors

THE EDITOR

Mark Jurik is the founder of Jurik Research and Consulting, a firm specializing in data modeling and time series forecasting. His greatest talent is integrating various disciplines as disparate as electrical engineering, psychology, and physics into unified theories useful for data pattern analysis. For his rapid problem-solving skills, he received a Letter of Appreciation from the U.S. Strategic Air Command in 1981. He has taught for several years at the University of California Extension at Santa Cruz and lectured at many conferences on aspects of neural net applications. Jurik has written for numerous publications related to financial data processing and was contributing author to the book *Virtual Trading* (Probus, 1995). He received a BA in Psychology and a BS in Electrical Engineering, both in 1978 from Cornell University.

Jurik Research and Consulting 408-688-5893
443 Los Altos Drive 408-688-8947 fax
Aptos, CA 95003 *office@jurikres.com* office e-mail
mgj@jurikres.com personal e-mail
www.jurikres.com Web site

Jurik Research and Consulting specializes in data modeling and time series forecasting. Technologies include advanced signal processing methods, neural networks, fuzzy logic, genetic algorithms, and data mining. Our mentoring program guides you through each stage of financial system building. Jurik Research also produces advanced indicators and special signal processing filters as add-in modules for both financial and scientific software applications.

THE CONTRIBUTORS

Joseph Alotta (Appendix D) is principle with Open Door Investment Advisors, Inc., a fee-only manager of portfolios using no-load mutual funds. Formerly, he was head of market risk management for First Union Corporation in Charlotte, NC. He held similar positions at First Chicago Corporation and First Options Corporation. He received a BS in Economics and a MBA in Finance, from New York University. He now practices in the greater Chicago area.

Open Door Investment Advisors, Inc.   630-969-2628
409 North Washington Street   630-969-2629   fax
Westmont, IL 60559   *designalotta@earthlink*.net   e-mail

Lee Ang (Chapter 5) is a fund manager and general partner of the Plasma Fund L. P. and the Aggressor Global Fund, specializing in macroeconomic investing. Plasma Fund L. P. is a U.S. domestic hedge fund. Plasma's approach includes strict money and risk management principles, tight stop loss, rapid executions of high reward/risk trades, optimal application of leverage and market neutrality, low portfolio risk, and effective drawdown management. Mr. Ang develops back-tested trading systems for use in the fixed-income, equity, and foreign exchange markets. He has written articles for *Technical Analysis of Stocks & Commodities*. He was graduated with top honors from New York University in 1991 with a BS in Economics and Accounting. He received an MBA in Finance in 1993 from NYU's Stern Graduate School of Business.

Plasma Fund, L. P.   212-604-4610
200 E. 82 Street, Suite 4F
New York City, NY 10028

Gary S. Antonacci (Chapter 13) is a professional trader, analyst, and portfolio manager. He also serves as an asset allocation and risk management consultant to brokerage firms, financial advisors, and institutional investors. Mr. Antonacci is the author of *Optimal Commodity Investing*, which describes his application of modern portfolio theory concepts to managed futures trading. He received an MBA from the Harvard Business School.

2517 Clinton Avenue   510-232-7007
Richmond, CA 94804   Aniruddha7@aol.com   e-mail

Michael de la Maza (Chapter 8) is the President of Redfire Capital Management Group, a money management firm. He has published over a dozen academic papers on optimization, genetic algorithms, neural networks, and commodities trading. De la Maza borrows ideas from the field of artificial intelligence to create fully automated trading strategies for bond, currency, and equity markets. He received a PhD in Computer Science from the Massachusetts Institute of Technology in 1997.

Redfire Capital Management Group   617-441-3258
950 Massachusetts Avenue, Suite 209   617-876-7236   fax
Cambridge, MA 02139-3174   *RedfireGrp@aol.com*   e-mail

Redfire Capital Management Group is a money management firm that offers consulting and advisory services; its clients include Goldman Sachs, Swiss Bank, and Furman Selz. Their consulting service gives large organizations, including the U.S. government, access to Redfire's proprietary artificial intelligence techniques.

Joe DiNapoli (Chapter 1) is a registered CTA, and President of Coast Investment Software, Inc. A veteran trader for over 25 years, he conducts a limited number of private tutorials each year and makes his trading approach available to others via software and trading course materials. His articles have appeared in a wide variety of national and international technical publications. Joe DiNapoli was a contributing author to *High Performance Futures Trading: Power Lessons from the Masters,* (selected as 1990 book of the year by *Super Trader's Almanac*), and is the author of *Fibonacci Money Management and Trend Analysis in Home Trading Course,* which has been lauded by professional and novice traders alike. His most recent book, *Trading with DiNapoli Levels,* promises to be his most important work to date. He received a BS in Electrical Engineering with a minor in Economics, from the University of Massachusetts, in 1967.

Coast Investment Software, Inc.,	941-346-3801	
6907 Midnight Pass	941-346-3901	fax
Sarasota, FL 34242	*coast@fibtrader.com*	e-mail
	www.fibtrader.com	*Web site*

Coast Investment develops and deploys "high accuracy" trading methods, using a combination of leading and lagging indicators in unique and innovative ways. These techniques have been presented to international clients for over 10 years.

Keith C. Drake (Chapter 17) is Director of Business Solutions at AbTech Corporation. He is responsible for identifying cost-effective solutions to clients' data mining challenges. He has 15 years' experience applying advanced computing technologies to intelligent decision aiding systems. He managed and led $4 million in advanced research for academia, government, and industry. Prior to joining AbTech, Drake served as an Air Force officer at Wright Laboratory, Wright-Patterson Air Force Base, Ohio, where he was instrumental in developing several pilot decision aiding systems including DARPA's Pilot's Associate pilot aiding system. He received the BS in Electrical Engineering (EE) with distinction in 1983, the MS in EE in 1985, and the PhD in EE in 1993, all from the University of Virginia.

AbTech Corporation	888-822-8324	
1575 State Farm Boulevard	804-977-9615	fax
Charlottesville, VA 22911	*sales@abtech.com*	office e-mail
	kcdrake@abtech.com	personal e-mail
	www.abtech.com	Web site

AbTech Corporation provides its financial data mining customers with the world's best predictive modeling tools and services. Over the past 10 years, AbTech has become a recognized leader in advanced modeling technologies, pioneering Statistical Networks, and many other data mining methods. AbTech's products have been applied in finance, marketing, business, telecommunications, banking, manufacturing, aerospace, and health care.

Timothy W. Hayes (Chapter 11) is a chartered market technician (CMT) and the Senior Equity Strategist of Ned Davis Research, Inc., an institutional research firm. In May 1996, Tim won the Charles H. Dow Award for groundbreaking research in technical analysis. After joining NDR in 1986, he became editor of NDR's flagship publication, *Stock Market Strategy.* Hayes also produces the firm's on-line Stock Selection Focus and coordinates asset allocation. His research articles have appeared in the *MTA Journal, Technical Analysis of Stocks & Commodities,* and other publications. His market commentary has been featured by the *Wall Street Journal, Barron's* and *Investor's Daily,* and he has made numerous appearances on CNBC. He received a BA from Kenyon College.

Ned Davis Research	941-484-6107	
600 Bird Bay Drive West	941-484-6221	fax
Venice, FL 34292	*sales@ndr.com*	business e-mail
	www.ndr.com	Web site

Ned Davis Research, Inc. (NDR), is an institutional investment research and advisory firm founded in 1980. NDR provides timely, broad-based market investment research information to institutional money managers. NDR's primary objective is to provide the very best, most reliable and accurate investment advisory support possible through research, publications, and charts. The focus of NDR research is timing the financial markets.

Cynthia A. Kase (Chapter 12) is a registered Commodity Trading Advisor and Chartered Market Technician. A veteran energy trader, she is president of Kase and Company, launched in 1992. Kase now actively advises about 50 major corporations. She has also developed comprehensive risk management programs for over two dozen firms across the energy industry. With a documented record of better than 94 percent accuracy as a forecaster, she is known by many as the top trading and hedging adviser practicing in the field. Her book, *Trading with the Odds,* has been hailed as the first new approach in 40 years. Kase has written for many publications. The Market Technicians' Association recently presented her with the prestigious Best of the Best Award for momentum. She holds a BS from Lowell Tech (1973) and ME from Northeastern University (1977), both in Chemical Engineering.

Kase and Company, Inc.	505-237-1600	
1000 Eubank Boulevard, NE, Suite C	505-237-1659	fax
Albuquerque, NM 87112	*kase@kaseco.com*	e-mail
	www.kaseco.com	Web site

Kase and Company, Inc. offers market forecasting, and the planning, design and implementation of innovative strategies for trading and hedging. Kase designs practical methods for managing price risk, and develops analytical software to support these processes.

Jeffrey Owen Katz (Chapter 18) is a professional trader and consultant. He is president and founder of Scientific Consultant Services, Inc., a firm that specializes in custom programming, provides expert consultation on systems development and the use of Omega Research's tools, and develops publicly available cutting-edge software for traders. He has taught at several universities, consulted for major institutions (both private and government), and has been a guest speaker for a wide range of organizations. Dr. Katz has published in journals of psychology and zoology, in trade publications, such as *PC AI, NeuroVe$t Journal,* and was a contributing author to the book *Virtual Trading* (Probus, 1995). Since 1996, he has been a Contributing Writer for Technical Analysis of Stocks & Commodities. He received a BA in mathematics in 1972 from the State University of New York at Stony Brook, and received a doctorate in psychophysiology in 1983 from the University of Lancaster, England.

Scientific Consultant Services, Inc.   516-696-3333
20 Stagecoach Road   516-696-3333   fax
Selden, NY 11784   *off@panix.com*   e-mail

Ari Kiev (Chapter 10) is a trading consultant to a number of Wall Street hedge funds, where he teaches stress management and maximum performance trading strategies. He is the author of *Trading to Win: The Psychology of Mastering the Markets* (John Wiley & Sons, 1998). A practicing psychiatrist and Medical Director of the Social Psychiatry Research Institute, Kiev has been a Clinical Associate Professor of Psychiatry at Cornell University Medical College for the past 30 years. He received his MD degree from Cornell University in 1958 and his law degree from New York Law School in 1988.

Suite 2H   212-249-6829
150 East 69th Street   212-249-8546   fax
New York, NY 10021   *niss33@AOL.com*   e-mail

Casimir (Casey) Klimasauskas (Chapter 16) is Vice President, Special Project, Advanced Control and Optimization Division, Aspen Technology, Inc. He also has taught occasionally at the Graduate School of Industrial Administration in the Masters in Computational Finance program at Carnegie Mellon University. He co-founded NeuralWare, which was acquired by Aspen Technology in 1998, and has spent the past eleven years combining neural networks, fuzzy logic, genetic algorithms, and statistics to solve complex business problems. Prior to NeuralWare he worked on a variety of projects in Electronic Computer Aided Design (ECAD), robotic vision systems, robotics, real-time operating systems, real-time data analysis and control. Casey received a BA degree in mathematics from the California Institute of Technology, and is a member of the International Neural Network Society and the Institute of Electrical and Electronic Engineers.

Aspen Technology, Inc.   412-787-8222
Advanced Control &
    Optimization Division   412-787-8220   fax
202 Park West Drive   *klim@sgi.net*   personal e-mail
Pittsburgh, PA 15275   *Casey.Klimasauskas@AspenTech.com*   office e-mail
                                www.AspenTech.com   Web site

Aspen Technology, Inc., is a leading supplier of software and services for the analysis, design, and automation of process manufacturing plants. AspenTech's solutions help improve plant design, operation, and management. These solutions enable customers to reduce their raw material, energy, and capital expenses, meet environmental and safety regulations, improve product quality, and shorten the time required to get new production processes on stream.

Joe Luisi (Chapters 5 and 6) has been involved with the financial markets for 7 years. He was Director of Research for a Maryland-based Commodity Trading Advisor and now trades for himself. He has written several articles for *Stock & Commodities Magazine.* He currently provides consultation for people interested in designing and trading a system personalized to suit their needs. He also offers several S&P 500 day-trading systems as well as currency swing trading systems. He received a BS in Finance from Kent State University, Ohio.

JAL Trading, Inc.   717-558-6407
1315 North Pitt Street   717-731-4785   fax
Carlisle, PA 17013

Kevin N. Marder (Appendix A) is president of Technical Analytics, a Los Angeles-based institutional equity research firm that specializes in sector/group analysis of the U.S. market. Kevin also heads up Marder Investment Counsel, Ltd., a registered investment advisor. Kevin has developed fixed-income portfolio analytic software for use by institutional portfolio managers. His continuous real-time stock and bond market commentary is syndicated to the Internet sites of CBS News, *USA Today, International Herald Tribune, Washington Post, Yahoo,* and AT&T, among others. He received an MBA with honors in Investments and Corporate Finance from the University of Southern California.

Technical Analytics   310-479-9715
8033 Sunset Boulevard, Suite 939   310-966-1456   fax
Los Angeles, CA 90046   *kmarder@cms.dbc.com* e-mail

Christopher T. May (Chapter 15) is the president of Kriya, Inc., a firm specializing in nonlinear technology in finance, generating revenues from financial software licensing and money management. Prior to this career on Wall Street, he served as a Captain in the United States Marine Corps. He received his MBA from New York University, where he was a Salomon Fellow and attended the International University of Japan. He received his BBA from Texas A&M.

Kriya, Inc.   212-213-2482
211 East 35th Street   212-888-7146   fax
New York, NY 10016   *kriya@interport.net*   e-mail

    Donna L. McCormick (Chapter 18) is vice president of Scientific Consultant Services, Inc. She was Administrative Director of The American Society for Physical Research for 15 years. She has published in a number of professional journals and financial trade publications. She has lectured to a variety of academic and institutional audiences, and has held memberships in professional organizations, including the American Association for the Advancement of Science. Since 1996, McCormick has been a Contributing Writer for *Technical Analysis of Stocks & Commodities.* She graduated cum laude from Brooklyn College of the City University of New York with a BS in experimental psychology.

Scientific Consultant Services, Inc.   516-696-3333
20 Stagecoach Road   516-696-3333   fax
Selden, NY 11784   *off@panix.com*   e-mail

    Robert M. Melancon, (Chapter 2) is a Registered Investment Advisor (RIA). He is President and Director of Technical Analysis for TymVest Investment Management, a position he has held since 1988. Prior to this, he was Managing Partner of a prominent regional management consulting firm in Dallas. He is a former President of the Association for Technical Analysis, member of Society of Asset Allocators and Fund Timers, frequent speaker on the theory and application of technical analysis methods, and publisher of a quarterly technical market analysis newsletter. Melancon has been actively engaged in the study of technical analysis for more than 18 years, and manages assets for individuals, institutions, and corporations throughout the country. He graduated cum laude from Loyola University with a BS in Business Administration.

TymVest Investment Management   972-231-9963
P. O. Box 2383
McKinney, TX 75070-2383   rmmel@compuserve.com   e-mail

    TymVest Investment Management is an investment advisory firm registered with the Securities and Exchange Commissions under the Investment Advisor's Act of 1940. The Dallas-based company provides technical market analysis, investment timing and mutual fund selection services on a discretionary basis to individuals, corporations, and pension and profit-sharing plans.

Dale Nelson (Chapter 17) is Chief of the Target Recognition Branch of the Sensor ATR Technology Division, Air Force Research Laboratory at Wright Patterson Air Force Base (WPAFB), Ohio. Prior to this, he held positions as the Program Objective Memorandum Database Administrator for Aeronautical Systems Division at WPAFB and as an aerospace engineer in the Flight Dynamics Laboratory, WPAFB. He was a structural fatigue engineer with Cessna Aircraft, Military Twin Division in Wichita, Kansas prior to assuming positions with the Air Force. Nelson is a member of the Institute of Electrical and Electronic Engineers (IEEE). He received his BS in Aerospace Engineering from Tri-State University in Angola, Indiana in 1969, and an MS in Computer Science from Wright State University, Dayton, Ohio, in 1981. He is currently completing his dissertation for a PhD in Electrical Engineering from Ohio University, Athens, Ohio.

Dale E. Nelson, Chief	937-255-1115, Ext. 4217	
ATR Technology Branch	937-656-4414	fax
Building 620 AFRL/SNAT	NelsonDE@sensors.wpafb.af.mil	e-mail
2241 Avionics Circle		
Wright-Patterson AFB, OH 45433-7321		

David C. Stendahl (Chapter 9) is Vice President of Financial Services with RINA Systems, Inc. He is an active trader and investment advisor specializing in trading S&P Futures, OEX Options, and Index mutual funds. *Barron's* recognized him as a leading options analyst. His investment and evaluation related articles have been published in *Technical Analysis of Stocks & Commodities, Traders' Catalog and Resource Guide,* and *Pinnacle Magazine.* Stendahl also speaks at national and international conferences, presenting his "Effective Methods for Evaluating Trading Performance" seminar at Dow Jones/Telerate TAG, Futures South and West, Futures Symposium International, Futures and Options Expo, and other conferences. He received a BA in Finance and Economics from Wittenberg University, Ohio.

RINA Systems, Inc.	513-469-7462	
8180 Corporate Park Drive, Suite 140	513-469-2223	fax
Cincinatti, OH 45242	*dsinvest@msn.com*	e-mail
	www.rinasystems.com	Web site

RINA Systems helps traders and investors make better, more informed investment decisions. The company combines mathematics, trading, and software development to design, develop, and deliver solutions to the trading and investment industry. The company evaluates trading system and trading performance in general by implementing statistical analysis of trading performance, risk analysis, money management and asset allocation using proprietary software packages.

Averill J. Strasser (Chapter 14) is a futures trader, an educator, an attorney, and a systems engineer. He is principal of Strasser Futures, a company dedicated to providing educational resources for traders. He began his work on computerized trading in the 1960s, when he was Professor of Engineering at the University of San Andres in La Paz, Bolivia. Although a long-time attorney, Strasser has retired from active litigation practice. He holds a BS degree in Mechanical Engineering, and a MS degree in Systems Engineering, both from the University of California at Los Angeles. He also holds a Juris Doctor degree from University of West Los Angeles and is a member of The State Bar of California.

Strasser Futures No. 1177	310-204-5551	
264 South La Cienega Boulevard	310-204-5551	fax
Beverly Hills, CA 90211	*mail@strasser.com*	e-mail
	www.strasser.com	Web site

Strasser Futures provides educational resources for the futures industry. The firm offers training for brokers, and courses and seminars for traders. It sells books, tapes, CD-ROMs, software, data and systems to enable traders to better understand and compete in the marketplace.

David Vomund (Chapter 3) is the chief analyst at AIQ Systems (www. AIQ.com) and is president of Vomund Investment Services. He worked four years at Target Inc. as a market analyst before joining AIQ Systems as chief analyst in 1991. He writes AIQ's highly acclaimed educational newsletter, *Opening Bell*. Vomund is a regular guest on financial television channels in Los Angeles and Chicago and his analyses and forecasts have appeared in *Personal Investor, Los Angeles Times, USA Today*, and *Barron's*. Vomund graduated from the University of California at Davis with a BA in Economics and from California Sate University at Hayward with an MBA in Finance.

Vomund Investment Services	702-831-1544	
P. O. Box 6253	702-831-6784	fax
Incline Village, NV 89450	*dvomund@visalert.com*	e-mail
	www.visalert.com	Web site

Vomund Investment Services publishes *VIS Alert*, a weekly newsletter that tracks the overall stock market, industry group rotation, sector fund switching, and individual stock selection.

Melvin M. Widner (Chapter 4) has had a long career in scientific research. For the past several years Dr. Widner has been studying and investigating financial markets, focusing on technical analysis. Drawing on his background, he has developed and published several new techniques for analysis. One of these is the Projection Band method, a means of determining when trend is changing, and another, the Mobility Oscillator method, the subject of his chapter. Most recently, he has developed a trend-following method called Rainbow Charts. He has many scientific publications and has considerable expertise in analysis and simulation. He has worked at two national

laboratories on research projects for national defense and energy programs. He holds
a PhD in Electrical Engineering from the University of Iowa.

Technical Strategies   703-492-3249
6500 Running Brook Road   703-791-5910   fax
Manassas, VA 20112   *techstrategies@msn.com*   e-mail

Technical Strategies is a research and consulting firm providing technical analysis software, educational materials, specific client-directed research and applications,
charting, and a weekly assessment of general market conditions for the OEX. Technical Strategies' unique and unconventional indicators give an independent assessment
of market conditions.

Index